DIE CHRISTIANISIERUNG DES KAUKASUS

THE CHRISTIANIZATION OF CAUCASUS
(ARMENIA, GEORGIA, ALBANIA)

ÖSTERREICHISCHE AKADEMIE DER WISSENSCHAFTEN
PHILOSOPHISCH-HISTORISCHE KLASSE
DENKSCHRIFTEN, 296. BAND

VERÖFFENTLICHUNGEN DER KOMMISSION FÜR

BYZANTINISTIK

HERAUSGEGEBEN VON

OTTO KRESTEN UND WERNER SEIBT

BAND IX

VERLAG DER ÖSTERREICHISCHEN AKADEMIE DER WISSENSCHAFTEN
WIEN 2002

ÖSTERREICHISCHE AKADEMIE DER WISSENSCHAFTEN
PHILOSOPHISCH-HISTORISCHE KLASSE
DENKSCHRIFTEN, 296. BAND

VERÖFFENTLICHUNGEN DER KOMMISSION FÜR BYZANTINISTIK
BAND IX

DIE CHRISTIANISIERUNG DES KAUKASUS

THE CHRISTIANIZATION OF CAUCASUS (ARMENIA, GEORGIA, ALBANIA)

Referate des Internationalen Symposions
(Wien, 9.–12. Dezember 1999)

HERAUSGEGEBEN VON
WERNER SEIBT

VERLAG DER ÖSTERREICHISCHEN AKADEMIE DER WISSENSCHAFTEN
WIEN 2002

Vorgelegt von w. M. Otto KRESTEN in der Sitzung am 6. Oktober 2000

Gedruckt mit Unterstützung des
Fonds zur Förderung der wissenschaftlichen Forschung

Die Deutsche Bibliothek – CIP-Einheitsaufnahme
Ein Titeldatensatz für diese Publikation ist bei der Deutschen Bibliothek erhältlich

Bild des Umschlags:
Taufe Christi im Jordan
(zum Kanon des 8. Tages der Epiphanie), aus einem armenischen Hymnarium
des 16. Jh. (Cod. Mech. Vind. 189)
Aus: Heide und Helmut BUSCHHAUSEN, mit Hilfe von Eva ZIMMERMANN,
Die illuminierten armenischen Handschriften der Mechitharisten-Congregation in Wien.
Wien 1976, Abb. 154

ISBN 3-7001-3016-3

Gesamtherstellung: Weitzer & Partner GmbH, A-8045 Graz

INHALTSVERZEICHNIS

VORWORT DES HERAUSGEBERS

Als Seine Heiligkeit, der Katholikos und oberste Patriarch aller Armenier, Karekin I., zu einer Konferenz nach Paris lud, um die internationalen Aktivitäten anlässlich des 1700 Jahr-Jubiläums der Christianisierung Armeniens, die im Jahre 2001 ihren Höhepunkt finden sollten, zu koordinieren bzw. weitere anzuregen, fand der Vorschlag Österreichs, ein hochkarätiges wissenschaftliches Symposion (mit einem primär ökumenisch ausgerichteten Rahmenprogramm und begleitenden Ausstellungen) zu organisieren, großen Beifall.

Als Veranstalter konnte die Österreichische Akademie der Wissenschaften/Kommission für Byzantinistik, die eben ihr 50jähriges Bestehen feierte, zusammen mit dem Institut für Byzantinistik und Neogräzistik der Universität Wien und der Österreichisch-armenischen Studiengesellschaft gewonnen werden; die Organisation übernahmen S. E. Erzbischof Hon.-Prof. Dr. Mesrob Krikorian und der Unterzeichnete. Die Eröffnung wurde auf jenen Tag gelegt, an dem der Altpräsident der Österreichischen Akademie der Wissenschaften und Ehrenpräsident der Association Internationale des Études Byzantines, Prof. Dr. Dr. h. c. mult. Herbert Hunger, dem nicht nur die österreichische Byzantinistik mehr verdankt als schlichte Worte auszudrücken vermögen, den 85. Geburtstag beging. Aus seinem überreichen Schaffen war nicht zuletzt das weit über Fachkreise hinaus bekannte Werk „Reich der Neuen Mitte. Der christliche Geist der byzantinischen Kultur“ richtungweisend für das Symposion. Aus gesundheitlichen Gründen musste sich Präsident Hunger aber dann doch die aktive Teilnahme versagen, ein halbes Jahr später wurde er aus unserer Mitte abberufen. Seinem Gedächtnis sei dieser Band in besonderer Weise gewidmet.

Es war uns eine große Freude, viele führende Fachvertreter als Referenten zu gewinnen, sodass das vielschichtige Gesamtphänomen der Christianisierung des südkaukasischen Raumes von verschiedenen Seiten her beleuchtet und vorbildlich aufbereitet werden konnte. Besonderes Augenmerk wurde den recht verworrenen Überlieferungssträngen geschenkt, denn es steht außer Zweifel, dass im Laufe der Zeit vorhandene mündliche und schriftliche Traditionen „angereichert“, „korrigiert“ und bewusst manipuliert wurden, um die jeweiligen ideologischen Positionen bzw. kirchenpolitischen Ambitionen besser abzusichern. In gemeinsamer Arbeit und fruchtbaren Diskussionen, deren Ergebnisse in die schriftlichen Endfassungen Eingang fanden, konnten beachtliche Fortschritte erzielt werden, wobei der chronologische Schwerpunkt im 4. Jh. lag (mit nur marginaler Berührung der in apostolische Zeit zurückreichenden Legenden).

So ist das Jahr 301 nun mit Sicherheit als Datum der Taufe des großarmenischen Königs Trdat/Tiridates auszuscheiden, vielmehr ist mit sehr hoher Wahrscheinlichkeit davon auszugehen, dass dieses wichtige Ereignis frühestens 314 stattfand. Die Taufe eines ostgeorgischen (iberischen) Königs erfolgte einige Jahrzehnte später, entweder in den 30er Jahren des 4. Jh., wie zumeist angenommen, oder erst um die Mitte dieses Jahrhunderts, wofür in letzter Zeit neue Indizien erarbeitet wurden. Im kaukasischen Albanien (auf dem Boden des modernen Azerbajdžan) setzte eine vergleichbare Entwicklung kaum vor dem späteren 4. Jh. ein, wogegen die Missionierung der Alanen im zentralen Kaukasusgebiet bzw. nordwestlich davon erst im 10. Jh. nennenswerte Erfolge zeitigen konnte.

Zwar war schon etwa ein Jahrhundert vor Trdat ein Fürst von Edessa Christ geworden, aber der Schritt König Trdats erhielt dadurch eine welthistorische Dimension, dass erstmals das Christentum durch königliches Dekret zur verbindlichen Staatsreligion erklärt wurde, während es im römischen Reich als Folge verschiedener Toleranzedikte im frühen 4. Jh. nur geduldet, erlaubt und nicht mehr wie zuvor verfolgt wurde, bis erst gegen Ende des 4. Jh. ein ähnlicher Zustand wie in Armenien erreicht wurde.

Der neue Forschungsstand entspricht sowohl den historischen Gegebenheiten des kaukasischen Raumes und der benachbarten Großreiche als auch den Voraussetzungen der „inneren Wahrscheinlichkeit".

Wir danken der Österreichischen Akademie der Wissenschaften, dass sie die Referate des Symposions zum Druck angenommen hat, sowie dem Fonds zur Förderung der wissenschaftlichen Forschung für die Drucksubvention. Für Unterstützung bei der redaktionellen Arbeit sind wir Mesrob K. Krikorian, Alexandra-Kyriaki Wassiliou, Christian Gastgeber und Hannes Weinberger ebenfalls zu Dank verpflichtet.

Wien, im Sommer 2001 *Werner Seibt*

ZAZA ALEXIDZE / TBILISI

FOUR RECENSIONS OF THE "CONVERSION OF GEORGIA"
(Comparative Study)

Georgia, one of the ancient Christian countries of the world has ended 18th c. without having written its Church history. Even the "Life of Georgia" (Georgian Annals, *Kartlis Tskhovreba*) entirely neglects the history of Church. King Vakhtang VI's "Committee of Learned Men" noticed this only in the 18th c.: "*The Life of Georgia* curtails the history of Church and gives a long lay story".[1] Nevertheless, neither they had thought of writing the history of Georgian Church, but have only written some additions to the corresponding places of the "Life of Georgia".

Why did not there arise the feeling of insufficiency? Why did everybody consider then as well as nowadays that the history of Georgian Church was well known to him? It seems that hagiograghical and polemical literature substituted the absence of the history of Church. Actually the most important works in this field mainly concerned some peaks of Georgian Church history.

The chronological succession of "St. Nino's Life", "13 Syrian Fathers' Lives", "Martyrdom of Abo", "Life of Grigol of Khandzta (Grigol Khandzteli)", "Life of the Hagiorites (Mtatsmindelis)", etc. represents an endless chain of the formation of Georgian Church, struggle for Christianity and the history of its clergy.

In this context let me remember polemical treatises written by Arseni of Sapara (Arseni Sapareli) "On the Separation of Georgia and Armenia" and Eprem Junior's (Eprem Mtsire) "About the Motives of Conversion of the Georgians". Though both of them were written to cover one short historical period, they still embrace vast historical and geographical area.

The "Conversion of Georgia" (*Moktsevai Kartlisai*) as it is known nowadays is neither pure historical work nor hagiographical, though being both at the same time. I consider that in order to determine its place one should bear in mind two aspects, synchronic (meaning what does it represent today?) and diachronic (what did it or they represent when they were being written?).

The "Conversion of Georgia" has even set the tradition to similar synthetic genre. All the versions of the "St. Nino's Life" written in the following periods, are at the same time hagiographical and historical works. It is evident by metaphrastic and periphrastic versions of the "St. Nino's Life", notwithstanding Leonti Mroveli's (Leonti of Ruisi) version that had been aimed to be inserted into long historical work. Both authors acknowledge their aims well. Arseni the Monk (the author of the metaphrastic version) writes and the author of the periphrastic work repeats in brief: "It is necessary to announce, my beloved people, that this King Mirian, as well as other kings of the Georgians, to what kid they belonged, and whose relatives' children we are".[2] This is the credo of "The Conversion of Georgia" though it is not declared overtly.

---

[1] Batonishvili Vakhushti, Aghtsera sameposa Sakartvelosa: Kartlis tskhovreba IV. Tbilisi 1973, p. 4; K. Grigolia, Akhali Kartlis tskhovreba. Tbilisi 1954, 215.

[2] Tskhovreba Ninoisi, in: Dzveli kartuli agiograpiuli dzeglebis krebuli, vol. III, 46.

Thus, all three ancient Georgian historical treatises, that deal with the specific though most important phenomenon, create one vast historical picture and describe other events than only those revealed in the title.

Presently, the "Conversion of Georgia" consists of two parts. The first part is conventionally called the "Annals" or the "Chronicles of the Conversion of Georgia"; the second one is called the "St. Nino's Life".

"The Annals of the Conversion of Georgia" is the history of Georgia from the time of establishment of the first Georgian monarchy till the first half of the 7th c. It also encloses the list of the Catholici and the Erismtavars (Princes, Dukes, Rulers) of Georgia (till the 9th–10th cc.).

"The Annals of the Conversion of Georgia" can be divided into five subgroups:

1. The legend of Alexander Macedonian's invasion of Georgia and establishment of Georgian statehood.
2. The Georgian kings' short chronicle, starting from the first King Parnavaz (the beginning of the 3rd c. B.C.), to the first Christian King Mirian (the beginning of 4th c. A.D.).
3. The story of conversion of Georgia into Christianity.
4. A brief chronicle of the Christian Kings of Georgia starting from the King Mirian including the first half of 7th c. Main events of this part are the reign of King Vakhtang Gorgasal (the most outstanding king of Georgia of the early medieval ages) and the campaign of Heraclius the Emperor of Byzantium (610–641) in Caucasia. The Catholicosat was established during the reign of King Vakhtang Gorgasal and Georgia was cleaned of heresy as a result of Heraclius' invasions.
5. An appendix: list of the Catholici and Erismtavars of Georgia from 650s till the turn of 9th–10th cc.

"The Life of St. Nino" is given twice in the "Conversion of Georgia". Once its short version is given in the so-called "Annals of the Conversion of Georgia" and a longer variant in the "St. Nino's Life" itself. These two "Lives" (shorter one given in the "Annals" and the longer one given in the "Life") though different in variants are intently fitted to each other.

There are three kinds of differences between these two "Lives":

1. The short version of the "Life" presents more information as compared to the long variant and it is noteworthy, that in case of shortening the long variant it cannot be expected.
2. The information in the short and long versions of "Lives" in some cases is different, excluding their dependence on each other.
3. The information in the short and long variants contradicts each other.

These three differences likely speak against their common origin.[3]

The existence of different variants in "St. Nino's Life" in the "Conversion of Georgia" is a most important fact for studying the origin of the texts.

The Manuscripts of "The Conversion of Georgia"

The Shatberdi collection (Institute of Manuscripts, S-1141) is undated, but according to the personalities mentioned there (King Bagrat, Ioane-Bera, Emperor of Byzantium John I Tzimisces) the collection is dated 973–976, in other words 970s or 960s–970s.[4] Such dating is on the whole acceptable but I consider 976 to be the lowest border.

---

[3] M. Chkhartishvili, Kartuli agiograpiis tskarotmtsodneobiti shestsavlis problemebi. Tbilisi 1987, 14–17.

[4] Shatberdis krebuli. Tbilisi 1979, 26.

Specialists were right to call one part of Shatberdi collection "the manual". This can be applied to the whole book. It really is a kind of encyclopaedic manual book and the scholars unanimously regard it to be so. But it is still unclear why the "Conversion of Georgia" has appeared to be in this collection. This question is quite natural to arise as far as there are similar collections in Georgian literature that coincides with the Shatberdi collection even compositionally. The only difference is that "Conversion of Georgia" is not among them.

It is evident that Georgian scholars' attention was at first attracted to the "Conversion of Georgia". It lacks some pages in the Shatberdi collection. Otherwise, the text has survived well.

The Chelishi collection (Institute of Manuscripts, H-600) consists of two parts:

1. The "Conversion of Georgia". The two beginning folios are missing.
2. The nativity of our Lord Jesus Christ in Bethlehem.
   According to the colophon the scribe of this part is a certain Basili. Palaeographically it is dated 14th–15th cc. by E. Taqaishvili.[5]
3. The "St. George's life" with a lot of folios missing at the beginning.
4. The "Martyrdom of the Holy, Glorious, and Great Martyr, George in April 23".

E. Taqaishvili dates this part to the first half of 16th c.[6] According to the colophon it must have been rewritten by the monk Okrop'iri. The Chelishi manuscript is binded by certain Tevdosia in the 17th c.

The principles of composing the Chelishi collection are difficult to judge as its two parts have been compiled irrespective of each other and both of them have missing pages, but it is clear that they were not mechanically compiled together. The "Conversion of Georgia" connects chronologically and by area St. George's life and the life of St. Nino. St. Nino's parents' life in Cappadocia starts here from the times of St. George's martyrdom.

To a greater extent this can be applied to the later tradition. In the so-called Arseni the Monk's version of "St. Nino's Life" (11th–12th cc.) the author eulogises St. George and declares him the patron of the Georgians.[7]

The same version of "St. Nino's Life" says that the Enlightener of the Georgians had erected a church of St. George on Mount Tkhoti (where King Mirian had acknowledged Jesus Christ).

Periphrastic version (13th c.) of "St. Nino's Life" declares the father of the Enlightener not only as the contemporary and the fellow citizen of St. George but as his friend as well.[8] Georgian mentality can easily link together the cult of St. Nino and St. George with the cult of Holy Virgin. Georgian ecclesiastical tradition, likewise St. George, represents Holy Virgin as the Protectress of the Georgians. Worshipping Holy Virgin and St. George together in Georgian chapels is a rather widespread tradition. It is well represented in Christoforo De Castelli's album that has the following inscription: "Praying to Holy Virgin to come and dwell in St. George's chapel".[9]

An important fragment of the manuscript *(N/Sin-48)* containing thirteen folios and two more fragments of the "Conversion of Georgia" were found in St. Catherine's Monas-

---

[5] E. Takaishvili, Opisanie rukopisei biblioteki "Obshchestva rasprostranenia gramotnosti sredi gruzinskogo naselenia. *CMOMPK* 40 (1909) 35–55.

[6] L. c. 705.

[7] Dzveli kartuli agiograpiuli dzeglebis krebuli. III, 11.

[8] L. c. 52.

[9] I. Surguladze, Mariamoba. In: Kartuli sabtchota entsiklopedia VI 52.

tery on Mount Sinai in 1990. The text is written on the parchment with black ink and in minuscule writing but the scribe uses also majuscule graphems to underline the most important text.

Palaeographically (taking into consideration lettering of both minuscule and majuscule writings) the manuscript can be dated early 10th century.

Sin-48 of the new collection had been initially bound into quaternions. At present, it only has the marking at the beginning of the third quaternion. This gives clear evidence that the "Conversion of Georgia" was not preceded by another work in the manuscript. Unluckily, it is not clear how much of the manuscript is missing at the end but it is evident that the size of the folios are so small and the graphemes are so big, that the manuscript could only contain the "Chronicles of the Conversion of Georgia" excluding even the "Life of St. Nino".

The text in N/Sin-48 starts from the episode when St. Nino after having prayed in the bramble created the cross from the vine twigs and it ends at the episode of Thirteen Syrian Fathers' arrival in Georgia.

The same year, on mount Sinai was discovered a manuscript (*N/Sin-50*) that contains the "Conversion of Georgia" and the "Thirteen Syrian Fathers' Lives".

The text is written in minuscule writing and sometimes majuscule writing as well. The captions are given in majuscule and vermilion.

Palaeographically the manuscript can be dated 9th–10th cc. The captions are most peculiar from this point of view and indicate on the turn of these centuries.

A certain monk Iovane (John) formerly called Arshusha to commemorate his soul and to pray for his sons (Demetri, Adarnerse and Nerse) has donated N/Sin-50 to the Mount Sinai. The anthroponyms given in the colophons also indicate that the manuscript is rather ancient. The same person who has also donated the wellknown Tchil-Etratis Iadgari (book of hymns) to St. Saba in Palestine in the 9th–10th centuries must have donated it. This is proved by the identical (palaeographically and according the contents) colophons made on N/Sin-50 and the Iadgari: "Christ, be merciful upon me, Iovane. Amen!"

N/Sin-50 can be dated precisely according to the data given in the text:

1. The list of the Catholici of Georgia that represents an appendix to the "Conversion of Georgia" lacks three Catholicis' names that are given in the list of Shatberdi collection (the last Catholicos is Arseni II, in about 955–985). The last Catholicos in the appendix of N/Sin-50 is Catholicos Basili who is the second Catholicos after Arseni I, the Great (860–887). Thus meaning that it cannot be dated later than the turn of the 9th and 10th centuries.
2. The list of Zedazeni Fathers with the dates of their Priority that is given in "The Life of Ioane (John) of Zedazeni" also indicates at the very beginning of the 10th century.
3. "The Life of John of Zedazeni (Ioane Zedazneli)" also mentions the Queen of Siunik (Sivnieti) called Amaspo (Armenian sources mention her name as Hamaspruh/Hamaspuh) as being alive at that time.[10] This is another evidence enabling to date the manuscript by the beginning of the 10th century.

Recensions of "The Conversion of Georgia"

The fact that the text of the Shatberdi and the Chelishi collections represent different recensions and not only different manuscripts has never been doubted. But the problem of their correlation has always been the subject of divergence of opinions.

---

[10] H. Atcharjan (Ačaṙean), Haiots andznanunneri baṙaran (Hayocʿ anjnanunneri Baṙaran) III. Erevan 1946, 26.

The Shatberdi and the Chelishi recensions were written in about the same period (10th c.), judging from the point of view of language, though of course, the Chelishi variant is badly distorted by the scribe. They must be originating from the 9th c. protorecension.[11] At present, after the discovery of N/Sin-50 it can be stated with great assurance that the protomanuscript of the Chelishi variant was made at the beginning of the 10th c., that is at about the same time as N/Sin-50. It is due to the fact that the list of the Catholici that is only summarised in the Chelishi redaction coincides with the Sinaitic recension. There is another great probability that the protorecension of 9th c. might imply only such text to which had been added the list of the Princes (Erismtavars) and the Catholici. The protovariants of the text must be coming from much earlier times.

When talking about the recensions of the "Conversion of Georgia" two problems must be singled out: the recensions of the whole collection of the "Conversion of Georgia" enclosing its two parts and the recensions of the "St. Nino's Life" as one separate part of the "Conversion of Georgia".

At present there exist four recensions of the whole collection of the "Conversion of Georgia". These are: the Shatberdi, the Chelishi, Sin-48 and Sin-50 of the new collection, and ten variants of the "St. Nino's Life" (except the synaxarial ones): short and long versions of the "Lives" in the Shartberdi and the Chelishi collections; short life in N/Sin-48 and long one in N/Sin-50; Leonti Mroveli's Georgian recension (divided into three variants: Queen Anna's, Queen Mariam's and King Vakhtang VI's variants) and its Armenian translation; metaphrastic or Arseni the Monk's version and the periphrastic one. The comparative study of the four versions of the "Conversion of Georgia" envisages studying of their textual relations with all the aforementioned variants in order to determine the archetype of the text of the "Conversion of Georgia".

The interrelation of all the abovementioned problems is, of course, impossible to deal with now, especially as, the reconstruction of the archetype means elucidating such textual details that can not be demonstrated here. That is why it would be more appropriate to deal with only most important subjects of the study and to give some brief conclusions.

Comparative Study

As it becomes evident, the "Conversion of Georgia" was not initially used as the title of a single work. It was used to denote a group of books describing the adoption of Christianity in Georgia.[12] Besides, under the adoption of Christianity was meant not a single act of Christianization (its adoption as the state religion) but the whole process till its end. This group included the work of Grigol the Deacon, "Annals of the Conversion of Georgia", "St. Nino's Life", "Acts of John of Zedazeni (Ioane Zedazneli) and his Disciples", "Martyrdom of Abibos of Nekresi" (Abibos Nekreseli) and may be some others as well that have not survived till nowadays, or else some others that had been included in this cycle and we are unaware of.

The "Conversion of Georgia" and "St. Nino's Life" were combined in one work at the end of the 10th c. This process of unification can be traced in N/Sin-50 where they are represented together not as one composition, but as the works dealing with the conversion of Georgia.

---

[11] Z. ALEXIDZE, Moktsevai Kartlisai. In: Kartuli sabtchota entsiklopedia VII. Tbilisi 1986, 86–87.

[12] Z. ALEXIDZE, Moktsevai Kartlisais strukturisatvis: Sakartvelos eklesiis, kartuli mtserlobis da kristanuli xelovnebis istoriis sakitxebi. Tbilisi 1998, 25–31.

The archetype of the "Conversion of Georgia" was a short version, presumably like the one (not identical) mentioned as the source in the Chelishi and Sinaitic recensions of the "Annals of Georgia": "A brief Description of the Conversion of Georgia described by Grigol the Deacon" (N/Sin 48).

Basing on the comparative study of the existing variants enables to restore the ancient shape of the "Annals of the Conversion of Georgia". It has become clear that the Chelishi recension presents an expanded narration of Georgian history from the beginning till the end of the 4th c. but is rather shortened when dealing from the 4th c. till the early 7th c., except the reign of King Vakhtang Gorgasal (late 450s). It is possible to determine the additions, motives and time. Most number of them was made in the late 1050s. It is noteworthy that among additions are such details of certain episodes that are most trustworthy for the historians because of their precise description. Here I mean following episodes: Constantine the Great (306–337) receiving King Mirian's envoys and Queen Helena sending letters to Mirian and Nino; St. Nino's death; the forceful conversion of Georgia highland; some details of the conflict between Vakhtang Gorgasal and Archbishop Michael. After having excluded the additions it became clear that the Illuminator of the Georgians, as expected, was never mentioned as the "Saint". On its part it indicates to the very old archetype.

The comparative study has also revealed absolutely unchanged places in the "Annals" like King Mirian's thanksgiving words to God for having Christ's Holy Chiton in Mtskheta. The absolute coincidence of all three variants at this place shows that it is the most ancient unaltered quotation. Especially as it also shows ancient traditions in regards with the content but its later variants have undergone serious changes.

The discovery of two new Sinaitic recensions of the "Conversion of Georgia" must contribute much to the Chelishi redaction. The coinciding passages, especially when they are backed by other later variants, must be considered to be deriving from the protorecension. The text given below and dealing with the core subject of Georgian Church history must be regarded as such.

The Caucasiologists cannot agree if the appointing of the Catholicosat in 470s–480s meant that Georgian Church was entirely autocephalous or not. Some of them regard that entire autocephaly can be achieved in the times when the Church is ruled by the Catholicos-Patriarch and not Catholicos. The first Catholicos-Patriarch is supposed to have been appointed in Georgia in the 11th c. when this title is first mentioned in Georgian documents.

To my opinion, there has never been such a strict demand for determining canonical autocephaly. Not any Georgian polemical treatises, specially written on this subject, reveal any inkling to prove this. The Catholici of Georgia used to have the title of the Patriarch since early Middle Ages using its Georgian word "Mamamtavari" (an exact parallel to the Greek "Patriarch" and Armenian "Hairapet"). This term is frequently used in Georgian historical documents and epigraphical monuments till 12th c. A direct indication to this is given in the Chelishi manuscript of the "Conversion of Georgia". But nobody took much interest in it on principle, as the same text was not given in the earlier Shatberdi recension. The Sinaitic recension (with the metaphrastic one) supports the Chelishi recension and in the restored archetype the text is read in the following way: since establishing the Catholicosat in Georgia "the Catholici started to act as Mamamtavars (Patriarchs) and to shepherd the nation". At present I am in no position to prove my statement with the corresponding materials but I want to assure the audience that "Mamamtavari" and "Patriarch" are used as synonyms in the 11th–12th cc. Georgian documents.

Approximately the same results were achieved after having performed comparative study of three recensions of the "St. Nino's life". The Sinaitic manuscript has served as the controlling material of the different places in the Shatberdi and the Chelishi recension. It has shown that both of them have additions and omissions. This has enabled us to restore the extent of the protorecension of these three redactions. It is noteworthy from this point of view that the fourteenth chapter of the Shatberdi recension, the "Setting up of the Holy Cross of Mtskheta and its Reappearance" is entirely added to the main text. The specialists long ago noticed the unintegrity of this chapter to the text.

The new way of reading of the text of the "Conversion of Georgia" was determined by the discovery of the Sinai manuscripts. One of the most important readings among them concerns when, and why, and who had built the "Klisura Wall" (meaning "Kelasuri" or the "Great Wall of Abkhazeti"). The Sinai manuscript has shown that the Persians during the Byzantine-Persian war in the middle of the 6th century had built it.

The Sinai manuscripts have enabled us to restore right and old variants of the toponyms and anthroponyms in the "Conversion of Georgia". For example: Kxhueti instead of Kukheti; the place names and the names of the principalities of the so called Branjs's Country (Branjeti); Karzam Khuar Barzabord instead of Kram Khuar Borzard; Astiron instead of Stereon or Astrion, etc. N/Sin-50 has almost unmistakably preserved the Persian phrase ("He, he, rast mebai Khojasta banog rasul psarzad") that had been restored by N. Marr[13] according to the translation given in the Shatberdi variant: ("You say the truth, the blissful Queen and the Apostle of God's Son"). It is interesting to note that the translation of this phrase must not have existed in the archetype and that it was made in the protovariant of Shatberdi manuscript. In that manuscript this phrase in Persian language must have been written correctly (it is badly distorted in the Shatberdi and the Chelishi manuscripts) because it was yet possible to translate it. The most interesting thing is that according to Shatberdi and Chelishi variants N. Marr identified the phrase as New Persian. But the variant of N/Sin-50 shows the transitive period between the Middle and New Persian languages. N/Sin-50 makes it certain now that in the archetype of the "Conversion of Georgia" we had Babylon instead of Bagdad. The existence of the New Persian phrase and toponym "Baghdad" in the Shatberdi manuscript was one of the strongest arguments in favour of dating the whole text later than 7th c.

N/Sin-48 gives the undissimilized form of the name of the King of Georgia Vakhtang Gorgasal ("Gorgasar"). The Shatberdi variant, mentioning King Vakhtang's name as "Golgasar" (< Gorgasar), also proves the use of this form in the protoredaction.

The comparative study of the four recensions of the "Conversion of Georgia" has solved an even more important problem in Georgian historiography and textology. It concerns the principles of determining the critical text of the "Life of Georgia" (*Kartlis Tskhovreba*) that is the main Georgian historical source.

The problem is that "The Life of Georgia" is preserved in varying manuscripts that often contain grave mistakes and totally different readings. It is divided into three groups according to the redactions: the so-called Queen Anna's variant, Queen Mariam's variant and King Vakhtang VI's Learned Men's variant. Chronologically, the first two groups precede the third one that was prepared by a group of scholars at the beginning of the 18th c. It is based on all the known manuscripts of those times and the material of the entire Georgian literature. Different readings of the text represent the main difficulty when determining the critical text of the "Life of Georgia". The lack of the means of control makes it difficult to give preference to any of the group of manuscripts. This can be achieved only by means of "St. Nino's Life" given in the "Conversion of Georgia". This becomes possible because the whole text of "St. Nino's Life", after having undergone

---

13 N. Marr, Khiton Gospoden v knighnikh legendakh armjan, gruzin i siriitsev. In: Sbornik statei uchenikov B. P. Rozen. St. Petersburg 1897, 72.

certain corrections, appears in Leonti Mroveli's "Life of the Kings of Georgia" (that is a part of the "Life of Georgia"). In this work the narration is given in the third person, the episodes are shifted, some places are shortened, etc. but the 11th c. historian mainly rewrites St. Nino's life from "The Conversion of Georgia".

The comparative study of all the variants of St. Nino's life has enabled us to draw two most important conclusions in Georgian historiography:

1. Leonti Mroveli's text represents all three recensions of the "Conversion of Georgia" that are known till nowadays. It is evident that Leonti Mroveli had at hand the variant that preceded all the redactions and that was their protovariant. Thus, we can state that in the times before Leonti Mroveli there existed at least five redactions of "The Conversion of Georgia".
2. The manuscripts of the cycle of Queen Anna's manuscript should be used as the main text in determining the critical text of the "Life of Georgia". The best among them is the so-called Chalashvili Manuscript.

The study of the newly discovered manuscripts of the "Conversion of Georgia" is still going on. There are lots of other novelties there and it is not possible to talk about all of them in one paper. I am sure that after all the recensions are published together the Caucasiologists of different fields will find lots of new and interesting things in it.

IRINA ARZHANTSEVA / MOSCOW

THE CHRISTIANIZATION OF NORTH CAUCASUS (RELIGIOUS DUALISM AMONG THE ALANS)

The mediaeval history of the North Caucasus must take into account Byzantine influence, in the political, cultural and social life of the peoples of the region. To understand what Obolensky has called the 'Byzantine Commonwealth', we must remember that its north-eastern border ran across the North Caucasus. It must be remembered that from circa 1000 AD to the beginning of XVIII century Christianity was the dominant religion in the North Caucasus. Naturally, the enormous influence of Byzantine culture was an important factor.

In the 1st-early 2nd mil. A.D. Central Ciscaucasia was inhabited by the Alans. There has been a lot of argument about the Alans: who they were, when and how they appeared in the Caucasus. The Alans were in fact a union of Iranian-speaking tribes; they emerged in the 1st c. A.D. and rose to become the main political force in the Caucasus for a thousand years. The Sarmatian tribe of Aorses became the basis for the formation of the Alanian union. The union also included other Iranian tribes, some of which had close contact with Central Asia. Thus the Alans were never at any point a mono-ethnic group. There is no sign of any ethnic consolidation until the second half of the 1st mil., and the process of consolidation involved the aboriginal tribes of the Caucasus, peoples speaking North Caucasian languages. If we simplify this complicated process, we can say that the Alanian ethnos came about as a result of the interaction of immigrant Iranian nomadic tribes with a local settled population.[1]

As the Alans held, geographically, a key position in the North Caucasus, which was the major cross-roads of Eurasian trading and military routes, they were, from the moment that they united into a coherent political group, constantly drawn into the orbit of the complicated relationships of the super-powers, whose interests clashed in the North Caucasus. In the V–VI centuries these powers were Iran and Byzantium, who fought for control over the caravan routes that ran across the North Caucasus through territory occupied by the Alans (fig. 1). The Alan union, even after this, remained intact as a coherent political entity with its ruler, even though its actual role was ambiguous and sometimes inconstant. "... the Alans always appear to be a separately defined political entity who are at times allies of the Khazars and at times closer to Byzantium or, very rarely indeed, to the Caliphate."[2]

Thus during the wars between Iran and Byzantium the Alans could fight for either the Persians or the Byzantines. The whole history of Alania reflects a certain political dualism. Thus, probably by the sixth century A.D. two major Alan groupings had appeared. A western group lived on the Upper reaches of the Kuban, close to Lazica and Abkhazia,

---

[1] About the ethnogenesis of Alan see more: V. A. Kuznetsov, Ocherki istorii Alan. Vladikavkaz 1992, 9–56; V. B. Kovalevskaja, Kavkaz i Alany. Moscow 1984, 74–92; A. V. Isaenko – V. D. Kuchiev, Nekotorye problemy drevnei istorii osetin. In: Alany. Istoriya i kul'tura. Vladikavkaz 1995, 10–30.

[2] A. P. Novosil'cev, Khazarskoe gosudarstvo i ego rol' v istorii Vostochnoi Evropy i Kavkaza. Moscow 1990, 105.

which were under Byzantine control. Therefore Western Alania also entered the sphere of Byzantine influence and often fought as an ally of Byzantium. The Eastern Alans were settled around the Darial Pass, which leads into Kartli, a country dependent on the Persians. In their politics they gravitated to Iran.[3] There were multilateral links between the Alans and the Byzantines, since the Byzantines attached great importance to the Alans and did all they could to consolidate the position of Byzantium in the Caucasus.

During the second half of the first millennium A.D. Alania was a sort of buffer between three world religions – Islam, Christianity and Judaism. Islam had been installed by Arabs in Azerbaijan and Dagestan in 8th century; Christianity was established in Armenia, Georgia and Abkhazia; Judaism was adopted by Khazars in the 9th century. The Arab-Khazar wars, where the Alans were allies of the Khazars, had a very strong anti-Islamic element. That is why the Alans also were anti-islamically oriented. Judging from the so called "Cambridge document" of the 10th century the penetration of Judaism to Alania was superficial and didn't much influence the Alan. Byzantine religious politics were more successful.

Saint Andrew, one of the Twelve Apostles, is said to have preached Christianity among the peoples of the North Caucasus, namely the Alans, the Abazgians and the Zichi in A.D. 40.[4] The tradition was first recorded by Origen and Eusebius in the 3rd–4th centuries A.D.[5] and subsequently taken up by Dorotheus, the Archbishop of Tyre, in the 4th century and Epiphanius of Constaninople in the 5th century as well as by the Georgian chronicles in the 11th century and the Eastern Orthodox Lives of the Saints in the 16th century.[6] Although it is merely a popular belief that cannot be regarded as a historical fact, it is indicative of the North Caucasus important position in the Christian world.[7]

According to Procopius of Caesarea, the Alans' first contacts with the Romans and Byzantines were in the second half of the fifth century in the reign of the Emperor Romulus Augustulus.[8] In the sixth and seventh centuries Alan-Byzantine relations were even closer and by the seventh century Christianity began to penetrate the Alans (a reference to the Caucasus of Maxim the Confessor, 662 A.D.).[9] The mass conversion of the Alans by Byzantium did not begin, however, until the tenth century, under Patriarch Nicholas the Mystic.[10] According to the letters of Nicholas, the Patriarch of Constantinople, there was a metropolitan see under the authority of Constantinople in Alania as early as in the 10th century A.D. A certain Peter was ordained its archbishop by Nicholas himself. The Patriarch paid considerable attention to the Alanian diocese and was worried about the archbishop Peter. The latter, apparently, felt wretched among the Alans

---

[3] S. G. Zeteishvili, Svedeniya ob alanakh v "Khronografii" Feofana. In: Drevneishie gosudarstva na territorii SSSR. Moscow 1976, 85; Kuznetsov, l.c. 155.

[4] Makarii, arkhiepiskop Khar'kovskii, Istoriya khristianstva v Rossii do ravnoapostol'nogo Knyazya Vladimira. St. Petersburg 1868, 11.

[5] Gedeon, mitropolit Stavropol'skii i Bakinskii, Istoriya khristianstva na Severnom Kavkaze do i posle prosoedineniya ego k Rossii. Moscow 1992, 15–16.

[6] V. Vasilevskii, Russko-Vizantiiskie otryvki. *Zhurnal Ministerstva narodnago prosveshcheniya* 1877/2; M. Dzhanashvili, Izvestiya gruzinskikh letopisei. *Sbornik materialov dlya opisaniya mestnostei i plemen Kavkaza* 26 (1899) 3; S. Petrovskii, Skazaniye ob apostol'noi propovedi po Severo-Vostochnomu Chernomor'yu. St. Petersburg 1898.

[7] About this legend see more: A. A. Tuallagov, Alaniya (Osetiya) i missionerskaya deyatel'nost' sv. Andreya. In: Alany: istoriya i kul'tura. Alanika III. Vladikavkaz 1995, 59–64.

[8] Prokopii Kesariiskii (Procopius of Caesarea), Voina s gotami. Moscow 1950, 77.

[9] Zhizn', dela i muchenichestvo prepodobnogo otca nashego ispovednika Maksima. *Bogoslovskii vestnik*. Sergiev Posad, november 1913, 162–165.

[10] Yu. Kulakovskii, Khristianstvo u alan. *VV* 5 (1898), 3–7.

who clung to their pagan beliefs. "I think constantly of the salvation of the people to whom you were sent as a guide and saviour", wrote Nicholas to Peter (letter 113).[11] The court at Constantinople also gave the Alans a great deal of attention, which is reflected in Constantine Porphyrogennetos's work *The Ceremonies of the Byzantine court*. Constantine Porphyrogennetos calls the ruler of Alania "his spiritual son" and sends him charts with golden seals, thus equating Alania such Christian kingdoms as Armenia and Bulgaria.[12] There are traces extant of a correspondence between Constantinople and Alania, which presupposes that the Alans knew Greek and had translators available.

It is clear that by the 10th century Alania had reached its political and economic prime, as state. In mid 10th century, with the fall of the Khazar Khaganate, which had also played an important role as a counterweight to Byzantium in the history of the Alans, the influence of Byzantine culture took on a new quality. This is expressed in the mass conversion of the Alans to Christianity, in the construction of the monumental church complexes in the tenth to thirteenth centuries. At present, in the territory once occupied by the Alan state we can list several dozen such complexes. Some of them are in a very good state of preservation, others have been less fortunate and only their foundations survive. – It is a sad fact that a few of these monuments are at present in a high risk zone. I mean not just the war in Chechnia (for instance, the extraordinary complexes of the Assa valley lie immediately next to the 'hot points'), but also illegal construction and forestry involving the destruction of archaeological monuments (including the ones we are concerned with) on a massive scale. For example, in an expedition we carried out in summer 1998 all we could do was to report that a whole series of small mountain fortresses had been destroyed; these included fortresses constructed with the help of Byzantine artisans in the Mzymta valley and on the North-Caucasian shores of the Black Sea (a very large Byzantine settlement at cape Utrish.

The most interesting of the Christian monuments of the tenth to thirteenth centuries are concentrated in the Upper Kuban-river basin (western Alania) (*fig. 1*). Once they accepted Christianity, an Alan eparchy was established, with its own bishop. The mapping of the monuments of the western group, when overlaid on the area of epitaphs written in Greek, has allowed researchers to place the boundaries of the territory of the Alan bishopric roughly between the Great Laba river in the west and the district of the town of Nalchik in the east.[13] An analysis of these complexes leads researchers to conclude that the main eastern Byzantine influence on Western Alania came mostly through Abkhazia. A major role in this cultural influence was, to judge by most indications, played by Trebizond.

The territory to which churches were confined belonged to the Alanian diocese. The churches served as bases for the missionary activity of the Byzantines. In the opinion of many specialists the centre of the Alan eparchy was at Lower Arkhyz, the valley of the Great Zelenchuk river.[14] In the course of Christianization of the Alans an ecclesiastic province was being formed in the early 10th century, with a Metropolitan in its head.[15]

[11] S. A. Ivanov, Vizantiiskoe missionerstvo X–XI vv. Moscow 2000 (in print).

[12] Constantinus Porphyrogenitus, De cerimoniis aulae Byz. 688 (Reiske).

[13] S. N. Malakhov, K voprosu o lokalizacii eparkhial'nogo centra v Alanii XII–XVI vv. In: Alany, Zapadnaya Evropa i Vizantiya. Ordzhonikidze 1992, 164–165.

[14] V. A. Kuznetsov, Nizhnii Arkhyz v X–XII vv. Stavropol' 1993, 228–255; idem, Durgulel' Velikii i Nizhnii Arkhyz. In: Metodika, issledovaniya i interpretaciya arkheologicheskikh materialov Severnogo Kavkaza. Ordzhonikidze 1988, 76–91; S. N. Malakhov, K voprosu o lokalizacii eparkhial'nogo centra v Alanii XII–XVI vv. In: Alany, Zapadnaya Evropa i Vizantiya. Ordzhonikidze 1992, 149–179, esp.164–165.

[15] V. A. Kuznetsov, Ocherki istorii Alan. Vladikavkaz 1992, 317–319.

Thus, the need arose to create the residence of Alanian Metropolitans and to found a cathedral. Hence the choice of the Lower Arkhyz, an ecologically favourable and sheltered in the heart of mountains valley was quite logical. It was situated on the great road "from the Alans to the Greeks", not far from Abkhazian Black Sea ports, which was conducive to the links with Byzantium. The erection of the Northern and Middle Churches with attached structures was begun there. The diocesan settlement gradually became a town. Large-scale church building, the influx of Byzantine missionaries and the enlivening of the economy and culture gave a strong impetus to the evolution of the Lower Arkhyz. The large complex of buildings has been preserved there: it consists of three churches of tenth century, the North, Central and South Zelenchuk churches. They all belong to the type of 'cross and dome' church typified by three apses, the cross shape within rectangular walls, and they have been constructed in the Anatolian (east Byzantine) architectural school tradition (*fig. 2*).

The North Zelenchuk church is the most monumental of any that survive: undoubtedly, it was the cathedral of the Alan bishopric. The inner walls of the church were covered with frescoes which survived to the end of the nineteenth century. Now only insignificant fragments of these frescoes survive. But we can get an idea of them from an album of drawings by the archaeologist and artist D. M. Strukov, who visited these areas in 1886 and made invaluable drawings of the frescoes and of virtually all the architectural monuments that still can be found today in the Great Zelenchuk gorge (Strukov's materials unfortunately are still not publihed, now it is in archive of the Institute of Material Culture, St. Peterburg). Specialists who have examined the frescoes in the North Church (*fig. 3*) believe that there is no doubt about the Byzantine influence (especially the influence of Byzantine manuscript ornamentation) in the ornaments.[16] Historians of architecture who have studied this monument have often pointed out the close parallels to this church to be found in the tenth century churches in Abkhazia, such as Lykhny, Loo, New Athos and the River Bzyb.[17] There is no doubt that all these churches belong to one architectural school, closely linked with the east Byzantine architectural school at Trebizond. It would be logical to suppose, as many specialists have done, that the Byzantine elements (at least in architecture) came to the North Caucasus via Abkhazia. This is only partly true. Recent research by L. A Perfil'eva has shown unmistakable eastern Byzantine sources for the genesis of the North Zelenchuk church and also its typological links with the tenth century church of St Sophia in Trebizond. It has been proposed, and on fairly solid grounds, that Greek builders (from Constantinople or Anatolia, in particular Trebizond) took part in the construction of the North Zelenchuk church. Moreover, there are many indications to show that the churches we have mentioned in Abkhazia are typological of a later period than the North Zelenchuk church, i.e. they were built during the same century, the tenth, but after the erection of the North Zelenchuk church and perhaps by the same builders.[18]

The Central Zelenchuk church is eight hundred metres to the south of the North church, on the northern edge of the mediaeval site of Lower Arkhyz. It is a little smaller than the North Church. Its interior was also once ornamented by frescoes, of which virtually none remain. Like the frescoes in the North Church, they were sketched by D.

[16] V. A. Kuznetsov, Zodchestvo feodal'noi Alanii. Ordzhonikidze 1977, 37; K. Weitzmann, Die byzantinische Buchmalerei des 9. und 10. Jahrhunderts. Berlin 1935 (Reprint Vienna 1996), pl. LXXVII.

[17] I. Adzinba, Arkhitekturnye pamyatniki Abkhazii. Sukhumi 1958, 194; L. G. Khrushkova, Lykhny. Srednevekovyi dvorcovyi kompleks v Abkhazii. Moscow 1998, fig. 46–47.

[18] L. A. Perfil'eva, K voprosu o vizantiiskom vliyanii na kul'tovuyu arkhitekturu Severo-Zapadnogo Kavkaza X–XI vv. In: Alany, Zapadnaya Evropa i Vizantiya. Ordzhonikidze 1992, 180–200.

M. Strukov in 1886 (a small part of these sketches was published by V. A. Kuznetsov (*fig. 3*). The material that has survived allows us to state that these frescoes too have unmistakable traces of Byzantine influence. The Central and North Zelenchuk churches have a lot in common in their layout, their proportions, in the design and building technique, so that there is really no doubt that they were erected at the same time or within a very short period. Nevertheless, the constructional peculiarities of the North Church make it similar to churches of the tenth to thirteenth centuries found in south-west Georgia (e.g. Zaki, Tsqarostavi, Enirabata, Doliskhana, Shoreti). From a territorial point of view all these similar churches are to be found in the provinces of Meskheti and Shavsheti, which were part of the princedom of Tao-Klarjeti, associated with the eastern provinces of Byzantium. In the beginning of the ninth century this territory, including Abkhazia, was a vassal state of the Byzantine empire. Thus the appearance of churches of this kind (with a transversely oriented basic interior and an elongated western branch) must inevitably be linked to the influence of a Byzantine building school, which has earlier prototypes from the fifth to seventh centuries in upper Mesopotamia and Anatolia.[19] The Central Zelenchuk church shows that this architectural composition has come to Alania via South West Georgia, but has here been re-worked in the spirit of Abkhaz-Byzantine traditions that had evolved locally.[20] The purpose of the Central Church was to be a central cathedral for the Christian population of a mediaeval town that then existed at Lower Arkhyz. There are indications to show that in the tenth century a monastery of John the Baptist existed around the Central Church, for the monastery is mentioned in written sources.

The South Zelenchuk Church is in the centre of the former township, surrounded by habitations. This is the smallest of the churches that have survived at Zelenchuk (*fig. 2*). The South Church suffered most from the time when the Alexander-Athos monastery was constructed. Nevertheless it is still possible to reconstruct the original plan of the building. It has many similarities with the plan and building techniques of the other Zelenchuk churches, especially the North Church, so that it too can be dated to a point in the tenth century. It has parallels in the tenth-century churches of Abkhazia, Chersonesus and eastern Crimea. Nevertheless, its closest analogies are with the Byzantine architecture of Trebizond (the Church of St Basil, church 'C'), yet another indication that the sources for the architecture of this church, and all the other Zelenchuk churches too, are to be found in Anatolian Byzantium.[21]

They all belong to the type of "cross and dome" church and they have been constructed in the Anatolian (east Byzantine) architectural school tradition. Other well preserved Christian churches – Shaona and Senta churches – of tenth-eleventh centuries are located not far from Lower Arkhyz and also have been constructed in the traditions of the eastern Byzantine school. The Senta church, one of the best examples of the so-called "cross-shaped" churches (*fig. 4*) is of particular interest. It is a pillarless, one-apse, cruciform plan church. There are but few similar churches, namely that of the former Chersonesos monastery in Sebastopol, those at Shiomgvime and Samtsevrisi in Georgia[22] and those at Lmbat and Talin in Armenia.[23] In the territory of the Byzantine Empire proper such churches are also few and date to the 5th–8th centuries, while those of the North Caucasus

---

[19] D. Boshkovich, Arkhitektura sredneg veka. Beograd 1957, 28–29, fig. 32, 36.

[20] Kuznetsov, Zodchestvo (n. 16), 61.

[21] N. I. Brunov, Pamyatniki rannevizantiiskoi arkhitektury v Krymu. *VV* 25 (1928) 98; A. L. Yakobson, Srednevekovyi Krym. Moscow-Leningrad 1964, 98.

[22] G. N. Chubinashvili, Voprosy istorii iskusstva. Issledovaniya i zametki. I. Tbilisi 1970, 53, 116–124.

[23] N. M. Tokarskyi, Po stranitsam istorii armyanskoi arkhitektury. Erevan 1973, 84, fig. 3-zh 3.

date mainly to the 10th–11th centuries. Among the latter those at the Arkhyz valley, the Kiafar and the Greater Zelenchuk river valleys are worth noting. It is believed that cruciform plan churches embodying the idea of the Saint Cross were erected primarily in "wild" places where the Christian faith was but recently practised. The simple design of such churches supposedly made the Christian symbolism clearer to the mass of the people.[24]

Apart from these major churches in the upper Kuban valley, there are several dozen simple mono-apsidal chapels which functioned as parish churches and can be also found on every township site of the tenth to thirteenth centuries. It is obviously that all the major churches of the tenth century were built with the direct use of Greek craftsmen who arrived together with missionaries. All the other small churches were very likely to have been built by local craftsmen who had undergone the necessary training by Byzantine builders.

The political environment of the conversion of the Alans was complicate. The conflict between Alania and Judaic Khazaria of 932 was provoked by Byzantium and ended in the defeat of Alania, a temporary abandonment of Christianity and the expulsion of Byzantine priests. According to the "Cambridge Anonymus" (60th years of X century) the Alans even converted to Judaism.[25] Either it is simply not true or the Judaism was adopted by only a small part of Alanian aristocracy. But the "Cambridge document" materials about a temporary abandonment of Christianity are confirmed by archaeology, in some Alans sites (e.g Ilyichevskoe, Pervomaiskoe) show traces of destructions and then reconstruction of Christian chapels, and these traces date to the middle of the 10th century.[26]

A syncretic outlook came with the official acceptance of christianity in the early 10th century. Missionaries and travellers both report that "the King of the Alans is a Christian at heart",[27] but that the population as a whole, though it was officially Christian and tolerant of Christianity, still remained pagan even in the 13th century. It seemed likely that the ruler himself didn't break complete with pagan beliefs. Theodore, a bishop who stayed in Alania in 1222–1225 in his famous "Epistle" describes vividly the fate of Christianity in Alania. "It was indeed a flock scattered over mountains, deserts and abysses, having neither enclosure nor hut, easy prey to wild beasts ... Alas, an apostolic foundation supported an edifice of straw and reed and it fell victim to fire ... Who am I to heal forcibly by my preaching the woes the Alanian state is beset with?"[28] The bishop further laments that "the Alans are Christians in name only".[29] All the "Epistle" abounds in quotations and parables from the Bible, primarily from the letters of St Paul who was the first to evangelize the heathen. However, the "Epistle" reveals some more mundane concerns of the bishop as well. Theodore is disturbed by the bloodthirst of the Alans, their

---

[24] G. K. Vagner, Iskusstvo myslit' v kamne. Moscow 1990, 23; V. I. Markovin, Issledovanie Sentinskogo khrama i nekropolya u reki Teberdy v Karachaevo-Cherkesii. *Istoriko-Arkheol. Al'manakh* (Moscow-Armavir 1996) 183.

[25] N. Golb – O. Pritsak, Khazarsko-Evreiskie dokumenty X v. Moscow–Jerusalem 1997, 132.

[26] V. N. Kaminskyi – I. V. Kaminskaya, Novye issledovaniya khristianskikh khramov malykh form v Zapadnoi Alanii. *Istoriko-Arkheolog. Al'manach* (1996) 175, 178.

[27] Rasskaz rimskogo katolicheskogo missionera dominikantsa Yuliana o puteshestvii v stranu privolzhskikh vengrov, sovershennogo im v 1235 godu. In: Osetiny glazami russkikh i inostrannykh puteshestvennikov (XIII–XIX vv.). Ordzhonikidze 1967, 13.

[28] Theodori episcopi Alaniae sermo epistolaris. *PG* 140, col. 393, 400. Episkopa Feodora "Alanskoe poslanie", trad. Yu. Kulakovskyi. *Zapiski Imp. Odesskogo obshchestva istorii i drevnostei* 21 (1898) 12; S. A. Ivanov, "Izdevayushchiesya nad lysinoi": episkop Feodor sredi alan. Moscow 2000 (in print).

[29] Col. 490.

polygamy and conjugal relations with neighbouring, probably pagan, tribes and their penchant for heresy. "Among the characteristic traits of my flock there are, first and foremost, murder and scores of other plagues".[30] "My flock not only lecher under the tree, as it is said in the Holy Scripture, they do it on stones and in waters as well. And they worship not idols but some demons on high grounds."[31] Although such a renowned scholar as S. Ivanov sees nothing but biblical allusions in these words, I tend to think that at least some features of Alanian beliefs, namely the worship of demons on raised ground, are described adequately by Theodore.

Let me touch very briefly upon pre-Christian beliefs of the Alans. Up to the 10th century they were under the sway of paganism. The latter (as we can judge according to archaeological and written data) continued to play an important role even after the conversion to Christianity up to the Middle Ages. Outstanding scholar Vassili Abaev has distinguished an Alanian cult of deities, among whom those of the sun and fire were the foremost.[32] The relevant Iranian tradition was intertwined with the equally widespread autochthonous fire cult in the Caucasus. Hence the dominance of fire and sun cult in Alanian (Sarmatian) beliefs mentioned by early authors.[33] Also there were other pagan cults – the cult of the dead, the cult of War-God, personified in the sword and others.[34] These Alanian cults are attested beyond doubt on the archaeological record.[35] We are more concerned, however, with a seemingly impossible interaction between heathen beliefs and Christianity. In this respect the Alanian site of Kiafar is, in my opinion, of particular interest (*fig. 1*).

Kiafar lies on a narrow ridge. It overlooks the junction of two rivers, the Kiafar and the Krivaia. Four years' work has resulted in us producing a large-scale plan of the city which maps all objects visible on the surface. We have investigated a total of some two hundred such objects. The length of the town from north to south is almost two kilometres. At some points the width reaches 200 metres. Even a cursory glance at the plan of the town shows its strikingly complex structure (*fig. 5*). The town has a lower and an upper part. If we include the river-bank part, which has disappeared, it was a tripartite city. There are almost no habitations in the lower part, but it is surrounded by a defensive wall. The lower part of the town does, however, have several complexes which I am inclined to interpret as religious. As for dating the monument, the bulk of the pottery we have recovered from excavations is dated to the 10th and 11th cc. Also we did some very general preliminary demographic calculations. The population of Kiafar was somewhere between 742 and 1781 persons. For its time it was a sizeable town. Next to the town was discovered a Royal Necropolis, which naturally was robbed in antiquity. But even today the tomb slabs with rich relief ornamentation survive. This is the place of origin for the famous royal tomb now in Stavropol museum. Pagan and Christian symbols are inextricably interwoven in the decoration of this tomb (*fig. 6*). This tomb belonged to one of the

[30] Col. 412 B.

[31] Col. 409 B-C.

[32] V. I. Abaev, Dokhristianskaya religiya alan. In: Doklady delegatsii SSSR na XXV mezhdunarodnom kongresse vostokovedov. Moscow 1960, 9; idem, Osetinskii yazyk i fol'klor. I. Moscow–Leningrad 1949, 70.

[33] Herodot/Gerodot, Istoriya v devyati knigakh, trad. F. G. Mishchenko. Sankt Petersburg 1888, 212, 216; V. N. Grakov, Perezhitki skifskikh religii i eposa u sarmatov. *Vestnik drevnei istorii* 1969/3, 71.

[34] Ammian Marcellin, Istoriya: V. V. Latyshev, Izvestiya drevnikh pisatelei o Skifii i Kavkaze. *Vestnik drevnei istorii* 1949/3, 305.

[35] Z. Kh. Albegova, Paleosociologicheskie issledovaniya religii alan V–XII vv. Dissertaciya na soiskanie uchenoi stepeni kandidata istor. Nauk (manuskript). Moscow 2000.

rulers. In the town we found several times slabs of dismantled tombs with similar reliefs (*fig. 7*).[36]

To which of the known Alan rulers of the 11th c. could this fortress town belong? And whose royal tomb is it? Prominent specialists in the Caucasus have suggested that the Alans reached their greatest power and their prime under the rule of Durgulel the Great, whose dates, according to Georgian sources, coincide with those of the Georgian King Bagrat IV (1027–1072). Durgulel is mentioned several times in *The Conversion of Georgia* as "the Great King of the Ovses Dorgolel". Durgulel the Great was also closely linked to the Byzantine imperial court. Naturally it is Durgulel the Great that is mentioned in many Byzantine sources of the time as "Ruler of Alania". Thus we have every reason to suppose that the largest town in western Alania, situated not far from the Alan Eparchy in the Lower Arkhyz, with such a complex structure and system of fortifications was the residence of Durgulel the Great.[37] Durgulel the Great had political and dynastic ties to Byzantium and Georgia and was a Christian, at least officially.[38]

The Kiafar site shows very well this syncretism of religious ideas among Alan aristocrats. The remains of several small churches and of Christian symbols in the decoration of buildings and mausoleum prove that much of the population professed Christianity (*fig. 7*).[39] There is, right by the upper town, to the right of the road, a rocky outcrop, which we have, for good reasons, decided to call the "Shrine" (*fig. 8*). Its sides are too steep to give access. This shrine is 10 metres high and has a flat top. Fifteen steps cut into the rock lead to this flat landing. We discovered and examined a structure there: it may have been a small single-apsis church or a chapel. This is suggested by the plan of the building, its orientation, the thickness of the wall, which are more solid than those of living accomodations, remains of a floor made of stone slabs, the construction techniques, which also differ from the techniques used in building living quarters and defensive structures. If this is a Christian church, then the closeness to sacrificial stones is all the more remarkable. These stones are placed in a half circle on the edge of the shrine, right by the entrance into the church. These stones, the church and the area between them are certainly parts of a single complex. Why do we think these stones are sacrificial? They are slabs of fairly large dimensions, artificially worked with an absolutely even surface. All of them stand on "feet" made of small slabs of sandstone. They are all placed at a slight slope. There are petroglyph signs, in the form of the so-called "Babylon" and tamgas of geometric form carved on a central slab which is right opposite the entrance to the building; next to the signs is a small hollow, perfectly hemispherical in shape (*fig. 8–2*). These slabs are absolutely identical externally to the slabs on which the local inhabitants – Karachai Turks (who are one part of contemporary descendants of Alans) – used to slaughter sheep until very recently. We thus have every reason to consider these slabs sacrificial. Other stones with petroglyphs and hollows were found on the shrine. It is clear that pagan religious

[36] I. Arzhantseva, From settlement to cities. Alanian proto-cities of the 1st–2nd mil. A.D. in the North Caucasus. In: Medieval Europe, vol. I. "Urbanism", p. 160; N. A. Okhon'ko, Izobrazheniya na stenakh grobnitsy s reki Krivoi. *Sovetskaya Arkheologiya* 1983/2, 79.

[37] V. A. Kuznetsov, Durgulel' Velikii i Nizhnii Arkhyz. In: Metodika, issledovaniia i interpretacia arkheologicheskikh materialov Severnogo Kavkaza. Ordzhonikidze 1988, 83–85.

[38] S. N. Malakhov, Alano-vizantiiskie zametki (I). In: Alany: istoriya i kul'tura. *Alanika* 3 (Vladikavkaz 1995) 376–383.

[39] K. F. Stal', Etnograficheskii ocherk cherkesskogo naroda. *Kavkazskii sbornik* 21 (1900) 110; Kuznetsov, Durgulel' (see note 37) 83; I. A. Arzhantseva, Otchet o rabotakh na Kyafarskom gorodishe v 1994 g. (Karachaevo-Cherkesiia). Archive of the Institute of Archaeology, Russian Academy of Sciences, 1995, R-1, 188845, album 72, fig. 2; eadem, From settlement to cities (see note 36) 160; I. A. Arzhantseva – Z. Kh. Albegova, Kul'tovye kamni Kyafarskogo gorodisha. In: Drevnosti Severnogo Kavkaza. Moscow 1999, 186.

rituals took place here. We found a large number of the same stone slabs on pedestal and with various signs on the surface over all the Kiafar-site. This suggests obligatory and widespread animal sacrifice or the use of animals augury (the use of animal organs for augury) among the population of Kiafar. I suggest that the slabs with "babylon" signs and chains of holes on their surfaces were also used for augury (*fig. 9*). Inside surfaces of these holes are very well polished, and it could be a result of frequent touching in certain places possibly, as a part of ritual. Most likely, the augury was conducted by throwing dice and sticks on the surface with signs, and the fortune depended on which of the "babylon" fields these objects ended up. Similar "babylons" exist in Western Europe till high middle ages as a field for a "fox game" (fr. "attrape – renard", sw. "svalta rav") (*fig. 10*). This game spread in Europe in the 1st mil. A.D.; it originates in the late-Roman game "lupus latrunculus"; and it is also based on the fortune-telling principle.

Numerous depictions of deer (stag) on the stones are clearly linked to ancient pagan rituals: "Hunter's magic" (*fig. 11*). Kiafar stones provided a striking example of intertwining of Christian and pagan mythology. The picture of deer (stag), the animal most respected by the Alans and their descendants, with a cross between the horns shows that the legend of the Miracle of St. Eustathius/Eustachius had been reworked locally. The image of St. Eustathius's deer and the cult of Apsati, Protector of Hunting and wild animals, who is depicted as a deer. The narrative of "St Eustachius Miracle" spreads in Europe somewhat later via Byzantium, and it is well represented in mediaeval art (cf. illustrations of Khludovskaya Psalter, at 14th-century painting of Pisanello, and so on). According to the Miracle, Eustachius (named Placidus before baptism) was a Roman high-rank officer, and he died as a martyr during the reign of the Emperor Hadrian (117–138 A.D.). Placidus converted to Christianity after he saw the image of the Saviour or a Cross between horns of deer that he pursued in hunting, and heard a voice saying "Placidus, why are your pursuing Me, Who wishes you salvation?" In Christian cultures, St Eustachius is considered patron of hunters.[40] This story gains popularity among the Alans and their descendant Osetians. It provides a plot for frescoes in the 11th-century church Khozita Mada Mairam (Godmother of the Khoziev Family) in the Zrug gorge of North Osetia and in the 14th-century Nuzal chapel which belonged to the Alan royal clan of Tsarazontovs.[41]

The Alans seemed to have a Christianised pantheon by the end ofthe 12th century: we see the same phenomenon in today's Osetians and the Balkars and Karachais who by origin and beliefs are the closest to them. Christian saints, today and then, carry out the functions of pagan gods. The Alans accepted only a veneer of Christianity. They were on the whole, at heart, still pagans. And, possibly, not completely relying on the grace of the new God, they continued making sacrifices to their old ones, and did so, ironically, nearby the new churches. In other words, the pagan rituals were not formally banished. In his letters of 914–916 to the Alan bishop Peter, Nicholas the Mystic advises against using force in conversion. Generally, he writes, the conversion from pagan life to the precise following the Scriptures is never easy. Therefore, one should bring them the teaching persistently, and [yet] with fatherly guidance and gently. But if you see, that they protest, bare this with patience – in particular, if the disobedient belong to the upper classes of the people (letter no. 52)[42]. The Alan nobility and rulers were mainly responsible

---

[40] Polnyi pravoslavnyi bogoslovskii enciklopedicheskii slovar'. I. St. Petersburg 1992, 826.

[41] V. A. Kuznetsov, Rekom, Nuzal i Tsarazonta. Vladikavkaz 1990, 66–67, fig. 28.

[42] Pribavlenie k izdaniyu tvorenii svyatykh otcov v russkom perevode. XX. Moscow 1861; S. A. Ivanov, Vizantiiskoe missionerstvo X–XI vv. Moscow 2000 (in print).

for this syncretic religion. Although they took the initiative in accepting Christianity, they could not fully renounce a pagan world-view.

List of illustrations

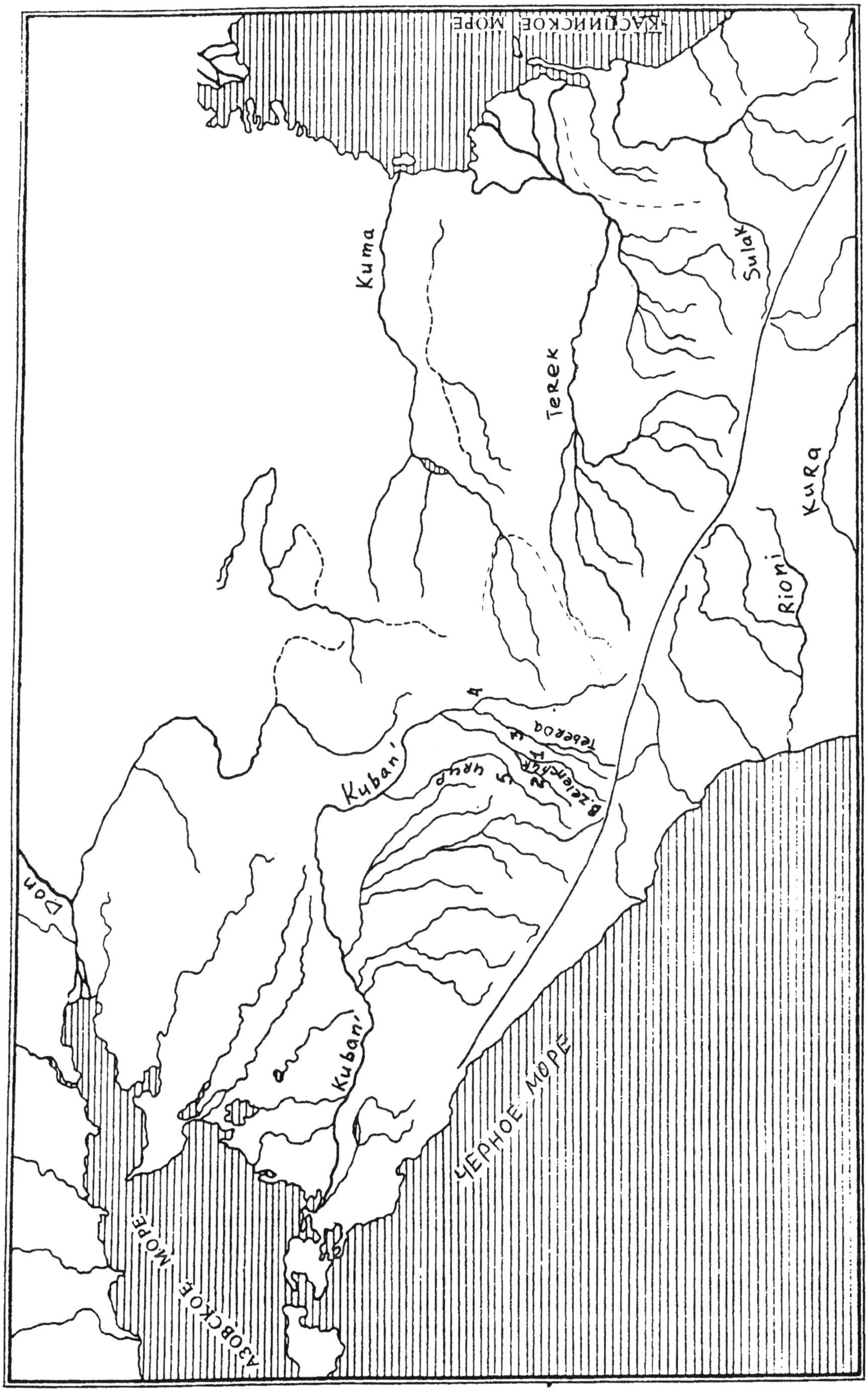

Fig. 1: Christian monuments of Western Alania: 1 Nizhnyi Arkhyz; 2 Kiafar; 3 Senta church; 4 Shaona church; 5 Il'ichevskoe site

Fig. 2: Zelenchuk churches: 1a Northern Church; 2b Central Church; 3 South Church (after V. A. Kuznetsov)

Fig. 3: The frescoes of the Zelenchuk churches (D. M. Strukov's sketches, published by Kuznetsov): 1–3 Northern Church; 4–5 Central Church

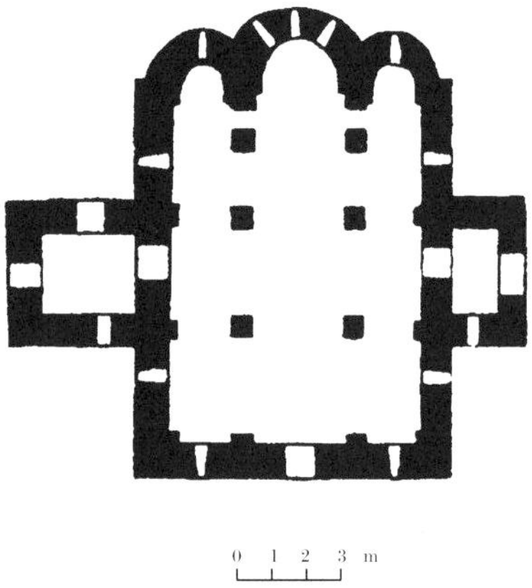

1a

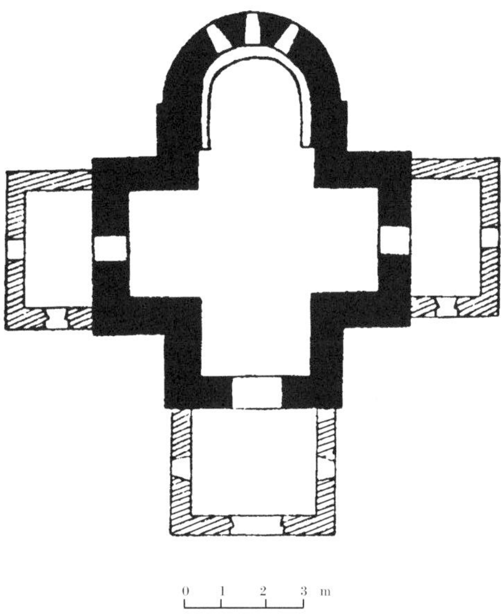

2b

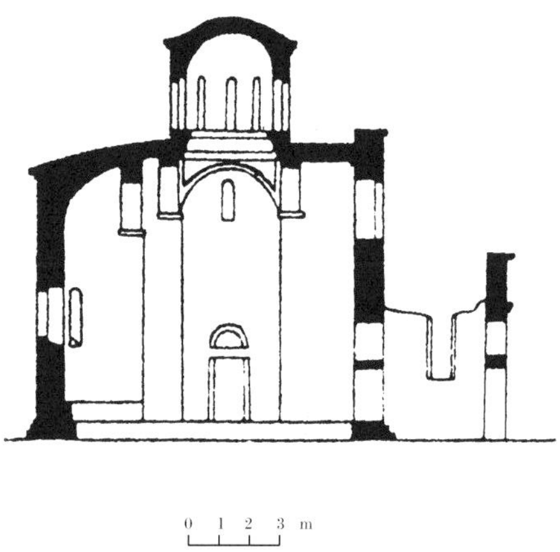

Fig. 4: 1a Shaona church; 2b Senta church (after Kuznetsov)

Fig. 5: Kiafar site. Plan

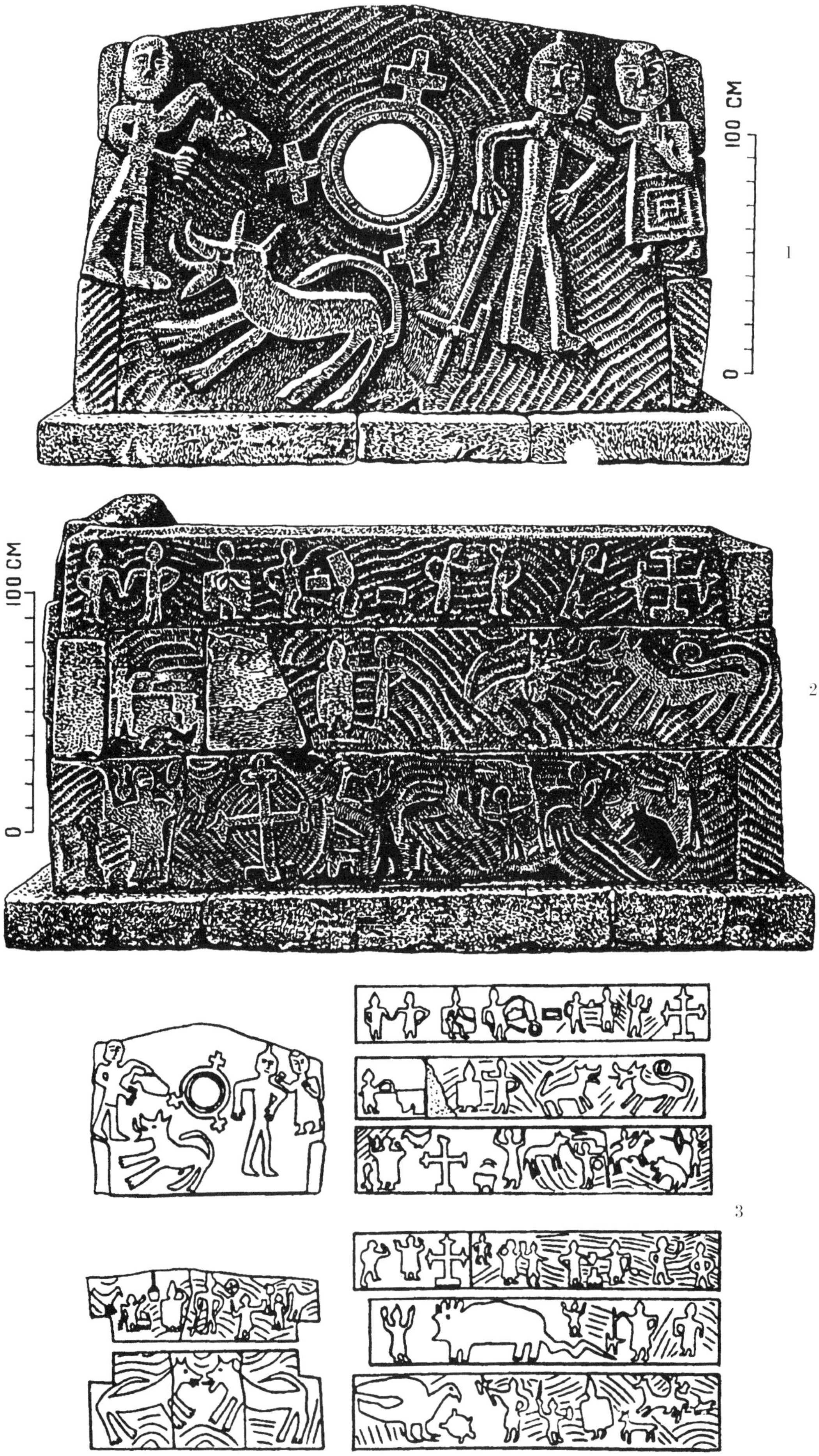

Fig. 6: Kiafar royal tomb: 1 Eastern side; 2 Northern side; 3 Traces of decoration (after N. A. Okhon'ko)

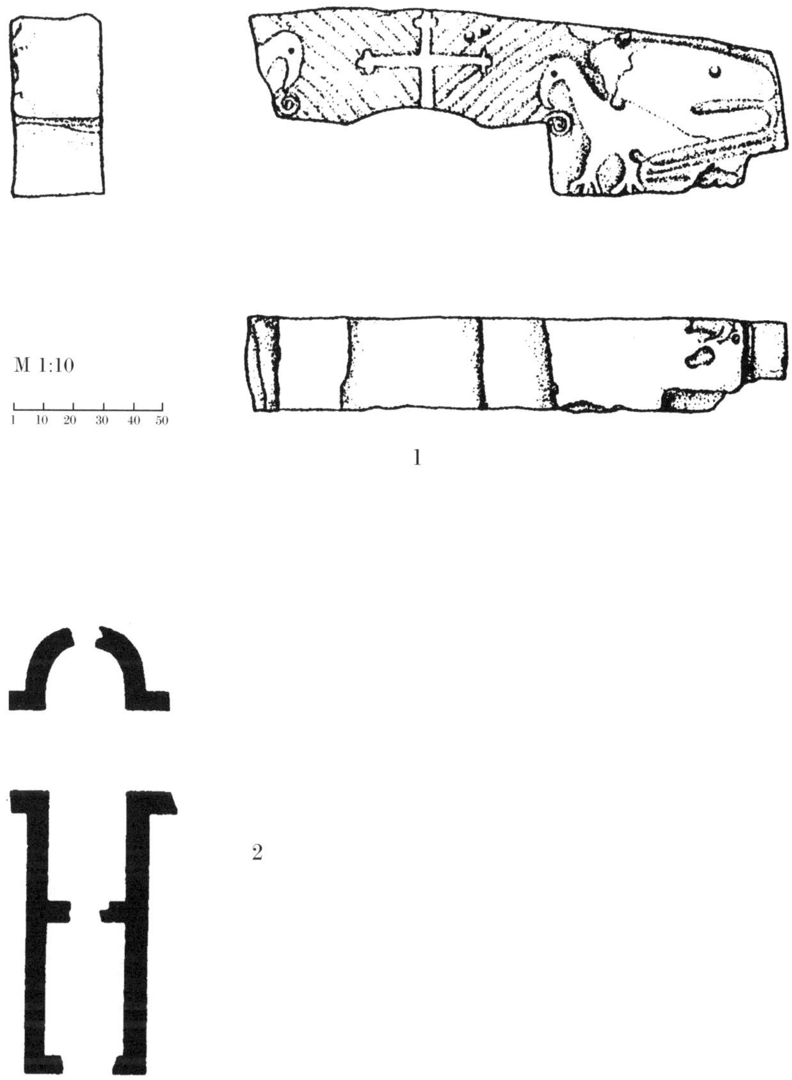

Fig. 7: Kiafar site: 1 Fragment of decorated slab (tomb); 2 Cruciform plan church (after Kuznetsov)

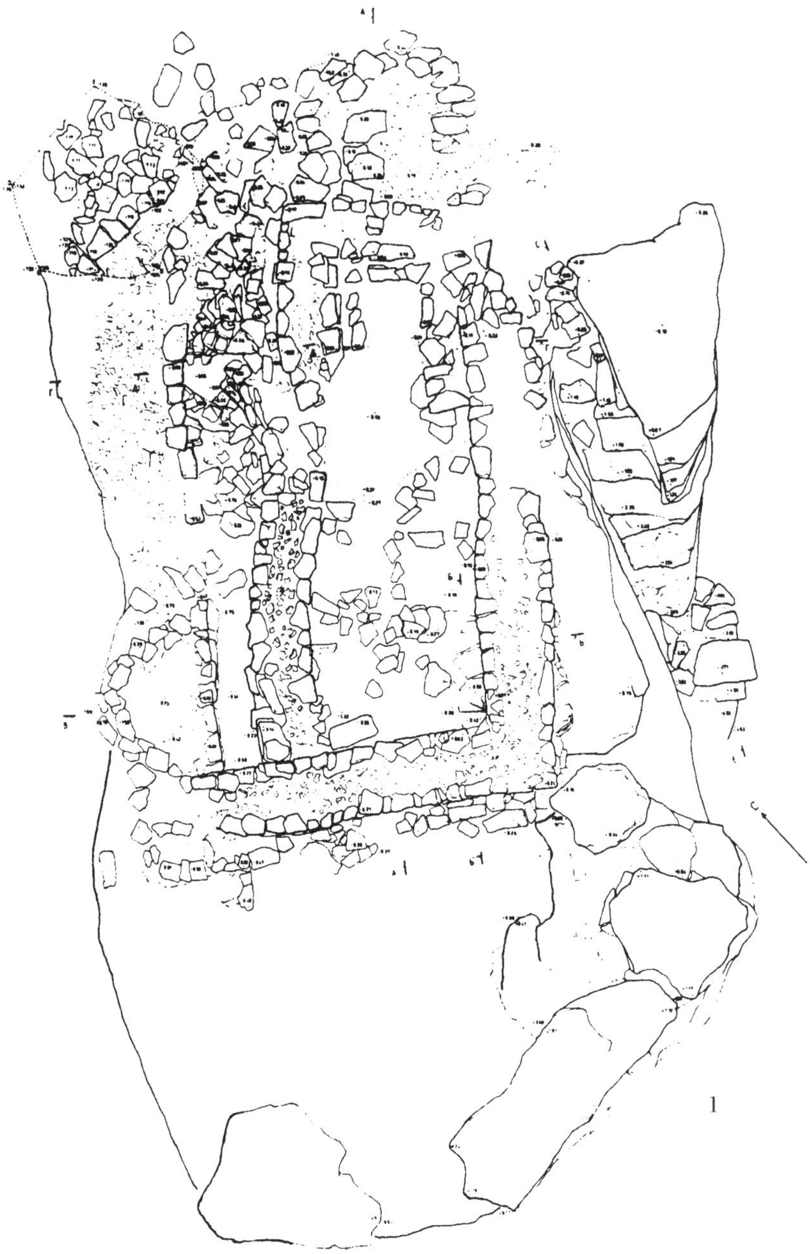

1

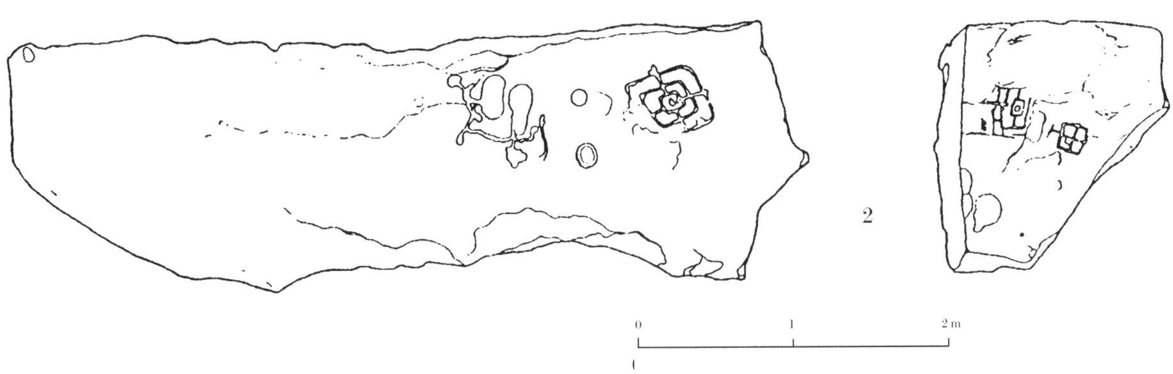

2

Fig. 8: Kiafar site: 1 "Shrine". Single-apsis church or chapel; 2 Sacrificial stones with "Babylon's"

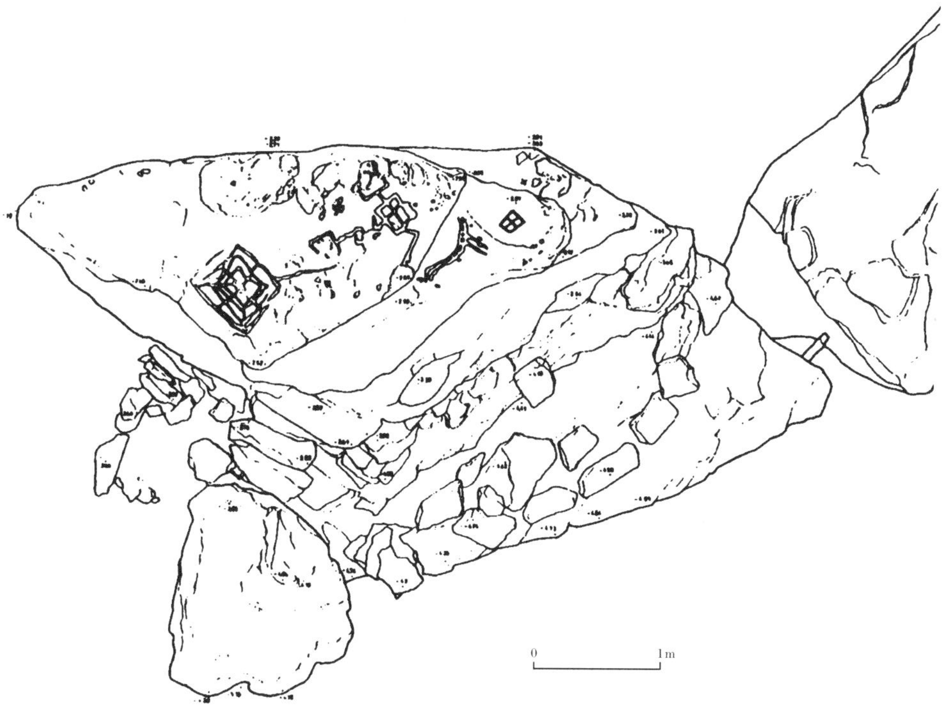

Fig. 9: Kiafar site: Sacrificial stone (for augury) with "Babylon" and other signs

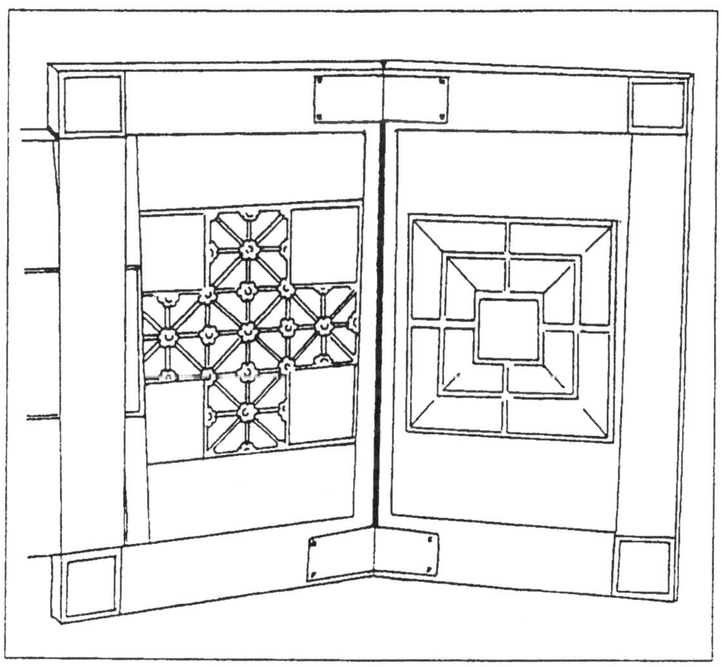

Fig. 10: Mediaeval wooden plates for the "fox game", XIV century (Museum Cluny, Paris)

Fig. 11: Kiafar site: "Hunter's magic" stone

WACHTANG DJOBADZE / CARLSBAD, CA

GEORGIANS IN ANTIOCH ON-THE-ORONTES AND THE MONASTERY OF ST. BARLAAM

The intensive flux of Georgian worshippers to the monasteries in Antioch begins in the sixth century A.D. These pilgrims were particularly attracted to the "wonderworker" St. Symeon Stylite the Younger (521–592) – sanctified already in his life time – and his famous monastery that was a model for the ascetic life; it exemplified the maximal detachment from the material world with its web of temptations and the approximation of celestial eternal bliss.

The Georgian pilgrims were drawn to this monastery not only to worship, but to seek a cure for various diseases from St. Symeon and to receive his blessings. The authors of the *vitae* of St. Symeon[1] and his renown mother, Martha,[2] offer ample information about those pilgrims who came to visit the monastery. Some of them even remained there like the priest Anton, who eventually was consecrated as Bishop of Seleucia by St. Symeon himself.

After the sack of Antioch by the Arabs in 637 the stream of Georgian pilgrims to these holy places in this region almost dried up; and even Georgia was occupied by the Arabs for three and a half centuries. The Arabs were defeated by Nicephorus II Phokas in 969, and after the liberation of Antioch the Georgians resumed their pilgrimages on a large scale.

They joined the still surviving monasteries like that of St. Symeon Stylites, and restored those that had been destroyed by natural calamities such as the monastery of St. Barlaam, or they built new lavras such as Dzeli C'xorebisa (Wood of Life). The Georgians established scriptoria in which a great number of books by Greek authors were copied, translated, and sent to Georgia to enrich their fatherland with Hellenic ideas and culture. The scope of the literary and educational activities carried out in some twelve monasteries and hermitages can be measured by the surviving manuscripts in the Institute of Manuscripts (Tbilisi), in the monasteries of Iviron in Athos, and in St. Catherine in Sinai. At the same time the number of monks increased steadily. The precise number of friars is not known, but toward the middle of the eleventh century in the monastery of St. Symeon alone lived some sixty Georgian monks; they also had their own library and even their own church, the remains of which we were able to trace along the south wall of the mandra. Eventually, the foot hold of Georgians in the western region of Antioch grew to a large colony and to the point of "quasi domination" – to use P. Peeters' expression – that became the cause for an ardent dispute between the Patriarch of Antioch, Theodosius III (1057–1059) and the Georgian church father George Athonite. The explicit account of this dispute has been recorded by the constant companion and biographer of George Athonite, Giorgi Mcire, who reports the following:

[1] P. Van den Ven, La Vie ancienne de s. Syméon Stylite le jeune, vol. I. Bruxelles 1962, 53–58*, 216–221*, and chap. 103, p. 80, 81.

[2] J. Garitte, Version Géorgienne de la Vie de Sainte Marthe. Louvain 1968, 53 and passim.

"Certain men from the monastery of the Holy Symeon, filled with devilish envy against us Georgians, attempted to eradicate our compatriots from said monastery, and slanderously intended to put some stain upon our holy and true religion, and thus to root us out from this glorious *lavra* where we were established from the very beginning by St. Symeon himself ... and with this evil conspiracy they approached the Patriarch Theodosius ... and told him, 'help us holy lord ... and rescue us from these alien men ... we do not know what their intentions are or what their religion is'. The astonished patriarch asked them, 'how is it possible that the Georgians do not adhere to orthodoxy?' ... And they replied that they did not know whether they were Armenians or Georgians, since their priest was not allowed to officiate."[3]

These accusations were exceptionally dangerous, since they concerned the "true" religion of the Georgians, and since the conversion of their country was clothed in mysticism. However, in the discussion with Patriarch Theodosius, George Athonite by quoting the writings of Greek theologians, was able to clear the accusations concerning the "true" religion of the Georgians and to convince the patriarch, the metropolitans, bishops and Antiochean eminences of the irreproachable integrity of their church and all they held supreme.

However, Athonite's victory seems to have been short-lived, because the Georgians had some substational shortcomings respecting the conversion of their country which needed to be overcome with more impressive arguments. This task was entrusted to another man of letters, Ephrem (Eprem) Mcire, who shortly after 1057 composed a "Report on the Conversion of Georgians, and the Books in which this is Mentioned". On this account he has the following to say:[4]

"For it was Eustathius (325–330), the Patriarch of Antioch himself who established the church built by Mirian in Mtskhetha (Mcxeta), and consecrated their Katholikos Archbishop. And the King of the Georgians, and all his dukes gave to the Patriarch of Antioch, as a payment for the holy chrism, towns comprised of a thousand households from the Georgian territory, so that the income from these should be the payment for the chrism. For at that time nowhere was the chrism holy but in Antioch, and from there it was distributed to everyone. From this time on the conversion is recognized, and because of their adherence to the church in Antioch, the archbishops of Kartli were consecrated by them. As to when they started the consecration of their own bishops and that it was done not without rule and decree, this we find described in the chronograph of Antioch which states:

At the time of Constantine Skoros (741–775) during the patriarchate of the blessed Theophylactus (Bar-Qanbara, 744–750) of Antioch, two messenger monks came from Kartli and reported to him that the Christian inhabitants of the Georgian land were in great difficulty, for since the time of the blessed Anastasios (559–570), Patriarch of Antioch, the katholikos (and) archbishop were not consecrated by them ... (since) no one dared to travel because of the Arabs. And he (Theophylactus), discussing the matter with the council of his archbishops, metropolitans, and bishops, gave to the Georgians the *protrepticon* which is (the document of) an exemption allowing the Katholikos of Kartli to be consecrated by the bishops of their country according to the ecclesiastical rule. And he (the Patriarch of Antioch) prepared for them descriptive reports; and one of these missionary monks by the name of John was consecrated as their katholikos at this time.

---

[3] Dzveli Kartuli agiograpiuli lit'erat'uris dzeglebi, ed. I. Abuladze, vol. II. Tbilisi 1967, 149 and passim. Some passages of Athonite's Life were translated into English by D. Lang, Lives and Legends of the Georgian Saints. London 1956, 165–168.

[4] Uc'q'ebaj mizezsa kartvelta mokcevisasa, tu romelta c'ignta sina moixsenebis, ed. T. Bregadze. Tbilisi 1959, 8 and passim.

Instead of the above-mentioned thousand households he ordained that they give every year to the Patriarch of Antioch one thousand *drahkan* which was given until the days of the holy Patriarch John, who conferred it on the holy Patriarch of Jerusalem, Orest, who came on a mission to the King of the Greeks, Basil, that this (tax) be given by the Georgians to their church in Jerusalem. And from these days it was decreed that the Georgians shall mention (in their liturgy) only the name of the Antiochean patriarch. And if heresy ever appears, only then should the exarch be dispatched there, to examine and straighten out heretical and spiritual errors, as in the days of the blessed Patriarch Theodoros, when Basil the Grammarian was sent there because of the heresy of the Akakians."

After the late fifties, despite occasional frictions with the authorities, lasting peace prevailed. The Georgian monasteries continued to grow and became formidable centers of literary activity. A great quantity of manuscripts were produced in their scriptoria which "flooded" Georgia with knowledge. Such a high standing was achieved at the fortunate time when the relations between Byzantium and Georgia were exceptionally favorable and considerable diplomatic gains were made: such as in 1031 the arrival of Queen Maria at the Byzantine court for her newly enthroned son in Georgia, Bagrat IV (1027–1072); the marriage of Bagrat IV with Helena, niece of the Byzantine Emperor, Romanus Argyrus III (1028–1034) in 1032; and conferring the title of Kuropalates on Bagrat IV; then came the marriage of Bagrat's daughter Martha to the Emperor Michael VII (1071–1078) and after his death her marriage to Nicephorus Botaniates (1078–1081).[5]

It is not the purpose of this paper to offer a full account of all the Georgian monasteries in the western outskirts of Antioch on-the-Orontes, but rather to concentrate on the monastery of St. Barlaam on Mt. Kasius, and to submit a condensed itemization of the documentary material found during our excavations *in situ* carried out from 1962–1966.

The location of St. Barlaam's monastery is suggested by the *bios* of the same saint and by objects collected there. In the Georgian version of St. Barlaam's *bios*, which I studied in the monastery of Iviron in Athos (A-84 after Blake's catalogue), is told that St. Barlaam was born on one of the summits of the Black Mountain north of Mt. Kasius in a place called Jubia.[6] More importantly, we learn from this manuscript that St. Barlaam, returning from Jerusalem to his native land, was guided by a pillar of fire, and that an angel appeared ordering him to ascend Mt. Kasius and to destroy the statue of Zeus and his sanctuary infested with devils, a task that Barlaam accomplished with great success.[7] The date of this event is not recorded, but since Julian the Apostate worshipped and made sacrifices to Zeus in this temple, Barlaam's exploits could have taken place sometime after the emperor's death in 363. Thus, Barlaam's *bios* compliments earlier literary

---

[5] See also the more extensive account by W. Djobadze, Materials for the study of Georgian monasteries in the Western environs of Antioch on the Orontes (*CSCO Subsidia* 48). Louvain 1976, 74–80. Thereafter quoted as "Materials".

[6] I am quoting Barlaam's *bios* from N. Marr, Agiografičeskie materialy po gruzinskim rukopisjam Ivera, II. *Zapiski Vostočnago Otdelenija Imp. Russk. Archeolog. Obščestva* 13/2–3 (1901) 113. In Jubia could have existed a monastery where a Georgian monk, Giorgi Jubieli (Giorgi from Jubia) was active. In 1140 he moved from Jubia to Iviron in Athos: E. Metreveli, Atonis Kartvelta monast'ris saağape c'igni. Tbilisi 1998, 87–217.

[7] Marr, op. cit. 118, 119. One should distinguish Barlaam of Jubia and Barlaam of Antioch, who was martyred during Numerianus (283–284). P. Peeters, *Bibliotheca hagiographica Orientalis*. Bruxelles 1910, 34; F. Halkin, *Bibliotheca hagiographica Graeca* I. Bruxelles 1957, 79. In honor of Barlaam of Antioch a church was built near the city and on March 9 in 479 in its baptistery the Patriarch of Antioch, Stephen, was attacked and stabbed to death with sharpened reeds by the monophysite clergy. His body was thrown into the Orontes river: G. Downey, A History of Antioch in Syria from Seleucus to the Arab Conquest. Princeton 1961, 489.

accounts about the existence of the sanctuary of Zeus and his statue. This was also confirmed by the material evidence found during the excavation.

This excavation on Mt. Kasius revealed various architectural fragments from the late Hellenistic to the late Roman period, that were reused in the walls of St. Barlaam's monastery; there were two fragments of a Doric frieze, triglyphs, plain metopes, Ionic and Corinthian capitals and their bases, architraves, and even an acroterion of a Roman sarcophagus,[8] as well as stamped mortar rims and stamped tiles.[9]

All these items corroborate the early literary sources and the *bios* that mentions on Mt. Kasius a sanctuary with the golden statue of Zeus,[10] who was not only the supreme divinity of the Greek pantheon, but the protector of the Seleucid dynasty. It is also related to the foundation of Antioch by Seleucos Nicator in 300 B.C., when he made appropriate sacrifices to Zeus on Mt. Kasius asking the deity where he should found his city.[11]

This temple of Zeus was highly venerated and the Roman emperors Titus, Vespasian, Hadrian, and Julian Apostate, who was the last emperor to do so, ascended the mountain to bring sacrifices on its summit.

After the destruction of the statue and sanctuary of Zeus and other exploits, St. Barlaam settled in a nearby cave to lead a solitary life and to occasionally perform miraculous healings. According to his *vita* he died on July 19 at the age of eighty. The year of his death is unknown, but it could have happened shortly after 363 and well ahead of the second half of the fifth century, when on the precinct of Zeus in honor of St. Barlaam a monastery and basilica were built. This monastic complex was short-lived and remained unknown. It must have been destroyed by the devastating earthquake that hit Antioch[12] in 526. This disastrous event that demolished many buildings and caused the loss of some 250 000 lives must have affected also the monastery of St. Barlaam which was near the epicenter.

The ensuing natural calamities which befell the area, such as the destruction caused by the invading Persians, and the final capture of Antioch by the Arabs in 637/8 left most monasteries unable to recover from the inflicted damages, and they remained in ruins. Only much later, after the expulsion of the Arabs by Nicephorus II in 969 Georgian monks arrived again in large groups and began with the restoration of the destroyed and abandoned monasteries, building anew their own churches or joining Greek monasteries.

One of the lavras which was rebuilt by Georgians toward the very end of the tenth or early eleventh centuries was that of St. Barlaam on Mount Kasius.

Georgian Literary Sources concerning St. Barlaam's Monastery

The Georgian literary sources concerning the *lavra* of St. Barlaam are rather scarce and all of these belong to the eleventh century. One of them is the afore mentioned "Life of George Athonite" written from 1066 to 1068 in which we are told that:

[8] W. Djobadze, Archeological Investigations in the Region West of Antioch on-the-Orontes (*Forschungen zur Kunstgeschichte und Christlichen Archäologie* 13). Stuttgart 1986, 7–9, 27–32, figs. X–XI; 22–26, 36–40, 41–44, 83. Thereafter: "Investigations".

[9] Op. cit., H. Seyrig's contribution pp. 201–204, figs. 383–393.

[10] Downey, op. cit. 128.

[11] Ibid. 67–77.

[12] For the detailed report of this earthquake see G. Downey, *TAPA* 89 81958) 87–89; idem, Antioch 519–533.

"Our God-loving King Bagrat[13] became aware that the translations of the holy books were completed, and that the churches in the Black Mountain were inundated by the river of those 'soul illuminating' books which had been copied in all the monasteries. But most of all toiled the blessed soul Ant'oni, having been Lip'arit'e, who made (the scribes) copy (books) for the monastery of St. Barlaam."[14]

One of these manuscripts, a *parakliton* preserved in St. Catherine's monastery in Sinai (Sin. 96),[15] was copied in the eleventh century by the "sinful Iovane" in Barlaam and was dedicated to St. Catherine's monastery. In another manuscript preserved in the same monastery, in a *menaion* (Sin. 56) copied in the XI–XII centuries, is revealed that on July 19th, the festival of the holy St. Barlaam[16] was celebrated in the monastery on Mt. Kasius. This date perfectly coincides with the date of the death given in St. Barlaam's *bios*.[17] Such a celebration on Mount Kasius is also confirmed by an *eulogia* mold showing the image of St. Barlaam with its accompanying inscription (see below).

St. Barlaam's Monastery on Mt. Kasius. Circuit walls

The monastery is located on the eastern slope of the mountain that originally had been leveled for the construction of the sanctuary of Zeus upon which in the second half of the fifth century the monastery of St. Barlaam was built.

In the second building period it was restored with minor modifications by Georgians. It is oriented toward east, and is enclosed by circuit walls in a square; its walls on the average are 2.00 m. high and their thickness typically is 0.80 m.; its exterior dimensions are 65.00 × 57.00 m. (*fig.* I).

The circuit walls rest on the foundation of earlier well dressed ashlar walls. The earlier walls on the monastery's north side are buttressed by several small rectangular compartments that are bonded with the walls. Originally they could have fulfilled the function of fortified towers which occur during the reign of Justinian.[18] For the interior face of the enclosure small size squared and roughly picked blocks are set in regular courses. Sometimes one finds inserted into the interior walls spoils from a Doric temple or late Roman buildings. Occasionally in the walls that were rebuilt by Georgians, blocks are set in mud mixed with straw. The hardened limestone used for the building was quarried on a nearby slope between the summit of the mountain and the monastery.

The mandra is accessible only from the south side, where the gate originally may have been provided with a barrel vaulted porch or some kind of propylaeum of which little remains.

The entire courtyard of the monastery (37.00 × 22.50 m.) was paved with evenly cut rectangular limestone slabs (*ca.* 1.00 × 1.20 m. and 0.20 m. thick) placed in regular rows. Large portions of this pavement still remain *in situ* especially on the north side. These slabs, while thicker by 0.05 m. than those reached by soundings in the basilica located in the south-east of the mandra, may have derived from the temple of Zeus where they may

---

[13] I.e. Bagrat IV (1027–1072).

[14] Agiograpiuli dzeglebi II 155.

[15] Kartul Xelnac'erta ağc'eriloba, Sinuri k'olekcia II. Tbilisi 1979, 116, and the testament on p. 130.

[16] Ibid. 215, Nr. 28.

[17] MARR, op. cit. 137 (fol. 123v).

[18] F. W. DEICHMANN – U. PESCHLOW, Zwei spätantike Ruinenstätten in Nordmesopotamien. Munich 1977, 9–14, fig. 1; see also C. KRAELING, The Walled City of the Gerasa Mosaics, in: Gerasa, City of the Decapolis. New Haven 1938, 341f., pl. LXXXVI-b.

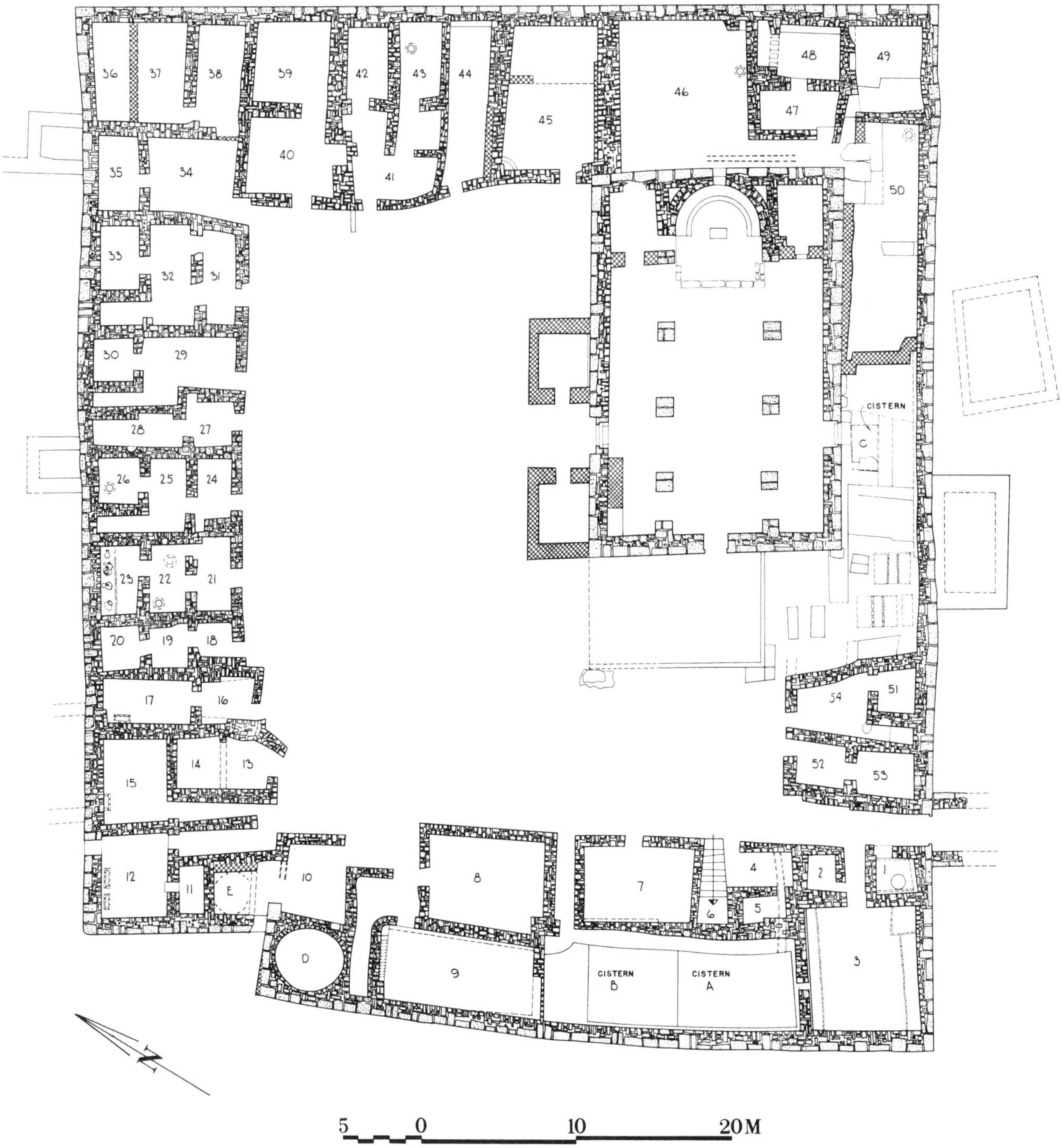

Fig. I: Plan of the Monastery

have comprised the temenos paving. The earliest identifiable coins found in this pavement belong to the second to third centuries A.D.[19]

Domestic Quarters and Church Annexes

Around the inner side of the circuit walls are lined up various compartments (*fig.*I) which mostly are built on the foundations of the first period (second half of the fifth century). Everywhere in these rooms an extensive damage from fire is evident.[20]

Room No. 1: This little room with a small cistern, coated with water proof plaster, suggests that it was the gate keepers chamber.

Room No. 2: Storage room for heating material containing a large amount of charcoal.

Room No. 3: On its north and south sides along the entire wall were long water proof troughs. The edges of the stone pavement were worn. Probably used as a wash room, an assumption that is supported by the two large cisterns (A and B) on the north side.

Room No. 8: Contained a large amount of thirteenth century glazed *sgraffito* sherds (tableware)[21] indicating that it was a refectory.

Room No. D: Domed oven.

Room No. 9: As room Nr. 8 it contained sherds of *sgraffito* table ware, but due to inflicted damages its precise function could not be ascertained (refectory or kitchen?).

The rooms along the north side consisting of two or three compartments were used as storage rooms or dwelling places for the monks or both. Several storage jars contained charcoaled grain, peas, walnuts, and garlic, typical items for a monk's diet. The biographer of Symeon the Younger tells us that he was nourished by natural products and peas soaked in water (*bios* ch. 13, 7–8) which formed the diet not only for Syrian but also Georgian monks residing aroung Antioch or in Palestine.[22]

Room No. 46: It is not only larger, but more solidly built und better preserved. It was also protected from the strong mediterranean winds and the scorching heat in the summer. It is equipped with a fireplace and an irregularly shaped storage bin. This room also revealed some artifacts (to be discussed later) suggesting that it and the other nearby compartments (nos. 47, 48) were reserved for the abbot of the monastery.

South of the southern entrance to the church below the ground level is another sizeable cistern (c) to catch rain water. The main source of water for the *lavra* was the spring that is located ca. 400 m. away on the southern declivity of the monastery.[23]

The Monastery Church

The monastery church is located in the south-eastern section of the mandra. It is a three naved basilica built partly on the foundations of the original church of the same type. Its exterior dimensions are 23.60 × 16.30 m. The thickness of its remaining walls reaches up to 1.22 m., and the building material is invariably locally quarried limestone. There are three entrances: west, north, and south. In the east it terminates in a semicircular apse flanked by two side chambers. Originally, there was no direct connection to

---

[19] M. HENDY, Roman Coins, in: DJOBADZE, Investigations (see n. 8) 217, 218.

[20] DJOBADZE, Investigations 17–21.

[21] Op. cit. 186–199, and fig. LX–LXVII.

[22] O. ZÖCKLER, Askese und Mönchtum I. Frankfurt 1897, 237ff.; E. LUCIUS, Das mönchische Leben des vierten und fünften Jahrhunderts in der Beleuchtung seiner Vertreter und Gönner, in:. Theologische Abhandlungen für H. Holzmann. Leipzig 1902, 131ff.

[23] DJOBADZE, Investigations 20, 21.

the pastophoria. The doorway leading to the northern pastophory with the apse is a later modification and should be ascribed to the second period. At that time the only apse window was also widened, and the eastern responds which are not bonded to the lateral walls of the presbytery were diminished in width, damaging the face of the capitals. The two-tired synthronon and the remains of a bishop's throne should be ascribed to the second period.

The exterior walls of the church were not richly ornamented, but the interior walls from the first period and the arch of the conch should have been lavishly embellished with various carved vegetal patterns. The lateral walls had brackets which were beautifully carved on three sides. From the first period were likewise the lavishly sculpted marble templon screens and richly adorned colonettes which had been cut from huge shafts of Corinthian columns (diam. 1.00 m.).[24]

Funerary Structures

South of the monastery along the exterior face of the circuit wall is a small funerary chapel consisting of three single, barrel-vaulted compartments on three levels (interior dimensions: 6.30 × 3.42 m.). On the east side of its lower chamber is an arcosolium containing a partially cut rock tomb (*fig.* II); its content had been plundered, and on its floor were scattered some human bones. The uppermost compartment – preserved only at the floor level – had a small semicircular apse on the east side.

On the westside of the basilica are five barrel-vaulted masonry tombs (*fig.* III), which also contained human bones.[25]

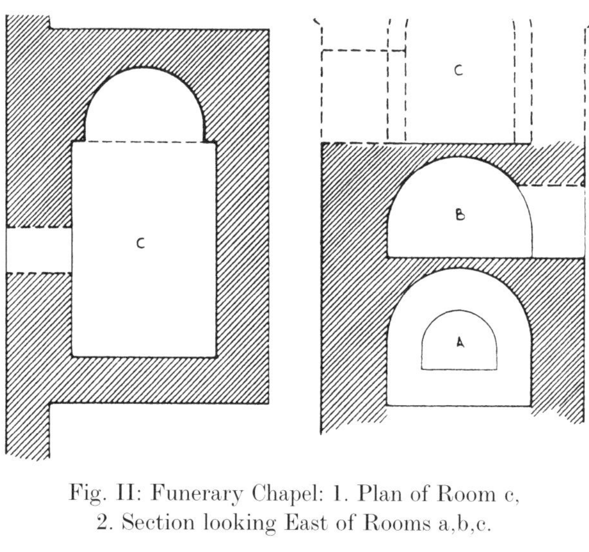

Fig. II: Funerary Chapel: 1. Plan of Room c, 2. Section looking East of Rooms a,b,c.

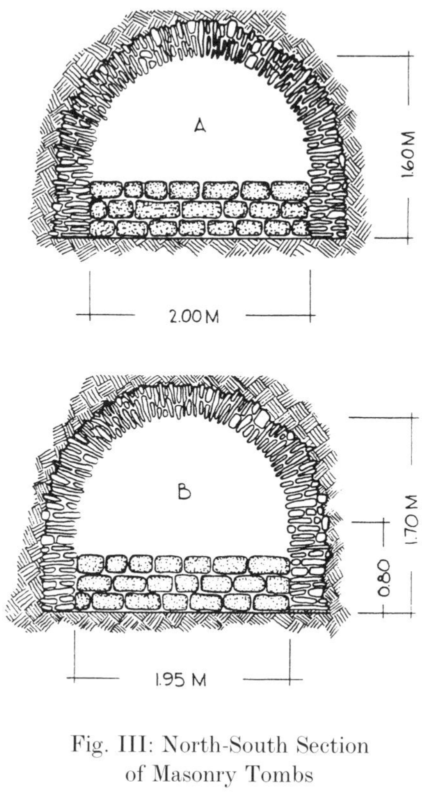

Fig. III: North-South Section of Masonry Tombs

[24] On this account see op. cit. 9–13, 38–49, figs. XV–XVIII; figs. 45–56 and 69–75.

[25] Op. cit. 21–23.

Fragments of Georgian Architectural Sculpture

The excavations in the monastery revealed some fragments of Georgian architectural sculpture and epigraphic material that compliment existing literary sources, while enriching our knowledge of the Georgian colonisation of this region. Below we offer a concise catalogue of this material.[26]

No. 1. Small impost base (*fig.* 1, *pl.* 1). Fresh water travertine, located in the northwest of the *mandra*. Broken off on two sides. H.: 0.05 m., sides at the bottom 0.16 × 0.142 m. It has a drilled hole (diam. 0.008 m., depth 0.023 m.). The two sloping remaining sides have a double-grooved interlace pattern.

No. 2. Fragment of a colonette (*fig.* 2). Fresh water travertine. Found in room No. 51. H.: 0.18 m., diam. 0.106 m. Its entire surface is covered with a double-grooved interlace pattern. There are two additional shorter fragments that coincide with No. 2 in every respect.

No. 3. Four fragments of a colonette with a square base (*fig.* 3). Fresh water travertine. Found in the north section of the courtyard. Maximum h. of the shaft 0.09 m., diam. 0.105 m., h. of the base 0.059 m. square. Three holes are drilled into the bottom at different angles. Fragments show traces of white oil paint and fire. Its square base is a panel decorated with a wavy tongue pattern with two graduated grooved strips below. A beaded molding is around the shaft. The dominant ornamental motif of this fragment as well as of its three smaller ones is interlaced circles; but the ornamental pattern, workmanship, and diameter of the shaft coincide perfectly with the shaft discussed above (*fig.* 2).

The closest – and only – parallel of these both items is in the church of Wood of Life in the Black Mountain, where bundle columns were found whose entire surface is decorated with an octagonal and square interlace double-grooved pattern (*figs.* 4, 5).

In 1924 Profs. H. Seyrig and Pedrizet investigating a monastery known in Georgian sources as the "Monastery of the Valley of the Reeds" situated in the outskirts of the Black Mountain, happened on a neatly carved limestone block.[27] This exceptionally revealing ornamental block was rediscovered, photographed, and published in 1965 by J. Mécérian[28] (*fig.* IV). Its panel displays a close similarity to the colonettes from Barlaam's monastery (*figs.* 2, 3) and to the bundle columns of Wood of Life (*figs.* 4, 5), not only by its octagonal interlace which – as the above mentioned items – is double grooved,[29] but also by other component elements which will be discussed below.

No. 4. Fragment of an ornamental panel (*fig.* 6, *pl.* 2). Fresh water travertine, found at the ground level between the south entrance to the basilica and the south circuit wall. H.: 0.13 m., max. l.: 0.24 m., w.: 0.061 m., with an ornamented front. Its back is very smoothly worked. The upper band consists of a chevron molding, a triple grooved ribbon, a bead molding, and a double grooved band. The lower portion is filled with a double grooved rinceau which encloses palmettes with spoon-shaped lobes, two of which extend as scrolls beyond the rinceau.[30] The rinceau closely resembles the ornamental panel found in the monastery of the "Valley of the Reeds" (*fig.* IV) and the ornamental base of the

---

[26] All items found in the process of the excavation have been deposited in the Archaeological Museum in Antakia.

[27] Personal communication from Prof. Seyrig.

[28] J. Mécérian, Expédition archéologique dans l'Antiochène occidentale. Beyrouth 1965, 38, 39.

[29] Ibid., figs. 42, 43.

[30] We discovered also two additional badly damaged component fragments, indicating the ferocity of the destruction that the monastery had to endure.

Fig. IV: Stele from the Valley of the Reeds

western porch (*fig.* 7) of Wood of Life. The beaded frames and the cruciform inscription on figure IV are common correlated features that will be discussed below.

I suppose that the ornamental prototype of the three panels discussed above is to be found in the cathedrale of Samtavisi (*fig.* 8) built in 1030 in Georgia.

No. 5. Fragment of an ornamented cusp (*fig.* 9) of the same material as the previous panels. It was found at the ground level in the lowest room of the funerary chapel. Max. h. 0.107 m., w. 0.105 m., th. 0.035 m. The front is embellished and the top shows traces of Georgian letters to be analyzed below. Underneath the letters is a narrow, curved chevron molding between double grooved ribbons from which hang paired stylized leaves with a bunch of grapes in its center. On both sides of the grapes are the remains of beaded curved strips. This diminutive fragment perfectly coincides with the cusps of the porch in the afore mentioned church Wood of Life that was published by Mécérian and which we are reproducing here (*figs.* 10, 11).[31] These pearl molded trefoil cusps originally had been

[31] Mécérian, op. cit., figs. 199–201.

fitted into the slot of the western archivolt of the porch[32] of Wood of Life. The cusps of Barlaam's monastery and those from Wood of Life have numerous parallels in Georgia, the closest of which again occurs in the cathedral of Samtavisi (*fig.* 12, *pl.* 3). Here again we have unmistakable evidence that the masons, who in 1030 constructed the cathedral of Samtavisi, were also active in the Black Mountain and on Mount Kasius.

Georgian Inscriptions from St. Barlaam

No. 1. Fragment of an ornamental panel[33] (*figs.* 13, V), presumable part of fig. 6 found at the floor level of the lowest compartment in the funerary chapel. Remains of a *mrgvlovani* inscription on its narrow upper edge (w. 0.042 m.). The h. of the letters varies from 0.009–0.02 m. Only three lines survive. Below we offer the reconstruction of this inscription:

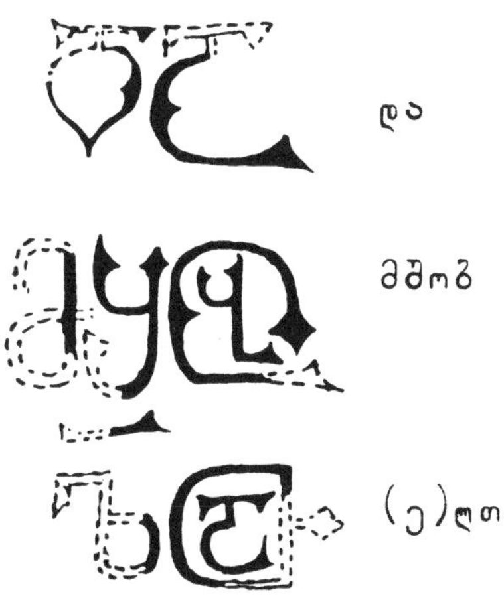

"... and (the) parents"

Fig. V: Inscription on Ornamental Panel

This fragment suggests that it is part of a dedicatory or commemorative inscription. The almost calligraphic execution of the letter leaves no doubt that it had been carved by an exceptionally skilled craftsman. Its outstanding paleographic feature – the placement of one letter into another – is rather unique in this region, although a similar treatment of letters, as well as a vertical arrangement of the inscription dictated by the available space, can be found in Georgia. It is the inscription of Bishop Melchisedek in the cathedral in Mtskhetha (A.D. 1029).[34] Another symptom of this inscription are the triangular (or arrowhead) terminations of its letters and the placement of triangular accents on the end and in the middle of some letters.

The closest parallel for our inscription is again in the church of the Wood of Life (*fig.* 14) and on the east facade of the cathedral in Samtavisi (*fig.* 15), where the incorpo-

[32] See the reconstruction in DJOBADZE, Investigations 141–144, fig. XLIV and figs. 319–321. As Mécérian indicates (fig. 10) the cusp spandrels were alternating the circular geometric interlace with bunches of grapes.

[33] DJOBADZE, op. cit. 209, 210, figs. 86, 87, 403, LXXI.

[34] L. MUSXELIŠVILI, The Earliest Inscriptions in the Church of Sveti Cxoveli at Mcxeta (in Georgian). *Ars Georgica* 1 (1942) 133f., fig. 1; W. DJOBADZE, Medieval Inscriptions in the Vicinity of Antioch on-the-Orontes. *Oriens Christianus* 49 (1965) 129f., figs. VIII, IX.

ration of one letter into another does not occur, because the mason was not restricted by the lack of space.

No. 2. Fragment of the decorated panel (*figs.* 9 [*pl.* 2], VI) discussed above. The dimensions, above all the thickness of the panel, and the paleographic characteristics of the letters suggest that it belongs to the inscribed fragment mentioned above (No. 1, *fig.* V).

Only three partial *mrgvlovani* letters (h. 0.024m., l. 0.062 m., h. of the letters 0.021 m.) remain. They are located above the ornamented surface on a narrow strip.

დე მ.;. "...de m..."

Fig. VI: Inscription on Ornamental Panel

They have exactly the same paleographic features as the preceding inscription. The first two letters are the suffix of a word, while the third letter, which is separated from the second one by an interval of 0.013 m., is the beginning of the second word. Due to the affinity to Nos. 1 and 2 and to the inscription of the Samtavisi cathedral (*fig.* 15) built in 1030, the inscription of Melchisedek (1021), and that of the church of Wood of Life (early forties of the eleventh century), and above all with the cruciform inscription from the monastery of the Valley of the Reeds (*figs.* 16, IV), our fragment could be comfortable placed in the early forties of the eleventh century.

No. 3. Fragment of a roof pan tile (*figs.* 17 [*pl.* 4], VII); reddish-yellow clay. Found in room No. 3; max. l. 0.21 m., w. 0.208 m., th. of the tile 0.02 m., th. of the border 0.034 m. In the middle is a single Georgian word in *nusxuri* script (l. 015m., h. of the letters 0.004–0.011 m.).

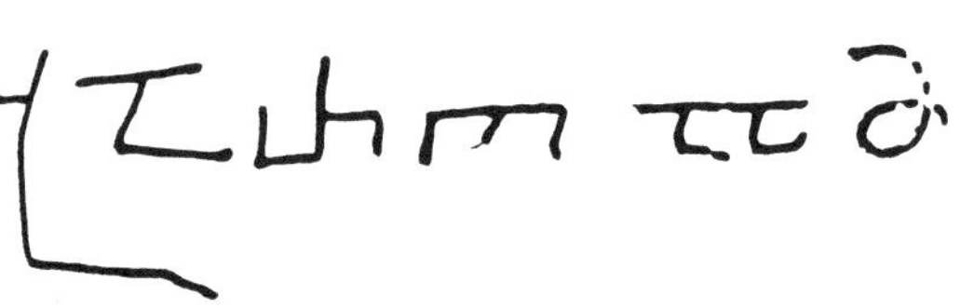

ბარლაამ Barlaam

Fig. VII: Inscription on Pantile Fragment

It is possible that the last restored letter "m" was not the end of the inscription, but that it continued in the genitive as "Barlaamis" or followed by the substantive "Saint" *e.g.* "Barlaamcmindis" ("of St. Barlaam") as it occurs in Georgian manuscripts produced in the western outskirts of Antioch. In this case the emphasis is placed not on the person Barlaam, but rather on the entire monastic complex dedicated to him. In any case, the fact that the tile was inscribed before it was fired could indicate that one of the Georgian monasteries retained a tile factory or kiln at the mouth of the Orontes, where there is a supply of clay.[35] The name Barlaam may therefore be a mark of distinction for the tiles ordered by the monastery, a custom that is still practiced in Antakya, by placing the

[35] Djobadze, Investigations 209.

name on every one thousandth tile to determine the owner. The paleographic features of the inscription suggest it belongs to the twelfth or thirteenth century.

No. 4. Three fragments of a reused stele (*figs.*18 [*pl.* 4], VIII) found in front of the north entrance to the church,[36] h. 0.77 m. Its upper portion is decorated with an incised cross with circular arms. Its lower portion contains an incised *mrgvlovani* inscription. The height of the letters varies from 0.047 m. to 0.11 m.; the first letter of the inscription is partly chipped off, but is easily reconstructed; the rest of the letters is well preserved. None of the two words is abbreviated. It reads:

წმიდაჲ კჳრიკე "Saint K'virik'e" (Kerykos)

Fig. VIII: Inscription on Reused Stele

The epigraphic characteristics are: The disappearance of the single lined neck in the letter *d*, placing one letter into another, and the overlapping of letters. They indicate the inscription belongs into the thirteenth century. Below the inscription there are two or three words written in *nusxuri*. The carving is shallow and chipped off which permits us to distinguish only a few letters.

No. 5. Circular mold for the preparation of the eucharistic bread (*figs.* 19, IX a, b). Limestone. Found in room no. 51. For its dimensions see *fig.* IX b. A relatively well preserved *mrgvlovani* inscription runs around the surface border. In the center of the mold are twelve incised squares (0.005–0.007 m. deep) arranged in the form of a cross, so that they rise on the stamped bread to facilitate the breaking of the eucharist. The four middle squares contain two abbreviated *mrgvlovani* letters:

ი(ეს)ჳ	ქ(რისტ)ე
ძე	ღ(მრთის)ა

"Jesus Christ Son (of) God".

The second inscription runs around the mold's rim which can be easily read despite minor damage. It starts at the left corner of the cross and runs to the right.[37]

[36] Ibid. 206, fig. LXIX.
[37] Ibid. 207–208.

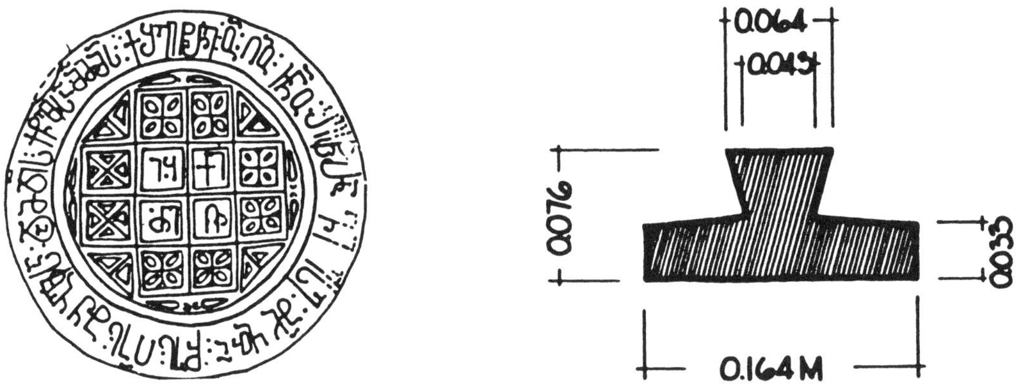

a b

Fig. IX a, b: Mold for Eucharistic Bread

«— შეიწ(ყნა)რე: ო(ჳფალ)ო: ღ(მერთ)ო: ჩ(უე)ნო: შეს(ა)წირავი: ესე: მ(ეო)ჳ(ე)ბ(ი)თა: წ(მიდ)ის: ღ(მრთ)ის: მშ(ო)ბ(ე)ლისა: და: მ(არა)დის: ქ(ალ)წ(უ)ლისა: მ(ა)რ(ია)მ(ი)ს:»

"O Lord our God, accept this offering through the intercession (of the) Holy Mother of God and Ever-Virgin Mary".

This text derives not from the Syro-Palestinian tradition, but from the Byzantine, and is taken from the liturgy of St. John Chrysostome.[38] In mentioning the mother of God as an intercessor and by directly alluding to the eucharist, this bread mold and its inscriptions is unique[39] among Georgian bread molds. Its paleographic features suggest the end of the twelfth to the first half of the thirteenth centuries, and imply that at this time the monastery of St. Barlaam was occupied by Georgian monks, and that the liturgy in the basilica was conducted in the Georgian language.

No. 6. Circular mold for the preparation of eulogia bread (*figs.* 20 a, b) of very soft limestone. Found in room No. 51. The diameter of the stamping surface is 0.137 m. In the middle is the full length, frontal figure of St. Barlaam flanked by a vertical inscription: Ὁ ἅ(γιος) [Βαρ]λ(α)άμ. His head is broken off, he wears a long girdled rope and a mantle. In the "positive" he holds a Latin cross in his right hand, in his left a scroll. Around the border is the circular legend:

[Εὐλ]ο[γ]ήα τοῦ ὁσήου πατρὸς ἡμῶ[ν] Β[αρλαάμ]

("The blessing of our holy father Barlaam").

This mold was not used for stamping eucharistic bread, but *eulogia* bread once a year.[40] It was given to monks and pilgrims alike on special occasions, such as the festival of St. Barlaam on June 19, which is the anniversary of St. Barlaam's birth as recorded in his *bios*, and in the colophon of a Georgian manuscript preserved in Sinai (Sin. 56). This bread was not broken into pieces as the eucharistic bread, but taken by the recipient

[38] On this account see M. Tarchnishvili, Liturgiae Ibericae Antiqua (*CSCO* 122). Louvain 1950, 64; F. E. Brightman, Liturgies Eastern and Western, I. Oxford 1965, 363, 365; G. Galavaris, Bread and the Liturgy. The Symbolism of Early Christian and Byzantine Bread Stamps. Madison 1970, 62–69.

[39] W. Djobadze, Medieval Bread Stamps from Antioch and Georgia. *Oriens Christianus* 63 (1979) 165.

[40] Ibid. 175f., and an extensive bibliography.

whole as a blessed object that possessed a miraculous potency. For instance in the monastery of St. Catherine in Sinai the monk Abba Sergius was able to chase away a lion[41] with this *eulogia* bread.

No. 7 Seal of Bohemond III (1163–1202) Prince of Antioch. Clay covered with lead, diam. 0.055 m.; found in room no. 23 in a niche of the north wall 2.00 m. above the floor level.

Obverse: Bohemond on horseback advances left; he wears a conical hat and bears a gonfalcon over his right shoulder; his left side is protected by a shield. Circular legend around the rim: +SIGILLUBOAMUNDI – PRINCIPISANTIOCENUS ("Seal of Bohemund Prince of Antioch").

Reverse: Two draped, nimbed busts. On the left St. Peter, distinguished by his broad head turned to the right, blessing with his right hand, with his left holding a long patriarchal cross. On the right St. Paul with a narrow face and long pointed beard, holding a five-studded book. Both apostles are identified by raised inscriptions in Greek.[42]

The reading of the seal, incorrectly spelled, seems certain, and the attribution to Bohemond III is also confirmed by an act dated 1163, to which at one time a seal was appended. The document to which our seal was attached has, of course, disappeared. However, it could have been associated with some historic event, since we know that in 1186 the monastery was under his jurisdiction.[43] The document may have granted some

Fig. X: Encolpion Cross

[41] For the full story see GALAVARIS, op. cit. 116.

[42] DJOBADZE, Investigations 53.

[43] E. REY, Les colonies franques en Syrie aux XIIe et XIIIe siècles. Paris 1883, 348.

privileges or autonomy of the monastery to the Georgians, who were at that time the inhabitants of the *mandra*.

Such an assumption may not be far fetched based on the cordial relations which existed between the Crusader rulers and the Georgian kings.[44] On the other hand it does not appear to have affected St. Barlaam's or any other Georgian monasteries located in this area. On the contrary the once ardent literary productivity seems to have almost dried up after the death of Bagrat IV (1072). In any event among the ca. fifteen surviving manuscripts there is not a single one that was produced during the Crusaders' domination in this area. Coincidentally after the middle of the eleventh century begins the migration of Georgian monks from the region around Antioch to the newly established monastery of Iviron in Athos (e.g. Giorgi the Hermit, his mentor, Giorgi Athoneli, and Giorgi Jubieli).

No. 8. Encolpion in form of a cross with flared arms (*fig.* X).[45] Silver and niello. Found in room no. 46. Total h. 0.103 m., w. 0.078 m. Its top is fitted with a ring for suspension; found with a silver chain. Niello representation on both sides.

Obverse: Crucified Christ without cross flanked by the busts in medallions of Mother of God and St. John the Evangelist. Both in the attitude of Deesis. Under the suppedaneum is Adam's skull.

Reverse:[46] Five busts in medallions. Mother of God in the center, and three military martyrs with arms. The uppermost an angel as on obverse. All figures on both sides are identified by Greek inscriptions.

The iconographic and stylistic symptoms of Christ, represented with closed eyes and bearded, wearing a loin cloth, and the posture of his twisted body and overlapping legs, suggest the late twelfth to early thirteenth centuries. This cross may have belonged to the last abbot of St. Barlaam's monastery, for such a reliquary had not only phylacteric potency but served as an insignium of the rank of its owner.[47]

Summary

The literary sources, architectural sculpture, epigraphic material, the two bread stamps, and the seal discussed above, allow us to arrive at the following conclusions:

1. In 300 B.C. on Mons Kasius Seleucos Nicator established the holy precinct dedicated to Zeus, and erected a Doric temple with his statue.
2. Sometimes after 363 A.D. the holy precinct of Zeus was destroyed.
3. In the second half of the fifth century in place of the holy precinct of Zeus was built the monastery of St. Barlaam with a basilical church.
4. Presumably during the great earthquake in 526 the monastery was destroyed and abandoned.
5. After 969 or in the first half of the eleventh century the monastery was rebuilt by Georgians.
6. From the end of the tenth to early eleventh centuries until the invasion of Bibars in 1268 the monastery of St. Barlaam belonged to Georgian monks and was operated by them.

---

[44] Z. Avališvili, Jvarosanta droidan. Paris 1929, 30–40; A. Sanders, Kaukasien. München 1944, 168–170; S. Badridze, Sakartvelos urtiertoba bizant'iasa da dasavlet evropastan. Tbilisi 1984, 122–125.

[45] Djobadze, Investigations 52f., figs. 95, 96.

[46] Ibid., fig. 96.

[47] O. Nussbaum, Das Brustkreuz des Bischofs. Mainz 1963, 7, 19ff.; H. Gerstinger, Enkolpion II: Enkolpion als Insigne. *RAC* 5 (1962) 327.

7. This monastery had a formidable scriptorium where numerous books were translated and copied. In its church the liturgy was conducted in the Georgian language.
8. Georgian masons who built the church "Wood of Life" in the Black Mountains were also active in St. Barlaam's monastery and in the "Valley of the Reeds" north of Seleucia Pieria.
9. During the time of the Crusaders in St. Barlaam and other Georgian monasteries the number of monks diminishes and the literary production ceases altogether.
10. After the sack of Antioch by Bibars in 1268 St. Barlaam's and all other Georgian monasteries were devastated. The monks abandoned their monasteries never to return.

List of Drawings

List of Figures (*pl.* 1–4)

ARMENUHI DROST-ABGARJAN – HERMANN GOLTZ
HALLE/SAALE

ZUR CHRISTIANISIERUNG ARMENIENS IM SPIEGEL DES HYMNARIUMS ŠARAKNOCʻ DER ARMENISCHEN APOSTOLISCHEN KIRCHE

Der Kanon auf den heiligen Erleuchter Grigor von Hovhannēs Erznkacʻi Pluz

Τὸν εὐκλεῆ ἱεράρχην ἅπαντες ὡς ἀθλητὴν ἀληθείας
σήμερον οἱ πιστοὶ θείοις ἐν ᾄσμασιν καὶ ὑμνῳδίαις εὐφημήσωμεν Γρηγόριον,
ποιμένα καὶ διδάσκαλον, τὸν ἔκλαμπρον φωστῆρα καὶ ὑπέρμαχον·
Χριστῷ γὰρ πρεσβεύει τοῦ σωθῆναι ἡμᾶς.

(Aus dem Kontakion zum Gedächtnistag Τοῦ ἁγίου ἱερομάρτυρος Γρηγορίου ἐπισκόπου τῆς μεγάλης Ἀρμενίας, Ὡρολόγιον τὸ μέγα, σεπτεμβρ. 30)

Ընտրեալ յաստուծոյ քահանայապետ ճշմարիտ.
և հովիւ հոգևոր բանաւոր հօտի...
Որ քրիստոսանուէր կոչմամբն ծագեցար որպէս զարեգակն.
և լուսաւորեցեր զհայաստան աշխարհս աստուածգիտութեամբ տէր սուրբ գրիգոր.
անդադար բարեխօսեա վասն անձանց մերոց:[1]

(Aus dem Kanon[2] des hl. Erleuchters Grigor, Šaraknocʻ[3], Edition Ējmiacin 1861, Nr. 75)

Die theologisch-hymnologische Reflexion der Christianisierung Armeniens wurde in der Forschung bisher kaum berücksichtigt. Neben den historischen und hagiographischen Quellen wäre es jedoch wichtig, auch das reichhaltige hymnographisch-homiletische Material zu diesem Thema einzubeziehen.

Es gibt im *Šaraknocʻ* mindestens neun Hymnen, die für das Thema der Christianisierung Armeniens relevant sind:

(1) *Šarakan auf den König Trdat* (**Շարական Տրդատայ թագաւորին**, *Mankunkʻ*-Gesang[4] im Kanon auf den hl. [Kaiser] Theodos[ios], Nr.16 in der Zählung der Ausgabe Eǰmiacin 1861, nach kirchlicher Überlieferung von Movsēs Xorenacʻi [traditionell ins

[1] Erwählt von Gott, Hoherpriester du wahrer, und Hirte der geistigen worthaften Herde... Der du durch die Berufung zu Christus aufgegangen bist wie die Sonne und erleuchtet hast das Land Armenien hier, mit Gotteserkenntnis, Herr, heiliger Grigor, unaufhörlich gutsprich für unsere Seelen.

[2] Dieser Kanon wird zum Gedächtnis auf den (wörtl.) „Ausgang aus der Grube“ am ersten Sonnabend nach Pfingsten gesungen und ist der ältere von den beiden Grigor gewidmeten Hymnen im *Šaraknocʻ*.

[3] *Šarakan hogewor ergocʻ surb ew ułłapʻaṙ ekelecʻwoys Hayastaneaycʻ*, Ējmiacin 1861 (arm. wörtl. *Reihen[folge] [vgl. ἀκολουθία] der geistlichen Gesänge der heiligen und rechtgläubigen Kirche der Armenier*).

[4] Eine der 9 Oden (Šarakane) des armenischen Kanons. Die Bezeichnung *Mankunkʻ* wurde diesem Gesang nach dem Anfangsvers des Musterpsalms ψ 112,1 gegeben: Αἰνεῖτε, παῖδες (**Մանկունք** [mankunkʻ]), κύριον, αἰνεῖτε τὸ ὄνομα κυρίου.

5. Jh. datiert], Yovhan Mandakuni [5 Jh.], Anania Širakac'i [7. Jh.] oder Nersēs Šnorhali [12. Jh.]).[5] Der Šarakan auf den König Trdat, ursprünglich für den 29. September, wird heute am Sonnabend vor dem 5. Sonntag nach Pfingsten, dem Gedächtnistag des Trdat, seiner Frau Ašxēn und seiner Schwester Xosroviduxt gesungen;[6]

(2) *Kanon des heiligen Grigor, unsres Erleuchters* (*Կանոն սրբոյն Գրիգորի մերոյ Լուսաւորչի*, zum Gedenktag des „Eingangs in die Grube" [Xor Virap], Nr. 40, nach kirchlicher Überlieferung von Hovhannēs Erznkac'i Pluz [13. Jh.]). Dieser Kanon wird am Sonnabend vor dem 6. Sonntag der Fastenzeit vor Ostern gesungen.

(3) *Kanon des heiligen Grigor, unsres Erleuchters* (*Կանոն սրբոյն Գրիգորի Լուսաւորչին մերոյ*, zum Gedenktag des „Ausgangs aus der Grube" [Xor Virap] und der berühmten Vision des hl. Erleuchters Grigor mit dem göttlichen Auftrag zum Kirchenbau, Nr. 75, nach kirchlicher Überlieferung von Yovhan Mandakuni [5. Jh.] oder Anania Širakac'i [7 Jh.]). Der Kanon wird am Sonnabend vor dem Festtag der Mutterkirche von hl. Ējmiacin gesungen.

(4) *Kanon der Söhne und der Enkel des heiligen Grigor des Erleuchters* (*Կանոն Որդւոց և Թոռանց սրբոյն Գրիգորի Լուսաւորչի*, Nr. 76, nach kirchlicher Überlieferung von Nersēs Lambronac'i [12. Jh.]). Der Kanon wird am 4. Sonnabend nach Theophanie gesungen;

(5) *Kanon des heiligen Patriarchen Nersēs des Großen* (*Կանոն սրբոյն մեծին Ներսիսի Հայրապետի*, Nr. 77, nach kirchlicher Überlieferung von Nersēs Lambronac'i oder Hovhannēs Erznkac'i, wird am 1. Sonnabend nach dem Festtag der Mutterkirche von hl. Ējmiacin gesungen);

(6) *Kanon der heiligen Hṙip'simeanerinnen* (*Կանոն սրբոց Հռիփսիմեանց*, Nr. 78, nach kirchlicher Überlieferung von Katholikos Komitas [7. Jh.]). Der Kanon wird am Montag der zweiten Pfingstwoche gesungen;

(7) *Šarakan auf die heilige Sanduxt* (*Շարական Սրբուհւոյն Սանդխտոյ*, *Mankunk'*-Gesang im Kanon auf hl. Hṙip'simeanerinnen, ohne zusätzliche Autorenangabe. Allgemein werden allerdings die *Mankunk'*-Šarakane Petros Getadarj [11. Jh.] oder Nersēs Šnorhali [12 Jh.] zugeschrieben). Der Gedächtnistag der hl. Sanduxt (ursprünglich im Dezember) fällt heute mit dem Festtag des hl. Apostels Thaddäus zusammen, d.h. ihrer wird am Sonnabend nach *Vardavaṙ* (Verklärung Christi) mit diesem Šarakan gedacht;[7]

(8) *Kanon auf die Lichtergießung* (*Կանոն Շողակաթին* [wörtl. Kanon des Schimmertropf], Nr. 83, nach kirchlicher Überlieferung von Katholikos Sahak Jorap'orec'i, [7.–8. Jh.], wird am 2. Sonntag nach Pfingsten, am Fest der Mutterkirche von hl. Ējmiacin, gesungen);

---

[5] Zusätzliche Informationen zu den Attributionen für diesen Šarakan und weitere Hymnen s. Gabriel AWETIK'EAN, Bac'atrut'iwn Šarakanac' (Erklärung der Šarakane), Venedig 1814, 115ff usw.; Grigor HAKOBYAN, Šarakanneri žanrë hay mijnadaryan grakanut'ean mej (Die Gattung der Šarakane in der mittelalterlichen armenischen Literatur), Erewan 1980, 134ff usw. sowie die bei Christian Hannick entstandene Untersuchung von Frau Alice ERTLBAUER, Armenische Kirchenmusik, Wien 1985, 37ff usw.

[6] Vgl. Šnorhk' GALUSTEAN, Hayazgi surber (Heilige armenischer Herkunft), Istanbul 1982, S. 138.

[7] Vgl. GALUSTEAN, Hayazgi surber, 154.

(9) *Kanon der heiligen Dolmetscher* (**Կանոն Սրբոց Թարգմանչացն**, Nr. 99, nach kirchlicher Überlieferung von Yovhan Mandakuni und Vardan Vardapet [13. Jh.]). Dieser Hymnus wird am 4. Sonnabend, nach dem Fest des Hl. Kreuzes, gesungen.

Nicht zu vernachlässigen sind auch die von Vardapet Sahak Amatuni herausgegebenen „außerkanonischen" Hymnen auf den Erleuchter Grigor, auf den König Trdat, auf den König Abgar, auf die Apostel Thaddäus und Bartholomäus, auf die heilige Jungfrau Sanduxt usw., die erstmals in der Zeitschrift des Katholikossats aller Armenier, „Ararat", in Ējmiacin ediert wurden.[8]

In diesem Beitrag möchten wir den umfangreichsten Hymnus im *Šaraknocʿ* zum Thema der Christianisierung Armeniens und zu Grigor dem Erleuchter, der neben dem *Kanon auf die Hřipʿsimeanerinnen* die feinste literarische Ausarbeitung erfahren hat, erstmals deutsch mit begleitendem armenischem *textus receptus* der breiteren Forschung zugänglich machen.
Es handelt sich dabei um den ersten *Kanon des heiligen Grigor, unsres Erleuchters*, der in der Ausgabe Ējmiacin 1861 die Nr. 40 trägt und zum Gedächtnis auf die Leiden Grigors und seine Grubenfahrt (der Gedenkanlass wird in Analogie zur Höllenfahrt wörtl. „Eingang in die Grube" genannt) in der fünften Woche der großen Fastenzeit am Sonnabend gesungen wird. Der Kanon besteht aus drei Teilen:

A. Erster Teil, **Այսօր զուարճացեալ**, ein *Ōrhnutʿiwn*-Gesang[9], umfaßt 36 Strophen, die ein alphabetisches Akrostichon bilden. Er wird Hovhannēs Vardapet Erznkacʿi Pluz (13. Jh.) zugeschrieben und stellt die hymnographische Bearbeitung der berühmten, nur im Altarmenischen existierenden Homilie[10] (nerbołean, „Lobrede") auf Grigor den Erleuchter vom selben Autor dar.

B. Zweiter Teil, **Լերինք ամենայն**, ein *Čašu*-Gesang[11] aus 11 Strophen, stammt ebenfalls aus der Feder des Erznkacʿi. Dieser Hymnus wird als *Ōrhnutʿiwn*-Gesang auch zum Fest der *Auffindung der heiligen Gebeine Grigors* gesungen.

C. Dritter Teil, **Որ ի Հօրէ առաքեալ**, eine *Harcʿ*-Reihe mit dem dazu gehörenden *Gorcatun*-Gesang (4 Strophen) und *Ołormea* (3 Strophen), *Tēr yerknicʿ* (4 Strophen) sowie *Mankunkʿ* (3 Strophen),[12] gilt als älterer Teil des Kanons und hat drei Attributionen erfahren: Yovhan Mandakuni, Movsēs Xorenacʿi und Nerses Šnorhali.

---

[8] Vgl. *Ararat* 1897/3, S. 121–127; 1897/5, S. 237–238; 1898/2, 93–95 usw., ebenso Sahak AMATUNI, Hin ev nor parakanon kam anvaver šarakanner (etwa. Alte und neue außerkanonische oder nicht bezeugte Šarakane), Vałaršapat, Druckerei von hl. Ējmiacin 1911.

[9] *Ōrhnutʿiwn* (arm. wörtl. Segen, Segnung): Erster Šarakan-Gesang in der Struktur eines armenischen Kanons. So heißt er nach dem Muster der ersten biblischen Ode Ἄισωμεν (**օրհնեսցուք** [ōrhnescʿukʿ]) τῷ κυρίῳ ἐνδόξως γὰρ δεδόξασται.

[10] *Sopʿerkʿ haykakankʿ* 5, Venedig 1853, S. 83–164.

[11] Šarakan-Gesang im Kanon, der zur *Čašu*-Stunde (wörtl. [Stunde] „der Mahlzeit" gesungen wird. Vgl. zu *Čašu* Norayr POŁAREAN, Cisagitutʿiwn (Liturgiewissenschaft), New-York 1990, S. 2.

[12] Die Bezeichnungen für diese im armenischen Kanon ihren festen Platz habenden Šarakan-Gesänge stammen von den biblischen Oden und Psalmen. Für „Harcʿ" (arm. wörtl. „der Väter") und „Gorcatun" (arm. wörtl. Haus/Oikos der Geschöpfe) vgl. die Oden 7 und 8: Προσευχὴ Ἀζαρίου (Dan. 3, 26; 52): Εὐλογητὸς εἶ κύριε ὁ θεὸς τῶν πατέρων (**հարցն** [harcʿn]) ἡμῶν) und (Ὕμνος τῶν τριῶν παίδων [Dan. 3, 57]: Εὐλογεῖτε, πάντα τὰ ἔργα (**գործք** [gorckʿ]) κυρίου, τὸν κύριον). Für *Ołormea* (wörtl. „Erbarme dich") und *Tēr yerknicʿ* (wörtl. „Herr vom Himmel her") vgl. die Psalmen ψ 50,1 und ψ 148,1: Ἐλέησόν (**ողորմեա** [ołormea]) με, ὁ θεὸς κατὰ τὸ μέγα ἔλεός σου und Αἰνεῖτε τὸν κύριον ἐκ τῶν οὐρανῶν (**տէր յերկնից** [tēr yerknicʿ]).

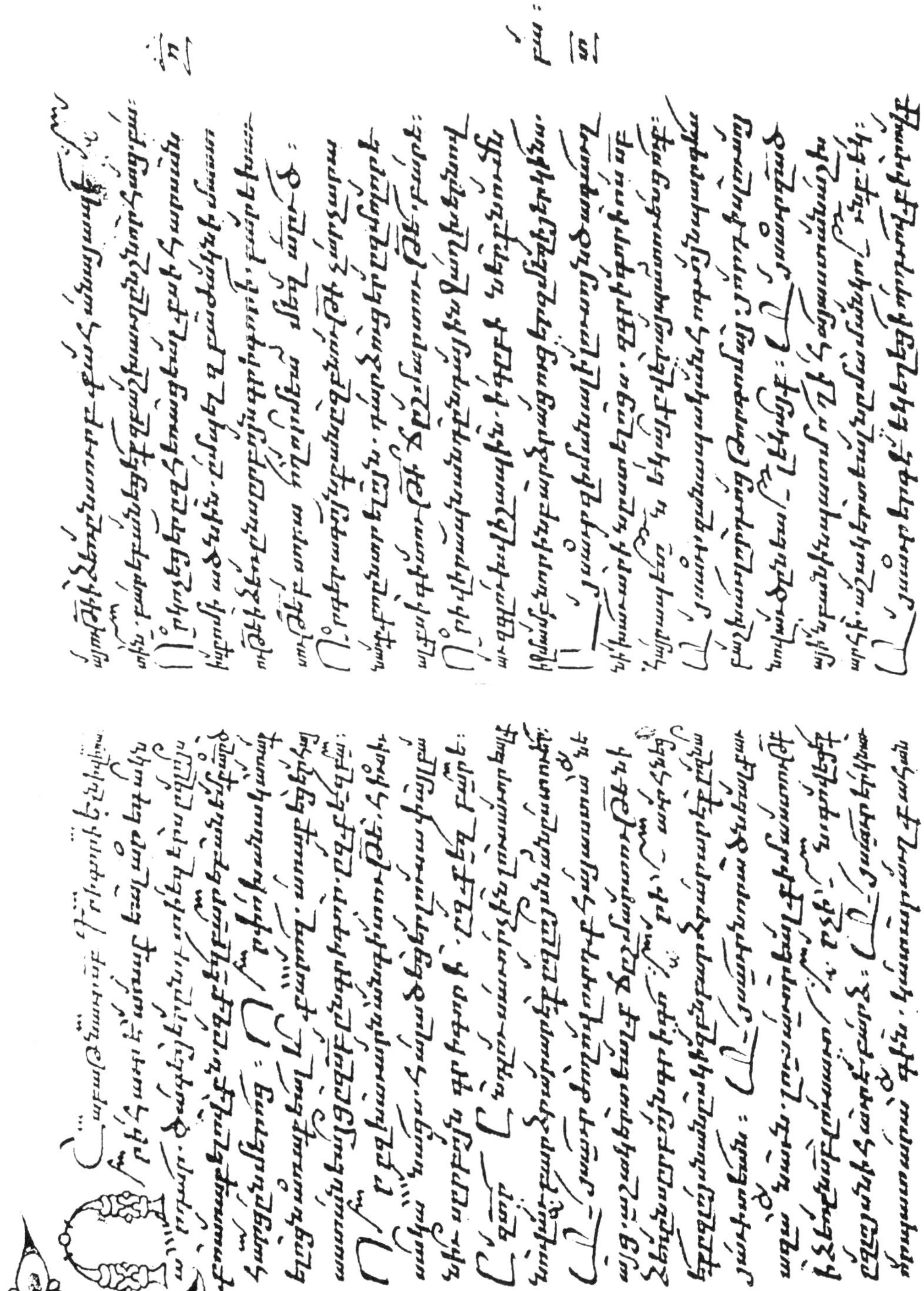

Armenisches Hymnarium aus Tübingen mit dem Grigor-Kanon (Ma XIII 22, f. 94[v]) (a. 1316).
Über dem Text jeweils armenische Musikzeichen (Xazen).

Unsere Edition wollen wir nur mit wenigen, für das Verständnis des Textes unbedingt notwendigen kommentierenden Anmerkungen begleiten. Sie soll eine Vorstufe für eine ausführliche Analyse der Theologie und Poetik dieses Kanons bieten, für die allein dieser Kanon genügend Stoff liefern würde, um eine ganze Monographie zu verfassen, besonders wenn sie im Vergleich mit den armenischen und byzantinisch-griechischen hagiographischen, homiletischen und hymnographischen Texten durchgeführt würde. Bei den Hinweisen auf Anklänge und Zitate von Bibelstellen ist hier noch keine Vollständigkeit angestrebt worden. Die wenigen Hinweise sollen nur in einigen Fällen Interpretationshilfen bieten.
Die im folgenden vorgelegte Übersetzung ist sorgfältig mit der Terminologie des gesamten *Šaraknocʿ* verglichen und abgestimmt worden. Sie ist Teil einer künftigen Ausgabe des gesamten *Šaraknocʿ*, die wir zur Zeit für den Druck vorbereiten.

Unser Übersetzungstext ist in sich in einem jahrelangen Arbeitsprozess philologisch und theologisch reflektiert und ausgeformt worden. Er bietet daher auch für die des Altarmenischen nicht kundigen Forscher und Forscherinnen eine zuverlässige sprachliche Grundlage für Analysen, Vergleiche, Interpretationen und Kommentare.

Կանոն սրբոյն Գրիգորի մերոյ Լուսաւորչի:
խ / օրհ[նութիւն] / դկ

Այսօր զուարճացեալ ցնծայ եկեղեցի.
դրախտ աստուածատունկ ծաղկեալ.
յորմէ տուաւ մեզ տունկն անմահութեան տէր գրիգորիոս.
և պըտղովն իւրով ելից ըզտիեզերս ամենայն:

Բարունակ ողկուզաբեր ճըշմարիտ որթոյն.
մըշակեալ հայրական աստուածային աջոյն.
յորմէ բըղխեաց բաժակն ուրախարար տըրտմեցելոյ ազինս.
որով արբեալ ըզմայլեցաք յուրախութիւն հոգևոր:

Գարնանաբեր հընչումըն հարաւային հողմոյն.
ճառագայթեալ հրով աստուածային հոգւոյն.
որով հալեցաւ սառըն կռապաշտութեան հիւսիսաբնակ ազանց.
և եղեն ծաղկեալք աստուածային գիտութեամբըն:

Դրախտ նորազուարճ տընկեալ յաշխարհիս հայոց.
բազմաջան քըրտամբք տէր գրգորիոս.
արբեալ ի վըտակաց հոսման քարոզի ճըշմարիտ բանին.
ծաղկաւէտ լըցեալ հրաշագեղ տընկօք:

Երկնային լոյս ծագեալ ի յերկրի ցուցար.
պայծառացեալ փայլմամբ ի յարփւոյն կենաց.
որով հերքեցաւ խաւար թանձրամած հայաստանեայց ազգի և տեսին ըզլոյս շնորհաց
սուրբ հոգւոյն:

Զօրաց հրեղինաց անմարմնական դասուց, պարակցեալ ցնծան ընդ հողանիւթ
բնութեանս, որ ընծայեաց տեառն աստուծոյ զտէր գրիգորիոս.
որով նուիրին ի փառս ուղղափառ հաւատոյ մանկունք:

KANON DES HEILIGEN GRIGOR UNSRES ERLEUCHTERS
(Übersetzung aus dem Altarmenischen)[1]

40/Ōrhnutʿiwn/3. Plagalton

Ա (Aysor)
Heute sich ergötzend jauchzt die Kirche,
von Gott gesetztes Paradies erblüht,
aus welchem ist gegeben uns der Setzling der Unsterblichkeit, Herr Grigorios[2],
und durch seine Frucht erfüllt hat er den Erdkreis ganz.

Բ (Barunak)
Rebe traubenbringend des wahren Weinstocks,
gepflegt von des Vaters göttlicher Rechten,
von welcher entsprungen ist der fröhlichmachende Becher betrübtem Volke hier,
durch welchen trunken, wir erquickt worden sind zu geistiger Fröhlichkeit.

Գ (Garnanaber)
Frühlingbringendes Klingen des südlichen Windes,
strahlend vom Feuer des göttlichen Geistes,
durch welchen getaut ist das Eis des Götzendienstes der nördlich wohnenden Völker,
und sie sind erblüht durch die göttliche Kenntnis.

Դ (Draxt)
Paradies, das neu ergötzliche, gesetzt im Land hier der Armenier
mit vieler Mühen Schweiß der Herr Grigorios,
getränkt von strömenden Bächen der Predigt des wahren Wortes,
von Blumen erfüllt, von wunderschönen Setzlingen.

Ե (Erknayin)
Himmlisches Licht aufgegangen, auf Erden dich gezeigt hast,
hellgeworden durch den Glanz von der Sonne des Lebens,
durch welches überwunden worden ist die dichte Finsternis des Armeniergeschlechts,
und sie haben gesehen das Licht der Gnaden des heiligen Geistes.

Զ (Zoracʿ)
Der feurigen Heerscharen körperlose Ränge, gemeinsam tanzen [und] jauchzen mit irdischer Natur hier, die geschenkt hat dem Herrn Gott den Herrn Grigorios,
durch welchen gewidmet werden den Ehren die rechtehrenden Glaubens Kinder.

---

[1] Der Übersetzung wurde die obenerwähnte Ausgabe Ēǰmiacin 1861 zugrunde gelegt, die wir im weiteren mit der Abkürzung „E“ bezeichnen.

[2] Hier wird die griechische Namensform des Erleuchters Grigor verwendet. Er ist der einzige armenische Heilige, dessen im byzantinischen Kirchenkalender und im byzantinischen Gottesdienst gedacht wird.

Էական բարւոյն կերպարան բարեաց.
հովուապետ բարի տէր գրիգորիոս.
քաղցրաձայն հընչմամբ դարձուցիչ մոլորեալ հօտին.
ժողովեալ ի հօտ ճըշմարիտ հովուին։

Ընտրեալ յաստուծոյ քահանայապետ անբիծ.
քարոզող ճըշմարիտ աստուծոյ բանին.
ընծայեցեր տեառն աստուծոյ զնոր ժողովուրդ մաքրեալ.
հրաւիրեալ ի փառս վերնոյն սիօնի։

Թագ պարծանաց արշակունեաց կազմեալ.
առաքելական վարուք տէր գըրիգորիոս.
յօրինեցար բազմագոյն ակամբըք հանդխից նահատակութեան.
վայելուչ պըսակ հիւսեալ սուրբ եկեղեցւոյ։

Ժառանգորդ եղեր հայրենի սեպհական հօտին.
վիճակեալ թադէոսի սուրբ առաքելոյն.
պարգեւական զաւակ կենդանի նըշխարաց նորին.
շառաւիղ շնորհաց աղօթիւք հայցեալ։

Ի փշաբեր արմատոյ վարդ կարմըրերփեան ծաղկեալ.
առաքելաշնորհ տէր գրիգորիոս.
անուշահոտ բուրմամբ լըցեր ըզհայաստան աշխարհս յայտնելով ի մեզ ըզհոտ
գիտութեան։

Լուսապայծառ ծաղիկ ի յերկրի ցուցար.
բըժիշկ հոգւոց մերոց տէր գրիգորիոս.
քաղցրաճաշակ արմաւենի ի տանն աստուծոյ տընկեալ.
պարարտացեալ պըտղով հաւատոյ մանկամբըք։

է (Ēakan)
Des wesenhaften Gütigen gütige Gestalt du,
Oberhirte gütiger, Herr Grigorios,
mit süßer Stimme Klingen Bekehrer der verirrten Herde,
versammelt zur Herde des wahren Hirten.

ը (Ëntreal)
Erwählt von Gott Hohepriester du ohn' Makel,
Prediger des wahren Gottesworts,
geschenkt hast dem Herrn Gott die neue Volksversammlung die gereinigte,
geladen zu den Ehren des oberen Zion.

թ (Tʻag)
Krone zum Ruhm der Aršakiden geformt,
in apostolischem[3] Leben, Herr Grigorios,
geziert worden bist mit vielfarbigen Edelsteinen der Kämpfe des Martyriums,
geziemender Kranz, geflochten für die heilige Kirche.

ժ (Žaṙangord)
Erbe geworden bist der väterlichen, eigenen Herde,
Los des Thaddäus, des heiligen Apostels
Nachkomme, geschenkt von dessen lebendigen Gebeinen[4],
Spross der Gnade, durch Gebete erheischt.

ի (I)
Aus dorniger Wurzel Rose leuchtendrot erblüht,
[wie die] Apostel begnadet, Herr Grigorios,
mit wohlriechendem Duft erfüllt du hast das Land Armenien hier, offenbarend unter uns den Geruch der Erkenntnis.[5]

լ (Lusapaycaṙ)
[Als] Lichthelle Blume auf Erden gezeigt dich hast,
Arzt unsrer Seelen, Herr Grigorios,
süßschmeckende Palme, im Hause Gottes gesetzt,
prangend mit Frucht, mit des Glaubens Kindern.

---

[3] Laut Gabriel AWETIKʻEAN, Bacʻatrutʻiwn Šarakanacʻ 193 existiert auch v.l. առաքինական, d.h. „tugendhaft". Der Kommentar des vorgelegten Kanons umfasst bei Awetikʻean die Seiten 191-201.

[4] Hinweis auf die Tradition über die Empfängnis Grigors am Grab des Apostels Thaddäus, des ersten Erleuchters Armeniens, zusammen mit dem Apostel Bartholomäus (vgl. AWETIKʻEAN, Bacʻatrutʻiwn Šarakanacʻ 193).

[5] Vgl. 2 Kor 2, 14ff.

Խոստավանող քրիստոսի ճըշմարիտ վըկայ.
բազմաչարչար նահատակ տէր գրիգորիոս.
զպակասութիւն չարչարանաց տեառն ի մարմնի քում կրեցեր.
որով ցընծայ եկեղեցի ի փառս որդւոց սիօնի։

Ծնող հոգևոր աստուածանման սիրով.
զորովագութ հայր պարծանաց տէր գրիգորիոս.
չարչարանօք մարմնոյդ մաքրեցեր ըզմեզ ի յաղտոյ մեղաց.
և ծընար որդիս լուսափայլ բանիւդ։

Կերպարան փառաց միածնի որդւոյն.
մարտիրոս յաղթող տէր գրիգորիոս.
բևեռս երկաթիս ընկալան երկնագնաց թաթք ոտից քոց սուրբ.
զի բևեռեսցես ըզմեզ յերկիւղըն աստուծոյ։

Հայաստանեայց հայր հաւատոյ հեղինակ ընտրեալ.
ճըգնողական վարուք տէր գրիգորիոս.
ի կոճեղս ոլորեալ հոսեալ յարենէ սրունք սըրբասնեալ մարմնոյդ.
հաստատելով ըզմեզ ի վէմ հաւատոյ։

Ձայնիւ մաղթանօք ըզյիշատակս քո տօնեմք.
լուսաւորիչ հոգւոց մերոց հայր գրիգորիոս.
կապիճս երկաթիս ծանունս և դառնակսկիծ կախաղանաւ ընկալեալ.
գետնամածնեալ ծընրադրութեամբ ծունկք մարմնոյ քոյ սուրբ։

Ղեկօք հաւատոյ ընդ ծով աշխարհիս անցեր.
վըշտակիր մարմնով տէր գըրիգորիոս.
տանջեալ ջարդեցան աստուածակիր բարձք անդամոց քոց սուրբ.
զի զլուծեալ անդամք հոգւոցս հաստատեսցես վերստին։

Ճըշմարիտ հոգւոյն հանճարով լըցեալ.
աղբերաբար շնորհիւ տէր գրիգորիոս.
ստորագլուխ եղեր ջրաչարչար պարպատմամբ և ուռուցմամբ ճըգնեալ.
զի լուացես ըզմեզ ի յաղտոյ մեղաց։

Խ (Xostavanoł)
Bekenner des Christos wahrer Zeuge,
vielleidender Vorstreiter, Herr Grigorios,
das [noch] Mangelnde an Leiden des Herrn in deinem Körper du ertragen hast,[6]
wodurch jauchzt die Kirche in Ehren der Söhne Zions.

Ծ (Cnoł))
Geistlich Gebärender in gottähnlicher Liebe,
innigerbarmender Vater [voll] Ruhm, Herr Grigorios,
durch die Leiden deines Körpers gereinigt hast uns vom Schmutz der Sünden
und geboren hast Söhne durch dein lichtglänzendes Wort.

Կ (Kerparan)
Gestalt der Ehren des eingeborenen Sohnes,
Martyrer siegreich, Herr Grigorios,
eiserne Nägel empfangen haben deine himmel[an]gehenden Füße heilig,
dass du annagelst[7] uns in der Furcht Gottes.

Հ (Hayastaneaycʿ)
Der Armenier Glaubensvater, erwählter Leiter,
in mühseliger[8] Lebensweise, Herr Grigorios,
im Stock festgespannt die von Blut überströmten Knöchel deines heiligen Körpers,
befestigend uns auf dem Fels[9] des Glaubens.

Ձ (Jayniw)
Mit dem Ton der Gebete dein Gedächtnis hier wir feiern,
Erleuchter unsrer Seelen, Herr Grigorios,
schwere Eisenstücke und den bitterschmerzlichen Galgen [haben] erlitten
die in Kniebeugung auf dem Boden haftenden Knie deines heiligen Körpers.

Ղ (Łekokʿ)
Mit dem Steuerruder des Glaubens das Meer der Welt hier durchquert du hast,
leidtragend am Körper, Herr Grigorios,
gequält [und] zerbrochen wurde das gotttragende Gerüst deiner heiligen Glieder,
dass die losgelösten Glieder der Seelen hier du wiederum befestigst.

Ճ (Čěšmarit)
Durch des wahren Geistes Einsicht erfüllt,
wie eine Quelle der Gnade, Herr Grigorios,
kopfüber mit Wasser gemartert worden bist durch Einflößen und Anschwellen, so Mühsal tragend,
dass du uns wäschst aus Schmutz der Sünden.

---

6 Vgl. Kol 1,24
7 Vgl. ψ 118,120
8 D.h. asketischer
9 Vgl. ψ 39,3

Մաքրողական աղ համեմիչ հայաստանեայց եղեր.
արփաբար հրսկող հայր գրիգորիոս.
աստուածային օրինացն բեռնաբարձ ողամբ կրեցեր ըզծանրութիւն աղին.
որով բարձեր ի մէնջ զբեռինըս մեղաց։

Ցեռեալ ընդ ոսկւոյ ակամբք պատուական մարգարտաշար հիւսեմք, զչարչարանաց քոց
թիւ տէր գրիգորիոս.
գելարանօք անուօք և առասանօք չարահնար տանջեալ.
դանդանաւանդըս և գայլս աստուածաբան բերանոյդ։

Նահատակ բարի քրիստոսի ընտրեալ.
արքային զինուոր տէր գրիգորիոս.
տորագլուխ կախմամբ դառնահոտ չընչմանն արիաբար տարար.
զի ուղղեսցես ըզգընացս ոտից մեր յերկինս։

Շառաւիղ լուսազարդ ճանապարհին կենաց.
երկրին աւետեաց հետևող տէր գրիգորիոս.
մոխրաշունչ եղեր քացախ ընկալեալ հոգիաշունչ ռունկամբդ.
պարգևելով ուրախութեան մեզ օծումն։

Ոսկիաձոյլ գերագոյն պատուական գըլխոյն, համանմանեալ հոգւով հայր գրիգորիոս.
կըռփեալ հարուածովք եղեալ ի մամուլս աստուածազարդ գլուխ քո.
որով բարձրացան գըլուխք կորացեալ մեղօք։

Ջնաշխարհիկ պարծանք հողեղէն բնութեանս.
չարչարանօք ժուժկալեալ տէր գրիգորիոս.
տատասկաւ տանջեալ քերանօք քերեալ և կապարաւ հալեալ, խանձողեցան նըշխարք քո
սուրբ ոսկերացդ։

Մ (Makʻrołakan)
Reinigendes Salz, Würze der Armenier geworden bist,[10]
tapfer wachender[11] Vater Grigorios,
mit dem des göttlichen Gesetzes Last aufhebenden Rücken ertragen hast die Schwere des Salzes,
wodurch aufgehoben hast von uns die Lasten der Sünden.

Յ (Yeṙeal)
Statt Ketten von Gold und Edelsteinen wert, in Perlenreihe wir flechten deiner Martern Zahl,[12] Herr Grigorios,
durch Schraubstock, durch Räder und durch Stricke böslistig gequält,
Stacheltrense und Wolfszacken am Gotteswort sagenden Munde dein.

Ն (Nahatak)
Vorstreiter gütiger, Erwählter des Christos,
des Königs Krieger, Herr Grigorios,
kopfüber aufgehängt die bitteren Dünste tapfer ertragen hast,
dass du richtest den Lauf unsrer Füße zum Himmel.

Շ (Šaṙawił)
Lichtgeschmückter Pfad[13] zum Weg des Lebens,
dem Land der Verheißung nachstrebend, Herr Grigorios,
Asche hast atmen müssen, Essig aufnehmen mit deiner geistatmenden Nase,
zu spenden uns der Freude [wohlduftende] Salbung.[14]

Ո (Oskiajoyl)
Dem goldschimmernd erhabenen ehrwürdigen Haupt verähnlicht durch den Geist, Vater Grigorios,
dein gottgeschmücktes Haupt, gefoltert durch Hiebe und gelegt in die Zwinge,
wodurch erhöht worden sind die Häupter, die gebeugt von Sünden.

Չ (Čnašxarhik)
Überweltlicher Ruhm für irdene Natur hier,
in Martern ausgehalten [hast], Herr Grigorios,
mit Disteln gequält, mit Kratzeisen gekratzt und mit geschmolzenem Blei gebrannt worden sind deine verehrten heiligen Gebeine.

---

[10] Vgl. Kol. 4,6

[11] Anspielung auf die Bedeutung des griechischen namens Γρηγόριος.

[12] Zur Erinnerung der 12 Folterqualen Grigors existierte ein Kloster südlich von Erznka (Erzincan), 2 Stunden entfernt, das den Namen „Leiden des Erleuchters“ (*Լուսաւորչի չարչարանաց վանք*) trug (vgl. Galustean, Hayazgi surber, 21). Hier dürften inhaltliche Verbindungslinien zwischen dem Kanon des Hovhannēs Erznkacʻi und dem erwähnten Kloster bei Erznka zu vermuten sein.

[13] Vgl. Jes. 61,3

[14] Vgl. Jes. 61,3

Պարակից հոգեղինաց երկնային զօրացն սրբափայլ զգեստիւք տէր գրիգորիոս.
ի խոր վիրապին իջեր ի տղմին ի մէջ դառնաշունչ օձիցն.
զի փրկեսցես զմեզ ի չար վիշապէն։

Ջերմեռանդն աղօթիւք և հոգևոր սիրով, փաստակեալ յուսով տէր գրիգորիոս.
զանկեալքս ի յերկնից ի խորս անդընդոց զվիրաւորեալքս մեղօք.
վերաբերեա ընդ քեզ յերկնային խորանսն։

Ուետին քաղցրութեան մեզ ի վերուստ շնորհեալ.
երիւք հընգօք ամօք ի վիրապին ճըգնեալ.
աստուածային տեսլեամբն ելեալ բըժըշկէր ըզհարուածեալսն ի դիւաբաղխ սաստիցն.
և լուսափայլ բանիւ բըղխմամբ հաստատելով ի հաւատս։

Սոսկալի տեսլեանն ի վերուստ յայտնեալ, մարգարէահրաշ հոգւով տեսանօղ եղեր.
բացման խորանին վերնական յարկին և երկնային լուսոյն.
խառնելով մարդկան ընդ հրաբուն զօրացն։

Վարդագոյն արեամբ վըկայիցն տեառն.
մաքրեցաւ երկիրս ի յաղտոյ մեղաց.
որ և հիմնեցաւ խորան խորհրդոյ տաճար տէրունեան շինեալ.
յորմէ բղխեաց աղբիւր քաւութեան մեղաց։

Տանն աստուծոյ տեսանող բարի.
արժանացեալ շնորհիւ տէր գրիգորիոս.
կործանիչ բագնեաց քակտիչ մեհենեաց զօրութեամբ խաչին.
քահանայապետ ընտրեալ աստուածային յայտնութեամբն։

Բաբունւոյն հրամանաւըն ի վերուստ կոչեալ, յառաքելական աթոռ տէր գրիգորիոս.
յորդառատ բանիւ հոգևոր ծնընդեամբ լուսաւորեցեր ըզհայաստան աշխարհս.
ընդ ամենայն տեղիս շինեալ խորան փառացն աստուծոյ։

Պ (Parakicʻ)
Gemeinsam tanzend mit den geistigen himmlischen Heerscharen in heiligglänzenden Kleidern, Herr Grigorios,
ins tiefe Loch hinabgekommen bist in Schlamm inmitten bitteratmender Schlangen,
dass du rettest uns vom bösen Drachen.

Ջ (J̌ermeṙandn)
In heißen Gebeten und geistiger Liebe dich mühend in Hoffnung, Herr Grigorios,
uns, die gefallen wir sind von den Himmeln in die Tiefen der Abgründe, die verwundet wir sind durch Sünden,
hinaufbringe mit dir in die himmlischen Hütten.

Ռ (Ṙetin)
Harz der Süßigkeit, uns von oben gnädig geschenkt,
durch drei[mal] fünf Jahre im Loch mühsalgetragen,
durch das göttliche Traumgesicht herausgekommen, heilte er die von dämonischen Einblasungen Besessenen
und durch lichtglänzenden Wortes Entspringen befestigte er [sie] im Glauben.

Ս (Soskali)
Als die schreckliche Schau von oben erschienen, bist durch den [in] Propheten wunderbar wirkenden Geist Seher du geworden
des Öffnens der Hütte der oberen Stätte und des himmlischen Lichtes,
da sich mischten die Menschen mit den feuerartigen Heerscharen.

Վ (Vardagoyn)
Durch rosenfarbnes Blut der Zeugen des Herrn
gereinigt worden ist dies Land von Schmutz der Sünden,
wo auch gegründet worden ist die Hütte des Rates, der Tempel des Herrn erbaut,
von welchem entsprungen ist Quelle der Sühnung der Sünden.

Տ (Tann)
Des Hauses Gottes Seher gütig,
gewürdigt durch Gnade, Herr Grigorios,
Umstürzer der Opferaltäre, Zerbrecher der Götzentempel durch die Kraft des Kreuzes,
Hoherpriester erwählt durch die göttliche Offenbarung.

Ր (Rabunwoyn)
Auf des Rabuni Befehl von oben berufen auf apostolischen Stuhl, Herr Grigorios,
durch reichlich fließendes Wort, durch geistige Geburt erleuchtet hast dies Land Armenien,
an alljeglichem Ort erbaut die Hütte der Ehre Gottes.

Ցանկալի սրօբէից անմարմնական վարուք.
մաքրափայլ մարմնով տէր գրիգորիոս.
յանապատի բնակեցար հանգոյն յօհաննու և եղիայի ճըգնեալ.
օրէնըսդիր աստուածային պատգամաց նըման մեծին մովսիսի։

Իւծելոցս մեղօք տառապեալ որդեացս, աստուածագութ ծընող հայր գրիգորիոս.
հայցմամբ աղօթիւք առ հայրն երկնաւոր խնդրեա.
կատարել զընթացըս մեր ուղղափառութեամբ։

Փըրկաւէտ մահուան կենարար բանին, կենդանի վըկայ տէր գրիգորիոս առ ծընեալն ի
    հօրէ որդին միածին լոյսն ճըշմարիտ հայցեա.
լուսաւորել զանձինս մեր աստուածային գիտութեամբըն։

Քընար քաղցրախօս աստուածային հոգւոյն.
յօրինեալ մարմնով և մասամբ հոգւոյն.
առ բղխեալն ի հօրէ փառակից որդւոյ սուրբ հոգին մաղթեա.
զի մաքրեսցէ ըզմեզ ի մեղաց մերոց։

ճ[ա]շ[ո]ւ / գկ

Լեռինք ամենայն այսօր ցընծացէք ընդ մեծապայծառ փառսն սեպուհոյ
    գերազանց լերինն.
քանզի ի նմա բնակեցաւ սուրբն գրիգորիոս սիւն լուսոյ հայաստանեայց
    սուրբ եկեղեցւոյ.
որով ցընծայ ի փառս վերնոյն սիօնի։

Որ առաւել խորին խորհըրդով խընդայ քան զարարատեանըն բարձր մասիս.
քանզի ի նմա հանգեաւ սուրբն գրիգորիոս տապանըն ապրեցուցիչ ի հոսանաց մեղաց
    հայաստան ազանց.
որով փրկեմք[1] միշտ ի ջուրց հոսանաց։

Գեղապանծ լուսով բերկրեալ զուարճանայ լեառն սեպուհոյ հանգոյն սինայի.
յորում եկաց կամարն ամպեղէն սուրբն գրիգորիոս գերահրաշ լուսով զարդարեալ
    նըման մովսիսի.
որով փայլին երեսք շնորհօք սուրբ հոգւոյն։

[1] In der *Šaraknoc'* Ausgabe Konstantinopel 1853: փըրկիմըք (d.h. Passiv). In E offenbar Druckfehler (փրկեմք, „wir retten" statt փրկիմք, „wir werden gerettet").

Ց (C̲ʿankali)
B̲egehrter von den Seraphen wegen des unkörperlichen Wandels,
reinglänzend im Körper, Herr Grigorios,
in der Wüste gewohnt hast gleichwie Johannes und Elia, Mühsal tragend,
Gesetzgeber der göttlichen Weisungen, ähnlich dem großen Mose.

Ւ (W̲iwceloc‘s)
Die wir uns h̲ärmen und durch Sünden gedrückt sind, wir Söhne, gottbarmherziger Gebärer,
Vater Grigorios,
durch Heischen und Beten beim himmlischen Vater ersuche,
zu vollenden unsren Lauf in Rechtgläubigkeit.

Փ (P̲‘ërkawēt)
Vom r̲ettenden Tode des lebenschaffenden Wortes lebendiger Zeuge, Herr Grigorios, bei
dem aus dem Vater Geborenen, dem eingeborenen Sohn, dem wahren Licht heische
zu erleuchten unsre Seelen durch die göttliche Erkenntnis.

Ք (K̲‘nar)
Süß redende H̲arfe des göttlichen Geistes,
zusammengefügt aus Körper und Zuteilung des Geistes,[15]
bei dem aus dem Vater entsprungenen, dem Sohn ehrengleichen heiligen Geiste bitte,
dass er reinige uns von unsren Sünden.

Čašu/ 3. Plagalton[16]

[Ihr] Berge alle, heute jauchzt über die großhellen Ehren des Sepuh, des ausgezeichneten
Berges,
weil auf ihm wohnunggenommen hat der heilige Grigorios, Säule des Lichts der armenischen
heiligen Kirche,
mit welchem sie jauchzt zu Ehren des oberen Zion.

Welcher[17] tieferen Geheimnisses sich freut als im [Lande] Ararat der hohe Masis,
weil auf ihm geruht hat der heilige Grigorios, die Arche rettend aus Fluten der Sünden die
armenischen Geschlechter,
mit welchem wir gerettet[18] werden immer aus den Wasserfluten.

Durch ruhmvoll schönes Licht erfreut, ergötzt sich der Berg des Sepuh gleichwie der Sinai,
auf welchem gestanden hat das wolkige Gewölbe, der heilige Grigorios
mit überwunderbarem Licht geschmückt ähnlich Moses,
mit welchem [sein] Antlitz[19] glänzt von den Gnaden des heiligen Geistes.

[15] Vgl. Hebr. 2,4
[16] Z. 14 f.: vgl. 2. Kön 6
[17] Sc. der Berg Sepuh.
[18] Wir übersetzen hier ausnahmsweise nach der konstantinopolitanischen Lesart, da die aktive Form in E grammatisch unerklärbar ist.
[19] Pluraletantum; vgl. aber auch 2 Kor 3,18.

Զօրօք հրեղինաց պարփակեալ պահիր լեառըն հանդստեան սրբոյն գրիգորի
տեսլեամբ կարմելայ.
զորս պարսպեն կառքն կենդանի մաքրափայլ աղօթք սուրբ լուսաւորչին հօրն հոգւոր.
զոր առ տէր ունիմք միշտ բարեխօս։

Համանմանեալ ամովսածնին եսայեայ կայծակնամաքուր սուրբ մարգարէին
տէր գրիգորիոս.
վեցթեւեան սրօբէից կիզիչ կենդանեացն եղև տեսանող հոգւով կենդանին.
զանդընդախոր զձորն երկնից կամար յօրինեալ։

Շնորհաբաշխ աջովն յիսուսի պատուեցաւ լեառըն սեպուհոյ ի տիպ սանիրայ և
ահերմոնի.
յորմէ բղխեաց աղբիւրն լուսոյ ջուրս բարեհամս և վըտակըս յորդախաղաց հոսանօք.
որով ցընծայ երկիրս ի բերս արմտեաց։

Ծնընդեամբ սուրբ կուսին յայրն բեթղեհէմ յորդորեցան դստերքն ևայի լինիլ
կուսութեամբ ի մայր քրիստոսի յորում ծագեցաւ խորհուրդն պայծառ երկնանըման
լերինն ի յայրն մանեայ մաքրական վարուք.
որով սըրբիմք միշտ ի յաղտոյ մեղաց։

Խորհուրդ խաչելոյն գերահրաշ տեղւոյն գողգոթայ ծածկապէս ի սմին լերին տեսանի.
զէնն արքայական սպանմանն գործի կենաց արքային ի կենաց գործիսն նուիրեալ.
որով փրկեսցէ զմեզ յաւիտենից մահուանէն։

Զխորհուրդ սեպուհոյ սեպհական փառաց հոգւովն սրբով մարգարէին ծանուցեալ.
զոր և հարցանէր զխորանն աստուծոյ և զլեառն տեառն թէ ով բնակիցէ.
զոր և տեսաք առ սուրբն գրիգոր կատարեալ։

Durch die Heerscharen der Feurigen umschlossen, wurde bewahrt der Berg der Ruhe des heiligen Grigor in Art des Karmel,
welchen hier umwallen lebendige [Kampf]Wagen, reinglänzende Gebete des heiligen Erleuchters, des geistigen Vaters,
den beim Herrn wir haben als steten Fürsprech.

Verähnlicht dem amozgeborenen Jesaja, dem durch die Glut reinen heiligen Propheten, der Herr Grigorios
der sechsflügligen Seraphen, der brennenden Lebewesen Seher geworden ist, im Geist lebendig,
die abgrundtiefe Schlucht zu der Himmel Gewölbe gemacht.[20]

Durch die gnadenverteilende Rechte Jesu geehrt worden ist der Berg Sepuh als Abbild des Senir und Hermon,[21]
aus welchem sie entspringen lassen hat die Quelle des Lichts, das Wohlschmeckende Wasser[22] hier und Flüsse mit munterspielenden Fluten,
mit welchen die Erde hier jauchzt beim Hervorbringen der Gewächse.

Durch die Geburt [aus] der heiligen Jungfrau in der Höhle von Bethlehem ermuntert worden sind die Töchter Evas, durch Jungfräulichkeit zu Müttern[23] des Christos zu werden, worin aufgegangen ist der helle Ratschluss[24] des himmelähnlichen Berges in der Höhle der Mane durch reinlichen Lebenswandel,
mit welchem wir gereinigt werden immer vom Schmutz der Sünden.

Das Geheimnis des Gekreuzigten, des überwunderbaren Ortes Golgotha verborgenerweise auf diesem Berg geschaut wird,
die königliche Waffe, Mordwerkzeug[25] des Lebens des Königs, zum Lebenswerkzeug bestimmt,
mit welchem es möge retten uns von dem ewigen Tode.

Das Geheimnis der dem Sepuh selbsteigenen Ehren durch den heiligen Geist dem Propheten bekanntgegeben,
wonach er auch fragte: Die Hütte Gottes und den Berg des Herrn, wer wird [sie] bewohnen,[26]
welches auch wir geschaut haben beim heiligen Grigor vollendet.

---

[20] Nach der Vita ist auf die Gebete des Grigor von Gott ein Seraph in die tiefe Schlucht gesandt worden, um die „unkörperliche“, engelartige Askese des Heiligen im irdischen Leib zu sehen und den Engeln darüber zu berichten (vgl. Awetikʻean, Bacʻatrutʻiwn Šarakanacʻ, 199).

[21] Vgl. Hoheslied 4,8; Senir und Hermon; beide Namen meinen denselben Berg.

[22] Eigennamen von Gewässern am Sepuh (vgl. Lobrede für Grigor, *Sopʻerkʻ haykakankʻ* 5, Venedig 1853, 137).

[23] Eigentlich sing.: „zur Mutter des Kʻristos“; Anspielung auf die Stelle in der Lobrede, S. 139 (dort expressis verbis im Sinne von Mt 12,50; Mk 3,35).

[24] Damit ist die Kirche des Ratschlusses bzw. des Geheimnisses (auch „Tempel der Ehren“) gemeint, die der hl. Grigor lt. Lobrede (*Sopʻerkʻ haykakankʻ* 5, 132) in der Höhle der Mane geweiht und benutzt hat.

[25] G. Awetikʻean sieht in diesem Bild entweder direkt die Waffe Trdats, die er als Kreuz auf dem Berg Sepuh aufgerichtet hat, oder im übertragenen Sinn Grigor, der als Sohn Anaks ein Instrument der Vernichtung des Lebens des armenischen Königs Xosrov wurde (vgl. Awetikʻean, Bacʻatrutʻiwn Šarakanacʻ, 199).

[26] Vgl. ψ 15,1

Անբիծըն վարուք արդարն հոգւով բանիւ ճշմարիտ և սուրբն սըրտիւ տէր գրիգորիոս.
որում ցանկացան զօրքն սրօբէից բերանք հրեղէնք յերկնից ի յերկիր[2] խոնարհեալ
ի տես մարմնով ճգնողին.
որ և պատիւ տեղւոյն անուամբըն կոչի:

Հովուին հսկողին ճշմարիտ և քաջ հովուին պատկերի հովիւքն եղեն հետևողք.
զոր ամփոփեցին զմարմինն մաքուր մերձ ի յայրն մանեայ մեզ դեղ ախտից
մաքրութեան.
որով սրբիմք հոգւով ի թունից վիշապին:

հ[ա]րց / դկ

Որ ի հօրէ առաքեալ արեգակն արդար.
ծագեցեր ընդ տիեզերս ըզլոյս քո առաքելովքն
զքեզ բարեբանեմք աստուած հարցըն մերոց:

Որ փոխանակ առաքելոցն առաքեալ և քարոզ, առաքեցեր հայաստանեայց
ըզսուրբն գրիգոր.
ըզքեզ [բարեբանեմք աստուած հարցըն մերոց]:

Որ ըզխաւարն անգիտութեան հիւսիսականացս,
հալածեցեր լուսափայլ բանիւ սրբոյն գրիգորի.
ըզքեզ [բարեբանեմք աստուած հարցըն մերոց]:

գ

Ըզտէր

Ընդ լուսաւորչին լուսաւորեալք նովաւ բարձր արարէք ըզլոյսն անըստուեր:

Այսօր ժողովուրդք հայաստանեայց աշակերտեալք ճըշմարտութեան
ի ձեռըն սրբոյն գրիգորի.
օրհնեցէք զլոյս անըսկիզբըն, բարձր արարէք ըզնա յաւիտեան:

Այսօր նորածնեալք աւազանաւն
լուսաւորեալք իմաստութեամբ ի ձեռըն սուրբ լուսաւորչի.
զովեցէք ըզլոյսն ի հօրէ.
բարձր [արարէք ըզնա յաւիտեան]:

---

[2] In E Druckfehler: յիրկիր

Der in makellosem Lebenswandel Gerechte im Geist, im wahren Wort und der Heilige im Herzen, der Herr Grigorios,
nach welchem begehrt haben die Heerscharen der Seraphen, die feurigen Münder von den Himmeln zur Erde niedergebeugt, zu schauen im Körper den Mühsaltragenden,
was auch [als] Ehre des Ortes im Namen[27] genannt wird.

Des wachthabenden Hirten,[28] des wahren und mutigen Hirten Abbildes, sind die Hirten geworden Nachfolger, [29]
den sie einhüllten, den reinen Körper nahe der Höhle der Mane, uns Arznei zur Reinigung von Leiden,
mit welcher wir gereinigt werden im Geist von den Giften des Drachens.

Harcʿ/4. Plagalton

Der du vom Vater gesandt, gerechte Sonne,
aufgehenlassen hast über dem Erdkreis dein Licht durch Sendung der Apostel, dich preisen wir, Gott unsrer Väter.

Der du anstelle der Apostel [als] Apostel und Prediger gesandt hast den Armeniern den heiligen Grigor,
dich [preisen wir, Gott unsrer Väter].

Der du die Finsternis der Unwissenheit der Nördlichen hier vertrieben hast durch das lichtglänzende Wort des heiligen Grigor,
dich [preisen wir, Gott unsrer Väter].

Gorcatun

Den Herrn [lobet und hoch hebt ihn ewiglich][30]

Mit dem Erleuchter, ihr, durch ihn Erleuchtete, hoch hebt das schattenlose Licht.

Heute, ihr Volksversammlungen der Armenier, die Schüler ihr geworden der Wahrheit durch den heiligen Grigor,
segnet das anfangslose Licht, hoch hebt ihn ewiglich.

Heute Neugeborene ihr durch das Becken,
Erleuchtete mit Weisheit durch den heiligen Erleuchter,
lobt das Licht aus dem Vater,
hoch [hebt ihn ewiglich].

---

[27] Sc. das Seraphim-Kloster in einer der Bergschluchten des Sepuh.

[28] Wieder Anspielung auf die Bedeutung des griechischen Namens Γρηγόριος.

[29] Die Hirten, die den Leichnam des hl. Grigor gefunden haben.

[30] Ergänzt nach Dan. 3,57.

Այսօր երկնաւոր պատարագին, կատարողք քահանայութեան
ի ձեռըն սուրբ քահանայապետին.
բարեբանեցէք զբաշխողըն շնորհաց.
բարձր [արարէք ըզնա յաւիտեան]:

ող[ո]ր[մեա]

Որ կոչեցեր ըզհեռացեալսն ի հարսանիս քո միածնին.
ըմպել զբաժակն իմաստութեան ի ձեռըն սըրբոյն գրիգորի.
բարեխօսութեամբ սորա ողորմեա մեզ աստուած:

Որ գերագոյն քան ըզբնութիւն չարչարանօք քո ընտրելոյն,
դարձուցեր ըզմոլորեալսն ի գիտութիւն ճըշմարտութեան.
բարեխօ[սութեամբ սորա ողորմեա մեզ աստուած]:

Որ ի վիրապն անդընդային ջաղխեր նովաւ զգլուխ վիշապին.
ի գբի ներքնումն իջմամբ նորին բարձրացուցեր զմեզ ի յերկինս.
բարե[խօսութեամբ սորա ողորմեա մեզ աստուած]:

տէր

Այսօր զիմանալի լուսոյն ծագողն ի խաւարի նըստելոցս.
զգրիգորիոս սուրբ հայրապետն, եկայք վերապատուեսցուք:

Այսօր զանապական հոգւոյն պարգեւսն բաշխող որդւոց թորգոմայ.
յորդիս լուսոյ նովաւ ծնեալք.
եկայք վերա[պատուեսցուք]:

Այսօր զաստուածային բանին պատմողն ի հայաստան աշխարհի.
աշակերտեալք նըմա մանկունք.
եկայք վե[րապատուեսցուք]:

Այսօր երգէ եկեղեցի որդւովք իւրովք ընդ հըրեշտակս.
յիշատակի լուսաւորչին փառք ի բարձունս աստուծոյ:

Heute ihr die himmlische Opfergabe Vollziehenden, Priester durch den heiligen
Hohenpriester,
preist den Verteiler der Gnaden,
hoch [hebt ihn ewiglich].

Ołormea

Der du gerufen hast die Fernen zur Hochzeit deines Eingeborenen,
zu trinken den Becher der Weisheit durch den heiligen Grigor,
durch dessen Fürsprache erbarm dich unser, Gott.

Der du durch Natur übersteigende Martern deines Erwählten umkehrenlassen hast die
Verirrten zur Erkenntnis der Wahrheit,
durch dessen Fürsprache [erbarm dich unser, Gott].

Der du im abgründigen Loch zermalmt hast durch ihn das Haupt des Drachens,
durch desselben Herabkunft ins Innere der Grube erhöht hast uns zu den Himmeln,
durch dessen Für[sprache erbarm dich unser, Gott].

Tēr

Heute den, der das geistige Licht aufgehen lässt den in Finsternis Sitzenden hier,
den heiligen Patriarchen Grigorios, kommt hochehren lasst uns.

Heute den, der die unverderbten Geistes Spenden verteilt den Söhnen Thorgoms,
die zu Söhnen des Lichts durch ihn geboren,
kommt, hoch[ehren lasst uns].

Heute den, der des göttlichen Wortes erzählt er im Lande Armenien,
die ihr ihm Schüler geworden, Kinder,
kommt, ho[chehren lasst uns].

Heute singt die Kirche durch ihre Söhne mit den Engeln
zum Gedächtnis des Erleuchters: Ehre in den Höhen Gott.

մ[ա]նկ[ունք] / գձ

Այսօր տօնէ եկեղեցի ուրախութեամբ ըզյիշատակ սըրբոյն գրիգորի.
որով լուսաւորեալ պայծառացաւ վայելչապէս.
ի հանդերձըս յոսկէհուըս զարդարեալ և պըսակեալ.
օրհնեցէք մանկունք զքըրիստոս թագաւորն։

Այսօր ցընծան նորածնեալ որդիք լուսոյ յիշատակաւ սուրբ լուսաւորչին.
որով հրաւիրեցան ի հարսանիսն անապական.
մըտանել ընդ փեսային երկնաւորի ի յառագաստըն լուսեղէն.
օրհ[նեցէք մանկունք զքըրիստոս թագաւորն]։

Այսօր քահանայք հոգևոր պատարագին սպասաւորք
վերապատուեն զքահանայապետըն սուրբ.
որով երկնայնոց քահանայութեան հաղորդեալք.
յոր վերափոխեալ այսօր մըտանէ ի սըրբութիւն սրբոց
միշտ բարեխօսել առ տէր վասըն մեր.
օրհնե[ցէք մանկունք զքըրիստոս թագաւորն]։

Mankunkʿ/3. Ton

Heute feiert die Kirche mit Fröhlichkeit das Gedächtnis des heiligen Grigor,
durch welchen erleuchtet, sie lichtgeworden ist gebührend,
in goldgewebten Gewändern geschmückt und bekränzt,
segnet ihr Kinder den König Christos.

Heute jubeln die neugeborenen Söhne des Lichts beim Gedächtnis des heiligen Erleuchters,
durch welchen sie geladen worden sind zur unverderblichen Hochzeit,
einzugehen mit dem himmlischen Bräutigam zum lichten Gemach,
seg[net ihr Kinder den König Christos].

Heute die Priester, der geistigen Opfergabe Diener, hochehren den heiligen Hohenpriester,
durch welchen sie des Priestertums der Himmlischen teilhaftiggeworden,
zu dem hinübergegangen heute er eingeht zur Heiligkeit der Heiligen, immer fürzusprechen
beim Herrn für uns,
segne[t ihr Kinder den König Christos].[31]

[31] NB! Hymnos triadikos.

BABKEN HARUTYUNYAN / EREVAN

DIE DIÖZESAN-GLIEDERUNG DER ARMENISCHEN KIRCHE IM ZEITALTER GREGORS DES ERLEUCHTERS

Die armenische Kirche wurde schon 301 (nach dem traditionellen Datum) in einzelne Diözesen, d. h. eparchisch geteilt. Das war vielleicht keine weitgehende Gliederung, in den Urquellen blieben leider keine Mitteilungen erhalten. Aber darauf weisen einige indirekte Indizien hin, wie die Geschichte der christlichen Kirchen der Nachbarländer des Königreichs von Großarmenien und die jüngsten archäologischen Ausgrabungen, die auf die Existenz christlicher Kirchen in Armenien schon vor der Proklamierung des Christentums als Staatsreligion hinweisen. Danach nimmt die eparchische Teilung der armenischen Kirche eine endgültige Form an, aber „Patmutʿiwn Hayocʿ" („Geschichte Armeniens") von Agathangelos hat darüber nur fragmentarische Mitteilungen. Deswegen fußt die Untersuchung der eparchischen Einteilung der armenischen Kirche vorwiegend auf den Angaben von Ełišē, Łazar Pʿarpecʿi, Uxtanēs und Stepʿanos Ōrbelean, sowie auch auf den Protokollen der Konzilien (insbesondere derer von Dwin in den Jahren 506 und 554).

In der auf uns gelangten redigierten Fassung des Werks von Agathangelos/ Agatʿangełos wird erwähnt, dass Gregor der Erleuchter in verschiedenen Regionen Großarmeniens angeblich 400 Bischöfe geweiht hätte.[1] Im Grunde genommen wiederholt diese Mitteilung auch der Geschichtsschreiber Uxtanēs. Nach ihm hat Gregor der Erleuchter 30 Bischofsstühle gegründet. Nach deren Aufzählung fügt Uxtanēs hinzu, dass Gregor der Erleuchter noch 370 Bischöfe geweiht hat.[2] Nach Stepʿanos Ōrbelean, der seine Angaben von Samuēl Kamrǰajorecʿi (X. Jh.) übernommen hatte, gründete Gregor der Erleuchter nicht 30 sondern 36 Bischofsstühle, deren Inhaber jeweils zur Hälfte links, zur Hälfte rechts des Katholikos ihren Platz haben sollten. Dabei war der erste rechterseits der Bischof von Harkʿ, der erste linkerseits der Bischof von Basean, der siebte rechterseits der Bischof von Siwnikʿ.[3] Aber St. Ōrbelean teilt noch etwas mit, was, unserer Meinung nach, für die weitere Untersuchung interessant sein könnte. Nach dem Autor „befiehlt Gregor der Erleuchter Tiridates dem Großen, sein Königreich nach dem Beispiel griechischer Kaiser zu organisieren und den Fürsten Thron und Rangstufe zu geben, was er bei jedem zur rechten und zur linken Seite entsprechend ihrer Würde tun sollte. Er hat das in einer sehr schönen Weise erfüllt. [Er setzte fest:] Beim Mittagsmahl sollen 400 Fürsten auf den Polstern sitzen, auf den obersten Plätzen der *Bdešx* (Markgraf) von Gugarkʿ und der Fürst von Ałjnikʿ, der Fürst von Angełtun und der Fürst von Kordukʿ, der Ritter Bagratuni und der Fürst von Arcrunikʿ, der Fürst von Siwnikʿ und der Fürst Mamikonean."[4]

N. Adontz hat in seiner Untersuchung der eparchischen Teilung der armenischen Kirche argumentiert, dass die Weihe der 400 Bischöfe einfach ein Missverständnis sei, das durch die Schuld von Redaktoren sowohl im Werk von Agathangelos als auch in den

[1] Agatʿangełeay Patmutʿiwn Hayocʿ. Tbilisi 1909, § 856 (S. 448).
[2] Uxtanēs Episkopos, Patmutʿiwn Hayocʿ. Vałaršapat 1871, 100.
[3] Patmutʿiwn nahangin Sisakan, arareal Stepʿannosi Ōrbelean arkʿepiskoposi Siwneacʿ. Tbilisi 1910, 25.
[4] L.c. 24.

Werken einiger späterer Autoren wiederholt wurde. Nach der Lebensbeschreibung von Nersēs dem Großen hat der Katholikos 400 Sitze um den Esstisch des Königs Aršak II. festgesetzt. Dann versuchte der Autor, namentlich die Fürsten aufzuzählen, die diese Sitze einnehmen sollten. Er konnte aber nur 132 Namen bieten, unter denen es einige Wiederholungen gibt, 13 Namen, die keinen Thron besitzen, sowie auch Namen solcher Stämme und Länder, die zu Großarmenien keine Beziehung hatten. Er schreibt, dass er die Namen der anderen Fürsten nicht aufschreiben konnte.[5] Wie bereits erwähnt, schreibt auch St. Ōrbelean über die 400 Fürsten, die diese Sitze innehatten. Aus dem Vergleich der Angaben verschiedener Geschichtsschreiber zieht der große Armenologe die Folgerung, dass als Quelle für dieses Missverständnis eine Mitteilung von Zenob Glak diente, die folgende Information bietet: Gegen die Invasion der nördlichen Völker hat Tiridates der Große dem georgischen Fürsten als Hilfskontingent 30.000 Soldaten unter dem Oberkommando des Fürsten von Apahunikʿ geschickt. Es gelang letzterem, nur einen kleinen Teil der Gefangenen zurückzuführen, drei Fürsten des Nordens und 400 Adelige gefangenzunehmen, die er nach Armenien brachte und dem König vorstellte. Der König setzte sie in der Festung Ołakan gefangen, nahm sie später nach Apahunikʿ mit und trug sie in die Liste der Würdenträger (Diwan) ein.[6] Wie N. Adontz zurecht betont, kann diese Mitteilung bei einer gewissen Unaufmerksamkeit so verstanden werden, als ob diese Fürsten und 400 Adeligen des Fürstentitels gewürdigt worden wären, was zum Entstehen der Sage über die 400 Throne geführt haben könnte.[7] Folglich hat die Mitteilung über die Weihe der 400 Bischöfe durch Gregor den Erleuchter keinen besonderen Wert, um so mehr, als sie durch keine anderen Angaben erhärtet wird.

Adontz stellt deutlich die Unmöglichkeit der Weihe der 400 Bischöfe durch Gregor den Erleuchter dar, irrt sich aber, wenn er denkt, dass die von Gregor dem Erleuchter geweihten Bischöfe nur insgesamt 12 waren. Nach Agathangelos hat der erste armenische Katholikos in Wirklichkeit 12 Bischöfe aus heidnischen Familien geweiht: Ałbianos, der zum geistlichen Aufseher der Euphratregionen ernannt wurde, Euthalios, als Hirten von Basēn und Umgebung, Bassos, Movsēs, Eusebios, Yovhannēs, Agapēs, Artitēs, Arsukēs, Antiokʿēs, Tirikēs und Kiwrakos.[8] Dass es auch andere geweihte Bischöfe gab, ist in derselben Mitteilung von Agathangelos deutlich zu erkennen, wo er schreibt: „Und die Namen der anderen kann niemand aufzählen, der es tun möchte."[9] Darauf wird noch zurückzukommen sein, jetzt aber soll versucht werden, die wirkliche Zahl der Bischofsstühle zu klären.

Wie oben bereits erwähnt, war diese nach Uxtanēs und nach Ōrbelean 30 bzw. 36. N. Adontz, der das Werk von Samuēl Kamrǰajorecʿi oder irgendeine andere gemeinsame Quelle für den Ursprung der Mitteilungen beider Verfasser hält, ist der Meinung, dass die Nichtübereinstimmung der Zahlen vielleicht durch diejenige Fassung des Werks Samuēls erläutert werden könnte, von der Ōrbelean Gebrauch gemacht hat. Der Verfasser denkt, dass sich die Liste Samuēls vom Verzeichnis des Uxtanēs kaum unterscheiden würde, und dass die Einteilung der Bischöfe in eine rechte und eine linke Gruppe vielleicht Ōrbeleans Vermutung sei, wobei er auf der Einteilung der Fürstenthrone in eine rechte und eine

---

[5] Patmutʿiwn Srboyn Nersisi Partʿewi Hayocʿ Hayrapeti. Venedig 1853, siehe *Sopʿerkʿ Haykakankʿ* VI 32–39.

[6] Yovhan Mamikonean, Tarōnoy Patmutʿiwn. Erevan 1980, 50–59.

[7] N. Adonc (Adontz), Armenija v epochu Justiniana. St. Petersburg 1908 (Erevan [2]1971) 240f. Vgl. zu diesem Werk auch die wertvolle Überarbeitung: N. Adontz, Armenia in the Period of Justinian. The Political Conditions Based on the Naxarar System. Translated with partial revisions, a bibliographical note and appendices by N. G. Garsoïan. Lissabon 1970.

[8] Agatʿangelos § 845.

[9] L.c.

linke Seite basierte.[10] Wenn es im Werk Samuēls eine Bischofsliste gegeben hat, die von Ōrbelean nicht übernommen wurde, dann entsprechen einander auf den beiden Listen nur folgende Daten: rechterseits ist der Bischof von Siwnikʽ auf der Liste von Uxtanēs auch der siebte, und der Bischof von Harkʽ ist auf beiden Listen der erste.[11] Einerseits scheint diese Ähnlichkeit bedeutend zu sein, aber andererseits gibt es Gründe für die Annahme, dass die im Werk von Uxtanēs aufgezählten Bischofsstühle nicht den Zeiten Gregors des Erleuchters zugeschrieben werden dürfen. Demnach handelt es sich entweder um eine zufällige Ähnlichkeit, oder ist die Mitteilung Ōrbeleans auch nicht auf die Zeiten des ersten armenischen Katholikos zu beziehen, eine Hypothese, die, wie wir später sehen werden, unbegründet ist.

Wir wollen jetzt versuchen, die Liste der Bischofsstühle von Uxtanēs zu analysieren, die folgenderweise aussieht:

1. Der Bischof von Harkʽ
2. Der Bischof von Ostan
3. Der Bischof von Taykʽ
4. Der Bischof von Mardałi
5. Der Bischof von Aršamunikʽ
6. Der Bischof von Arcrunikʽ
7. Der Bischof von Siwnikʽ
8. Der Bischof von Ṙštunikʽ
9. Der Bischof von Mokkʽ
10. Der Bischof von Amatunikʽ
11. Der Bischof von Basēn
12. Der Bischof von Mamikonean
13. Der Bischof von Bagrewand
14. Der Bischof von Xorxoṙunikʽ
15. Der Bischof von Wanand
16. Der Bischof von Apahunikʽ
17. Der Bischof von Aršarunikʽ
18. Der Bischof von Gnunikʽ
19. Der Bischof von Gołtʽan
20. Der Bischof von Gardman
21. Der Bischof von Akē
22. Der Bischof von Bažunikʽ
23. Der Bischof von Erutak
24. Der Bischof von Asorikʽ (Assyrien)
25. Der Bischof von Anjewacʽikʽ
26. Der Bischof von Pałunikʽ
27. Der Bischof von Mehnunikʽ
28. Der Bischof von Eli
29. Der Bischof von Zarehawan
30. Der Bischof von Miws Asorikʽ (dem „Anderen Assyrien")

„Das sind diejenigen 30 Bischöfe, die von Gregor dem Erleuchter geweiht wurden und den Thron bestiegen. Außerdem wurden noch 370 Bischöfe geweiht, die mit Gottes Segen in verschiedenen Orten zum „Aufseher" und in jeder Provinz zum geistlichen Führer ernannt wurden."[12] Wenn diese vielleicht unvollständige Liste mit der Bischofsliste von Samuēl Kamrǰajorecʽi identisch wäre, dann sollte der Name des Bischofs von Basēn an der 19. Stelle sein, in Wirklichkeit ist er aber an der 11. Stelle. Diese Tatsache zieht sogar die unvollständige Identität der beiden Listen in Zweifel. Es gibt aber auch einen anderen Faktor. Die namentlich erwähnten Bischofssitze, deren Gründung der Geschichtsschreiber Gregor dem Erleuchter zuschreibt, besetzen in Wirklichkeit diejenigen Regionen Großarmeniens, die nach 428 zum armenischen Marzpanat (Statthalterschaft) gehörten. Ist es nicht erstaunlich, dass Gregor der Erleuchter in Ałjnikʽ, Kordukʽ, Copʽkʽ, Gugarkʽ und in vielen anderen Orten, deren Existenz bereits am Anfang oder in der Mitte des IV. Jahrhunderts fixiert wurde, keine Bischöfe eingesetzt hätte? Es fehlen auf der Liste die Namen aller Grenzbezirke, die Namen der östlichen Regionen Großarmeniens und die Namen derjenigen Regionen, die nach der Teilung im Jahre 387 zum Römischen Reich gehörten. Es ist nicht schwer, zu verstehen, dass diese Liste nichts anderes als ein Dokument aus der Marzpan-Zeit von 428 bis 451 ist. Dies beweist auch die Tatsache, dass

---

[10] Adonc, l.c.

[11] Bei Ōrbelean ist der erste Bischof rechts der von Harkʽ, der siebte der von Siwnikʽ. Bei Uxtanēs ist der erste Bischof der von Harkʽ, der siebte der von Siwnikʽ. Wenn also der Bischof von Siwnikʽ auf der rechten Seite ist, dann soll auch der von Harkʽ auf der rechten sein. Bei Samuēl ist der erste Bischof rechterseits allerdings der von Basēn.

[12] Uxtanēs Episkopos, Patmutʽiwn Hayocʽ 100.

auf der Liste die Bischofswürde von Gardman erwähnt wird, die nach 451 unter der Herrschaft des Katholikosats von Ałuank‘ (Kaukasisches Albanien) sein sollte. Ohne auf Einzelheiten einzugehen, wollen wir nur erwähnen, dass die Bischofswürden von Assyrien und Miws Assyrien, die vielleicht die Bevölkerung von Tmorik‘ und irgendeiner weiteren von Assyrern bewohnten Region repräsentierten, nicht zur assyrischen sondern zur armenischen Kirche gehörten, da die obenerwähnten Territorien administrativ dem armenischen Marzpanat angehörten. Wir werden später sehen, dass diese in allen Ländern vorhandene Erscheinung den Schlüssel zur Klärung der Frage nach der Zahl der Bischofseparchien Großarmeniens in sich trägt.

Die Bischofsliste von Uxtanēs zeugt davon, dass die Bischofsstühle nach der feudalen administrativen Gliederung gegründet wurden. Wenn wir folglich diese Liste mit den Bischofslisten von Ełišē und Łazar P‘arpec‘i sowie auch mit der Teilnehmerliste der Synoden von 506 und 554 in Dwin vergleichen, dann sehen wir, dass in all diesen Listen das Prinzip der feudalen administrativen Organisation typisch ist, der der feudale Besitz zugrunde liegt.

Im folgenden wollen wir die Listen der Bischöfe vergleichen, die an den Versammlungen, die im Jahre 450 in Artašat und in den Jahren 506 und 554 in Dwin stattfanden, teilgenommen haben.

Die Versammlung von 450

1. Katholikos Yovsēp‘, nach Ełišē Bischof von Ayrarat
2. Anania von Siwnik‘
3. Mušē von Arcrunik‘
4. Sahak von Tarōn
5. Sahak von Ṙštunik‘
6. Melitē von Manazkert[13]
7. Eznik von Bagrewand
8. Surmak von Bznunik‘
9. T‘at‘ik von Basēn
10. Eremia von Mardastan
11. Gag von Wanand
12. Basil von Mokk‘
13. Ełbayr von Anjewac‘ik‘
14. Tačat von Tayk‘
15. K‘asu von Tarberunik‘
16. Zawen von Mananałi, nach Ełišē Eułał von Mardałi
17. Ełišē von Amatunik‘
18. Eremia von Apahunik‘[14]

Die Versammlung von 506

1. Katholikos Babgēn von Ot‘mus
2. Meršapuh von Mamikonean
3. Nersēs von Mardpetakan
4. Teaṙntur von Hark‘
5. Samuēl von Bznunik‘
6. P‘ovkas und Samuēl von Basēn
7. T‘at‘ul von Aršarunik‘
8. Ałan von Xorxoṙunik‘
9. Atat von Tayk‘
10. Tačat von Aršamunik‘
11. Daniēl von Ṙštunik‘
12. Yapik von Mokk‘
13. Xabib von Arcrunik‘
14. Šahē von Amatunik‘
15. Sahak von Pałunik‘
16. Pawłos von Gnunik‘
17. Movsēs von Zarehawan
18. Dawit‘ von Tmorik‘
19. Daniēl von Anjewac‘ik‘
20. T‘emur von Mehnunik‘[15]
21. <Siwnik‘>
22. <Mardałi>

Die Versammlung von 554

1. Katholikos Nersēs von Bagrewand
2. Der Bischof Meršapuh von Tarōn und Mamikonean
3. Grigor von Sephakan Gund (Mardpet-Regiment)
4. Pargew von Hark‘
5. Tirak von Bagrewand
6. Grigor von Basēn
7. Nersēs von Mardałi
8. Vałot von Aršamunik‘
9. Petros von Siwnik‘
10. Grigor von Arcrunik‘
11. Markos von <Bznunik‘>
12. Maštoc‘ von Xorxoṙunik‘
13. Yovhan von Apahunik‘
14. Abdišo von Orthodoxen Assyrern
15. Yovnan von Wanand
16. Hawuk von Aršarunik‘
17. K‘ristap‘or von Pałunik‘
18. Yuys von Gołt‘an
19. T‘adēos von Mehnunik‘[16]

---

[13] Bei Ełišē Bischof Melet von Manazkert und Bischof K‘asu von Turuberan.

[14] Ełišēi Vasn Vardanay ew Hayoc‘ Paterazmin. Erevan 1957, 27f. Łazaray P‘arpec‘woy Patmut‘iwn Hayoc‘ ew T‘ułt‘aṙ Vahan Mamikonean. Tbilisi 1904, 41–45.

[15] Girk‘ t‘łt‘oc‘. Tbilisi 1901, 41f.

[16] L.c. 73.

Die Versammlung von 506

23. <Wanand>
24. <Apahunikʿ>[17]

Die Versammlung von 554

20. Xosrov von Amatunikʿ
21. Sahak von Ṙštunikʿ
22. Sołomon von Mokkʿ
23. Stepʿanos von Anjewacʿikʿ
24. Hoṙomanos von Akē
25. Mikʿaēl von Zarehawan
26. Astuacatur von Bznunikʿ[18]
27. <Taykʿ>
28. <Gnunikʿ>[19]

Im Jahre 450 haben also an der Versammlung der Geistlichen und weltlichen Fürsten, die auf das Edikt von Yazkert (Jesdikert) II. (mit der Forderung nach dem Religionswechsel) eine Antwort geben sollte, insgesamt 18 Bischöfe teilgenommen. Diese Zahl kann unverändert bleiben, wenn wir Yovsēpʿ nach dem Werk von Ełišē für den Bischof von Ayrarat halten, und andererseits kann diese Zahl kleiner werden, wenn wir ihn nach dem Werk von Łazar Pʿarpecʿi für den armenischen Katholikos halten. Man wird aber kaum denken, dass an der Versammlung alle Bischöfe des Armenischen Marzpanats teilgenommen haben. Sogar ein flüchtiger Versuch der Fixierung der Bischofssitze auf der Karte deckt Lücken auf, die indirekt die Existenz weiterer Bischöfe postulieren. Es ist schwer zu sagen, wie hoch die Zahl der Bischofseparchien wirklich war, aber man kann sicher davon ausgehen, dass sie mehr als 18 waren. Die Teilnehmerlisten der Versammlungen in Dwin in den Jahren 506 und 554 lassen auch daran denken, dass nicht alle Bischöfe an diesen Synoden teilgenommen haben. Jedenfalls wird man kaum glauben, dass im Jahre 506, als die Versammlung in Dwin einberufen wurde, in Siwnikʿ keine Bischofseparchie existierte. Wenn wir nach dem Beispiel von N. Adontz annehmen, dass Aršamunikʿ im Jahre 450 der Diözese von Mardałi angehörte, und auch Mardałi im Jahre 506 zu Aršamunikʿ gehörte, was theoretisch möglich ist, dann kann man doch auf keine Weise annehmen, dass auch Siwnikʿ irgendeiner anderen Diözese angehörte. Deswegen sollte man postulieren, dass es zu Zeiten der Dwiner Versammlung außer den 19 an der Versammlung teilnehmenden Bischöfen (der 20. war der armenische Katholikos), die die armenischen Marzpanats-Eparchien repräsentierten, noch 4 Bischöfe gab, die ihren Sitz in Siwnikʿ, Mardałi, Wanand und Apahunikʿ[20] hatten. Eine Tatsache, die N. Adontz auch zurecht betont hat. Hiermit erreicht die – noch nicht vollständige – Zahl der Bischofswürden mit hoher Wahrscheinlichkeit 23.

Es scheint, dass man von den Verhältnissen zur Zeit der Synode von Dwin im Jahre 554 ein vollständigeres Bild der armenischen kirchlichen Eparchien erhalten könnte. An der von Katholikos Nersēs einberufenen Versammlung haben 18 Bischöfe teilgenommen. Das ist aber auch keine verlässliche Zahl. Man sollte sie wenigstens um 9 vergrößern, wovon 7 in der Anklageschrift des Katholikos Nersēs erwähnt sind. Ausgehend von der letzten Liste könnte man annehmen, dass auch in Taykʿ und im Herrschaftgebiet von Gnunikʿ Bischofsstühle existierten. Damit erreicht die Bischofszahl 27, die sich von der Mitteilung des Uxtanēs nicht viel unterscheidet und sogar deren Richtigkeit stützen kann, wenn man annimmt, dass auch andere Bischöfe an der Versammlung nicht teilnehmen konnten. Jetzt wollen wir versuchen, die Liste der Bischofseparchien im Werk von Uxtanēs mit denen der Jahre 450 und 554 zu vergleichen.

---

[17] Es wird angenommen, dass diese Bischofswürden zur Zeit der Synode von Dwin im Jahre 506 existierten.

[18] Die folgenden sieben Namen kann man in der Anklageschrift des Katholikos Nersēs finden (S. 70).

[19] Man nimmt an, dass diese Bischofswürden zur Zeit der Synode von Dwin im Jahre 554 existiert haben. Eine vergleichende Untersuchung dieser Listen bei N. Adonc, Armenija v epochu Justiniana 331.

[20] Adonc 331.

Die Liste von Uxtanēs

1. Der Bischof von Harkʿ
2. Der Bischof von Ostan
3. Der Bischof von Taykʿ
4. Der Bischof von Mardałi
5. Der Bischof von Aršamunikʿ
6. Der Bischof von Arcrunikʿ
7. Der Bischof von Siwnikʿ
8. Der Bischof von Ṙštunikʿ
9. Der Bischof von Mokkʿ
10. Der Bischof von Amatunikʿ
11. Der Bischof von Basēn
12. Der Bischof von Mamikonean
13. Der Bischof von Bagrewand
14. Der Bischof von Xorxoṙunikʿ
15. Der Bischof von Wanand
16. Der Bischof von Apahunikʿ
17. Der Bischof von Aršarunikʿ
18. Der Bischof von Gnunikʿ
19. Der Bischof von Gołtʿan
20. Der Bischof von Gardman
21. Der Bischof von Akē
22. Der Bischof von Bažunikʿ
23. Der Bischof von Erutak
24. Der Bischof von Asorikʿ (Assyrien)
25. Der Bischof von Anjewacʿikʿ
26. Der Bischof von Pałunikʿ
27. Der Bischof von Mehenunikʿ
28. Der Bischof von Eli
29. Der Bischof von Zarehawan
30. Der Bischof von Miws Asorikʿ

Die Synode von 450

2.[21] 1. Yovsēpʿ von Ayrarat
12. 2. Sahak von Tarōn
1. 3. Melitē von Manazkert
13. 4. Eznik von Bagrewand
5. Surmak von Bznunikʿ
3. 6. Tačat von Taykʿ
11. 7. Tʿatʿik von Basēn
21. 8. Kʿasu von Turuberan
9. Eremia von Mardastan
4. 10. Eułał von Mardałi
7. 11. Anania von Siwnikʿ
6. 12. Mušē von Arcrunikʿ
8. 13. Sahak von Ṙštunikʿ
9. 14. Basil von Mokkʿ
15. 15. Gag von Wanand
10. 16. Ełišē von Amatunikʿ
25. 17. Ełbayr von Anjewacʿikʿ
16. 18. Eremia von Apahunikʿ[22]

Die Synode von 554

12. 1. Der Bischof Meršapuh von Tarōn und Mamikonean
2. Grigor von Sephakan Gund (Mardpet-Regiment)
1. 3. Pargew von Harkʿ
13. 4. Tirak von Bagrewand
11. 5. Grigor von Basēn
4. 6. Nersēs von Mardałi
5. 7. Wałot von Aršamunikʿ
7. 8. Petros von Siwnikʿ
6. 9. Grigor von Arcrunikʿ
10. Markos von <Bznunikʿ>
14. 11. Maštocʿ von Xorxoṙunikʿ
16. 12. Yovhan von Apahunikʿ
24. 13. Abdišo von Orthodoxen Assyrern
15. 14. Yovnan von Wanand
17. 15. Hawuk von Aršarunikʿ
26. 16. Kʿristapʿor von Pałunikʿ
19. 17. Yuys von Gołtʿan
27. 18. Tʿadēos von Mehnunikʿ
10. 19. Xosrov von Amatunikʿ
8. 20. Sahak von Ṙštunikʿ
9. 21. Sołomon von Mokkʿ
25. 22. Stepʿanos von Anjewacʿikʿ
21. 23. Hoṙomanos von Akē
29. 24. Mikʿael von Zarehawan
22. 25. Astuacatur von Bznunikʿ
3. 26. <Taykʿ>
18. 27. <Gnunikʿ>

Die vergleichende Behandlung zeigt an, dass auf der Liste von Uxtanēs die Bischöfe von Bznunikʿ und Mardastan fehlen, die während der im Jahre 450 einberufenen Versammlung erwähnt werden. Andererseits fehlen auf der Liste von Ełišē die Bischofswürden von Aršamunikʿ, Xorxoṙunikʿ, Aršarunikʿ, Gnunikʿ, Gołtʿan, Gardman, Akē, Bažunikʿ, Erutak, Assyrern, Pałunikʿ, Mehnunikʿ, Eli, Zarehawan und Miws Asorikʿ. Die Bischofswürden von Mehnunikʿ und Turuberan sind eigentlich identisch. Das Fehlen von Mardastan wurde immer noch nicht begründet, weil es keine dafür nötigen Grundlagen gibt, wenn nur Mardastan nicht mit Erutak identisch ist, eine Hypothese, die nicht besonders zuverlässig ist.

Was die Existenz anderer Bischofswürden in der Mitte des V. Jahrhunderts betrifft, so denken wir, dass darauf die in den Werken von Ełišē und Łazar Pʿarpecʿi aufbewahrten Fürstenlisten ein Licht werfen können. Es reicht bereits, die Liste der vom persischen Hof nach Tisbon/Ktesiphon gerufenen armenischen Fürsten mit der Namenliste der an der Versammlung in Artašat teilnehmenden Bischöfe zu vergleichen, damit es klar wird, dass diejenigen Bischöfe in Artašat anwesend waren, die hauptsächlich die Regionen unter der unmittelbaren Herrschaft des armenischen Marzpan und die Besitzeparchien der gegen die Abtrünnigkeit gestimmten Fürsten vertraten. So sind Ayrarat, Manazkert, Bznunikʿ, Basēn, Turuberan-Mehnunikʿ, Mardastan und Mardałi Königs-, Marzpans- oder teilweise Kirchenbesitz, und die Bischöfe von Tarōn und Taykʿ, Siwnikʿ, Arcrunikʿ, Ṙštunikʿ,

[21] Vor den Reihenzahlen der Bischofslisten von 450 und 554 sind die Nummern der Liste von Uxtanēs angegeben.

[22] Die Bischofsliste von 450 nach Ełišē.

Mokkʿ, Amatunikʿ, Anjewacʿikʿ und Apahunikʿ repräsentieren die erblichen Besitztümer und teilweise auch die unter ihrer Herrschaft liegenden Gaue von Vardan Mamikonean, Vasak Siwni, Neršapuh Arcruni, Aršak Ṙštunik, Artak Mokacʿi, Ełišē Amatuni, Šmawon Anjewacʿi und Manēč Apahuni. Folglich wird die Abwesenheit etwa des Bischofs von Xorxoṙunikʿ bei der Synode von Dwin im Jahre 450 dahingehend zu erklären sein, dass er der Versammlung fernblieb, wohl ein Ergebnis der gegen den Aufstand eingestellten Position von Gadišo Xorxoṙuni. Nach unserer Meinung hat die Abwesenheit des Bischofs von Gardman in der obenerwähnten Versammlung denselben Grund. Was die anderen Abwesenden betrifft, deren Namen wegen des Fehlens der nötigen Materialien nur mit Schwierigkeiten zu eruieren wären, kann man folgendes sagen: Ihre Abwesenheit war entweder in Einstellungen ihrer Fürsten gegen den Aufstand oder in deren Gleichgültigkeit bzw. Behutsamkeit in bezug auf den Kampf mit den Sasaniden begründet.

Wie oben erwähnt, fehlt auf der Liste von Uxtanēs die Bischofswürde von Bznunikʿ. Dieses Faktum, das auf den ersten Blick keine große Bedeutung zu haben scheint, hilft in Wirklichkeit herauszubekommen, wann die Liste der Bischofsstühle von Uxtanēs erstellt wurde. Im Jahre 428 hat der persische Königshof den letzten Vertreter der armenischen Königsdynastie der Aršakunikʿ, Artašēs Aršakuni, und den Katholikos Sahak Partew entthront, wonach den Thron des Katholikos ein Priester namens Surmak von Arckē bestieg.[23] Surmaks Herrschaft dauerte nur ein Jahr. Bald hatte er mit seiner Lebensweise die armenischen Nacharare (Lehnsherren) verärgert, die ihn vertrieben, und mit deren Unterstützung ein Assyrer namens Brkʿišoy den Thron des Katholikos bestieg. Aber am persischen Königshof hatte man die „Dienste“, anders ausgedrückt den Verrat von Surmak nicht vergessen, und auf Befehl des persischen Königs wurde ihm die Bischofseparchie von Bznunikʿ anvertraut.[24] Unter den Versammlungsteilnehmern im Jahre 450 wird der Name eines Bischofs Surmak von Bznunikʿ erwähnt, der, unserer Meinung nach, derselbe Surmak (von Arckē) sein sollte. Demnach kann man, ausgehend von den obenerwähnten Tatsachen, vermuten, dass die Liste zur Bischofszeit von Surmak ausgestellt wurde, der sich die Bischofswürde von Bznunikʿ früher angeeignet hatte, als er sie vom persischen König bekam. Deswegen wurde die Bischofswürde von Bznunikʿ in die Liste von Uxtanēs aufgenommen.

Wenn wir nach dem Gesagten auf die obenerwähnte Liste der Bischofswürden zurückkommen, können wir folgern, dass es bereits in den 20er Jahren des V. Jahrhunderts, verbunden mit der sozial-politischen Entwicklung des Landes auf dem Territorium des armenischen Marzpanats, ungefähr 30 oder etwas mehr Bischofswürden gab. Entweder verfielen damals einige Bischofswürden unter unbekannten Umständen und wurden neue gebildet, oder es wurden zwei Eparchien vereinigt und der Verantwortung eines gemeinsamen Bischofs übergeben. Sowohl für die Liste von Uxtanēs als auch für alle anderen später aufgestellten Bischofslisten ist charakteristisch, dass sie der speziell feudalen administrativen Teilung Armeniens und des armenischen Marzpanats entsprechen. Da erhebt sich die Frage, ob auch die administrative Einteilung Großarmeniens am Anfang des IV. Jahrhunderts einen ausgeprägt feudalen Charakter hatte.

Es sei erwähnt, dass die kirchlichen eparchischen Gliederungen in der Regel entweder der administrativen Einteilung der unabhängigen Staaten oder der Unterteilung des Römischen Reiches in Provinzen entsprochen haben. Als etwa die Provinz Kappadokien in das Erste und das Zweite Kappadokien geteilt wurde (im Jahre 371), brachte man kurz darauf auch die Kirchenverwaltung mit der neuen administrativen Ordnung in Übereinstimmung. Ausgehend von diesem Grundsatz sollte man annehmen, dass für die Klärung

---

[23] Movsisi Xorenacʿwoy Patmutʿiwn Hayocʿ (Tbilisi 1913), III 63.

[24] L.c.

der von Gregor dem Erleuchter gegründeten Bischofssitze die Materialien der Konzilien im V.–VII. Jahrhundert nicht als sichere Stützen dienen können, denn die administrative Teilung des Königreichs Großarmenien am Anfang des IV. Jahrhunderts unterschied sich prinzipiell von der administrativen Ordnung im V.–VII. Jahrhundert, die, wie wir bereits gesehen haben, einen typisch feudalen Charakter hatte.

Wie sah die administrative Gliederung Großarmeniens im früheren IV. Jahrhundert aus? Die Materialien der „Geographie" des großen Alexandriner Geographen Claudius Ptolemaeus, von „Ašxarhacʻoycʻ" (Armenische Geographie) und der „Geschichte Armeniens" von Agathangelos helfen, die administrative Teilung Großarmeniens aufzuklären.

Nach der Beschreibung Großarmeniens von Claudius Ptolemaeus wurde das armenische Königreich administrativ in 20 Gebiete oder Strategien geteilt: Catarzene – (Kłarǰkʻ), Obarene = Gogarene (Gugarkʻ), Otene (Utikʻ), Colthene = Caspiene (Kaspkʻ), Sodukene (Cawdēkʻ = Arcʻax), Sibakene = Sisakene (Sisakan – Siwnikʻ), Sacapene = Sacasene (Šakašēn), Basilissene = Basilikene (Königsland oder Ostan), Bolbene = Bolxene (Bołxa/Buxa), Arsesa (Arsik oder Xałtikʻ), Akilisene (Ekełikʻ), Astaunitis (Hašteankʻ), Sophene (Copʻkʻ), Anzitene (Anjit = Ałjnikʻ), Thospitis (Copʻkʻ oder West-Vaspurakan), Coriaia = Cortaia (Korčaykʻ I), Bagrauandene (Bagrewand), Gordyene (Kordukʻ), Cotaia = Co[r]taia (Korčaykʻ II) und Mardi (Mardpetakan).[25] Nach „Ašxarhacʻoycʻ" bestand das Königreich Großarmenien aus 15 Gebieten: Hocharmenien, Copʻkʻ (das „Vierte Armenien"), Ałjnikʻ, Taruberan oder Turuberan, Mokkʻ, Korčaykʻ, Persarmenien, Vaspurakan, Siwnikʻ, Arcʻax, Pʻaytakaran, Utikʻ, Gugarkʻ, Taykʻ und Ayrarat.[26] Die Beschreibung Großarmeniens im „Ašxarhacʻoycʻ" zeigt an, dass sie auf Grund der Verhältnisse des III. Jahrhunderts abgefasst wurde, die chronologisch der Epoche des Ptolemaeus nahe sind. Aber da es im V. Jahrhundert niedergeschrieben wurde, haben darin viele administrativ-politische Bedingungen des V. Jahrhunderts Platz gefunden. So wurden Katarsene-Kłarǰkʻ und Obarene-Gogarene-Gugarkʻ vereinigt, und so entstand das Gugarkʻ in „Ašxarhacʻoycʻ"; durch die Vereinigung mit Thospitis-Copʻkʻ wurde das neue Vaspurakan gebildet; die Gebiete Utikʻ und Ayrarat von „Ašxarhacʻoycʻ" haben sich jeweils durch die Vereinigung von Sakasene-Šakašēn mit Utikʻ und von Bagrewand mit Basilikene-Ostan formiert; ein Teil von Arsesa-Xałtikʻ wurde mit Akilisene vereinigt und so entstand Hocharmenien, und ein anderer Teil wurde mit Buxa vereinigt und so entstand Taykʻ des „Ašxarhacʻoycʻ". Ptolemaeus schreibt nichts über die Existenz von Mokkʻ, weil es sich erst im IV. Jahrhundert formiert hat.

Wenn man die Angaben von „Ašxarhacʻoycʻ" und der „Geographie" von Ptolemaeus mit den Berichten der „Geschichte Armeniens" von Agathangelos vergleicht, wird es offensichtlich, dass die Mitteilungen des Geschichtsschreibers der Christianisierung chronologisch eine mittlere Position zwischen den beiden obenerwähnten Quellen beziehen. Das, was bei Agathangelos praktisch unverständlich ist, wird im Licht der Angaben von Ptolemaeus und „Ašxarhacʻoycʻ" völlig klar.

Was zeigen die Berichte des Agathangelos an? Nach des Geschichtsschreibers Bezeugung „hat damals der König alle Hauptnacharare und Gebietsstatthalter eilends, angstvoll und mit großer Freude zusammengerufen. Das waren: 1. der Fürst von Angełtun; 2. der Fürst von Ałjnikʻ, der große Bdešx (Markgraf); 3. der Fürst von Mardpetutʻiwn; 4. der das Vorrecht der Krönung besitzende Herr des Fürstentums der Aspet-Würde (Rittertum); 5. der Fürst der Sparapet-Würde, der Heerführer des Landes Armenien;

---

[25] Claudii Ptolemaei Geographia (ed. Müller) I/2, V, cap. XII 1–10.

[26] Ašxarhacʻoycʻ Movsisi Xorenacʻwoy. Venedig 1881, 29. Zu dieser Quelle vgl. auch R. H. Hewsen, The Geography of Ananias of Širak (Ašxarhacʻoycʻ). The Long and the Short Recensions (*Beihefte zum TAVO* B 77). Wiesbaden 1992.

6. Der Fürst von Korduk'; 7. Der Fürst von Cop'k'; 8. der Fürst von Gugark', welcher „der andere Bdešx" (Markgraf) genannt wird; 9. der Fürst von Ṙštunik'; 10. der Fürst von Mokk'; 11. der Fürst von Siwnik'; 12. der Fürst von Cawdēk'; 13. der Fürst von Utik'; 14. der Fürst-Šahap (Stadthauptmann) von Zarewand und dem Gau Her; 15. der Fürst des Hauses Małxazut'iwn (die Garde); 16. der Fürst von Arcruni.

Dies sind die Auserwählten, die Statthalter, die Herren der Tausenden und Myriaden im Land Armenien, im Hause von T'orgom (Togarma), die der König Tiridat zusammengerufen und in die Gebiete Kappadokiens geschickt hat, damit sie in der Stadt Caesarea, die auf Armenisch Mažak' heißt, Gregor zum Bischof ihres Landes weihen lassen."[27]

Es ist nicht schwer zu erkennen, dass die namhaftesten Fürsten von Großarmenien Gregor den Erleuchter zur Weihe nach Caesarea begleiten sollten. Es ist interessant, dass sie als Statthalter, als Führer von Tausenden und Myriaden bezeichnet werden. Unter den Begleitern waren die Bdešx (Markgrafen) von Ałjnik' und Gugark' und die Fürsten von Mardpetut'iwn, Korduk', Cop'k', Ṙštunik', Mokk', Siwnik', Cawdēk' und Utik' Statthalter bestimmter Gebiete, jene acht, die der Autor eindeutig für Gebietsfürsten hält. Obwohl der Bdešx von Ałjnik' und der Fürst von Mardpetakan nicht als unmittelbare Statthalter bezeichnet werden, vertreten sie trotzdem das Gebiet von Ałjnik', genauer gesagt den östlichen Teil von Ałjnik' und das Gebiet von Mardpetakan, das nach den Angaben des „Stammvaters der armenischen Geschichtsschreibung", Movsēs Xorenac'i, Ost-Vaspurakan entsprochen hat. Es ist nicht weniger interessant, dass die obenerwähnten Gebiete in den Beschreibungen Großarmeniens, zuerst in der „Geographie" von Ptolemaeus und dann auch in „Ašxarhac'oyc'" ihre Parallelen finden. Aber bevor an diese Parallelen herangegangen wird wäre festzustellen, über welche Gebiete die „Geschichte" des Agathangelos noch berichtet.

In verschiedenen Zusammenhängen erwähnt der Autor den Fürsten von Angełtun,[28] das Land oder Bdešxut'iwn (die Markgrafschaft) von Nor Širakan[29], Kaspk' oder die kaspischen Gebiete mit der Königsstadt P'aytakaran[30], Kłarǰk'[31], das Gebiet von Xałtik'[32], das Land von Tarōn[33], das Land der feudalen Herrschaft des armenischen Königs in Atrpatakan[34] und den Gau Ayraratean oder Ayrarat[35]. Wenn über Angełtun irgendwelche Zweifel bestehen können, dann steht jedenfalls fest, dass Bdešxut'iwn von Nor Širakan, die Länder von Xałtik', Kłarǰk' und Tarōn, das Land der feudalen Herrschaft von Atrpatakan, Kaspk' und Ayrarat Gebiete sind. Aber im wesentlichen ist es auch sicher, dass Angełtun – aus uns unbekannten Gründen – von Ałjnik' getrennt und in ein separates Gebiet umgewandelt wurde, das sich von Groß-Cop'k' bis zu den Euphrat-Territorien erstreckte. Wenn wir die Ergebnisse der obigen Untersuchungen zu kartographieren versuchen, gelangen wir zur folgenden administrativen Ordnung.

---

27 Agat'angełos, § 795f.
28 L.c. § 873.
29 L.c. § 842, 873, 877.
30 L.c. § 842. Die andere Erwähnung von Kaspk' (§ 19) betrifft Großarmenien nicht.
31 L.c. § 842.
32 L.c. § 785, 842.
33 L.c. § 809.
34 L.c. § 842.
35 L.c. § 21, 31, 122, 150, 776, 791, 803, 817, 841, 873 und 881.

Die administrative Einteilung Großarmeniens am Anfang des IV. Jahrhunderts	*Nach der „Geographie" von Ptolemaeus*	*Nach „Ašxarhacʿoycʿ"*
1. Angeltun	–	–
2. Aɫjnikʿ (der östliche Teil)	Ansitene	Aɫjnikʿ
3. Mokkʿ	–	Mokkʿ
4. Das Gebiet von Ṙštunikʿ	Tospitis	West-Vaspurakan
5. Das Gebiet von Kordukʿ	Gordyene	[der westliche Teil von Korčaykʿ]
6. Das Gebiet von Arcrunikʿ	Kortaia I	Korčaykʿ (der östliche Teil)
7. Bdešxutʿiwn von Nor Širakan	–	Persarmenien (der südliche Teil)
8. Mardpetakan	Mardoi (Mardi)	Ost-Vaspurakan
9. Kaspkʿ	Kolthene (= Kaspkʿ)	Pʿaytakaran
10. Utikʿ	Otene	Utikʿ
11. Cawdēkʿ	Sodukene	Arcʿax
12. Siwnikʿ	Sisakene	Siwnikʿ (Sisakan)
13. Gugarkʿ	Obarene (= Gogarene)	Gugarkʿ (der östliche Teil)
14. Kɫarǰkʿ	Katarsene	Gugarkʿ (der westliche Teil)
15. –	Bolchene	Taykʿ
16. Xaɫtikʿ	Arsesa	–
17. Copʿkʿ	Sophene	Copʿkʿ (das Vierte Armenien)
18. Zarewand und šahaputʿiwn vom Gau Her	Kortaia II	Persarmenien (der nördliche Teil)
19. –	Akilisene	Hocharmenien
20. Das Land von Tarōn	Astaunitis	Taruberan
21. Atrpatakan	–	–
22. Ayrarat	Basilikene und Bagrauandene	Ayrarat

Unter Berücksichtigung aller Angaben könnte man feststellen, dass die Trennung des Hauses Angeɫ von Aɫjnikʿ im III. Jahrhundert stattfand und im Jahre 298 im Friedensvertrag von Nisibis zum Ausdruck kam[36]. Auf jeden Fall war Angeltun im II. Jahrhundert und in der ersten Hälfte des III. Jahrhunderts keine separate administrative Region, wie Ptolemaeus und „Ašxarhacʿoycʿ"nachweisen. Aus den Mitteilungen von Agathangelos und Buzandaran sowie auch aus den Berichten von Xorenacʿi, Eɫišē und Ɫazar Pʿarpecʿi könnte man folgern, dass die angesehenen Fürsten Gebietsstatthalter waren. Folglich lässt die Erwähnung des Fürsten von Angeltun unter den Angesehenen keinen Zweifel daran, dass Angeltun ein Gebiet war. Die Identifizierung des Gebiets von Ṙštunikʿ mit Tospitis bei Ptolemaeus sei folgendermaßen erläutert: Bekanntlich haben ziemlich viele Fürsten des Königreichs Großarmenien je 1000, die Bagratunis sogar 1500 Soldaten ins Schlachtfeld geführt. Aber die Fürsten von Ṙštunikʿ und Arcrunikʿ, die anscheinend die gleiche Kriegsmacht hatten, spielten im Leben des Landes eine sehr wichtige Rolle, im Unterschied zu den Fürsten von Wanand, Apahunikʿ, Anjewacʿikʿ und zu vielen anderen Fürsten, die auch 1000 Soldaten anführten. Ein Grund dafür war die Tatsache, dass sie nicht nur die Erbfolge hatten, sondern auch Gebietsstatthalter waren. Dass der Gau Ṙštunikʿ zu Vaspurakan gehörte, setzt voraus, dass West-Vaspurakan

[36] Petros Patrikios, Fragm. 14 (Dindorf, Historici graeci minores I, S. 443). Zum Datum des Friedens von Nisibis vgl. W. Seibt, Der historische Hintergrund ..., u. S. 127 mit Anm. 13.

„Gebiet von Ṙštunikʿ“ heißen sollte, weil den östlichen Teil von Vaspurakan das Fürstentum bzw. das Gebiet von Mardpetakan besetzte[37]. Was die Arcruni betrifft, muss man – ausgehend von zahlreichen wertvollen Bezeugungen von Tʿovma Arcruni[38] – annehmen, dass sie die Statthalter von Korčaykʿ, genauer gesagt von Ost-Korčaykʿ waren, denn Kordukʿ bildete zusammen mit Nachbarregionen ein separates Gebiet. Dass Kaspkʿ dem Pʿaytakaran von „Ašxarhacʿoycʿ“ entsprach, wird durch alle Quellen bewiesen, und dass es mit Kolthene bei Ptolemaeus zu verbinden ist, wird durch dessen geographische Reihenfolge bewiesen, weil es nach Otene-Utikʿ und vor Sodukene-Cawdēkʿ-Arcʿax beschrieben wird[39]. Die Identifikation von Cawdēkʿ mit Sodukene und Arcʿax von Ptolemaeus wird durch die Mitteilung von Xorenacʿi bewiesen, sowie auch durch jenen Bericht der „Geographie“ des Ptolemaeus, dass Sodukene in der Nachbarschaft von Siwnikʿ lag[40]. Xałtikʿ liegt in Čorox-Basēn, wo sich der Gau Arseacʿ Pʿor befindet, und danach Xałtikʿ auch Arsessa genannt wurde[41]. Unter den von Agathangelos erwähnten Gebietsnamen fehlen zwei Regionen: Taykʿ und Akilisene-Ekełikʿ. Die historisch-geographische Untersuchung von Großarmenien am Anfang des IV. Jahrhunderts und das Kartographieren der obenerwähnten Materialien zeigen an, dass diese Gebiete im Zeitraum der Proklamierung des Christentums als Staatsreligion wirklich existierten, weil ihre Territorien nicht den Nachbargebieten angehören konnten.

Für die Behandlung dieser Frage sind auch die arabische und die griechische Fassung des Werks von Agathangelos von Interesse. Wenn man an die Richtigkeit dieser Fassungen glaubt, dann sollte man annehmen, dass Gregor der Erleuchter nicht nur in die armenische Gebiete und Gaue, sondern auch nach Virkʿ und in die Länder der Durjuken (Vorfahren der Čečenen) und Alanen Bischöfe geschickt hat. Dann klärt sich auf, dass er auch nach Angełtun, Arsan oder Ałjnikʿ, Groß-Copʿkʿ, Copʿkʿ Hašteankʿ, Siwnikʿ, Mokkʿ und Mardpetakan Bischöfe geschickt hat; den Söhnen der heidnischen Priester, die das Christentum angenommen hatten und zum Bischof geweiht worden waren, hat Gregor der Erleuchter Eparchien anvertraut. So übergab er Ałbianos als Eparchie Bagrewand und die Euphrat-Regionen, Eutʿałios die Eparchie von Basēn, Bassos die Eparchie von Koł oder Kołtʿ, Movsēs die Eparchie von Ekełikʿ und Derǰan, Eusebios die Eparchie von Daranałi, Yovhannēs die Eparchie von Karan oder Karin, die N. Adontz als Karanitia bezeichnete, Xabib die Eparchie von Suspir, Ałbios die Eparchie von Tarōn und Bznunikʿ, Artites die Eparchie des Landes Małxasen, Arsukes die Eparchie von Širak, Antiokʿēs die Eparchie von Kordukʿ, Tirikēs die Eparchie von Atrpatakan und Kiwrakos die Eparchie von Aršamunikʿ[42]. Die armenische Fassung des Werkes von Agathangelos erfasst die Namen aller obenerwähnten Bischöfe außer Ałbios, doch werden nur die Eparchien von Ałbianos und Eutʿałios (Euphratgebiete bzw. Basēn) spezifiziert[43]. Wie N. Adontz zurecht betont, können diese Angaben nicht ohne eine Vorprüfung benutzt werden, aber gleichzeitig soll betont werden, dass darin einige wertvolle Informationen enthalten sind. Wenn Ałbios keine Entstellung von Ałbianos ist, dann stehen die Angaben der armenischen Fassung über die aus heidnischen Familien geweihten Bischöfe mit denen der arabischen und griechischen Fassung des Werkes von Agathangelos in völligem

[37] Movsēs Xorenacʿi II, c. 7.
[38] Tʿovma Arcruni ew Ananun, Patmutʿiwn Tann Arcruneacʿ. Erevan 1985, 212.
[39] Claudii Ptolemaei Geographica V, cap. XII 4.
[40] Movsēs Xorenacʿi II 8; Ptolemaeus, l.c.
[41] Ptolemaeus V, cap. XII 6.
[42] Vgl. Adonc, Armenija v epochu Justiniana 328f.
[43] Agatʿangełos, § 845. Über die verschiedenen Fassungen des Werkes „Agathangelos“ vgl. G. Garitte, Documents pour l'étude du livre d'Agathange. Vatikanstadt 1946; M. van Esbrœck, Agathangelos. *RAC* Suppl. 1/2 (1985), Sp. 239–248.

Einklang. Wenn das Werk von Agathangelos ziemlich spät ins Arabische und ins Griechische übertragen wurde, haben die Übersetzer oder Redaktoren die Geschichte über die Christianisierung von Virkʿ, Durjuken und Alanen künstlich hinzugefügt. Andere Berichte, die nach unserer Meinung beachtenswert sind, weisen nach, dass in Angełtun, Ałjnikʿ, Copʿkʿ, Hašteankʿ (das damals mit Turuberan identisch war[44]), Siwnikʿ, Mokkʿ, Mardpetakan, Kordukʿ, Atrpatakan (= die feudale Herrschaft der armenischen Könige in Atrpatakan) wirklich Bischofssitze organisiert waren, anders ausgedrückt wurden also zehn von 22 Gebieten Großarmeniens in diese Liste aufgenommen. Das ist natürlich keine vollständige Liste, es ist sogar offensichtlich, dass die obenerwähnten Bischofswürden, verbunden entweder mit chalcedonensischen oder irgendwelchen anderen Umständen, hauptsächlich im Osten Großarmeniens liegen. Bedeutend ist aber die Tatsache, dass an dem wichtigen Prinzip der Organisierung der Bischofswürden in den Gebieten Großarmeniens festgehalten wurde.

Auf der Basis des Obenerwähnten und von Protokollen des Konzils in Nikaia und an anderen Orten, sind unseres Erachtens die Berichte von Stepʿanos Ōrbelean über die Gründung der 36 Bischofsstühle durch Gregor den Erleuchter gar nicht haltlos.

Ausgehend von der administrativen Teilung des Landes sollte Gregor der Erleuchter in 22 Gebieten Großarmeniens Bischofseparchien gründen. Aber hier erhebt sich die Frage, welche die übrigen 14 Bischofsstühle waren. Hier helfen uns die Angaben des „Gahnamak“ („Thronliste“) [„Zōranamak“ (Militärliste)] über das militärische Aufgebot der Fürstenfamilien. Es ist naheliegend und verständlich, dass zunächst Bischofswürden in den Besitzen der mächtigeren Naxarar-Familien (naxarar – Lehensherr) gegründet werden konnten. Wenn wir hypothetisch die Fürstentümer, die im Kriegsfall über 500 Soldaten stellten, und die insgesamt 27[45] waren, für diejenigen Fürstentümer halten, die Bischofswürden haben konnten, sehen wir, dass der bedeutende Teil dieser Naxarare Gebietsstatthalter waren, wie zum Beispiel der Fürst von Angełtun, der Bdešx von Ałjnikʿ, der Bagratuni (der Statthalter von Xałtikʿ), Copʿacʿi, der Bdešx von Gugarkʿ, Kaspecʿi, Utēacʿi, Cawdeacʿi, Tayecʿi, Mamikonean (das Land von Tarōn), Siwni, Kadmēacʿi (= Bdešxutʿiwn von Nor Širakan), Korduacʿi, Arcruni, Ṙštuni, Mokacʿi. Infolge eines Missverständnisses, als man beim Abschreiben die Buchstaben „M“ und „T“ verwechselte und so die Zahl 200 in 4000 verwandelte, wurden Fürstentümern, die keine besonders große Kriegsmacht besaßen, 4000 Soldaten zugeschrieben[46]. Dies erlaubt uns, die Liste noch um einen Namen zu verkleinern. Nun stellt die Fürstenliste insgesamt 10 Naxararutʿiwn (Lehensherrschaften) dar: 1. Naxararutʿiwn von Bznunikʿ, 2. Naxararutʿiwn von Manawasean, 3. Naxararutʿiwn von Xorxořunikʿ, 4. Naxararutʿiwn von Wahunikʿ oder Wahewunikʿ, 5. Naxararutʿiwn von Apahunikʿ, 6. Naxararutʿiwn von Basēn, 7. Naxararutʿiwn von Kamsarakan, 8. Naxararutʿiwn von Wanand, 9. Naxararutʿiwn von Gardman und 10. Naxararutʿiwn von Orduni. Wenn unsere Annahme richtig ist, dann sollte Gregor der Erleuchter auch in den obenerwähnten Naxararutʿiwn Bischofswürden gegründet haben.

Diese Struktur regt natürlich einige Fragen an. Zum Beispiel: Hatten die Gnunis im frühen IV. Jahrhundert einen eigenen Bischof? Es ist schwierig, diese Frage eindeutig zu beantworten. Aber aller Wahrscheinlichkeit nach haben die Gnunis doch erst zur Zeit von Xosrov III. Kotak einen Bischofsstuhl erworben. Diese unsere Annahme wird, wenn nicht völlig, dann doch zum wesentlichen Teil durch die Materialien der arabischen und

[44] Vgl. Yovhan Mamikonean, Patmutʿiwn Tarōnoy. Erevan 1941, S. 46; Movsēs Xorenacʿi II, cap. 9, 22, 35, 62; III, cap. 31; Tʿovma Arcruni, S. 90, 134.

[45] Adonc 251f. (s. „Militärliste“).

[46] L.c. 251.

der griechischen Fassungen des Werkes von Agathangelos bestätigt, wo die Bischofswürden von Basēn (= Basenacʿi), Kol (vielleicht Vanand), Bznunikʿ (= Bznuniš), Širak (= Kamsarakan), dem Land der Małxasen (= Xorxoṙuni) erwähnt werden. Aber die Behandlung der Liste zeigt an, dass auch sie einigermaßen unter dem Einfluss der späteren Zeiten steht.

Bezüglich der übrigen 4 Bischofswürden haben die Materialien des Konzils von Nikaia erstaunliche Informationen aufbewahrt. Es stellt sich heraus, dass seitens Großarmeniens fünf Bischöfe die Beschlüsse unterschrieben haben: Aristakēs, der Sohn Gregors des Erleuchters, Atrikes aus Pompeiupolis (Peenpole nach den armenischen Manuskripten), Eutikʿianos aus Amaseia, Elpidios aus Komana und Heraklios aus Zela[47]. Es steht außer Zweifel, dass „Peenpole" eine Entstellung irgendeines Namens ist. Im Konzilsprotokoll von Nikaia heißt der Bischof Akrites – Acrites Diospontanus[48]. N. Adontz zeigte, dass Diospontos mit Amaseia in Pontos identisch ist, das zur Zeit Konstantins des Großen zu Ehren seiner Mutter Helene in Helenopontos umbenannt wurde[49]. Nach der „Notitia Basilii" war Amaseia das Zentrum von Helenopontos, und seine Bischofsstädte waren Amisos, Sinope, Ibora, Andrapa, Zalichos oder Leontopolis und Zela[50]. Nach den „Nova Tactica" hieß die Stadt Zalios von Helenopontos auch Pompeiupolis[51]. Der Vergleich der beiden Beschreibungen von Helenopontos zeigt an, dass ὁ Ζαλίου von „Nova Tactica" dem „ὁ Ζαλίχου" der „Notitia Basilii" entspricht und folglich Zalichos nicht nur Leontupolis sondern auch Pompeiupolis hieß. Und eben diese letztere Benennung wurde in der armenischen Fassung bis zur Unkenntlichkeit entstellt und verwandelte sich so in „Peenpole". In der Versammlung von Nikaia sollte Diospontos die Territorien von Amaseia, Komana, Zela, Zalichos sowie auch Amisos, Sinope, Ibora und Andrapa mit ihren Umgebungen repräsentieren. Wie bereits erwähnt, haben die ersten 4 Bischöfe beim Konzil von Nikaia die Kirche Großarmeniens vertreten. Warum? Es gibt nur eine Erklärung dafür: Die obenerwähnten Städte mit ihren Umgebungen haben im Kaiserreich die Landsitze der feudalen Herrschaft des armenischen Königs gebildet, und die Bischofswürden dieser Städte von Diospontos waren deswegen dem Katholikosat Großarmeniens untergeordnet. Das Zentrum der Landsitze der armenischen Könige war wahrscheinlich die Stadt Pompeiupolis, und folglich war der Bischof von Pompeiupolis das Oberhaupt der Bischöfe armenischer Landsitze von Diospontos; deswegen hieß Acrites Diospontanus und sogar Acrites Armeniae Disponti.

Es soll betont werden, dass als erster Cassius Dio über die feudale Herrschaft armenischer Könige im Kaiserreich berichtet, indem er schreibt, dass Tiridates am Anfang des III. Jahrhunderts von Kaiser Macrinus alle Länder zurückbekam, die sein Vater in Kappadokien erworben hatte[52]. Dieser Bericht ist unbestimmt, weil im III. Jahrhundert die Provinz Kappadokien ein ausgedehntes Territorium umfasste und sich bis in die armenischen Länder erstreckte, die am Ostufer des Euphrat lagen. Der obenerwähnte Tiridates war Tiridates II., dessen Vater Xosrov I. im Kaiserreich Landsitze bekam, weil er gegen die nordkaukasischen Bergbewohner gekämpft hatte[53]. S. Eremyan hatte ver-

[47] Kanonagirkʿ Hayocʿ, I. Erevan 1964, S. 141.

[48] I. D. Mansi, Sacrorum Conciliorum Nova et Amplissima Collectio, II. Graz 1960, 694.

[49] Adonc 85f.

[50] J. Darrouzès, Notitiae episcopatuum ecclesiae Constantinopolitanae. Paris 1981, Not. 4, 223–229; Georgii Cyprii Descriptio orbis Romani. Leipzig 1890, 13f.

[51] Georgii Cyprii Descriptio 67.

[52] S. ausführlicher B. H. Harutyunyan, Hay tʿagaworneri irakan išxanutʿyan harcʿi šurjë. *PBH* 1988/4, S. 54f.

[53] Cassii Dionis Cocceiani Historiarum Romanorum quae supersunt. Berlin 1895, CXXIX 27, 4.

sucht, den Landsitz der feudalen Herrschaft armenischer Könige in Kleinarmenien zu lokalisieren[54], aber die Berichte des Konzils in Nikaia lassen keinen Zweifel daran, dass sich diese Landsitze in Diospontos befanden. Als weiteres Indiz dient der Umstand, dass zur Zeit des Kaisers Herakleios Kappadokien (III) mit den Städten Amaseia, Ibora, Zalichos, Andrapa, Aminsos, Neokaisareia und Sinope den Namen Armeniakon bekam[55].

Hiermit wird die von St. Ōrbelean erwähnte Liste von 36 Bischöfen komplett. Es kann natürlich die Frage entstehen, warum unter den obenerwähnten 36 Bischofswürden die Katholikoi von Virkʿ und Ałuankʿ nicht erwähnt werden. Die Werke von Movsēs Xorenacʿi und Buzandaran geben darauf eine Antwort[56]. Die 36 Bischofssitze wurden zur Zeit der Proklamierung des Christentums als Staatsreligion gegründet. Und der zum Bischof von Iberien (Virkʿ) und dem kaukasischen Albanien (Ałuankʿ) geweihte Enkel Gregors des Erleuchters, Grigoris, war erst 15 Jahre alt, als er am Ende der Herrschaft Tiridates' III. in die östlichen Gebiete Armeniens, nach Virkʿ und Ałuankʿ oder in das Königreich der Maskʿutʿen geschickt wurde, um dort zu predigen. Bislang gibt es keinen Beleg, der von der Existenz des iberischen und albanischen Bischofssitzes in dieser Zeit zeugen könnte. Noch mehr, Grigoris wurde auf Befehl des Königs der Maskʿutʿen, Sanesan, getötet, und der Versuch, das Christentum in Iberien und Albanien zu etablieren, scheiterte zeitweilig.

Zusammenfassend sollte man die Richtigkeit der Mitteilung von St. Ōrbelean annehmen, nach der in den Zeiten der Proklamierung des Christentums als Staatsreligion in Großarmenien 36 Bischofsstühle gegründet wurden, und zwar nach zwei Prinzipien: Erstens war das die administrative Teilung des Königreichs, und zweitens sollte man den namhaften Fürstenfamilien des feudalen Großarmenien ein Recht auf Bischofseparchien einräumen. Aber die weitere Feudalisierung Großarmeniens, die Teilung im Jahre 387 und das Ende des Königtums der armenischen Arsakiden haben in der kirchlichen eparchischen Teilung wesentliche Korrekturen bewirkt.

---

[54] S. T. Eremyan, Paymanakan hołatirutʿyan aṙajacʿman harcʿi šurǰë feodalakanacʿoł Hayastanum. *PBH* 1971/1, S. 6.

[55] Constantinus Porphyrogenitus, De thematibus II (S. 65, 65–67 Pertusi).

[56] Movsēs Xorenacʿi III, cap. 3–6; Pʿawstos Buzand III, cap. 6–7.

MESROB K. KRIKORIAN / WIEN

ADDENDUM ZUR DIÖZESAN-GLIEDERUNG ARMENIENS IM IV. JH.

In Zusammenhang mit der Entstehung der armenischen Bistümer ist die Geschichte „Pʻawstos Buzandaran“[1] aus dem V. Jh. sehr wichtig. Nach der Überzeugung von Heinrich Gelzer ist „für die Geschichte des IV. Jahrhunderts von Trdats Tode bis zur Reichstheilung das Geschichtswerk des Faustos eine historische Quelle ersten Ranges.“[2] Aus diesem Grund habe ich, der Forderung eines Gutachters zum Beitrag von B. Harutyunyan folgend, dieses Geschichtsbuch untersucht, um der Frage der Errichtung der Bistümer Armeniens im IV. Jh, besonders aber zur Zeit Gregors des Erleuchters, auch von dieser Seite her nachzugehen.

Die erste Erkenntnis auf Grund der Daten von Buzandaran Patmutʻiwnkʻ ist, dass Gregor der Erleuchter Anfang des IV. Jhs. keine Bistümer oder Diözesen gegründet hat. Allem Anschein nach hat er vielmehr Missionsstationen eingerichtet, für die Evangelisierung des Landes. Zu diesem Zweck hat er Prediger/Lehrer aus Sebasteia nach Armenien mitgebracht (314), um die Bekehrung des Volkes erfolgreich zu organisieren. Dafür haben wir ein gutes Beispiel aus der Zeit des Königs Tiran Aršakuni (339–350), Enkelsohnes Tiridates des Großen (298–330). Nach dem Ableben des Patriarchen Yusik (341–347), Sohnes des Vrtʻanēs und Enkels des Gregor, wurde Daniel als Nachfolger zum Chorepiskopos/Missionsbischof von Tarōn/Taraun gewählt. Der Abstammung nach war er ein Syrer in hohem Alter, der in Persien das Evangelium gepredigt hatte und danach von Gregor dem Erleuchter zu seinem Generalvikar ernannt worden war. Noch vor seiner Inthronisierung hatte er den König Tiran wegen dessen sündhafter Lebensführung streng getadelt, und deswegen wurde er auch ermordet. In diesem Zusammenhang erzählt das Buzandaran-Geschichtsbuch, dass zwei Schüler des verstorbenen Chorepiskopos Daniel, nämlich Šałita und Epiphan, den Leichnam nach Tarōn in die Ortschaft „Hacʻeacʻ Draxt“ getragen und dort beerdigt hätten. Wortwörtlich heißt es:

„Da hoben seinen Leichnam seine geliebten Schüler auf, deren vornehmster Šałita hieß, der von ihm ja der Provinz Kordukʻ zum *Vardapet*/Lehrer gegeben war, und der zweite Epipʻan, welcher dem Gau Ałdznikʻ/Ałjnikʻ und Gross-Copʻkʻ von ihm ja als Lehrer gegeben war, und mit ihnen die Diakone des Lagers. Sie zogen ab, trugen weg, setzten seinen Leichnam an dem Orte bei, wo früher der Sitz seiner Zelle (gewesen) war im Lande Taraun, wo die Mutter der Kirchen Armeniens war, nahe bei dem Quellborn, wo Grigor die Taufe der aus dem Reichsheere bestehenden Menge vollzogen (hatte), an dem Orte, der benannt Hacʻeacʻ Draxt (Eschengarten) heißt. An jenem Orte bestatteten sie den

---

[1] Pʻawstosi Buzandacʻwoy Patmutʻiwn Hayocʻ oder Buzandaran Patmutʻiwnkʻ, Venedig 1889/90; Nina G. GARSOÏAN, The Epic Histories (Buzandaran Patmutʻiwnkʻ), Übersetzung und Kommentar, Harvard Univ Press, Cambridge Mass. 1989.

[2] H. GELZER, Die Anfänge der armenischen Kirche, *Berichte der Kgl. Sächsischen Gesellschaft der Wissenschaft* 1895, 111.

Leichnam des hl. Daniel unter der Erde, gemäß dem früheren Gesichte (Vision) und gemäß dem ihnen gegebenen Befehle."[3]

Den Namen nach war Šałita selbst auch ein Syrer und Epiphan ein Grieche. Höchstwahrscheinlich gehörten sie zu den Predigern, die der Hl. Gregor aus Sebasteia mitgebracht und in verschiedene Landesteile gesandt hatte. Es ist interessant, dass zur Zeit des Katholikos Nersēs des Parthers (353–373) diese zwei Sprengel als Bischofssitze oder Diözesen erwähnt werden, was unsere Vermutung, ja Überzeugung stärkt, dass erst Mitte des IV. Jhs. Bistümer in Armenien entstanden sind. P'awstos Buzandaran erzählt, dass, nachdem König Aršak II. (351–367) und Nersēs der Große miteinander gestritten hatten, auf Anordnung des Königs ein gewisser Č'unak[4] oder Šahak[5] zum (Anti)-Patriarchen ernannt wurde. Alle Bischöfe haben es abgelehnt, an der Bischofsweihe des Šahak teilzunehmen, „nur die Bischöfe von Ałjnik' und Korduk' sind gekommen", sagt Buzandaran. Das bedeutet, dass Anfang der zweiten Hälfte des IV. Jhs. diese zwei Regionen, wo früher Missionar-Vardapeten gewirkt hatten, schon zu Diözesen umstrukturiert waren.[6] Auf Grund der Angaben des Buzandaran Patmut'iwnk' kann man nicht behaupten, dass „in den Zeiten der Proklamierung des Christentums als Staatsreligion in Großarmenien 36 Bischöfsstühle gegründet wurden", wie Babken Harutyunyan meint. Vielleicht hat es 36 Missionsstationen gegeben, unter der Führung von Predigern oder Kirchenlehrern (Vardapeten), aber auch diese Zahl kann man nicht mit Sicherheit angeben. Nur soviel ist klar, dass Gregor der Erleuchter seinen Sohn Aristakēs zum Ko-Adjutor und den Chorepiskopos Daniel als Generalvikar bzw. Verwalter von Tarōn/Taraun ernannt hat. Tarōn bzw. die Stadt Aštišat war der Ort, wo sich die Haupt- oder Mutterkirche befand und wo der Hl. Gregor feierlich auf seinen patriarchalen Thron gesetzt worden war. Zur Zeit des Erleuchters gab es keine anderen Bischöfe, zumindest werden keine in „Buzandaran" erwähnt.[7]

Auf dem Konzil von Nicaea (325) werden zwei Teilnehmer aus Armenia Maior genannt: Arista[r]ces et Acrites/'Ακρίτης. Aristakēs ist der jüngere Sohn des Hl. Gregor und Akrites könnte Artit', ein Schüler des Chorepiskopos Daniel sein, der später zum Bischof von Basean ernannt worden ist.[8] Im Jahre 325 war er dann vielleicht noch ein Diakon oder ein junger Mönch, der im Namen seines Lehrers Daniel mit dem Bischof Aristakēs nach Nicaea zum ersten ökumenischen Konzil gefahren ist. Markwart glaubt dagegen, Akrites/Acrites entspräche dem armenischen „Wahrič", und möchte dahinter den Bischof Daniel erkennen.[9]

Anfang des IV. Jhs. gab es in Armenien zahlreiche Christen, aber das Volk im ganzen war noch nicht evangelisiert. Die Geschichte bis zum Patriarchen Nersēs dem Großen (353–373) zeigt, wie heidnisch und wild die Menschen noch in ihren Sitten und in ihrer

[3] Josef Markwart, Die Entstehung der armenischen Bistümer, (*Orientalia Christiana*, XXVII-2, No 80), Rom 1932, 192; Buzandaran Patmut'iwnk', 43.

[4] Buzandaran, 127.

[5] Malachia Ormanian, *Azgapatum* (Geschichte der armenischen Nation), I, Konstantinopel 1912, 186–87. Nach der Meinung von Ormanian stammt Šahak aus dem Hause des Albianos, der früher ein heidnischer Priester gewesen war und später vom Hl. Gregor in die Hierarchie der armenischen Kirche integriert wurde. Siehe auch Markwart, *ibid.*221–22.

[6] Markwart, Die Entstehung der armenischen Bistümer, 222–23, bezweifelt, dass es im Jahre 359/60 in Ałjnik' und Korduk' Bischofssitze gegeben habe, weil damals die erste Provinz noch zu den von Rom abhängigen Satrapien gehörte, und die zweite Provinz unter der Gewalt der Perser stand.

[7] Markwart, *ibid.* 197.

[8] Markwart, *ibid.* 169; Buzandaran Patmut'iwnk', 274.

[9] Markwart, *ibid.* 199–209.

Lebensführung waren. Der jüngere Sohn des Hl. Gregor, Patriarch Aristakēs (325–333) wurde vom Fürsten Ark'ełayos aus Cop'k' ermordet. Grigoris, Missionsbischof für Georgien und Albanien, wurde im Jahre 337 von den Massageten oder Mazk'ut'k' brutal umgebracht. Auch der Patriarch Vrt'anēs (333–341) wurde einmal in der Mutterkirche von Aštišat in Tarōn von den Bewohnern der Bergregion Sasun attackiert. Der Katholikos Yusik (341–347) sowie der Chorepiskopos Daniel wurden von König Tiran (339–350) zum Tode verurteilt. Der Grund für die Ermordung dieser Märtyrer war ihre kritische und tadelnde Haltung gegenüber noch nicht christianisierten Königen, Fürsten und dem Volk. Natürlich wäre unter solchen Umständen die Gründung der Bistümer gleich Anfang des IV. Jhs. kaum möglich. Auf alle Fälle haben die Bemühungen der Prediger oder Lehrer nach etwa 35 Jahren gute Früchte gebracht, weil zum ersten mal bei der Wahl oder Ernennung des Katholikos Nersēs des Parthers (353–373), „auch eine Menge armenischer Bischöfe sich beim König für dieselbe Angelegenheit versammelt hat."[10] Danach hat man sich „mit der Zustimmung aller Bischöfe, des Königs und der weltlichen Würdenträger (Fürsten)" auf den Weg begeben, um in Caesarea/Kappadokien den Nersēs zum Bischof weihen zu lassen.[11]

Patriarch Nersēs selbst hat sich sehr um die Evangelisierung Armeniens und die Gründung weiterer Bistümer bemüht. Im Jahre 354 hat er in der Stadt Aštišat/Tarōn eine national-kirchliche Synode abgehalten, um die moralischen Sitten der Bevölkerung und den sozialen Zustand der Benachteiligten der Gesellschaft zu verbessern. In diesem Zusammenhang erzählt das Geschichtsbuch Buzandaran: „Und er ging und kam in der Region der Provinz Tarōn an und rief zu sich alle Bischöfe des Landes Armenien. Sie versammelten sich in der Dorfstadt Aštišat, wo die erste Kirche gebaut war."[12]

Die Bemerkungen von P'awstos Buzandaran, dass zur Zeit des Katholikos Nersēs das Ansehen und die Verehrung der Bischöfe überall in Armenia Maior erhöht wurde, der Gottesdienst bereichert und ordentlich gestaltet, und die Diakone und Mönche zahlreich wurden,[13] betreffen vielleicht die Gründung neuer Bistümer. Auch der folgende Satz deutet Ähnliches an, wo es heißt: „Und das alles hat Patriarch Nersēs ausgesprochen. Dann ging er vom König weg und bereiste alle Kantone und unterwies, leitete, organisierte und verstärkte die Kirchen in allen Kantonen Armeniens."[14]

Tatsächlich berichtet Buzandaran später (Buch V/Kap.21), dass Patriarch Nersēs „in allen Kantonen Bischöfe zur Aufsicht ernannte."[15] Ein Beispiel dafür ist die Weihe des Mönches Xad/Chad aus Karin für die Diözese von Bagrewand und Aršarunik'.[16] Gleichzeitig wurde er zum *Locum tenens/tełapah* ernannt. Wieviele Bistümer es Mitte des IV. Jhs. in der zweiten Phase der Entwicklung der Struktur der Diözesen gegeben hat, ist schwer zu beantworten, weil Buzandaran keine Liste bietet: vielleicht waren es 10 oder 12, höchstens 15, entsprechend den Hauptprovinzen des Landes. Die dritte Etappe der Entwicklung kann man in die Mitte des V. Jhs. setzen, wo schon 18 oder mehr Diözesen

---

[10] Buzandaran, *ibid.*72.

[11] *Ibid.* 72–73. Garsoïan, *ibid.* 111: "Then the mightiest princes gathered together so that they might take the much desired Nersēs and go [to the place] where it was the custom to consecrate the patriarch. And many Armenian bishops also assembled before the King over this matter and to counsel with unanimous consent of all that he be chosen; [for] it was pleasing to all that he be placed on the leading throne. With the unanimous agreement and consent of all the bishops, the King and the whole of the realm [the following] set forth and went" etc.

[12] Buzandaran Patmut'iwnk', 76.

[13] *Ibid.* 78.

[14] *Ibid.* 114–15; Garsoïan, *ibid.* 138.

[15] Buzandaran, 219, vgl. 236. Garsoïan, *ibid.*202: "And he placed bishops as overseers in every district."

[16] Buzandaran, 108.

bzw. Diözesan-Bischöfe bei der Synode von Artašat erwähnt werden. Diese Synode wurde im Jahre 449 versammelt, um eine Antwort an den Sasaniden-Großkönig Jazdegert/Jesdegerd II. (438/39–452) zu verfassen. Hier folgt die Liste nach dem Historiker Elišē[17]:

1. Ayrarat
2. Tarōn
3. Manazkert/Mantzikert
4. Bagrewand
5. Bznunikʿ
6. Taykʿ/Tao
7. Basean
8. Turuberan
9. Mardastan
10. Mardoyałi
11. Siwnikʿ
12. Arcrunikʿ
13. Ŕštunikʿ
14. Mokkʿ
15. Vanand
16. Amatunikʿ
17. Anjewacʿikʿ
18. Apahunikʿ

Dieselbe Liste der Provinzen und Regionen mit einem Bischofssitz kann man auch bei Łazar von Pʿarpi (V. Jh.)[18] finden, nur werden die achte (Turuberan) *Tarberuni* und die zehnte *Mananałi* genannt.

Die Zahl von 30 Diözesanbischöfen, die nach Uxtanēs (X. Jh.)[19] angeblich von Gregor dem Erleuchter geweiht wurden, stellt die endgültige Diözesangliederung der armenischen Kirche im VI. Jh. dar, wie wir sie bei der Synode von Dvin (553–555) vorfinden. Nach den Angaben von Pʿawtos Buzand/aran hat Gregor der Erleuchter keine Bistümer gegründet. Die Zahl 30 oder 36 stammt von späteren Quellen (Uxtanēs und Stepʿanos Ōrbelean[20]) und spiegelt die endgültige Struktur der Diözesen wider, aber erst ab dem VI. Jh. und nicht früher.

[17] Ełiše, Über Vardan und den Krieg der Armenier (altarmenisch), Kritische Edition von Eruand Tēr-Minasian (Minassians), Erevan 1957, 28.

[18] Łazar Pʿarpecʿi, Geschichte der Armenier (altarmenisch), Tiflis/Tbilisi 1904, 44–45.

[19] Uxtanēs Episkopos, *Patmutʿiwn Hayocʿ*/Geschichte der Armenier, Vałaršapat 1871, 100.

[20] Stepʿanos Ōrbelean, Patmutʿiwn Nahangin Sisakan/Geschichte der Provinz Sisakan (Siwnikʿ), Tbilisi 1910, 25.

MESROB K. KRIKORIAN / WIEN

THE FORMATION OF CANON LAW OF THE ARMENIAN CHURCH IN THE IVth CENTURY

The origins of the Armenian Canon Law is a subject which as yet has not been object of special research. The purpose of the present study is to investigate the formation of the Canon Law in the IVth century, to identify the sources and to present arguments in favour of the existence of certain documents of ecclesiastical law in Greek.

According to the latest scholarly studies Armenia was finally and officially evangelized in 314 through the efforts of St. Gregory the Illuminator and by the edict/proclamation of King Tiridates IVth (298–330). In the same year St. Gregory travelled to Caesarea/Kayseri and was ordained bishop by the Metropolitan Łevond/Leontios.

Surely, St. Gregory who organized the Church of Armenia, took care also of canonical regulations which were necessary for the development and prosperity of the Christian life. In the Book of Canon Law of the Armenian Church, *Liber Canonum*, there are kept 30 canons under the name of St. Gregory[1].

In the IVth century the Armenians did not possess an alphabet on their own, therefore it can be presumed that these canons were compiled in Greek and later, in the Vth century, after the invention of the Armenian alphabet, they were translated into Armenian. Malachia Ormanian suggests that Gregory Illuminator might have ordered regulations which becoming traditions were documented in written form "at a convenient time."[2] According to the ancient Armenian tradition, the first fathers or patriarchs who formulated or ruled ecclesiastical canons, were St. Gregory, St. Nersēs and St. Sahak. In the text of 55 canonical chapters written by St. Sahak the Parthian († 439) or attributed[3] to him, under canon No. 44 we find the following evidence recorded: "*This constitution of rules, written by command of the blessed (or departed) Sahak the great Patriarch of the country of Armenia, having received from the courageous martyr and lord Grigor/Gregory, was translated from the Greek into Armenian.*"[4]

In MS No. 659 of Matenadaran (written in 1368 at Kaffa, copied from "a very ancient Manuscript"[5]) in connection with Canon Nr. 36 delivers us an interesting information as

---

[1] *Kanonagirk Hayocʿ/Corpus Canonum of the Armenians*, ed. with introduction and notes by Vazgen Hakobyan/Yakobian, I, Erevan 1964 (in Armenian), 243–249 (vol. II 1971). In 1959 Ch. Mercier has translated the canons of the first three Ecumenical Councils and of Local Councils: Les Canons des Conciles oecumeniques et locaux en Version arménienne, *REArm* 15 (1981) 191–262, preface and notes by J. P. Mahé.

[2] Malachia Ormanian, *Azgapatum* / History of the Armenian Nation (Arm.), vol. I, Istanbul 1912, 103.

[3] Jakobus Daschian believes that the canons in the name of St. Sahak were compiled in the first decades of VIth century, see Joseph Catergian, Die Liturgien bei den Armeniern (Arm.), Vienna 1897, 141, note 103; 231, note 38; 323 and 733. See also Nerses Akinian, The Canons attributed to St. Sahak (Arm.), *Handes Amsoreay* 1946, nos 1–12, 48–70; 1947, no 1, 1–25. Vazgen Hakobyan accepts the authenticity of the canons of St. Sahak, *ibid.* (see above note 1) 623–626.

[4] *Corpus Canonum*, 402.

[5] V. Hakobyan, l.c., Introduction LXXVI.

follows: "*Constitution of rules, received from the martyr lord Grigor/Gregor, was translated by Eznik by order of the blessed Sahak patriarch of Armenia and his fellow-bishops*".[6]

Another witness concerning the ancient tradition can be found in the documents of the Synod of Šahapivan (444) as follows: The governors of provinces, grand princes and nobles of Armenia gathered together and unanimously stated: "*You should establish rules set up by St. Grigor, Nersēs, Sahak and Maštocʿ as well as other good ones in accordance with your will, and we commit ourselves to them willingly and delightfully, since the regulations of the Church are weakened and the people have returned to lawlessness. Consequently laws, which are pleasing to God and good for the building up of his Church, these you order and we shall obey and firmly observe them.*"[7]

The conclusion of these evidences is quite clear and truthful: St. Gregory Illuminator has left behind some ordinances of laws in Greek language which in the Vth century under the patronage of Catholicos Sahak were translated into Armenian by Eznik of Kołb[8] or by other pupils of St. Mesrop Maštocʿ. Of course I do not assume that the 30 canons of St. Gregory are literal or exact translation of the original text; most probably St. Sahak has redacted the translation adopting them to the life and situation of the time. The canons of Šahapivan, where the name of Gregory is mentioned as the first Armenian church-father who has set up ecclesiastical rules, show certain similarities with the regulations under discussion.

For instance compare:

Greg. Illum.	Šahapivan
No. 8	No. 7
No. 9	No. 7
No. 12	Nos. 9+10
No. 17	No. 11
No. 26	No. 16
Nos. 30/13	No. 15

A comparison of two groups of canons affirm that the regulations of St. Gregory are of primitive or earlier stage, whereas the canons of Šahapivan are achieved and prescribe severe punishment.

With the name of St. Gregory are connected also the canons of Nicaea (325). Agatʿangełos (Vth century) and Movsēs Xorenacʿi (V/VIIIth century) have recorded the participation of the Armenian Church in the first ecumenical Council of Nicaea. Agatʿangełos reports as follows:

"*Then after this great emperor, the Augustus Constantine, commanded that all the bishops should assemble in the city of Nicaea. Then the great King Trdat and the holy Catholicos Gregory made preparations and dispatched Aristakēs. He arrived at the great Council of Nicaea with all the bishops. There were defined the acceptable traditional Faith for the whole world, and the illuminating ordinances.*"[9]

Moses Chorenensis also devotes two chapters to the Council of Nicaea. He says: "*Then there arrived an edict of the Emperor Constantine to our King Trdat/Tidirates, that taking*

[6] L.c., 625, and Abel Mxitʿarian, Patmutʿiwn Žołovocʿ Hayastaneaycʿ Ekełecʿwoy / History of Synods of the Armenian Church, Etchmiadzin 1874, 25.

[7] V. Hakobyan, l.c., 428, Mxitʿarian, 59–60, and Tiran Nersoyan, A brief Outline of the Armenian *Liber Canonum* and its Status in modern Times, *Kanon (Jahrbuch d. Ges. f. d. Recht d. Ostkirchen)* 1 (1973) 81.

[8] *Azgapatum*, I, 114.

[9] Agathangelos, History of the Armenians, translation and commentary by Robert W. Thomson, New York 1976, 415–417. Armenian critical text edited in Tiflis/Tbilisi by Galust Tēr-Mkrtčʿean and St. Kanayan, 1909, chapt. 127, sections 884 and 885 (pp. 465–466).

Saint Gregory with him he should go to the council. But Trdat refused... Nor did Saint Gregory agree to go. ... But they sent in their place Aristakēs with the true confession of Faith signed by them both."[10]

At Nicaea 318 fathers anathematized and excommunicated the Arians. "*Then Aristakēs returned with the authentic creed*[11] *and the twenty canonical chapters of the council and met his father and the King in the city of Vałaršapat. Saint Gregory was delighted and added a few chapters of his own to the canons of the council to take greater care of his diocese."*[12]

Buzandaran Patmutʿiwnkʿ (Vth century) mentions the participation of Aristakēs very shortly in a sentence in connection with Jakob of Nisibis, as follows: "*But Yakob performed greatest miracles. And he was present at the great synod of Nikia/Nicaea, which took place in the days of Constantine, the emperor of the Romans and at which three hundred and eighteen bishops gathered together to anathematize the heresy of Arianos of Alexandria, who was from the province of Egypt. All the bishops took their seats there before Constantine; and Aristakēs, the son of wondrous Grigor, the first catholicos of Greater Armenia, was present from Greater Armenia."*[13]

The credibility of these witnesses has nobody challenged as yet. The Chalcedonian and Roman Catholic authors[14] also accept the participation of the representative of the Armenian Church in the Synod of Nicaea (325). The short remark of *Diegesis/Narratio* is not very clear in connection with the person of the participant. At the very beginning of this polemic writing against the Armenian Church, we read: "*During the time of the god-beloved and saint Constantine was held the holy Synod of Nicaea against Arios, in 34th year of the reign of Tiridates and in 20th year of the deliverance of St. Gregory from the dungeon; and during the time when St. Rostakes held the office of bishop and of his father who attended the Synod."*[15]

Apparently some Greek authors had the information that St. Gregory personally participated in the synod of Nicaea[16], but the Armenian tradition[17] clearly confirms that the son Aristakēs went to Nicaea, since St. Gregory was aged and probably at the end of 325 or in 326 he passed away.

All Armenian authors unanimously state that Aristakēs brought with him the 20 canons of the Council to Armenia and his father St. Gregory Illuminator "added a few

---

[10] Moses Khorenatsʿi, History of the Armenians, translation by Robert W. Thomson, Cambridge, Mass. 1978, 245–246. Armenian critical text edited in Tiflis/Tbilisi by Manuk Abełian and S. Yarutʿiwnian, 1913, 239–241.

[11] The Armenian term "aržanahawat" (*fide dignus, qui fidem meretur*) means "worthy of believing, worthy of acceptance". Thomson has translated it as "orthodox" in the sense of "rechtgläubig".

[12] Thomson, l.c. 246, Armenian text 240–241.

[13] The Epic Histories (*Buzandaran Patmutʿiwnkʿ*), translation and commentary by Nina G. Garsoïan, Cambridge, Mass. 1989, 79 (Book III, chapt. 10). Armenian text, *Pʿawstosi Buzandacʿwoy Patmutʿiwn Hayocʿ*, Venice 1889, 25.

[14] Pawłos Yovnanian, *Patmutʿiwn Tiezerakan Žołovocʿ Ekełecʿwoy* (History of the Ecumenical Councils of the Church), Vienna 1847, 23–24; Ałexandr Balčian/Balgy, *Patmutʿiwn Katʿołikē Vardapetutʿean i Hays* (History of the Catholic Teaching among Armenians and their Union with the Roman Church at the Synod of Florence), Vienna 1878, 7, and Sahak Gokian/Goky, *Hayocʿ Ekełecʿin* (The Armenian Church until the Council of Florence), Beirut 1961, 91 etc.

[15] Gérard Garitte, *La Narratio de Rebus Armeniae*, *CSCO*, CXXXII, *Subsidia* 4 (1952), 27. The dates given here are subject of discussion: now generally the reign of Tiridates is fixed to 298–330 and the Evangelization of Armenia in 314.

[16] For instance Nikephoros Kallistos, *Ekklesiastikes Istorias* / Nicephori Callisti Xanthopuli Ecclesiasticae Historiae, lib. VIII, *PG* 146, chapt. XIV, 60.

[17] See also Yovhannēs Drasxanakertcʿi, History of Armenia, translation and commentary by Krikor H. Maksoudian, Atlanta, Georgia 1987, 80–81 (has extracted the information of Xorenacʿi); Kirakos Ganjakecʿi, History of Armenia (Arm.), critical edition by Karapet Melik-Ohanǰanian, Erevan 1961, 13, and Vardan Vardapet, Collection of History (Arm.), Venice 1862, 41 etc.

chapters of his own to the canons of the Council to take greater care of his diocese".[18] Comparing the Greek/Latin and the Armenian versions we can ascertain that in fact St. Gregory has added only one chapter, canon 18 against homosexuality, which does not exist in the orginal text. Since canons 15 and 16 are very similar, they are integrated in one chapter (15); consequently in total the Armenian text also comprises 20 chapters[19] which surely were translated from the Greek in the Vth century, under the supervision of St. Sahak and St. Mesrop Maštocʿ. A comparison of the texts reveals that the translators in the Vth century have not achieved a verbatim translation of the Nicean Canons but they have rather accomodated them to their situation and customs.[20] For instance, in the first canon in connection with castration, the Armenian text adds, in case when it is done by freewill, the person concerned should repent 7 years out of the church, afterwards 4 years under superintendence, and if his penitence would be considered as sincere, he could enter into the church and receive communion; but in any case, he should continue his penitence 3 more years and at the same time take communion.[21] Another example: Canon 14 concerns lapsed catechumens: "*De cathecuminis lapsis – De cathecuminis sancto et magno concilio placuit, ut tribus annis sint inter audientes tantum modo, post haec autem cum cathecuminis orent*".[22] The Armenian editor has left out the term "lapsis"/lapsed and has compiled a general canon about the instruction of catechumens: these should learn three years the order and law and another year follow the prayer-service with penitents and then they could be baptized and get communion.[23] Whether such serious alterations were carried out in the Vth century at the time of translation of the canons or later, it is difficult to know, since there are no manuscripts from the earlier period (the oldest MS originates from 1098: MS No. 131 of New Julfa).

The next father after St. Gregory who has decreed canons, is Patriarch Nersēs the Great (353–373), grand-child of the grand child (Yusik, Patriarch 341–347) of the Illuminator. In 354 at the Synod of Aštišat he promulgated many rules in order to improve the Christian life in Armenia. These regulations are kept in the 4th chapter of Book IV (II) of *The Epic Histories*, where it is said that Catholicos Nersēs "*regulated many canonical rules of his fathers.*"[24] Movsēs Xorenacʿi explains his purpose and intention as follows: When Nersēs, Chief of the bishops, returned from Byzantia/Constantinople to Armenia, he renewed all ordinances of his ancestors, because the good discipline and order which he saw in the country of Byzantines, especially in the imperial capital city, he implemented them in his homeland.[25] The decisions of the synod of Aštišat can be arranged in two groups:[26]

---

[18] Movsēs Xorenacʿi, Book II, chapt. 90 (Arm. 240–241, Engl. 246); Agathangelos section 885. See also M. K. Krikorian, The first three Ecumenical Councils and their Significance for the Armenian Church, *The Greek Orthodox Theological Review* 16/1–2 (1971), 193–195.

[19] M. K. Krikorian, Die Rechtslage der armenischen Kirche heute, *Kanon* 3 (1977) 200 (199–213); idem in: Die Kirche Armeniens, ed. Friedrich Heyer, Stuttgart 1978, 140 (139–157).

[20] See Nersoyan, A brief Outline of the Armenian *Liber Canonum* and its Status in modern Times, 77. Ch. Mercier has not rightly understood and appreciated the differences of the Armenian version in comparison with the Greek text: see his letter in *REArm* 15 (1981), 187.

[21] *Corpus Canonum*, 116–117. The Nicene Canons see *ibid.*, 114–131 (–150).

[22] Fonti Fascicolo IX: Discipline Générale Antique (IVe–IXe s.), tome I, 1: Les Canons des Conciles Oecuméniques, par Périclès-Pierre Joannou, Rome 1962, 36: "*14. Des catéchumènes qui ont failli. Le saint et grand concile ordonne que les catéchumènes qui ont failli soient seulement audientes pendant trois ans; ils pourront après cela prier avec les autres catéchumènes.*"

[23] *Corpus Canonum*, 126–127. See the critical remark of Thomson, Early Armenian catechetical Instruction, in: Armeniaca. Mélanges d'Études arméniennes, Venice 1969, 101.

[24] *The Epic Histories* (see above note 13), 113–114.

[25] Movsēs Xorenacʿi / Moses Khorenatsʿi, History of the Armenians, English translation, 274; Armenian text (Tiflis/Tbilisi 1913), Book III, chapt. 20, 278–279.

[26] M. K. Krikorian, Die Rechtslage der armenischen Kirche heute, *Kanon* 3 (1977) 201; idem, in: Die Kirche Armeniens (Stuttgart), 141.

I. Foundation of charitable and ecclesiastical Institutions[27]

1. General hospitals
2. Hospitals for the leprous
3. Orphanages
4. Homes for the ages
5. Schools in Greek and Syriac
6. Monasteries and cells for the monks.

II. Prohibitions

1. To mourn hopeless on the dead
2. Prostitution, homosexuality, infidelity in the family
3. Murder and manslaughter
4. To eat from the flesh and drink from the blood of idol-sacrifice
5. To approach his wife during the menses
6. To marry close relatives.

It is noteworthy that these canons, the second group, which are so much appreciated and praised in the life and history of the Armenian Church, are not included in the *Corpus Canonum.*[28]

Malachia Ormanian, a great authority on the history of the Armenian Church, dignifies and exalts the Patriarch Nersēs for his social and charity canons of reforms with the following words: "*If St. Gregory is regarded "Illuminator of souls" in the first period, for spreading the light of faith, then Nersēs should be regarded "Illuminator of hearts" in the second period for his untiring efforts concerning the canons of reforms, whereas a third period was going to be opened through Sahak who in respect of the beginning and development of the Armenian Literature, can be accepted as "Illuminator of minds" by the Armenian nation.*"[29]

In 381, 8 years after the death of St. Nersēs the Parthian, was assembled the second Ecumenical Council in Constantinople, in order to examine the heresy of Macedonius who denied the Godhead of the Holy Spirit. At this synod not only the teaching of Macedonius was anathematized, but also the Nicene Creed was accomplished and proclaimed valid and binding for the whole Church. According to an old tradition recorded in the History of Moses Chorenensis / Movsēs Xorenacʿi, Catholicos Nersēs has personally participated in the Council of Constantinople. The Historian writes: "*He (Theodosius) freed all those holy fathers who because of their orthodox faith were captured in exile; among others he brought also Nersēs the Great to Byzantion / Constantinople and kept him in great honours until the true faith in connection with the blasphemies of the wicked Macedonius was ascertained. Macedonius did not confess the Holy Spirit as Lord, adorable and praiseworthy with the Father and the Son*" etc.[30]

The same information can be found in the "History of Synods of the Armenian Church" ascribed to Yovhannēs Ōjnecʿi (VIIIth century), as well as in some theological letters.[31] Apparently following Xorenacʿi, Yovhannēs of Drasxanakert (Xth century) too in his History of Armenia records the participation of St. Nersēs in the Council of

[27] These six decisions concerning the foundation of charitable and ecclesiastical institutions, in fact are not canons, but their intention is the same, namely the improvement of the social and family life.

[28] The reason why those canons of the Synod of Aštišat are not included in the *Corpus Canonum,* perhaps was the fact that in the IVth century the Armenians did not have their own alphabet, or in the Vth century the church-fathers thought that they were already documented in the Book of *Buzandaran* / The Epic Histories!

[29] M. Ormanian, Azgapatum, vol. I, 170.

[30] M. Khorenatsʿi, History of the Armenians, Armenian text, Book III, chapt. 33, pp. 297–298; English translation, 290–291; cf. *Patmutʿiwn srboyn Nersisi Partʿewi* (History of St. Nersēs the Parthian), Venice 1853, 61–62.

[31] *Girkʿ tʿltʿocʿ* (Book of Letters), Tiflis / Tbilisi 1901, 220, 295, 304, 492.

Constantinople as follows: "*After him Theodosius the Great, a pious and godly man, took over the Kingdom. He repelled all the shady snares and established the foundations of stainless faith. Subsequently he ordered those whom Valens had banished in fetters to return to their respective places. Together with them he also fetched Nersēs the Great whom he kept with him until he had with his help converted the sacrilegious blasphemy of Macedonius to the direction of the true faith. And then a council of alltogether one hundred and fifty bishops met in Byzantium and pronounced anathema on Macedonius and all the pneumatomachoi.*"[32]

Although communicated in various writings or sources, it is hard to believe that St. Nersēs has taken part in the ecumenical Synod of Constantinople, because according to reliable research he had already passed away in 373! However the Armenian Catholic author Vardapet Paułos Yovnanian in his History of Ecumenical Councils accepts as a fact the participation of St. Nersēs in the Synod of Constantinople and thinks that the name of the catholicos has been altered in the acts and documents of the Council.[33] Ormanian does not believe that Catholicos Nersēs has participated in the second Ecumenical Council, but he thinks that the decisions of the Synod were brought in the IVth century to Armenia, and since there were no differences or divisions between the Churches, "they were without any opposition accepted by Catholicos Aspurakēs and by the bishops of the Armenian Church."[34] Aspurakēs of Manazkert / Mantzikert reigned from 381 to 386 (or 383–387!), but there is no record at all that during his administration the acts of the Council of Constantinople were brought to Armenia. Most probably the documents were brought by Yovsēpʿ of Pałin, Eznik of Kołb, Łewondēs and Koriwn in 432/433 as they returned from their study journey via Constantinople. Koriwn in the Biography of his teacher and master Mesrop Maštocʿ, provides us interesting information about these events. He writes: "*After a while a few brethren came to the region of the Greeks, the name of the first one of which was Łewondēs, and the second was I, Koriwn. And as they drew near Constantinople, they joined Eznik, and as most intimate companions, together they performed their spiritual tasks. Then they came to the land of Armenia, having brought authentic copies of the God-given Book and many subsequent traditions of the worthy church-fathers, along with the canons of Nicaea and Ephesus, and placed before the fathers the Testaments of the Holy Church which they had brought with them.*"[35]

We have seen that the canons of Nicaea were already brought in 325, after the universal assembly, by Aristakēs, the younger son of Gregory Illuminator. Consequently under "the canons of Nicaea (and Ephesus)" we could understand the Nicene-Constantinopolitan Credo and the canons of Constantinople and Ephesus.[36] Finally we can conclude that the canons of the second Ecumenical Council were brought to Armenia not in 381, during the reign of Catholicos Aspurakēs of Manazkert,[37] but in 432/433 by

---

[32] Yovhannēs Drasxanakertcʿi, History of Armenia, translation by MAKSOUDIAN, 85.

[33] P. YOVNANIAN (see above note 14), 118.

[34] ORMANIAN, Azgapatum, I, 246; see also M. KRIKORIAN, The first three Ecumenical Councils and their Significance for the Armenian Church (see above note 18), 196–197.

[35] Koriwn (Koriun), The Life of Mashtots, translated by Bedros NOREHAD, 1964, 43; the Armenian text edited by Manuk ABELIAN, Erevan 1941, 74/76; Gabriele WINKLER, Koriwns Biographie des Mesrop Maštocʿ (*OCA* 245), Rome 1994, 112; M. KRIKORIAN, Das römische Dokument über den Ausgang des Heiligen Geistes aus orientalisch-orthodoxer Sicht, in: Vom Heiligen Geist, edited by A. STIRNEMANN and G. WILFINGER, Vienna 1998, 135, footnote 5.

[36] KRIKORIAN, l.c.

[37] Paul ANANIAN in his book, The Date and Circumstances of the Ordination of St. Gregory the Illuminator (in Armenian), proposes the period 383–387 for the reign of Aspurakēs and suggests the years 381–383 for Sahak Korčeay who usually is not included in the canonical list of catholicoi (see ORMANIAN, l.c. I, 243–244). For our study it does not make any difference whether in 381 the catholicos was Aspurakēs or Sahak, since we are convinced that the canons of the Synod of Constantinople were brought to Armenia not before the Vth century.

the disciples of St. Mesrop and they were immediatly rendered from the Greek into Armenian.

The last question in connection with the formation and development of the Armenian canon law in the IVth century, is the case of local Synods. In the fourth century were convened several special synods: Ancyra (314), Caesarea (314), Neo Caesarea (314/319), Gangra (ca. 340), Antioch (341), Laodicea (at the end of IVth century) and Sardice (343–344), the canons of which are incorporated in the *Liber Canonum*, but it is very difficult to ascertain whether any of them were utilized in Armenia before the invention of the alphabet in 406.

I would like to examine especially two local synods which were convened before the Council of Nicaea (325), namely those of Ancyra and Caesarea. In *Corpus Canonum* of the Armenian Church have survived ten canons under the title of the Synod of Caesarea (314) which exist only in the Armenian and Syrian tradition![38] Actually these rules correspond to canons 20–25 of the Council of Ancyra which in the Armenian version has only 20 articles.[39] Subsequently for an unknown reason the last canons (20–25) of the Greek text of Ancyra have been detached and ordered separatly under the name of Caesarea.[40] In fact it is now generally accepted that in 314, most probably in connection with the ordination of Gregory Illuminator, a synod was assembled in Caesarea. The Armenian *Corpus Canonum* has preserved the names of 20 bishops who participated in the Synod and in the consecration of St. Gregory, under the presidency of Archbishop Leontios.[41] It is not improbable at all that Gregory Illuminator brought with him the canons of Ancyra to Armenia which later in the Vth century were divided in two groups, canons 1–20 (of Ancyra) and 20–25 as separate canons of the synod of "Caesarea". This council had perhaps rather discussed problems of jurisdiction in general and relations of the Armenian Church with Caesarea in special. It is also probable that the setting of the canons in two groups was already carried out in the IVth century, because the last canons 20–25 of the Greek text of Ancyra (in Armenian ten chapters) concern morals and were very important for the newly evangelized Armenia, whereas the first 20 canons mostly are related with deacons, priests and bishops. Here I present the titles of the canons of Caesarea:[42]

1. Concerning women who are married and fornicate.
2. Concerning virgins who commit adultery before the wedding.
3. Concerning women who fornicate and kill their children (do abortion).
4. Concerning those who kill not the illegitimate, but the legitimate children.
5. Concerning those who kill (children) in sleep.
6. Concerning widows who commit adultery.
7. Concerning those who wish to learn sorcery.
8. Concerning sorcerers.
9. Corcerning those who abandon their fiancée and get another woman.
10. Concerning thieves, robbers and murderers.

Summing up our evidences, commentary, arguments and remarks, we can conclude that the Book of Canons of the Armenian Church in the IVth century in Greek language comprised the following:

[38] J. Lebon, Sur un concile de Césarée, *Muséon* 51 (1938), 89–132; Ananian, l.c., 152–153 and Nersoyan, A brief Outline of the Armenian *Liber Canonum* and ist Status in modern Times, 80–81.

[39] *Corpus Canonum*, I, 150–167.

[40] L.c. 168–176.

[41] *Corpus Canonum*, I, 150; Ananian, l.c., 156–161, and Nersoyan, l.c., 81.

[42] *Corpus Canonum*, I, 168–169 (text 169–176); Ch. Mercier, l.c., 212–215: "Les dix Chapitres des Canons de Césarée."

1. The Canons of St. Gregory
2. The Canons of Nicaea
3. The Canons of St. Nersēs the Great, and most probably
4. The Canons of Ancyra and
5. "Caesarea".

In general the scholars believe that the compilation of the Armenian *Corpus Canonum* was initiated in the Vth century. For the first time the present study affirms that the formation of the Canon Law had already begun in the IVth century, during the days of St. Gregory Illuminator. In the Vth century the short Book of Canons was translated into Armenian under the guidance of St. Sahak and St. Mesrop and adapted to the life and circumstances of the Armenian people.

In a recent essay[43] Dietmar Schon OP examines the problem of the origin of the Armenian Canon Law and calls in question even the date of the Vth century.[44] In his extremly negative approach not only he refuses the reliability and authenticity of evidences of the early Armenian historians, but also neglects several important facts and arguments which are discussed in our present study. One of the main arguments of Schon is his distorted dispute in connection with the anti-byzantine position of the Armenians in the second-half of the IVth century during the reign of King Pap (367–374), who rejected the primacy of the Metropolitan See of Caesarea, and later in the V–VIth century in connection with the Council of Chalcedon. The scholar ignores totally the fact that the Armenians regardless to their anti-byzantine political and ecclesiastical attitude, they have in the V–VIth century and at all times translated numerous works from Greek, beginning with the Bible and continuing with exegetical, historical, philosophical, liturgical and grammatical treatises. Schon does not deny the existence of early canons in the Armenian Church, but he does not accept the existence of any collection of canons before the VIIIth century. He writes: "*Ein Meilenstein der armenischen Rechtsentwicklung ist mit dem Namen des Katholikos Johannes von Ōdzun (717–728) verknüpft. Er sammelte das frühere armenische Kirchenrecht, sorgte für eine Fortsetzung nach den Bedürfnissen der Zeit und gab das so aktualisierte Kirchenrecht in einer Kanonessammlung heraus.*"[45]

It is true and generally accepted that the first comprehensive Collection of Canons of the Armenian Church was edited by Catholicos John of Ōdzun / Ōjun, but this does not negate the early formation of Canon Law in the IVth century in Greek language and the compilation of the first *Corpus Canonum* in Armenian in the Vth century.

---

[43] Der Codex Canonum Ecclesiarum Orientalium und das authentische Recht im christlichen Orient, in: Das östliche Christentum, new series, vol. 47, Würzburg 1999, 270–318.

[44] L.c., 270–278.

[45] English translation: "*A milestone of the development of the Armenian ecclesiastical law is connected with the name of Catholicos John of Ōjun (717–728). He collected the early (!) Armenian canon law, cared for a continuation in accordance with the needs of the time and edited in this way the actualized church-law in a collection.*"

JEAN-PIERRE MAHÉ / PARIS

DIE BEKEHRUNG TRANSKAUKASIENS: EINE HISTORIOGRAPHIE MIT DOPPELTEM BODEN

Die Historiographie der drei christlichen Länder Transkaukasiens (Albanien[1], Armenien[2] und Georgien[3]) erwähnt zwei aufeinander folgende Wellen der Christianisierung, zuerst im Apostolischen Zeitalter, dann während der konstantinischen Epoche[4].

Diese zwei Bekehrungen sind quantitativ und qualitativ durchaus unterschiedlich: die erste wird als sporadisch, vielgestaltig und nicht offiziell gekennzeichnet; ganz im Gegenteil dazu ist die zweite massiv, systematisch und institutionell. Wichtig ist aber, dass diese Überlieferung in zwei historiographischen Schichten dargestellt wird, die sowohl durch die Daten wie durch den geschichtlichen Wert sehr ungleich sind. Die Bekehrung im vierten Jahrhundert wird üblicherweise in alten Quellen erzählt, die trotz aller späteren Bearbeitungen (5.–10. Jh.) manche authentische Gegebenheiten enthalten. Dagegen sind die das apostolische Zeitalter betreffenden Erzählungen meistens spätere Erfindungen, die sich im Zusammenhang der nationalen Streitigkeiten um die Autokephalie der Kirchen entwickelt haben. Obwohl sie manchmal die Erinnerung an wirkliche Tatsachen widerspiegeln, werden diese in fabelhafte Darlegungen eingebettet.

Sehr früh sind sich die Armenier dieser doppelten Historiographie bewusst gewesen. So erzählt Movsēs Xorenacʿi eine mündliche Überlieferung, die ihm vom heiligen Patriarchen Sahak (387–438), dem letzten männlichen Abkömmling des heiligen Gregorius, übermittelt worden sei: „Als Anak (der Vater unseres Illuminators) in der Ebene von Artaz wohnte, befand sich zufällig die Stelle, wo er schlief, ... sehr nahe bei der Ruhestätte des heiligen Apostels (Thaddäus). Eben dort, so meint man, wurde unser großer und heiliger Illuminator von seiner Mutter empfangen. Daher ergänzte er, ... was von der Ernte seines Vorgängers übrig geblieben war, nachdem die Gnade des heiligen Apostels auf ihn übergegangen war“[5].

Da er zwei verschiedene Historiographien der Bekehrung Armeniens vorfindet, versucht der Geschichtsschreiber sie als komplementär darzustellen. Dieses Verfahren ist ziemlich alt. Auch unter der kritischsten Hypothese kann Movsēs Xorenacʿi nicht später als im 8. Jh. gelebt haben[6]. Überdies wird das, was er einer angeblichen Überlieferung

---

[1] Die Historiographie Albaniens kennen wir nur durch die *Geschichte Albaniens*, die im Spätmittelalter dem Movsēs Dasxurancʿi (oder Kałankatuacʿi) zugeschrieben wurde (cf. Dowsett 1961).

[2] Über die armenische Historiographie s. Mahé 1992, Toumanoff 1963, S. 15–205. Einen äußerst kritischen und negativen Gesichtspunkt bietet Kettenhofen 1995, S. 48–135 und 1998 dar. Die bei den armenischen Autoren von diesem Verfasser aufgezeigten Unrichtigkeiten und Anachronismen sind an und für sich unbestreitbar. Doch scheint mir recht fraglich, ob er irgendwie versucht hat zu verstehen, was diese Historiographie überhaupt bedeutet.

[3] Über die georgische Historiographie s. Toumanoff 1943. 1963 (S. 20–27) und die kritischen Bemerkungen von Lang 1966, S. 157–159.

[4] Die Tatsachen sind von Outtier 1996 knapp dargestellt worden.

[5] Mahé 1993, S. 226.

[6] Er wird erst von Geschichtsschreibern des 10. Jhs. erwähnt, kann aber wohl ein Zeitgenosse des letzten Sahak Bagratuni (752–770) gewesen sein (Mahé 1993, S. 13. 89).

zuschreibt, schon in der im 6. Jh. verfassten Karšuni-Version des Agathangelos erzählt[7].

Die Geschichte des Illuminators zeigt ein paradoxes Beispiel dafür, wie sich eine in ganz sagenhafte Erfindungen eingehüllte Überlieferung auf unbestreitbare geschichtliche Tatsachen stützen kann – trotz einiger chronologischer Unsicherheiten.

Im mittelalterlichen Armenien ist die offizielle Erzählung der Bekehrung Trdats die angeblich aus dem Griechischen übersetzte und dem Agathangelos zugeschriebene Geschichte Armeniens (*A*). Man weiß, dass dieser von einem sogenannten Augenzeugen verfasste Bericht nichts anderes als die Bearbeitung einer älteren, zur Zeit nur durch griechische und arabische Versionen erreichbaren armenischen *Vita Gregorii* ist[8].

Indem er danach strebte, den Rahmen der Hagiographie zu übertreffen, um eine echte Geschichte Armeniens zu schreiben, reicherte der Redaktor des Agathangelos seine Quelle mit – der Wirklichkeit nicht entsprechenden – Ausschmückungen an. Mit Einzelheiten, die dem *Leben des hl. Maštocʿ* entlehnt sind, zog er die Schritte des Illuminators auf Wegen nach, die erst hundert Jahre später der heilige Übersetzer der armenischen Bibel einschlagen sollte[9]. Außerdem glich er seine Erzählung den antiken Romanen[10] an, die er höchstwahrscheinlich nur indirekt durch apokryphe Apostel-Akten kannte.

Tatsächlich ist in manchen Beziehungen die Geschichte des Agathangelos den griechisch-lateinischen Romanen – etwa dem *Esel* des Lukianos oder den *Metamorphosen* des Apuleius – so ähnlich, dass von Zufall keine Rede sein kann. Die Themen sowie die Struktur des Werkes sind gleich. Zum Beispiel lässt sich die Umgestaltung des armenischen Trdat zu einem Wildschwein in allen Einzelheiten der Erzählung auf die Verwandlung des römischen Lucius in einen Esel beziehen. In beiden Fällen erlangt ein durch seine Sünden erniedrigter, ja zu einer tierischen Gestalt herabgesetzter Mensch sein eigentliches Aussehen und seine wirkliche Persönlichkeit durch die Gnade eines fremden Gottes wieder. Beide Male vernichtet die Vorsehung die vom blinden und grausamen Schicksal gestellten Fallen, indem sie die überholte Welt durch eine neue ersetzt.

Es gibt keinen Roman ohne Liebe und keinen Liebhaber ohne rivalisierenden Graukopf. Obwohl die irdische Liebe einer Nonne wie Hṙipʿsimē, die ihre Jungfräulichkeit für Jesu bewahrt, untersagt ist, findet man bei Agathangelos alle diese romanhaften Elemente, u. z. in den von den Apokryphen bestätigten Varianten, wieder. Zum Beispiel pflegt der Graukopf, der in unserer „Komödie" kein anderer als der Kaiser Diokletian ist, die Damen „per Katalog" zu bestellen. Daher lässt er das Bildnis der schönen Nonne zwangsweise malen. Dasselbe Missgeschick erlebt auch die heilige Thekla, diese mit dem Apostel Paulus umherziehende christliche militante Aktivistin[11]. Später scheitert der „Olympiasieger" Trdat daran, die vom Heiligen Geist gestärkte Hṙipʿsimē zu vergewaltigen. Er erleidet eine unehrenhafte Niederlage. Über dieselben geistigen und körperlichen Kräfte verfügt auch die heilige Thekla, sobald es darum geht, ihre Tugend zu verteidigen[12].

Überdies hat Robert Thomson richtig bemerkt, dass die Geschichte Grigors und Trdats nach der Abgar- und Thaddäussage geformt wurde. In beiden Erzählungen meldet sich ein ausländischer Missionar am königlichen Hof. Dann lässt er sich nach kompli-

---

[7] Esbroeck 1971, S. 24, § 8.

[8] Garitte 1946; Winkler 1980.

[9] Die von Tēr Mkrtčʿean – Kanayeancʿ 1909 (Appendix S. XIV–XV) ausführlich verzeichneten Parallelen zwischen Koriwn und Agathangelos sind von Winkler 1994 unzulänglich berücksichtigt worden.

[10] Vgl. Mahé 1996, S. 32–35, wo wir Agathangelos im Einzelnen mit den antiken Romanen verglichen haben. Schon bei Peeters 1942, S. 102–103 war vom „Roman de Ste Hṙipʿsimē" die Rede.

[11] Leben und Wunder der heiligen Thekla, § 4 (Calzolari 1995).

[12] Akten der heiligen Thekla, § 26 (Niederlage eines gewissen Alexander); Leben und Wunder der heiligen Thekla, § 3 (Niederlage eines Götzenpriesters); vgl. Calzolari 1995.

zierten romanhaften Umwegen erkennen. Beide Male wird der König infolge einer übernatürlichen Heilung bekehrt. Der Apostel trägt eine lange Katechese vor. Endlich erbaut er die ersten Kirchen und weist auf seinen Nachfolger hin[13]. Es fällt sofort auf, dass schon um 451 Agathangelos die Thaddäussage gekannt hat.

Daher hat er einige Umstände der Erzählung entweder verstärkt oder neue hinzugefügt. Diese Elemente betrachten wir zwar als romanhaft; er dagegen hat sie als bezeichnend für die apostolische Legitimität Grigors angesehen.

Passt man aber besser auf, so erkennt man, dass nicht der Redaktor des Agathangelos (*A*) für alle „Erfindungen" verantwortlich ist, sondern manche schon in seiner Quelle (*V*) gefunden hat[14]. Eigentlich gehörte die *Vita Gregorii* zur Gattung der sogenannten „epischen Leidensgeschichten"[15], die von der historischen Wirklichkeit ziemlich entfernt sind. Auch von der übernatürlichen Verwandlung Trdats abgesehen, wie kann man sich die unwahrscheinlich lange Widerstandskraft des heiligen Grigor oder seine auch in den albernsten Positionen unerschöpfliche Beredsamkeit vorstellen? Wie kann er eigentlich am Fuße der tiefen Grube überleben ? Auch die älteste Variante des Textes ist schon recht fabelhaft.

Wir dürfen uns aber nicht darüber wundern, dass eine mehr als hundert Jahre nach den Ereignissen verfasste Chronik von der Wirklichkeit stark abweicht. Nach der Erfindung der armenischen Schrift (um 400) wurde die *Vita Gregorii* wohl nach der zweiten Bibelübersetzung (435) und vor Agathangelos (am frühsten 451) geschrieben.

Zu jener Zeit hatte Armenien schon seine Könige verloren (428). Der letzte Grigoride war 438 gestorben. Die Erinnerung an die Bekehrung Trdats wurde dann von schwermütiger Sehnsucht nach dem verlorenen Ruhm, ja nach dem endgültig abgelaufenen Zeitalter der Größe gefärbt. Die Grigor'sche Historiographie rekonstruiert eine durch die Wechselfälle des nationalen Gedächtnisses gesehene Vergangenheit. Zurückblickend richtet sie sich auf den verhängnisvollen Ausgang eines unerbittlichen Schicksals[16].

Doch verbergen die fabelhaften Elemente dieser Überlieferung ihren historischen Wert nicht. Zwar kann man fragen, ob sich der erste christliche Arsakide mit dem 293 in der persischen Inschrift von Païkuli genannten Trdat (III.?) oder mit einem hypothetischen Trdat IV. identifizieren lässt, der ihm 298 nach dem Friedensvertrag von Nisibis nachgefolgt sein sollte[17]. Dennoch darf man nicht die Tatsache bezweifeln, dass sich ein vom Kaiser Diokletian (284–305) auf den Thron erhobener armenischer König[18] zum

---

[13] Thomson 1994, IV, S. 141.

[14] Die Unterschiede zwischen den verschiedenen Fassungen sind von Garitte 1946 systematisch untersucht worden.

[15] Der Begriff der „epischen Leidensgeschichte" ist zuerst von Delehaye (1966, S. 171. 222–223) entwickelt, dann von Garsoïan (1985, XII, S. 152) auf Agathangelos angewandt worden.

[16] Mahé 1999, S. 64.

[17] Nach Toumanoff (1969, S. 11–14. 16. 261–275) ist der in der Paikuli Inschrift erwähnte „Tirdât der König" Trdat III., der Bruder Xosrovs II., der unter römischer Schutzherrschaft zuerst Westarmenien (287–293), dann aber das wiedervereinigte Reich von Großarmenien regierte (293–298). Nach dem römisch-persischen Friedensvertrag von Nisibis (298) wurde er von seinem Neffen Trdat IV., dem Sohn Xosrovs II., ersetzt (298–330). Nach Kettenhofen (1995, S. 158) kann „eine wirklich befriedigende Rekonstruktion der Ereignisse in Armenien nach 293 wohl aufgrund der Quellensituation nicht mehr vorgelegt werden. Welche Rolle tyldt mlk' gespielt hat, ist kaum zu beantworten".

[18] In der Zeittafel am Ende seines Buches druckt Kettenhofen (1995, S. 170) die folgenden Daten fett (was bedeuten soll, dass er sie vertritt): „15. Jahr Diokletians – 298 – Rückführung Trdats nach Armenien (Ps.-Sebēos). Trdat (IV.) wird König in Armenien (in Abhängigkeit Roms). Iberien wird von Rom abhängig, Albanien bleibt sāsānidisch".

Christentum bekehrt und den Bischof Aristakēs zum Konzil von Nizäa (325) gesandt hat[19].

Wann fand dieses wichtige Ereignis statt? Da Agathangelos keine präzisen Daten angibt, haben viele moderne Historiker die vom späteren Geschichtsschreiber Movsēs Xorenacʿi mitgeteilten Auskünfte übernommen: Trdat wird im dritten Jahre Diokletians, also 287, gekrönt[20], und Grigor wird im 17. Jahre Trdats, also 304, zum Bischof geweiht[21]. Da aber vor dieser Weihe die Katechese Grigors, die Heilung des Königs und die Zerstörung der heidnischen Tempel erwähnt werden, datieren einige Verfasser die Bekehrung Armeniens auf den Anfang des vierten Jahrhunderts vor[22].

Dennoch hat P. Ananean[23] richtig beobachtet, dass diese Ergebnisse nur dann gelten dürfen, wenn man voraussetzt, dass Movsēs Xorenacʿi die richtige Regierungszeit Diokletians gekannt hat. Das ist leider nicht der Fall. Nach Movsēs Xorenacʿi wird Diokletian nicht 284 sondern 260 zum römischen Kaiser. Stimmt man mit diesem Datum überein, so ergibt sich, dass Trdat 262 gekrönt und Grigor 279 geweiht wird, was sicher viel früher ist als in Wirklichkeit. Die anderen historiographischen Quellen, u. z. Uxtanēs (10. Jh.), Pseudo-Zenob Glak (10. Jh.) und Pseudo-Sebēos (7. Jh.) bringen so widerspruchsvolle Angaben bei, dass nur unerschrockene Arithmologen wie Toumanoff daraus vernünftige Schlüsse zu ziehen wagten[24].

Indem er die Bekehrung in den politischen Zusammenhang setzt, hält es Hakob Manandyan[25] für unmöglich, dass der von Rom eingesetzte und verteidigte Trdat einen von den Kaisern verbotenen Glauben angenommen hätte. Nach seiner Meinung soll diese Entscheidung erst nach dem Mailänder Edikt (313), wahrscheinlich aber erst 315 stattgefunden haben[26].

Neuerdings hat Ruben Manaseryan[27] angemerkt, dass, wenn man prinzipiell voraussetzt, dass Armenien sich erst dann bekehren darf, wenn das Christentum in den östlichen Provinzen des römischen Kaiserreiches wenigstens toleriert wird, das Datum 313 überhaupt nichts bedeutet. Es solle vielmehr das Datum 324 gelten, als Konstantin seinen Gegner Licinius, „den geilen und ekelhaften Greis, der sich die Haare gefärbt und die Selige Glaphyra gemartert hat"[28], besiegte. Denn dieser war ebenso christenfeindlich wie die vorigen Gebieter des römischen Ostreichs, Galerius (305–311) und Maximinus Daïa (311–313). Nun liegt es klar auf der Hand, dass Armenien am Vorabend des Nizäer Konzils schon jahrelang christlich gewesen ist, da Trdat als Bischof nicht Gregorius *Illuminator*, sondern dessen Sohn und Nachfolger Aristakēs entsandte.

Was das offiziell für die Abhaltung der Feier des 1700-jährigen Jubiläums gewählte Datum 301 betrifft, so möchte ich ganz bescheiden anmerken, dass es kaum mit den historiographischen Gegebenheiten übereinstimmt, dass Trdat in diesem Jahre die heilige Hṙipʿsimē und deren Genossinnen auf Anregung Diokletians hin gemartert habe. Sollte man vermuten, dass der Name Diokletian in diesem Zusammenhang eher symbolisch als

---

[19] Hakobyan, Bd. I, 1964, S. 141 und Gelzer et alii 1898, p. LII, § 106.

[20] Movsēs Xorenacʿi II, 82 (Mahé 1993, S. 233).

[21] Movsēs Xorenacʿi II, 91 (Mahé 1993, S. 245).

[22] Nach Ōrmanean (1912, § 52. 59, S. 82. 89) findet das Martyrium Hṙipʿsimēs und ihrer Genossinnen 301 und die Zerstörung der heidnischen Tempel 302 statt.

[23] Ananian 1961.

[24] Toumanoff 1969, S. 274–281. Man vergleiche diese Zeittafeln mit Kettenhofen 1995, S. 169–171.

[25] Manandyan, Bd. II, 1978, S. 131.

[26] Nach Ps. Sebēos wird Trdat im 15. Jahre Diokletians (also 298) König Armeniens, und nach Movsēs Xorenacʿi wird Gregorius Illuminator im 17. Jahre Trdats (also 315) geweiht.

[27] Manaseryan 1997, S. 178–179.

[28] Movsēs Xorenacʿi II, 88 (Mahé 1993, S. 241).

historisch zu verstehen sei, so ergibt sich sogar ein späteres Datum: dem notorischen Christenverfolger würde dann ein Frevel seiner weniger bekannten Nachfolger zugeschrieben worden sein. Allenfalls war der Arsakide gleich nach dem Abtreten Diokletians im Jahre 305, während Galerius den Krieg im Westen führte, in der Lage, seinem Reich eine neue, nämlich christliche Richtung zu geben, ohne sich vor dem Zorn seiner römischen Verteidiger zu fürchten. Ob der Feldzug des Maximinus Daïa (wohl im Sommer 312) gegen armenische Christen, die doch „Freunde und Bundesgenossen" des römischen Volks waren, eine Reaktion der Tetrarchen auf den Übertritt Trdats zum Christentum darstellt, lässt sich aufgrund des ziemlich vagen Zeugnisses von Eusebius kaum entscheiden[29].

Daher denkt R. Manaseryan, dass das wahrscheinlichste Datum der Bekehrung Trdats 304–306 sei. Man könnte dazu bemerken, dass auch der christenfeindliche Galerius, im Frühling 311, kurz vor seinem Tode, ein Toleranzedikt erließ. Vielleicht hat sich Trdat erst dann zum Christentum bekehrt[30]. Überdies soll die Weihe Grigors im Sommer 314 stattgefunden haben. Damals wurde eben die in der griechischen Übersetzung der *Vita Gregorii* erwähnte Synode der 20 Bischöfe in Cäsarea um den Erzbischof Leontius versammelt[31]. Sobald die Vita ihres epischen und romanhaften Charakters entkleidet wird, lässt sie Tatsachen erkennen, die datierbar sind.

Nun zur armenischen Thaddäussage[32]. Sie macht einen viel weniger günstigen Eindruck. Auf den ersten Blick könnte man glauben, dass die Armenier die Edessener Sage schlicht und einfach übernommen und auf sich bezogen haben. An und für sich ist diese Sage schon in geschichtlicher Hinsicht nicht einwandfrei, denn sie verwechselt Abgar VIII. (177–212), den ersten christlichen König von Edessa, der ein begeisterter Verteidiger des Ketzers Bardesanes war, mit seinem Vorgänger Abgar V. Ukhama (13–50)[33]. Zweifellos nimmt sich der armenische Übersetzer des Labubna mit seiner syrischen Quelle manche Freiheiten heraus, denn er lässt den Apostel Thaddäus nicht in Edessa, sondern im Orient sterben. Somit kann man ihn später in Artaz in Armenien ansiedeln. Dort wird er von König Sanatruk gemartert.

Doch sind diese Abweichungen vom Urtext nicht völlig willkürlich. Schon im 4. Jh. betrachtet die allerälteste griechische Fassung der syrischen *Thaddäusakte* Edessa als eine armenisch-syrische Stadt. Demgemäß wird berichtet, dass der Apostel nicht nur Syrer, sondern auch eine Menge von „Hebräern, Griechen und Armeniern" zum Christentum bekehrt habe. Außerdem besiegt sein angeblicher Henker Sanatruk, obwohl er in der

---

[29] Eusebius, *Kirchengeschichte* IX, 8, 2. Über diese Eusebiusstelle s. Kettenhofen 1995, S. 81–84. 103–104. Es ist klar, dass der Name Trdat nicht erwähnt wird, und dass Eusebius nicht weiß, wann die Christianisierung dieser Armenier stattgefunden hat. Die modernen Historiker, die die Bekehrung Armeniens später als 311 datieren, erläutern diesen Text auf zweierlei Art. Sie vermuten entweder wie Duchesne (Bd. II, 1908, S. 32) und Manandyan (1978, S. 130), dass Eusebius über armenische Provinzen spricht, die zum römischen Reich gehören (das passt aber mit dem Kontext nicht überein, denn die erwähnten Armenier sind keine Untertanen, sondern „Freunde und Bundesgenossen des römischen Volkes"), oder, wie Toumanoff (1969, S. 271), dass Maximinus Daia bei diesem Feldzug die gemeinsame Politik bei seinen armenischen Bundesgenossen unterstützte.

[30] Vgl. Seibt unten S. 128–131. Manaseryan lehnt diese Zeitangabe ab, denn er meint, die Bekehrung zum Christentum sei eine politische, von den Römern völlig unabhängige Entscheidung Trdats, womit er das Prestige des armenischen Königs erneuern wollte, indem er nicht mehr als Vertreter des göttlichen Cäsars sondern des allmächtigen Gottes herrschte.

[31] Thomson 1976, LXV (Anmerkung 136).

[32] Emine 1867 (für die armenische Fassung) und Desreumaux 1993 (über den syrischen Urtext). Der Name Thaddäus ist ein Lesefehler von syrischem Addai.

[33] Pierre 1999, S. 14.

Suda „König Armeniens" genannt wird, die Römer nicht in Großarmenien, sondern im Taurusgebirge, in Nisibis, Edessa und Hatra. All dies lässt vermuten, dass sich sein Königreich nicht direkt in Armenien, sondern im Grenzgebiet zwischen Armenien und der syrischen Welt befunden hat. Es gab also ganz ernste Gründe dafür, die Christianisierung der Osrhoene mit der Südarmeniens zu verknüpfen[34].

Wenn wir die *Vita Gregorii* und Agathangelos mit Aufmerksamkeit lesen, ergibt sich, dass die Bekehrung Trdats nur das arsakidische Königreich, sogar nur dessen nördlichen Teil betrifft[35]. Ausgeschlossen sind Kleinarmenien (westlich des Euphrat, unter römischer Herrschaft), Südarmenien und die sogenannten transtigritanischen Satrapien im Südwesten, worauf bald die Römer und bald die Perser Anspruch erhoben. Demzufolge unterscheidet der *Buzandaran* ganz deutlich zwischen „dem Sitz des heiligen Grigor", der im 4. Jh., von Kappadokien aus, die Evangeliumsverkündigung empfing, und dem „Sitz des heiligen Thaddäus" im Süden, der von den Syrern begründet wurde[36].

Mit voller Sicherheit dürfen wir behaupten, dass es dort ein Bistum vor der Zeit des heiligen Grigor gegeben hat. Höchstwahrscheinlich gehörte der Bischof Meruzanes, an den Dionysius von Alexandrien 251 einen *Brief über die Busse*[37] gesandt hat, zur Familie Arcruni, die in der Umgebung des Van Sees große Gebiete besaß[38]. Früher zurückgehen kann man nur durch die Analyse des armenischen kirchlichen Wortschatzes. Solche Vokabel wie *kʿahanay*, „Priester", *abełay*, „Mönch", *urbatʿ*, „Freitag", usw. weisen, wegen der syrischen Etymologie, auf eine syrisch-mesopotamische Christianisierung Südarmeniens hin[39].

Abercius bezeugt, dass sich das Christentum schon im 2. Jh. in Syrien und Mesopotamien ausgebreitet habe[40]. Die armenischen Grenzgebiete sind wohl gleichzeitig christianisiert worden. Doch erteilt uns die armenische Thaddäussage keine rein historische Auskunft über den Ursprung und die Umstände jenes Prozesses.

Schon in der Mitte des 5. Jhs. arbeiten Agathangelos sowie der *Buzandaran* die Fiktion eines über die Grenzen des königlichen Gebietes und des arsakidischen Reiches hinausgehenden, vereinigten Armenien aus. Daher strebt die Historiographie danach, die beiden Überlieferungen zu verschmelzen. Demnach stellt man als zwei Entwicklungsstufen eines und desselben Prozesses dar, was eigentlich zwei chronologisch und geographisch ganz verschiedene, ja voneinander völlig unabhängige Wellen der Christianisierung gewesen sind. Diese Synthese findet man schon in der armenischen Quelle der karšunischen Übersetzung der *Vita Gregorii* vor, die jedenfalls älter ist als Movsēs Xorenacʿi[41].

Letzterer kennt auch andere, spätere apostolische Sagen, u.z. die des heiligen Bartholomäus, der zuerst, nach der Teilung Armeniens im Jahre 387, zum Verteidiger der westarmenischen Grenze wurde. Dann breitete sich sein Ruhm auch in Ostarmenien aus. Mit diesen Legenden versuchte der Katholikos Yovhannēs V. Drasxanakertcʿi (899–929) die vom 6. Jh. an von den Byzantinern bestrittene apostolische Herkunft und Autokephalie seines Sitzes zu bestätigen[42].

*

[34] Esbroeck 1972, S. 254.
[35] Garsoïan 1999, S. 5–14.
[36] Buzandaran IV, 3: Nersēs sitzt auf dem Thron des Apostels Thaddäus und (auf dem) der Erbschaft seines Vorfahren Grigorius (Garsoïan 1989, S. 110).
[37] Eusebius, *Kirchengeschichte* VI, 46, 2.
[38] Garsoïan 1999, S. 20.
[39] Meillet 1977, S. 259–264, über einige syrische Lehnwörter im Bereich des christlichen Kults.
[40] Pierre 1999, S. 14.
[41] S. o. Anm. 7.
[42] Movsēs Xorenacʿi II, 34 (Mahé 1993, S. 191). Über den Ursprung der armenischen Bartholomäussage s. Esbroeck 1983.

Obwohl die Geschichtsschreibung der Iberer und Albaner nicht so reichlich und verfeinert wie die armenische ist, bietet sie doch dieselbe Zweiheit, ja dieselbe Zerrung, zwischen der mit dem konstantinischen Zeitalter verknüpften Überlieferung und den mehr oder weniger sagenhaften Ansprüchen auf apostolische Herkunft.

Die in der *Kirchengeschichte* des Rufinus von Aquileia eingeschlossene älteste Erzählung der Bekehrung der Iberer wird dem Bacurius zugeschrieben. Dieser war, während des Aufenthaltes des Rufinus in Jerusalem (390–397), Dux der palästinischen Grenze. Dann wurde er am Anfang des 5. Jhs. zum König Iberiens[43].

Er berichtete, dass seine Heimat von einer ausländischen Gefangenen zum Christentum bekehrt worden sei. Diese Frau habe in einer Hütte in der Umgebung der Hauptstadt gewohnt. Ihre strenge Askese habe die Aufmerksamkeit der Bewohner angezogen. Sie fragen sie über ihren Gott. Dann heilt sie ein Kind im Namen Christi. Auch die Königin besucht sie und wird durch ihre Gebete von schwerer Krankheit befreit. An Christus glaubt die Königin sofort, aber der König zweifelt immer noch. Eines Tages geht er auf die Jagd. Plötzlich wird er von dichter Finsternis umgeben. Die Sonne sieht er erst dann wieder, wenn er den Namen Christi angerufen hat. Demzufolge bittet er die Gefangene darum, ihn zu belehren, worauf er das Volk zur Bekehrung ermutigt. Auf Anregung der heiligen Frau, und nach ihrer Anweisung, beginnt man eine Kirche zu bauen. Als die äußeren Wände schon stehen und zwei innere Säulen errichtet sind, versucht man vergebens, die dritte Säule aufzustellen. Auch kräftigen Ochsenjochen gelingt es nicht. Die Gefangene betet die ganze Nacht im Heiligtum. Am nächsten Morgen stellt sich die während der Nacht in der Luft schwebende Säule bei der Ankunft des Königs spontan auf ihren vorgesehenen Platz. Nach der Vollendung des Kirchenbaus sendet die Gefangene dem Kaiser Konstantin einen Brief, um die Bekehrung anzukündigen und Priester zu erbitten[44].

Außer dem Erzähler Bacurius und dem Kaiser Konstantin erwähnt Rufinus keine Eigennamen. Die Gefangene sowie der König, die Königin und die Hauptstadt des Reiches bleiben namenlos.

F. Thélamon hat gezeigt[45], dass die Erzählung des iberischen Königs über die Christianisierung seiner Heimat eine mit heidnischen Ideen gemischte mündliche Überlieferung wiederholt. Darin spielt die Gefangene die Rolle dieser georgischen Schamanen, die man heutzutage *kadagi* nennt. Dieses verhältnismäßig neue Wort bedeutet „Herold“. Früher hat man dazu *kandara* gesagt, was einen hölzernen Querriegel bedeutet, der als Vogelstange benützt wird[46]. In der Tat steigt die Gottheit (*xafi*) vom Himmel herab, um sich auf den Schamanen zu setzen, ebenso wie ein Vogel auf der Stange sitzt. Dann wird der Wahrsager (oder die Wahrsagerin) ein Sklave (*mona*) des Gottes. Er wird ja vom ihm gefangen (*dač'erili*) und besessen, so dass er den göttlichen Willen sowie die Einzelheiten des göttlichen Kults verkünden muss. Er allein kann im Namen des Gottes heilen und retten. Eben das tut die heilige Ausländerin unter den Iberern.

Aber der Kult darf nur vom Priester (*Mk'adre*) durchgeführt werden. Dieser trägt den symbolischen Mast (*droša*), der wie ein heiliger Baum die menschliche Umwelt mit dem göttlichen Universum verbindet. Demzufolge besteht der Hauptritus bei der Gründung eines Heiligtums darin, den symbolischen Mast aufzupflanzen. Diesen rammt der Priester in den Boden so ein, dass er einen Winkel von 45 Grad formt. Das sonderbare Zeichen der sogenannten lebendigen Säule erinnert uns wohl an diesen Ritus[47].

---

[43] Thélamon 1981, S. 93–94.

[44] Lateinischer Text und französische Übersetzung bei Thélamon (1981, S. 87–90).

[45] Ebd. S. 107–122.

[46] Charachidzé 1968, S. 117.

[47] Thélamon 1981, S. 118.

Aber dieser Ursprungs- u. Begründungsmythos des georgischen Christentums wird von Rufinus zu einer Missionserzählung umgedeutet. Dabei wird die Quelle nach der Abgar- und Thaddäussage gestaltet, die auch den armenischen Agathangelos beeinflusste. Die Ankunft eines ausländischen Apostels, die Heilung des Königs, das Erbauen des ersten Heiligtums sowie die Einrichtung der kirchlichen Hierarchie werden getreulich übernommen. Doch erscheinen spezifische Veränderungen, die dem einheimischen Substratum entsprechen. Nicht der König, sondern die Königin wird geheilt. Der König wird von der Finsternis befreit. Diese Zweiteilung des Wunders, als individuelle Heilung einerseits und kosmisches Zeichen andererseits, spiegelt zweifellos die uralten Vorstellungen der Iberer wider, wie die Rollen unter den beiden Geschlechtern verteilt sind, soweit es sich um die Beziehung zum Göttlichen handelt[48].

Vom Rufin'schen Text wird schon am Ende des 4. Jhs. die *Kirchengeschichte* des Gelasius von Cäsarea abgeleitet[49]. Im 5. Jh. ist die Erzählung mehreren Geschichtsschreibern, Sokrates[50], Sozomenos[51] und Theodoretos[52], bekannt. Sokrates scheint eine der Quellen des armenischen Chronisten Movsēs Xorenacʿi[53], sowie der georgischen Schrift *Die Bekehrung Kartlis*[54] gewesen zu sein. Diese beiden vertreten aber schon eine spätere Entwicklungsstufe. Die einst namenlosen Personen der lateinischen Fassung haben jetzt Namen bekommen: so heißt die heilige Gefangene Nune auf armenisch und Nino auf georgisch[55], der König Mirian und die Königin Nana. Auf das Oratorium der Heiligen, sowie auf die Stellen der heidnischen Götzen und der frühesten christlichen Heiligtümer wird nun ganz genau auf dem Gebiet der Stadt Mcxeta hingewiesen. Der heidnisch durchtränkten Geschichte der lebendigen Säule wird jetzt die erbauliche Sage eines jenseits der Kura befindlichen Wunderkreuzes hinzugefügt. Offenbar wird das frühere heidnische Sinnbild des Gründungsholzes des Heiligtums durch den rein christlichen Kultus des Kreuzes verdoppelt (aber doch nicht ersetzt).

Um diese Entwicklungsstufen zu begreifen, sollte man die komplizierte Textgeschichte der Bekehrung Kartlis ausführlich rekonstruieren. Zweifellos wird diese Arbeit durch die Veröffentlichung der zwei neu entdeckten sinaïtischen Fassungen erleichtert werden[56].

In der heutigen Form vereinigt die Bekehrung Kartlis zwei unterschiedliche redaktionelle Blöcke, u. z. die Chronik der Bekehrung im engen Sinne[57] und eine Sammlung von verschiedenartigen Überlieferungen über das Leben und die Tätigkeit der heiligen Nino[58]. Der zentrale Teil der Chronik[59] läuft im wesentlichen parallel mit der Rufin'schen Erzählung ab. Doch wird die Christianisierung der Iberer in einem breiteren historischen

[48] Ebd. S. 99–101.

[49] Gelasius von Cäsarea, *Kirchengeschichte* III, 10.

[50] Sokrates, *Kirchengeschichte* I, 20.

[51] Sozomenos, *Kirchengeschichte* II, 7.

[52] Theodoretos, *Kirchengeschichte* I, 24.

[53] Movsēs Xorenacʿi II, 86 (Mahé 1993, S. 238–239). Es gibt zwei altarmenische Übersetzungen des Sokrates. Die längere Redaktion wurde von Pʿilo Tirakacʿi im Jahre 693 verfasst. Die kürzere wird keinem bestimmten Übersetzer zugeschrieben (Tēr Movsēsean 1897). Welche Fassung Movsēs Xorenacʿi benützt hat, bleibt noch umstritten.

[54] Pätsch 1975.

[55] Nunē und Nino sind wohl Entstellungen des Wortes „Nonne". Der Name der Predigerin bleibt also unbekannt. Auf koptisch wird sie „Theognoste" und auf lateinisch „Christiana" genannt.

[56] S. o. S. 9–16 den Beitrag von Z. Alexidze, und Martin-Hisard 1997, S. 53–80.

[57] Kapitel 1, 1–9 (Pätsch 1975, S. 290–297; s. a. Martin-Hisard 1998, S. 1181–1182.

[58] Bekehrung, Kapitel 2, 15 (Pätsch 1975, S. 302–335).

[59] Bekehrung, Kapitel 1, 3–9 (Pätsch 1975, S. 293–297).

Rahmen dargestellt: Davor wird die Genealogie der heidnischen Könige und die Geschichte ihrer Götzen seit Alexander dem Großen erläutert[60]; danach wird die Chronik des christlichen Iberiens bis zum Fall der Sasaniden im Jahre 651 fortgesetzt[61]. Am Ende der Erzählung sind zwei Verzeichnisse hinzugefügt worden: die Könige (*mepe*) und die Prinzen (*eristavi*) Kartlis, sowie die iberischen Patriarchen bis zum 10. Jh.[62]

Von diesen Hinzufügungen abgesehen, bietet die „Chronik der Bekehrung" eine in der Mitte des 7. Jhs. verfasste synthetische und einheitliche Erzählung der Geschichte Kartlis dar. Was die Bekehrung selbst betrifft, so ist es klar, dass der Verfasser sich auf eine Quelle gestützt hat, die er „das abgekürzte Büchlein des Diakons Grigol" nennt[63]. Da es sich auf das Zeitalter Mirians und Ninos konzentrierte, ging dieses Buch wohl viel mehr ins Einzelne als die heutige Chronik, die sich von der hellenistischen Epoche bis zur arabischen Eroberung erstreckt. Die Verkürzung spürt man ganz deutlich, wenn der Verfasser nur andeutungsweise die Wunder der Erleuchtung Mirians und der lebendigen Säule erwähnt: „Im siebten Jahre", so schreibt er, „bekehrte (Nino) durch ein Wunder den König. Dieser beeilte sich, die untere Kirche im Garten zu erbauen. Dort war die hölzerne Säule, die sich spontan errichtete"[64]. Hätten wir die oben erwähnte detailliertere Fassung nicht zur Verfügung, so würden wir die genaue Bedeutung des Textes nicht verstehen. Das sogenannte „Büchlein Grigols" war in Wirklichkeit länger als die Schrift, die wir jetzt besitzen.

Wann diese verlorene Quelle verfasst wurde, wissen wir nicht genau. B. Martin-Hisard[65] meint, dass diese dem Rufinus noch unbekannte Geschichte des heiligen Kreuzes von Mcxeta im Laufe des 5. Jhs. ausgearbeitet wurde. Jedenfalls pilgerten schon im 6. Jh. und bis zur Trennung der beiden kaukasischen Kirchen am Anfang des 7. viele Armenier zu diesem heiligen Kreuz, dessen Ursprung wahrscheinlich im „Büchlein Grigols" erzählt war[66]. Demzufolge muss dieses Werk etwas früher als die Pilgerfahrt, also an der Wende vom 5. zum 6. Jh. entstanden sein. Damals errichtete auch König Vaxtang Gorgasal das iberische Patriarchat[67].

Dank dieser Chronik, welche die Tätigkeit ihrer Gründerin erzählt, den geographischen Rahmen ihres Apostolats umgrenzt, den Ursprung der Hierarchie erläutert und die wichtigsten Heiligtümer beschreibt, verfügt die Kirche Iberiens über ein nützliches Zeugnis ihrer Legitimität[68]. Es blieb nur noch übrig, die Chronik auf dem Laufenden zu halten, indem man die Namen der neuen Patriarchen und Könige hinzufügte.

Zum ersten Mal wird diese Schrift in der zweiten Hälfte des 7. Jhs. bearbeitet. So entstand der Prototyp der heutigen vier Fassungen. Damals genoss Iberien noch unter arabischer Herrschaft ein ziemlich günstiges Statut der Autonomie. Infolge der erzwungenen Unterbrechung der Verbindung mit dem Patriarchat von Antiochia[69] war die iberische Kirche um so mehr unabhängig, als sie sich 610 auch von Armenien getrennt hatte. Selbstverständlich versuchte sie, ihre eigene nationale Überlieferung zu verstärken.

---

[60] Bekehrung, Kapitel 1, 1–2 (Pätsch 1975, S. 290–293).

[61] Bekehrung, Kapitel 1, 10–28 (Pätsch 1975, S. 297–301).

[62] Bekehrung, Kapitel 1, 29 (Pätsch 1975, S. 301).

[63] Bekehrung, Kapitel 1, 5 (Martin-Hisard 1998, S. 1182: „sowie es geschrieben ist im kleinen abgekürzten Büchlein des Diakons Grigol". Diese Stelle ist nur von der Čeliš Handschrift überliefert. Daher wurde sie nicht von Pätsch 1975 übersetzt). Über das Büchlein Grigols s. Tarchnišvili – Assfalg 1955, S. 87f.

[64] Bekehrung, Kapitel 1, 4 (Pätsch 1975, S. 294).

[65] Martin-Hisard 1997, S. 71.

[66] Bekehrung, Kapitel 1, 5 (Pätsch 1975, S. 295, Anm. 31 und Martin-Hisard 1998, S. 1182).

[67] Bekehrung, Kapitel 1, 18 (Pätsch 1975, S. 299; vgl. Martin-Hisard 1998, S. 1195–1196).

[68] Martin-Hisard 1997, S. 70.

[69] Über die Beziehungen der Kirche Kartlis zu den anderen Kirchen (Konstantinopel, Antiochia, Armenien) s. Martin-Hisard 1998, S. 1188–1192.

In der *Bekehrung Kartlis* wird Nino als eine Genossin der von Trdat gemarterten Hṙipʿsimē beschrieben[70]. Nach dem *Buzandaran* erscheint Grigoris, der Enkel des Gregorius Illuminator, als Bischof Iberiens und Albaniens[71]. Movsēs Xorenacʿi meint sogar, dass nach der Bekehrung Mirians Nino den heiligen Grigor um Rat fragte, ob sie die Götzenbilder zerstören und das Kreuz errichten solle[72]. Endlich, in der Chronik des georgischen Schriftstellers Arsen, behaupten die Iberer: „Aus Griechenland hat uns der heilige Grigor den Glauben gebracht“[73]. In der Tat hat der iberische Patriarch Kyrion während der christologischen Erörterung mit den Armeniern keine Schwierigkeiten, seinen vom heiligen Grigor eingeführten orthodoxen Glauben zu bekennen[74]. Offensichtlich verlangte die Trennung der Iberer von den Armeniern (im Jahre 610) die Ausarbeitung einer neuen Historiographie, die, ohne die frühere Überlieferung zu verneinen, die Initiative der heiligen Nino, sowie die Unabhängigkeit ihres Apostolats ganz deutlich hervorheben würde.

Das verwirklicht der zweite Teil der *Bekehrung Kartlis*, wo verschiedene Überlieferungen über das Leben der Heiligen zusammengestellt sind. Vielleicht sind einige von diesen Erzählungen dem früheren Büchlein Grigols entnommen worden. Zum Beispiel liest man neue Einzelheiten über die lebendige Säule[75] oder über die Errichtung des Kreuzes[76]. Diese zur ältesten und wesentlichsten Schicht der Erzählung gehörenden Umstände waren in der Kompilation vom Jahre 651 sehr verkürzt worden. Andere Auskünfte über die Geburt und die Jugend Ninos oder die heilige Tunika Christi oder die jüdische Gemeinde[77] von Mcxeta kommen von unabhängigen mündlichen oder schriftlichen Überlieferungen, die der Urerzählung durchaus fremd sind.

Wann wurde diese Sammlung verfasst und dem ersten Teil hinzugefügt? Sicher vor dem Ende des 8. Jhs. Man könnte aber vielleicht noch etwas früher zurückgehen. So hat die Historiographie der Christianisierung der Iberer im Zeitalter Konstantins einerseits tiefe und alte Wurzeln, andererseits hat sie sich langsam und allmählich entwickelt, je nachdem wie sich die politischen Umstände des 4. bis zum 7. Jh. geändert haben. Außerdem behält sie ein starkes, sofort spürbares mythologisches und hagiographisches Substrat.

Doch darf man die Wirklichkeit der wesentlichen Tatsachen nicht anzweifeln. Am Anfang des 4. Jhs. hat eine christliche Frau unbekannten Namens Mirian III. und sein Königreich zum Christentum bekehrt. C. Toumanoff[78] hat sogar bewiesen, dass die chronologischen Gegebenheiten des Textes mit dem Datum des 17. Juli 334 ziemlich gut zusammenpassen. Damals soll die totale Sonnenfinsternis stattgefunden haben, weswegen Mirian die Hilfe Christi angefleht habe. Die übrigen Einzelheiten der Erzählung, u.z. die von Konstantinopel gesandten Priester, die Orte der Heiligtümer, der Säulenkult, die Missionen der heiligen Nino zu den Gebirgsvölkern usw. scheinen an und für sich ganz wahrscheinlich. Speziell die Auskünfte über die jüdische Gemeinde von Mcxeta, ihren Friedhof, die Bekehrung einiger Juden zum Christentum und die Beziehungen der übrigen zum König und zur christlichen Gemeinde tragen wohl das Siegel der Echtheit.

---

[70] Bekehrung, Kapitel 1, 3 (Pätsch 1975, S. 293).
[71] Buzandaran III, 5–6 (Garsoïan 1989, S. 70–73).
[72] Movsēs Xorenacʿi II, 86 (Mahé 1993, S. 238).
[73] Arseni Sapareli, „Über die Trennung der Iberer und der Armenier“, Kapitel 5 (Aleksidze 1980, S. 81).
[74] Buch der Briefe, 1906, S. 171.
[75] Bekehrung, Kapitel 9/B6 (Pätsch 1975, S. 322–323).
[76] Ebd., Kapitel 14 (Pätsch 1975, S. 330–334).
[77] Ebd., Kapitel 3. 6. 7. 12 (Pätsch 1975, S. 304–307. 311–318. 325–328).
[78] Toumanoff 1963, S. 374–377.

Bis jetzt wurde nur über Iberien, d. h. Ostgeorgien, gesprochen. Dennoch hatte sich damals das Christentum auch in Westgeorgien, in der pontischen Gegend ausgebreitet. Aber darüber existiert keine uralte georgische Historiographie. Man soll nämlich nicht vergessen, dass die georgische Literatur in Iberien entstanden ist. Erst am Ende einer langwierigen Entwicklung wird das Georgische zur Schriftsprache des ganzen Landes Sakartvelo[79]. Zum ersten Mal wird diese Tatsache 951 von Giorgi Merčuli bezeugt. Im Leben des heiligen Grigol von Xanjta (759–861) bemerkt er: „Jetzt ist Georgien zu diesem ausgedehnten Länderkomplex geworden, wo man alle Gebete auf Georgisch hersagt. Nur zwei Worte spricht man immer noch auf Griechisch, u.z. *Kyrie Eleison*“[80]. Nun betreffen die vom 11. Jh. an der Konstantinischen Historiographie hinzugefügten apostolischen Sagen ausschließlich West- und Südgeorgien.

Im (um 1070 verfassten) Leben des Giorgi Mtac'mindeli (1009–1065) erzählt sein Schüler Giorgi Mcire die Besprechung seines Meisters mit dem Patriarchen von Antiochia, über die Autokephalie der georgischen Kirche. Da die seit dem 7. Jh. unterbrochenen Beziehungen zur syrischen Metropole wieder aufgenommen worden waren, wurde diese lang verdrängte Frage plötzlich am Ende des 11. Jhs. zum Zankapfel. So verteidigt der Georgier Teopile die apostolische Herkunft seiner Nationalkirche: „Wir sind die Herde Andreas des Erstberufenen, der auch seinen Bruder rief. Vom ihm wurden wir bekehrt und erleuchtet. Außerdem ist einer der zwölf Apostel, Simon der Cananäer, in unserer Heimat in Abchasien, u.z. in Nicopsia, bestattet worden“[81].

In der Tat erzählt ein ins *Leben der Könige* Leont'i Mrovelis eingesetzter apokrypher Akt des Andreas[82], wie der Apostel, bevor er nach Skythien ging, auf Antrag der Gottesmutter das Evangelium in Westgeorgien verkündet habe. Dabei soll er auch ein wundertätiges Bild der Jungfrau hinterlassen haben. Diese Mission erfüllte er in zwei Stufen: zuerst war er allein, dann kam Simon der Cananäer auch mit[83]. Die Lebenszeiten Leont'i Mrovelis sind umstritten: man schwankt zwischen dem 9. und 11. Jh.[84]. Doch ist hier die Frage belanglos, denn die Andreasgeschichte ist sicher eine Interpolation[85].

Die interessantesten Auskünfte, die diese recht sagenhafte Erzählung enthält, bestehen aus Ortsnamen, die alle auf West- und Südgeorgien hinweisen: Trapezunt, Adscharia, Samcxe, Mesxeti, T'ao Klarǰeti und Abchasien. Dieses Apostolat soll unter der Regierung Aderks (1–57) stattgefunden haben. Nun hatte dieser König Iberiens aber überhaupt keine Beziehung zu Westgeorgien. Nur die Erwähnung dieses unzutreffenden Synchronismus genügt zum Beweis, dass der Text nach der Entstehung des vereinigten Reiches von Georgien – also nach Bagrat III. (975–1014) – verfasst worden ist[86]. Ganz anachronistisch glaubt der Autor, dass schon am Anfang der christlicher Ära ein und derselbe König ganz Georgien beherrscht habe.

Andreas lässt den Sohn einer in der Gegend von Ac'qur im Samcxe regierenden Witwe auferstehen. Wie G. Charachidze[87] richtig bemerkt hat, gehört der angebliche Name

---

79 Tarchnišvili – Assfalg 1955, S. 19–40.

80 Lang 1956, S. 146.

81 Ebd. S. 154–155. 165–168.

82 Die Andreasakten sind ins Georgische von Euthymius (Ektime) Mtac'mindeli (955–1028) übersetzt worden. Sie enthielten „die Reisen und Predigten des Apostels Andreas“, welche „der ehrwürdige Mönch und Philosoph Niketas (9. Jh.) gesammelt und zusammengestellt hat“ (Tarchnišvili – Assfalg 1955, S. 135).

83 Französische Übersetzung bei Tamarati 1910, S. 120–124. Deutsch bei Pätsch 1985, S. 91–99.

84 Lang 1966, S. 158.

85 In der kritischen Ausgabe Leont'i Mrovelis ist diese erst im frühen 18. Jh. bezeugte Interpolation vom Originaltext getrennt und klein gedruckt (Q'auxčišvili, Bd. I, 1955, S. 37–42).

86 Jedenfalls nach der Übersetzung der Andreasakten (s. o. Anm. 74 bzw. 82).

87 Charachidze 1968, S. 559ff.

dieser Frau, Samjivari, eigentlich einer berühmten Göttin, der dämonischen Buhlerin der Schamanen, die, in der Form einer schönen Frau, mit ihrem Glasperlenhalsband (*mjivi*) die Männer anlockt und erotische Träume verursacht. Aber dieser Mythos ist viel älter als das georgische Heidentum. Denn die Gestalt dieser sich für sehr junge Männer interessierenden Dame reiferen Alters ist auch in Armenien bezeugt. Dort verliebt sich Šamiram, die geile Königin der Assyrer, in den armenischen König Ara den Schönen. Zuerst wird dieser von ihren Soldaten getötet, dann aber von den hundsköpfigen Dämonen, den Aralezen, wiederbelebt. Als Zauberei benützt Šamiram ein aus wirbelförmigen azurblauen Glasperlen bestehendes Halsband[88]. Einen solchen Schmuck trug auch die assyrische Liebesgöttin Ištar/Inanna, als sie in die Unterwelt hinabstieg, um ihren Geliebten, den Hirten Dumuzi/Izdubar, zu befreien[89]. So enthält die Erzählung gar keine geschichtlichen Tatsachen. Sie lässt nur ahnen, was für heidnische Kulte in dieser Gegend existierten.

Doch darf man behaupten, dass sich das Christentum im Pontischen Georgien und in Abchasien schon vor dem konstantinischen Zeitalter ausgebreitet hat. Am Nizäer Konzil nahmen die georgischen Bischöfe von Trapezunt und Pizunda teil. Letzterer namens Stratophilos erbaute um 312–325 eine einschiffige Kirche, die 1972 von A. Apakidze untersucht wurde[90]. Viele andere archäologische Überreste bezeugen eine frühe Christianisierung der pontischen Küste. Trotz mancher durchaus fabelhafter Erfindungen widersprechen die Erzählungen, die eine Verbreitung des Evangeliums in Westgeorgien während des frühchristlichen Zeitalters beschreiben, der geschichtlichen Wirklichkeit nicht direkt[91]. Dennoch passen ihre apostolischen Referenzen viel zu gut zur Polemik des 11. Jhs., um nicht apokryph zu sein.

*

Mit Ausnahme der von Sasa Aleksidze im sinaïtischen Kloster der heiligen Katharina 1996 entdeckten zwei Palimpseste[92] besitzen wir keinen Text in kaukasisch-albanischer Sprache. Der Inhalt dieser neuen Handschriften bleibt noch unbestimmt. Wir verfügen bis jetzt noch über keinen Hinweis darauf, dass es sich um geschichtliche Werke handeln könnte. Wir haben also keine direkten Auskünfte über die Historiographie des kaukasischen Albanien.

Doch vernehmen wir davon einen fernen und sicher entstellten Widerhall in der armenischen Schrift, deren Titel *Geschichte Albaniens* ist (GA). Vom 10. bis zum 13. Jh. wird dieses Werk normalerweise ohne Verfassernamen angeführt. Aber schon vom Ende des 12. Jhs. an wird es einem bestimmten Movsēs, bald Dasxuranc'i und bald Kałankatuac'i zugeschrieben[93]. Dieser letztere Name ist eine auf falscher Auslegung des Textes begründete Erfindung von Kirakos Ganjakec'i[94]. Der erste Name ist – im günstigsten Falle – eine spät entwickelte lokale Überlieferung[95]. Da die spätmittelalterlichen

[88] Movsēs Xorenac'i I, 15–18 (Mahé 1993, S. 130–131. 135–136 und 335, Anm. 1. 3).

[89] Bottéro – Kramer 1989, S. 277: „Elle s'ajusta au cou le Collier de lazulite; disposa élégamment sur sa gorge les Perles-couplées; se passa aux mains les Bracelets d'or; tendit sur sa poitrine le Cache-seins, 'Homme, viens! viens!'".

[90] Khrouchkova 1989, S. 90; Lang 1956, S. 94.

[91] Doch haben wir keinen archäologischen Beweis für die Verbreitung des Christentums während des 1.–2. Jhs., wie die Apokryphen behaupten.

[92] Aleksidze – Mahé 1997.

[93] Dowsett 1961, S. XV–XVIII.

[94] Ebd. S. XVIII. Kirakos Ganjakec'i (13. Jh.) hat wahrscheinlich GA II, 11 (ebd. S. 84) missverstanden.

[95] Ebd. S. XVII. Etwas früher als Kirakos nennt Mxit'ar Goš den Verfasser der GA Movsēs Dasxuranc'i.

Chronisten es wahrscheinlich zu schwierig fanden, ein anonymes Buch anzuführen, haben sie sich darum bemüht, um jeden Preis einen Verfasser zu entdecken.

Betrachtet man aber den Inhalt des Werkes, so verliert die Frage der Autorschaft jede Bedeutung. Es fällt sofort auf, dass wir es hier mit keiner homogenen, einem bestimmten Individuum zuzuschreibenden Schrift zu tun haben. Vielmehr handelt es sich um eine Kompilation, ja um eine Sammlung verschiedenartiger Chroniken und Dokumente, deren Umfang und buchstäblicher Text nicht immer unverändert geblieben sind. Zum Beispiel hat der armenische Katholikos Anania um 958 wohl eine andere Fassung als Uxtanēs dreißig Jahre später gelesen[96].

In den drei Büchern des heutigen Werkes erkennt A. Hakobyan drei Hauptquellen:
1) eine „Erzählung über den König Vačʿagan III. den Frommen" (485–510);
2) eine um 630 verfasste „Geschichte des Katholikos Viroy";
3) eine im Jahre 684 beendete Chronik.

Doch soll man dazu bemerken, dass die Bücher II und III wohl später, u.z. bis zum Anfang des 12. Jhs., bearbeitet worden sind[97], denn sie erwähnen spätere Ereignisse. Die endgültige Redaktion des Textes wurde erst am Anfang des 12. Jhs. fertiggestellt[98].

Auch die nach dem Tode Vačʿagans des Frommen geschriebene älteste Quelle der Kompilation ist um etwa anderthalb Jahrhunderte jünger als die Entstehung eines großalbanischen Königreiches im Jahre 387, das aus zwei durchaus heterogenen Teilen bestand: einerseits, auf dem nördlichen Ufer der Kura Albanien im eigentlichen Sinne (*Bun Ałuankʿ*); andererseits, auf dem südlichen Ufer die armenischen Bezirke von Arcʿax und Utikʿ[99]. Obwohl das armenische Element im neuen Reiche die Oberhand gewinnt, muss doch Maštocʿ, der Erfinder der armenischen Schrift, ein eigenartiges Alphabet von 56 Buchstaben speziell für die Albaner um 422 erschaffen haben[100]. Dann übersetzt man die Bibel ins Albanische. Gab es damals auch eine Historiographie in derselben Sprache? Das wissen wir nicht. Jedenfalls betrachtet die direkt auf Armenisch verfasste klassische Historiographie Albaniens die Ereignisse vom armenischen Standpunkt aus, ebenso wie die Bevölkerung der südlichen Bezirke. Die Christianisierung des Königreiches wird ganz besonders mit der Bekehrung Armeniens verbunden.

Doch findet man auch Überreste unabhängigerer Zeugnisse vor. Zum Beispiel bestreiten unter dem Patriarchat des armenischen Katholikos Abraham (607–611) die Albaner den Iberern den Vorrang, indem sie behaupten: „Einer der Jünger des Herren, namens Ełišay, der vom heiligen Jakob dem Herrenbruder geweiht wurde, kam in früherer Zeit nach Albanien. Dort predigte er; dann erbaute er eine Kirche, als es noch keine in Armenien gab. Das ist die Kirche von Giš[101], die allererste Mutterkirche des Morgenlan-

---

[96] Ebd. S. XVI.

[97] Donabédian 1988–89, S. 491.

[98] Dowsett 1961, S. XX: Die meisten Daten in GA sind nicht später als 944. Doch erwähnt GA III, 22 den König Senekʿerim von Siwnikʿ (um 1080–1105).

[99] Doch glauben bestimmte Verfasser, dass die Gebiete südlich der Kura erst nach 428, teilweise sogar erst nach 451 zu Albanien kamen (Winkler 1994, S. 345).

[100] Koriwn, Kap. 24–26 (Winkler 1994, S. 108–109. 340–348).

[101] Die Lokalisierung von Giš ist bestritten worden. Dowsett 1961, S. 5, Anm. 5, identifiziert die Ortschaft mit dem heutigen Kiš, nördlich von Nukha. Andere Autoren haben dazu bemerkt, dass sich nach GA II, 33 (Dowsett 1961, S. 138–139) Giš in Utikʿ befinden soll. Daraus schließen sie, dass es sich nur um Giš (Giši) im Rayon Martuni von Bergkarabach handeln kann. Doch widerspricht diese Lösung GA II, 33, denn dieses Dorf befindet sich nicht in Utikʿ, sondern in Arcʿax. Übrigens ist keineswegs bewiesen, dass die verschiedenen Quellen von GA I, 6, II, 33 und II, 48 eine und dieselbe Ortschaft meinen. Eigentlich zeigt die Landkarte Eremyans zwei Giš: eines nördlich der Kura im Bezirk von Beł (B7) und das andere in Utikʿ nördlich von Amaras (G7). Nicht sehr weit von diesen beiden Dörfern befinden sich Ortschaften, deren Namen auf Ełišay bezogen sind, u. z. Ełišay – Kʿurmux neben Giš (B7) und Ełišēivankʿ südlich von

des“[102]. Nach dieser Überlieferung soll Ełišay vom heiligen Jakob direkt nach Albanien abgeordnet worden sein. Sein Apostolat ist also von der Christianisierung Armeniens völlig unabhängig und findet auch früher statt.

Später haben sich die Armenier darum bemüht, diese Historiographie zu „verbessern“, indem sie Ełišay dem heiligen Thaddäus, dem ersten Apostel Armeniens, unterordneten. Sie geben an, dass Ełišay zuerst in Albanien zu einem Jünger dieses Apostels wurde. Nachdem Thaddäus von Sanatruk gemartert worden war, ging der Jünger nach Jerusalem, um seinen Tod zu verkünden. Erst dann wurde er vom heiligen Jakob geweiht und anstatt seines Meisters nach Albanien gesandt. Zuerst predigte er in Čʿoł (d. h. Derbent), dann in Utikʿ und in Giš; schließlich wurde er in der Ebene von Zargun gemartert[103].

Diese zweite, ziemlich verschlungene Fassung scheint absichtlich erfunden worden zu sein, um die erste zu neutralisieren, um die Kirche Albaniens in den Schoß der armenischen Kirche zurückzuführen. Ełišay geht nicht nur nach Čʿoł/Derbent, nördlich der Kura, sondern auch nach Utikʿ, auf das südliche Ufer. Diese anachronistische Geographie Albaniens beweist, dass die Urüberlieferung entstellt worden ist. Aber diese Bearbeitung ist ziemlich alt, da wir sie schon in der am Ende des 6. Jhs. geschaffenen „Erzählung über Vačʿagan“ lesen. Daher lässt sich wohl die frühere Überlieferung auf das 5. Jh. zurückführen. Demzufolge kann sie zur ältesten Schicht der albanischen Historiographie gehören.

B. Outtier hat bemerkt, dass die Anwesenheit von Juden in Albanien am Anfang der christlichen Ära ziemlich wahrscheinlich ist; doch muss man gestehen, dass sie nirgendwo bezeugt ist. Die im albanischen kirchlichen Wortschatz erhaltenen syrischen Vokabeln (soweit man es indirekt durch das Udische wissen kann) lassen ahnen, dass syro-persische Missionen nach Albanien kamen, wohl im 2. und 3. Jh. Mehr kann man aber kaum vermuten[104].

Was die Bekehrung Albaniens im 4. Jh. betrifft, so haben wir zwei verschiedene historiographische Überlieferungen. Die eine bezieht sich auf den Süden und die andere auf den Norden. Es ist auffallend, dass das Apostolat des Grigoris, des um 330 gemarterten Sohnes des Aristakēs und Enkels des Grigor Illuminator in der armenischen Hälfte des späteren Königreichs von Großalbanien ausgeübt wird. Der *Buzandaran* (III, 6) nennt Grigoris „den Katholikos der Länder Iberiens und Albaniens“[105], was eigentlich seine Diözese im Gugarkʿ, also im sogenannten Grenzgebiet der Mazkʿutʿkʿ[106] liegen lässt.

Giš(i) (G7). Lässt sich die Sage des Ełišay bis zu einer alten lokalen Überlieferung zurückführen (s. GA II, 48), so muss sie sich ursprünglich auf ein echtalbanisches (also nördlich der Kura gelegenes) Giš beziehen. Später wurde die Sage aber armenisiert (GA I, 6); dabei verlegte man Giš in die Umgebung Amaras, nicht weit vom Grabmal des armenischen Märtyrers Grigoris. Will man diese zweite Lokalisierung als die ursprüngliche und einzig gültige ansehen, so muss man damit auch behaupten, dass die Sage Ełišays eine nach 387 (bzw. 428 oder 451) entstandene armenische Erfindung sei.

Die Kirche von Giš/ Kiši nördlich der Kura ist kein Gebäude des 5. Jhs., wie man falsch vermutet hat. In ihrem jetzigen Zustand ist sie wahrscheinlich im 11. Jh. entweder erbaut oder umgebaut worden. Diese Auskünfte verdanke ich Frau Dr. Annegret Plontke-Lüning aus dem Institut für Altertumswissenschaft der Friedrich-Schiller-Universität Jena, die mir die entsprechenden Seiten ihrer noch unveröffentlichten Dissertation großzügig gesandt hat. Dort bespricht sie, samt allen literarischen Quellen, auch die archäologischen Daten, und identifiziert Giš mit Giši in Bergkarabach.

102 GA II, 48 (Dowsett 1961, S. 177).

103 GA I, 6 (Dowsett 1961, S. 5).

104 Outtier 1996, S. 557.

105 Buzandaran III, 6 (Garsoïan 1989, S. 72).

106 Ebd. III, 5 (Garsoïan 1989, S. 70). Garsoïan 1989, S. 466, identifiziert das Grenzgebiet der Mazkʿutkʿ mit der iberischen Mark von Gugarkʿ (vgl. die Landkarte Hewsens 1989 am Ende desselben Bandes, G 3).

Von dort aus erstreckt sich seine Tätigkeit bis Atrpatakan, weit südlich der Kura, und er wird vom Arsakiden Sanēsan, dem König der Mazkʿutkʿ, getötet[107]. Sein Grabmal befindet sich in Amaras im Bezirk Haband, immer noch südlich der Kura[108]. Obwohl er in einem Teil Großalbaniens tätig gewesen ist, hat er doch im eigentlichen Albanien gar nichts getan. Darüber hinaus gehörten die Bezirke, wo er predigte, vor seinem Tode noch nicht zu Albanien. Nur anachronistisch könnte man sie Albanien nennen.

Im Gegensatz dazu betrifft die Bekehrung des um 370 gestorbenen Arsakiden Uṙnayr[109] das nördliche Königreich[110]. Selbstverständlich bleibt die neue Religion lange ziemlich schwach, denn sie muss der mazdäischen Unterdrückung und Verfolgung widerstehen. Zum Beispiel empört sich der zuerst abgefallene König Vačʿē II. (457–463) gegen die Perser. Dann tritt er ab, um Mönch zu werden[111].

Wann wurde Uṙnayr getauft ? Sollten wir der *Geschichte Albaniens* glauben, so geschah es zu Lebzeiten des Grigor Illuminator, sogar vor der Mission des Grigoris. Aber diese Chronologie stimmt nicht mit der Lebenszeit des im Jahre 359 gegen Armenien kämpfenden Königs Uṙnayr überein[112]. Letzterer kann kein anderer sein als der erste christliche König Albaniens[113]. Er muss sich also zwei oder drei Menschenalter später als Trdat, völlig unabhängig von seinem armenischen Vorgänger, zum Christentum bekehrt haben. Vielleicht berief er den ersten Bischof – wie der iberische König Mirian III. – direkt aus Konstantinopel. Aber ganz anachronistisch lässt der Brief des armenischen Katholikos Giwt (461–478) diesen Bischof über den Hof Trdats in Albanien ankommen[114].

Zweifellos sind die früheren albanischen historischen Überlieferungen stark armenisiert worden. Sicher ist das Apostolat Grigoris' wirklich, doch nur in den erst später ins Königreich Albanien eingeschlossenen südlichen Bezirken ausgeübt worden. Irreführend war es, diese Verkündigung in die nördlichen Bezirke zu verlegen. Aber dadurch wurde der erste christliche König Uṙnayr zu einem Zeitgenossen des Gregorius Illuminator.

Ebenso wurde auch Ełišay dem Thaddäus untergeordnet. In beiden Fällen wurde die Christianisierung Albaniens zu einer bloßen Fortsetzung der Bekehrung Armeniens. Somit wurde die jeder eigenen historischen Legitimität beraubte albanische Kirche zu einem Satelliten des armenischen Patriarchats, vom dem sie sich, trotz mancher Bemühungen vom 7. bis zum 10. Jh., nie befreien konnte[115]. Vom 11. Jh. an verschwand die albanische Sprache ziemlich schnell. Dann wurde das albanische Patriarchat zu einer der verschiedenen Prälaturen, die sich im spätmittelalterlichen Armenien um den Vorrang stritten.

*

In den drei christlichen Staaten des Kaukasus bietet die Entwicklung einer das apostolische Zeitalter und die konstantinische Epoche umschließenden doppelten Historiographie eine so deutliche und präzise Übereinstimmung dar, dass man sie zuerst kaum

[107] Die Lokalisierung der Vatnean Ebene, wo Grigoris gemartert wurde, ist bestritten. Entweder befindet sie sich südlich vom Gugarkʿ, neben dem „nördlichen See" (Cildir See, Hewsen 1989, Landkarte G 3), oder südlich der Kura, neben Pʿaytakaran (Hewsen 1989, L 5), oder nördlich der Kura, im Königreich der Mazkʿutkʿ (Hewsen 1989, M 2). Garsoïan 1989, S. 377, vertritt die erste Lokalisierung, die aufgrund der ältesten Quellen die wahrscheinlichste ist.

[108] Hasratian 1977.

[109] Toumanoff 1990, S. 91 (10. 4). 568. – Vgl. auch K. N. Yuzbachian, Einige Bemerkungen, u. S. 185.

[110] GA I, 9. 11 (Dowsett 1961, S. 8. 11).

[111] GA I, 10 (Dowsett 1961, S. 9–10).

[112] Buzandaran V, 5 (Garsoïan 1989, S. 194–196) und Ammianus Marcellinus XVIII, 6, 22. XIX 2, 3, der zwar einen albanischen König, aber nicht dessen Namen erwähnt.

[113] Dowsett 1961, S. 7, Anm. 6.

[114] GA I, 11 (Dowsett 1961, S. 11).

[115] Mahé 1994, S. 479. 492. 514. 517. 518.

vor dem Verdacht verteidigen kann, dass eine solche Konvergenz künstlich sei, als ob die drei nationalen Überlieferungen nachträglich miteinander in Einklang gebracht worden wären. Schreitet man von der Vermutung zur Anklage über, so würde man dazu neigen, diese Bearbeitung einerseits den politischen Absichten Armeniens, und andererseits dem frühen Aufblühen einer armenischen Geschichtsschreibung zuzuschreiben.

Im 4. Jh., als das Christentum zur überwiegenden religiösen Macht des römischen Kaiserreichs wird, ist Armenien der erste der drei kaukasischen Staaten, der den neuen Glauben empfängt. Am Anfang des 5. Jhs. schafft Armenien es wieder, vor den anderen sein nationales Alphabet und seine eigene Literatur zu haben. Die älteste historiographische Quelle über diese Zeitperiode gibt sogar an, dass der Armenier Maštocʿ die drei kaukasischen Alphabete erfunden habe[116]. Auch gegen die mazdäischen Verfolgungen stellt sich Armenien an die Spitze des Widerstandes. Somit gewinnt es bei den Schwesterkirchen unbestreitbares Ansehen und mächtigen Einfluss.

Demzufolge war Armenien wohl in der Lage, die Historiographie Iberiens und Albaniens zu beinflussen oder sogar zu ändern. So wird Uṙnayr zum Jünger des Grigorius Illuminator und Nino zur Genossin Hṙipʿsimēs. Doch behalten die iberischen und die albanischen Überlieferungen eine unbeugsame historische Realität, eine auffallende Eigentümlichkeit und eine materiell überprüfbare Echtheit, auch wenn Sie sekundär mit der Bekehrung Armeniens verknüpft und nach denselben literarischen Mustern umgeformt sind.

Während die christologischen Erörterungen des 5. und 6. Jhs. das Auftauchen von Nationalkirchen, die ihre Unabhängigkeit betonen, begünstigen, beginnen letztere vom 7. Jh. an, auf ihre apostolische Herkunft Anspruch zu erheben. Wieder kommt Armenien als erstes: die Thaddäussage war schon am Anfang des 5. Jhs. übersetzt und bearbeitet worden. Etwas später verfügt Albanien über die Geschichte Ełišays. Georgien arbeitet die Andreassage viel langsamer aus. Vom 7. bis zum 9. Jh. konzentriert es sich lieber auf das *Leben Ninos*.

Soll man daher diese apostolischen Erzählungen als opportunistische Mythen und fabelhafte Erfindungen ansehen? In manchen Fällen ist die Feststellung der Tatsachen viel schwieriger und weniger beweiskräftig als für die Christianisierung im 4. Jh. Die Texte enthalten sicher viel Sagenhaftes.

Doch finden die erwähnten Ereignisse in Gebieten statt, deren Beschreibung eine echte Ortskenntnis verrät und auf die lokale mündliche Überlieferung hinweist. Betrachten wir es näher, so fußt die Zweiheit der transkaukasischen Historiographie mehr auf geographischen als auf chronologischen Faktoren. Jeder der drei betroffenen Staaten besitzt sozusagen ein doppeltes Gebiet und übt eine Geopolitik mit doppeltem Boden aus. So vereinigt Großalbanien das rein albanische nördliche Ufer der Kura mit den früher armenischen Bezirken des Südens. Georgien verteilt sich auf zwei verschiedene Länder beiderseits des Imeretier Gebirges. Auch Armenien setzt dem Norden den Süden, d. h. der Öffnung nach Kappadokien die nach Syro-Mesopotamien gegenüber.

So hat die Bekehrung im 4. Jh. nur Nordarmenien und Iberien betroffen. Südarmenien und Westgeorgien sind einzeln christianisiert worden. Aber die Ausarbeitung einer unitarischen Nationalhistoriographie hat dazu geführt, die beiden Überlieferungen zusammenzuschmelzen, indem man sie anachronistisch einem und demselben Gebiete zugeschrieben hat. Thaddäus und Grigor, von welchen der erstere nur den Süden und der

[116] Koriwn, Kap. 9. 17. 24 (Winkler 1994, S. 99. 105. 109). Dass Maštocʿ, der Erfinder der armenischen Schrift, auch das albanische Alphabet geschaffen hat, ist kaum zu bezweifeln. Was das georgische Alphabet betrifft, so unterscheidet sich seine Struktur vom Armenischen und Albanischen. Daher wird die Autorschaft des Maštocʿ von manchen Spezialisten verneint.

zweite nur den Norden des Landes bekehrt hatte, sind zu zwei aufeinanderfolgenden Aposteln ganz Armeniens geworden. Dasselbe gilt auch für Andreas und Nino in Georgien. Was Armenien betrifft, so gehörte die nationale Einheit im 4. Jh. schon der Vergangenheit an; in Georgien war dagegen diese Einheit noch nicht verwirklicht. Aber die nationale Ideologie überholte die Chronologie.

Der Fall Albaniens lässt sich auf dasselbe Muster zurückführen, obwohl es etwas komplizierter ist. Das Apostolat Ełišays und die Bekehrung Uṙnayrs betreffen den nördlichen Teil des Landes. Das Martyrium des Grigoris findet im Süden statt. Aber nach der Entstehung des vereinigten Königreiches geht die Historiographie nicht mehr auf Einzelheiten ein. Da man nach dem Jahre 387 die Mission des Grigoris in Albanien lokalisieren durfte, war man der Überzeugung, das ganze Land als eine Erweiterung des Grigor'schen Bereiches in Anspruch nehmen zu dürfen. Zwischen Thaddäus und Ełišay musste auch eine Verbindung entstehen.

Wie bei allen ostchristlichen Völkern gehört auch im Kaukasus der Glaube zur nationalen Identität. Da die Nation sich ihrer Einheit stark bewusst ist, wird jede Christianisierung eines einzelnen Bezirks auf das ganze Gebiet bezogen. Geographische Fixierungen werden vernachlässigt. Bestehen bleibt nur eine Chronologie des kollektiven Gedächtnisses und der mündlichen Überlieferung, die man summarisch auf zwei Epochen aufteilt. Aus dieser in letzter Instanz auf mündlichen Quellen begründeten Überlieferung entsteht die doppelte Historiographie der Transkaukasischen Königreiche.

Bibliographie

AKOPJAN (A. A.) 1987 = Albanien-Ałuankʿ in den griechischen, lateinischen und altarmenischen Quellen, Jerewan [auf russisch]

ALEKSIDZE (Z.) 1980 = Arseni Sapareli: Über die Trennung der Iberer und der Armenier, Tbilisi [georgisch; kommentierte kritische Ausgabe]

ALEKSIDZE (Z.) – MAHÉ (J.-P.), Découverte d'un texte albanien: une langue ancienne du Caucase retrouvée, *Comptes rendus de l'Académie des Inscriptions et Belles-Lettres* (1997), S. 517–532, Paris

ANANIAN (P.) 1961 = La data e le circostanze della consecrazione di S. Gregorio Illuminatore, *Muséon* 74 (1961), S. 43–73. 317–360

BOTTÉRO (J.) – KRAMER (N. S.) 1989 = Lorsque les dieux faisaient l'homme. Mythologie mésopotamienne, Paris

Buch der Briefe = ed.1906 Tiflis [armenisch; Sammlung der dogmatischen Briefe der armenischen Patriarchen]

CALZOLARI (V.) 1995 = La leggenda di Santa Tecla nella letteratura armena antica (*Tesi dell'Università Cattolica del Sacro Cuore di Milano*), Mailand

CHARACHIDZE (G.) 1968 = Le système religieux de la Géorgie païenne, Paris

DELEHAYE (H.) 1966 = Les passions des martyrs et les genres littéraires, Brussels

DESREUMAUX (A.) 1993 = Histoire du roi Abgar et de Jésus, Turnhout [französische Übersetzung des syrischen Textes der Lehre Addais und der griechischen und äthiopischen Versionen]

DONABÉDIAN (P.) 1988–89 = Une nouvelle mise au point sur l'Albanie du Caucase, *REArm* 21 (1988–89), S. 485–495 [kritische Zusammenfassung von Akopjan 1987]

DOWSETT (C. F. J.) 1961 = The History of the Caucasian Albanians by Movsēs Dasxuranc'i, London

DUCHESNE (L.) 1908 = Histoire ancienne de l'Église chrétienne, Bd II, Paris

EMINE (J.-R.) 1867 = Histoire d'Abgar et de la prédication de Thaddée, in: LANGLOIS (V.), Collection des historiens anciens et modernes de l'Arménie, Bd. I, Paris, S. 313–321

EREMYAN (S. T.) 1979 = Das Königreich Großarmenien, Jerewan [Landkarte]

ESBROECK (M. VAN) 1971 = Un nouveau témoin du texte d'Agathange, *REArm* 8 (1971), S. 13–167

ESBROECK (M. VAN) 1972 = Le roi Sanatrouk et l'apôtre Thaddée, *REArm* 9 (1972), S. 241–283

GARITTE (G.) 1946 = Documents pour l'étude du livre d'Agathange, Vatican

GARSOÏAN (N. G.) 1985 = Armenia between Byzantium and the Sasanians, Aldershot [Aufsatzsammlung I–XII]

GARSOÏAN (N. G.) 1989 = The Epic Histories Attributed to Pawstos Buzand, Cambridge (Ma) [Kommentierte englische Übersetzung]

GARSOÏAN (N. G.) 1999 = L'Église arménienne et le grand schisme d'Orient, *CSCO* 574, Leuven

Gelzer (H.) – Hilgenfeld (H.) – Cuntz (O.) 1898 = Patrum Nicaenorum Nomina, Leipzig

Hakobyan (V.) 1964 = Armenisches Kanonbuch, Bd. I, Jerewan [armenisch]

Hasratian (M.) 1977 = L'ensemble architectural d'Amaras, *REArm* 12 (1977), S. 243–259

Hewsen (R. H.) 1989 = Armenia upon the Death of King Trdat the Great ca. 330 [Landkarte in Garsoïan 1989]

Kettenhofen (E.) 1995 = Tirdâd und die Inschrift von Paikuli. Kritik der Quellen zur Geschichte Armeniens im späten 3. und frühen 4. Jh. n. Chr., Wiesbaden

Kettenhofen (E.) 1998 = Die Arsakiden in den armenischen Quellen, in: Wiesehöfer (J.), Das Partherreich und seine Zeugnisse, Wiesbaden, S. 325–354

Khroutchkova (L. G.) 1989 = Les édifices paléochrétiens en Transcaucasie occidentale, *Byzantion* 59 (1989), S. 88–127

Lang (D. M.) 1956 = Lives and Legends of the Georgian Saints, London

Lang (D. M.) 1966 = The Georgians, London

Mahé (J.-P.) 1992 = Entre Moïse et Mahomet: réflexions sur l'historiographie arménienne, *REArm* 23 (1992), S. 121–153

Mahé (A. et J.-P.) 1993 = Histoire de l'Arménie par Moïse de Khorène, Paris

Mahé (J.-P.) 1994 = Die armenische Kirche von 611 bis 1066, in Vauchez (A.) et alii, Die Geschichte des Christentums, Bd. IV, Freiburg i. B., S. 473–542

Mahé (J.-P.) 1994–95 = Agathange et la destruction des sanctuaires païens, *École Pratique des Hautes Études* (*Sciences historiques et philologiques*), Livret 10 (1994–95), S. 32–35, Paris

Mahé (J.-P.) 1999 = Le premier siècle de l'Arménie chrétienne (298–387): de la littérature à l'histoire, in: Mutafian (Cl.), Roma-Armenia, S. 64–72, Rom

Manandyan (H.) 1978 = Werke II, Jerewan [armenisch; kritische Theorie der Geschichte des armenischen Volkes II,1]

Manaseryan (R.) 1997 = Armenien von Artawazd bis Trdat dem Großen, Jerewan [armenisch]

Martin-Hisard (B.) 1997 = Jalons pour une histoire du culte de sainte Nino (fin IVe–XIIIe s.), in: Mahé (J.-P.) – Thomson (R. W.), From Byzantium to Iran. Armenian Studies in Honour of Nina G. Garsoïan, Atlanta (Ga), S. 53–80

Martin-Hisard (B.) 1998 = Le christianisme et l'Église dans le monde géorgien, in: Mayeur (J.-M.) et alii, Histoire du christianisme, Bd. III (de 432 à 610), Paris, S. 1169–1239

Meillet (A.) 1977 = Études de linguistique et de philologie arméniennes, Bd. II, Leuven [Aufsatzsammlung]

Ōrmanean (M.) 1912 = Nationale Geschichte, Bd I, Konstantinopel [armenisch]

Outtier (B.) 1996 = La christianisation du Caucase, in: Il Caucaso: cerniera fra culture dal Mediterraneo alla Persia, secoli IV–XI (*Settimane di studio del Centro italiano di studi sull'alto Medioevo* XLIII), Spoleto, Bd. I, S. 553–570

Pätsch (G.) 1975 = Die Bekehrung Georgiens, *Bedi Kartlisa* 33 (1975), S. 288–337

Pätsch (G.) 1985 = Das Leben Kartlis, Leipzig

Peeters (P.) 1942 = Saint Grégoire l'Illuminateur dans le calendrier lapidaire de Naples, *Analecta Bollandiana* 60 (1942), S. 91–130

Pierre (M. J.) 1999 = Les premières missions à l'est. La génération apostolique, *Le Monde de la Bible* n° 119 (mai-juin 1999), S. 11–15

Q'auxčišvili (S.) 1955 = Das Leben Kartlis, Bd. I, Tbilisi [georgisch; kritische Ausgabe der altgeorgischen Chroniken]

Tamarati (M.) 1910 = L'Église géorgienne des origines jusqu'à nos jours, Rom

Tarchnišvili (M.) – Assfalg (J.) 1955 = Geschichte der kirchlichen georgischen Literatur, Vatican

Tēr Mkrtč'ean (G.) – Kanayeanc' (St.) 1909 = Agat'angełay patmut'iwn Hayoc', Tiflis

Tēr Movsēsean (M.) 1897 = Sokrates, Kirchengeschichte, Vałaršapat [Kritische Ausgabe der zwei altarmenischen Redaktionen]

Thélamon (F.) 1981 = Païens et chrétiens au IVe siècle. L'apport de l'Histoire Ecclésiastique de Rufin d'Aquilée, Paris

Thomson (R. W.) 1976 = Agathangelos. History of the Armenians, New York [armenischer Text und kommentierte englische Übersetzung]

Thomson (R. W.) 1994 = Studies in Armenian Literature and Christianity, Aldershot [Aufsatzsammlung I–XII]

Toumanoff (C.) 1943 = Medieval Georgian Historical Literature (VIIth–XVth centuries), *Traditio* 1 (1943), S. 139–182

Toumanoff (C.) 1963 = Studies in Christian Caucasian History, Georgetown University

Toumanoff (C.) 1969 = The Third Century Armenian Arsacids. A Chronological and Genealogical Commentary, *REArm* 6 (1969), S. 233–281

Winkler (G.) 1980 = Our Present Knowledge of the History of Agathangelos and its Oriental Versions, *REArm* 14 (1980), S. 125–141

Winkler (G.) 1994 = Koriwns Biographie des Mesrop Maštoc', Rom

WERNER SEIBT / WIEN

DER HISTORISCHE HINTERGRUND UND DIE CHRONOLOGIE DER CHRISTIANISIERUNG ARMENIENS BZW. DER TAUFE KÖNIG TRDATS (CA. 315)

Durch jahrhundertalte Traditionen fast geheiligte Überlieferungen auf ihre historische Stichhaltigkeit und Verlässlichkeit kritisch zu hinterfragen, ist zwar unabdingbare Pflicht des forschenden Geschichtswissenschaftlers, wird aber nicht immer den Beifall derer finden, die aufgrund neuer, vielleicht überraschender Ergebnisse ihr Geschichtsbild etwas abändern sollten. Das gilt nicht zuletzt für das Datum der Taufe des armenischen Königs Trdat/Tiridates – das „offizielle" Jahr 301, an dem weite Kreise immer noch festhalten wollen, ist jedoch heute höchst unwahrscheinlich geworden[1].

Armenier werden – ohne lange nachzudenken – *Agathangelos/Agatʿangełos* als Hauptquelle für die Christianisierung ihres Landes angeben. Das ist sicher richtig, wobei aber bei manchen die Frage, welcher Agathangelos gemeint ist, Erstaunen hervorrufen wird. Heute wissen wir, dass es mehrere Redaktionen gibt, wobei vielfach redaktionelle Eingriffe, Umarbeitungen und vor allem Erweiterungen vorgenommen wurden, um bestimmte ideologisch-kirchenpolitische Zielsetzungen der jeweiligen Zeit zu verfolgen bzw. durch Projektion in die Vergangenheit mit dem Glanz von *mos maiorum* zu versehen, oder einfach dadurch, dass man solche Positionen unangefochtenen Persönlichkeiten der Vergangenheit unterschob, über jede Diskussion zu stellen[2].

Agathangelos, der in vielen Sprachen erhalten ist[3], natürlich auch in Armenisch[4], fußt auf einer älteren Quelle, die wir gewöhnlich als *Vita Gregorii* bezeichnen, die in einer alten

---

[1] Eine kritische Bewertung vieler älterer Datierungen bietet E. KETTENHOFEN, Tirdād und die Inschrift von Paikuli. Kritik der Quellen zur Geschichte Armeniens im späten 3. und frühen 4. Jh. n. Chr. Wiesbaden 1995, bes. 92–104.

[2] Sehr hilfreich ist die präzise Analyse von M. VAN ESBROECK, Agathangelos, in: *Lexikon für Antike u. Christentum*, Suppl.-Lieferung 1/2. Stuttgart 1985, 239–248. Vgl. auch G. WINKLER, Our present knowledge of the history of Agatʿangełos and its oriental versions. *REArm* 14 (1980) 124–141.

[3] Immer noch sehr wertvoll G. GARITTE, Documents pour l'étude du livre d'Agathange (*Studi e Testi* 127). Vatikanstadt 1946. Zur griechischen Version s. G. LAFONTAINE, La version grecque ancienne du livre arménien d'Agathange. Édition critique (*Publ. Inst. Orient. Louvain* 7). Louvain-la-Neuve 1973. Die aus dem Griechischen übersetzte arabische Version des Cod. Sinait. arab. 395 edierte A. N. TER-ŁEVONDYAN, Agatʿangełosi arabakan nor χmbagrutʿyunë. Erevan 1968. Eine sehr reiche (ältere) Bibliographie findet sich bei H. S. ANASYAN, Haykakan matenagitutʿyun. I. Erevan 1959, 151–213, eine neue bei R. W. THOMSON, A Bibliography of Classical Armenian Literature to 1500 AD. Turnhout 1995, 90–95. Ἀγαθάγγελος, der „Bringer der guten, frohen Botschaft des Evangeliums" (wobei das εὐ, „gut", des Wortes Evangelium bewusst durch ἀγαθός, eher in Richtung „tugendhaft", ersetzt wurde), wäre durchaus als griechischer Beiname Gregors sinnvoll.

[4] Agathangeli historia Armeniae (Agatʿangełay patmutʿiwn Hayocʿ), edd. G. TĒR-MKRTČʿEAN – ST. KANAYEANCʿ. Tbilisi 1909; vgl. dazu GARITTE, Documents 2f. Agathangelos, History of the Armenians. Translation and Commentary by R. W. THOMSON. New York 1976 (enthält auch den armenischen Text).

griechischen (*Vo*)[5], einer jüngeren griechischen (*Vg*)[6] und einer – weniger wertvollen – arabischen Version (*Va*)[7] vorliegt, leider nicht in einer armenischen, weshalb von vielen Armenologen insbesondere *Vo* bislang zuwenig oder gar nicht zur Kenntnis genommen, geschweige denn ausgewertet wurde[8]. Und doch ist davon auszugehen, dass die älteste Version nicht nur deshalb, weil sie den Geschehnissen näher ist, im Zweifelsfalle den Vorzug verdient, sondern auch weil sie weniger bewusste Retuschen erwarten lässt als die späteren. Nur ist auch diese Vita von den Ereignissen, die sie erzählt, deutlich entfernt[9].

Vo, die somit älteste, uns heute greifbare Erzählung über die Christianisierung Armeniens, scheint das Ergebnis der zusammenschauenden Verarbeitung mehrerer früher, z.T. wohl auch divergierender bzw. widersprüchlicher Quellen zu sein, wie etwa einer ersten *Vita Gregorii*, einem Martyrium der hl. Jungfrauen um Rhipsimē und Gaianē, Gründungslegenden einzelner Kirchen und anderer „Wallfahrtsorte", wohl auch Berichten über die Christianisierung südarmenischer Regionen aus dem syrischen Raum her usw., mit intendierter besonderer Betonung der Bedeutung Gregors als entscheidendem Kristallisationspunkt der Gesamtentwicklung. Zumindest einige dieser Texte mögen in griechischer Sprache abgefasst gewesen sein und vielleicht sogar in das 4. Jh. zurückreichen.

Was die historische Relevanz der mannigfaltigen Nachrichten betrifft, muss man sich stets vor Augen halten, dass hagiographische Werke anderen Gesetzen gehorchen als strenge, wissenschaftliche Geschichtsschreibung, denn christliche Erbauung und Stärkung im Glauben bzw. Gottvertrauen sind hier allemal wichtiger als „positivistische Tatsachenberichte" und Verwandtes[10].

---

[5] G. Garitte, La vie grecque inédite de saint Grégoire d'Arménie (Ms. 4 d'Ochrida). *AnBoll* 83 (1965) 233–290, Text 257–290.

[6] S. Garitte, Documents 23–116.

[7] Am besten in der lateinischen Übersetzung von Garitte, Documents 27–116 zu benützen; vgl. auch S. 141–149 und A. N. Ter-Łevondyan, Agatʽangełosi arabakan χmbagrutʽyan norahayt amboljakan bnagirë. *Patma-banasirakan Handes* 1973/1, 209–237.

[8] Während manche Rezensionen der Vita tätsächlich jüngere Veränderungen aufweisen, halten wir die Ohrider Version für die älteste erhaltene Variante, älter als alle Versionen des Agathangelos. Auch J.-P. Mahé, Die Bekehrung Transkaukasiens: Eine Historiographie mit doppeltem Boden, o. S. 108f., stuft Versionen der *Vita Gregorii* als älter als Agathangelos ein. Anders z. B. N. Garsoïan, L'église arménienne et le grand schisme d'Orient (*CSCO* 574, Subsidia 100). Louvain 1999, 4: „et les recensions de la *Vie de saint Grégoire* (dites série V), sont probablement plus tardives."

[9] Eine Datierung in das späte 5. Jh. erwog v. Esbrœck, Agathangelos 244f. So auch V. Inglisian, Die armenische Literatur, in: Handbuch der Orientalistik I/7: Armenische und kaukasische Sprachen. Leiden – Köln 1963, 162 („um 491"). Andere setzen bereits Agathangelos früher an, etwa 460, vgl. Garsoïan, Schisme 9; Thomson, a.O. XC. Mahé, a.O. 109, erwägt für die *Vita Gregorii* eine Datierung nach 435, aber vor Agathangelos, der frühestens 451 geschaffen wurde. Sollte etwa der Tod des letzten Gregoriden im Mannesstamm (438), auf den möglicherweise ein Richtungsstreit über die zukünftige Orientierung der armenischen Kirche folgte, „Auslöser" für die *Vita*, die die Bedeutung Gregors nachdrücklich hervorhob, vielleicht sogar seine Rolle überbewertete, gewesen sein? Dass dieses Werk – jedenfalls bereits in der ältesten uns heute fassbaren Form – deutliche politisch-ideologische Aspekte aufweist, wird wohl niemand bezweifeln.
Andererseits kommen wir mit einem Datum um die Mitte des 5. Jh. in eine „heiße Phase" der christologischen Auseinandersetzungen. Es sollte sich lohnen, die vielen Predigten, die Gregor immer wieder in den Mund gelegt werden, bzw. deren Unterschiede in den einzelnen Versionen, unter diesem Gesichtspunkt genauer zu analysieren.

[10] Vgl. allgemein H. Delehaye, Cinq leçons sur la méthode hagiographique. Brüssel 1934; ders., Les passions des martyrs et les genres littéraires (*Subsidia hagiographica* 13 B). Brüssel ²1966; ders., L'ancienne hagiographie byzantine. Les sources, les premiers modèles, la formation des genres. Conférences prononcées au Collège de France en 1935, edd. B. Joassart – X. Lequeux (*Subs. hagiogr.* 73). Brüssel 1991; R. Aigrain, L'hagiographie. Ses sources, ses méthodes, son histoire. Poitiers 1953.

Eine der zentralen chronologischen Fragen ist, wann der armenische König Trdat als römischer Vasall die Macht in Großarmenien übernahm. Die Inschrift von Paikuli, die nun vorzüglich aufgearbeitet ist[11], macht jedes Datum vor 293 unmöglich, da damals noch der Sāsānide Narseh die Macht in Großarmenien innehatte, von wo er aufbrach, um persischer Großkönig zu werden – wie auch immer sein offizieller Titel in Armenien gelautet haben mag[12]. Es spricht alles dafür, dass Trdat erst im Zusammenhang mit den römischen Siegen und dem daraus resultierenden Frieden von Nisibis (eher 298–299 als 297–298[13]) König von Großarmenien wurde. Ich möchte dagegen nicht *a priori* ausschließen, dass Trat schon zuvor römischer Vasall in einem anderen, kleinen Teil Armeniens bzw. Subkaukasiens gewesen war[14] – das Rätsel um den König Trdat, der in der Paikuli-Inschrift (allerdings ohne geographische Angabe) genannt wird[15], ist weiterhin ungelöst. Sicherlich haben etwa die „Satrapien" im Süden Großarmeniens, südlich bzw. südwestlich des Van-Sees (z.B. Sophene, Anzitene, Arzanene, Korduene, Moxoene, Adiabene) eine gewisse Autonomie gegenüber Großarmenien besessen[16].

Was bedeutete diese Krönung aber *realiter*? Der König von Großarmenien war kein absoluter Herrscher, er teilte seine Macht mit den Häuptern der Fürstengeschlechter, die einzelne Regionen, Provinzen oder Gaue unter ihrer Kontrolle hatten, zumeist seit Generationen. Manche dieser *Nacharare* waren eher romfreundlich, andere eher iranfreundlich, wobei dann noch zwischen größeren Nahverhältnissen zu den Sāsāniden oder zu den Arsakiden zu unterscheiden war. Von „Parteien" im modernen Sinn kann man natürlich nicht sprechen, aber doch von einer traditionellen politischen Disposition, die allerdings auch auf die jeweiligen Machtverhältnisse Rücksicht zu nehmen imstande war. Nach jahrzehntelanger Vorherrschaft der Sāsāniden war eine – wohl eher kleine – Allianz mehr oder weniger romfreundlicher Geschlechter kaum eine entsprechend tragfähige Machtbasis – Trdat blieb also auf Jahre hinaus massiv auf die Unterstützung durch die römische Militärmacht angewiesen, denn schon allein die offene oder bedeckt agierende Opposition im eigenen Land sollte nicht unterschätzt werden. Das darf bei allen weiteren Überlegungen nicht aus den Augen verloren werden. Zudem erwecken die Quellen den Eindruck, dass Trdats Macht in den nördlicheren Regionen Armeniens erheblich größer war als im Süden[17].

An der Wende vom 3. zum 4. Jh. haben wir es im *Imperium Romanum* mit der *Tetrarchie* zu tun, jenem von Diokletian geschaffenen System der „vier Herrscher". Diokletian, der sich als *dominus et deus* fühlte und titulieren ließ, d. h. als Herr (wie ein

---

[11] Kettenhofen, Paikuli (s. Anm. 1) 1–47.

[12] Vgl. Kettenhofen, a.O. 42–45.

[13] Während man in der älteren Literatur (und teilweise bis heute) – den *Consularia Constantinopolitana* und der Oster-Chronik folgend – 297 als das Jahr der persischen Niederlage ansah, machte T. D. Barnes, Imperial Campaigns, A.D. 285–311. *Phoenix* 30 (1976) = Early Christianity and the Roman Empire. London 1984, XII, 182–186; 188; 193, das Jahr 298 für die römischen Erfolge und „the winter of 298/99 or the spring of 299" für den Friedensschluss wahrscheinlich; später sprach er sich eindeutig für das spätere Datum aus: Barnes, Constantine and Eusebius. Cambridge, Mass. – London 1981, 18: „Serious negotiation for a treaty began in the spring of 299". Vgl. auch R. C. Blockley, East Roman Foreign Policy. Formation and Conduct from Diocletian to Anastasius (*Arca* 30). Leeds 1992, 5–7.

[14] Zur Problematik vgl. etwa Kettenhofen 68–70.

[15] Tyldt MLK' / Tirdād Šāh; vgl. Kettenhofen 26, Nr. 12; 42–47; 144–164. Dieser Tirdād muss nicht unbedingt sāsānidischer Vasall gewesen sein; auch ein – diplomatisch geschickter bzw. politisch kluger – Vasall Roms konnte um gute Beziehungen zum mächtigen Nachbarn bemüht gewesen sein und eine entsprechende Botschaft bzw. Glückwunschadresse abgesandt haben.

[16] Zu ihrer Bedeutung in dieser Zeit allgemein bzw. für die Christianisierung aus dem syrischen Raum her vgl. Garsoïan, Schisme 8–22.

[17] Vgl. Garsoïan, Schisme 8f. (mit weiterer Lit.); 43.

Herr über Sklaven!) und Gott, hatte mit dem im Reich bereits erstarkten Christentum echte Probleme; nachdem er eine Zeit lang eher tolerant die starke Ausbreitung des neuen Glaubens geduldet hatte, wollte er als typischer Militär auch die religiöse Frage mit Gewalt lösen, sodass es zu großangelegten Christenverfolgungen kam, bei denen sich nicht zuletzt der Caesar Galerius hervortat, bes. ab 303[18] (nach ersten Aktionen bereits zwischen 299 und 301). Es ist denkbar, dass so manche römische Untertanen vor den Verfolgern in andere Provinzen, z.T. auch in Vasallenreiche auswichen, etwa nach Armenien. Es ist ferner gut möglich, dass in einzelnen Regionen diesseits und jenseits der Reichsgrenzen die dortigen Machthaber den Christen gegenüber zumindest zeitweise tolerant, ja sogar aufgeschlossen waren – manche Andeutungen in den Quellen könnten in diese Richtung weisen. Ich halte dafür, dass auch Gregor primär aus solchen Erwägungen nach Armenien kam, vielleicht auch nur in eine an das Römische Reich angrenzende Region, in der die Macht des großarmenischen Königs im allgemeinen nicht zu sehr zum Tragen kam.

Offenbar nahmen dergleichen Migrationen aber ein solches Ausmaß an, dass die Kaiser ihre Vasallen aufforderten, gegen die Christen, insbesondere wohl gegen römische Emigranten vorzugehen. Ein aus Kappadokien kommender Gregor[19], der später zum großen Missionar Armeniens werden sollte, wurde ein Opfer dieser Entwicklung – welche Martern er tatsächlich erleiden musste, ist nicht so sicher, denn die hagiographische Überlieferung hat hier oft „ausgeschmückt", aber jedenfalls wurde er eingekerkert, und das über mehrere Jahre. Das Martyrium der heiligen Jungfrauen um Gaiane und Rhipsime erfolgte im Zuge einer späteren Welle der Christenverfolgungen, vielleicht erst auf Druck oder sogar mit Mitwirkung des Maximinus Daia, etwa zwischen 311 und 313[20]. Im Osten des Reiches waren Galerius und sein Caesar Maximinus Daia erklärte Christenverfolger. Als sich Galerius im April 311, kurz vor seinem Tod, zu einem ersten Toleranzedikt entschloss, setzte Maximinus, den seine Truppen 310 ebenfalls zum Augustus ausgerufen hatten, die Verfolgungen unbeirrt fort[21]. Nachdem er gegen Licinius unterlegen war, beging er im Sommer 313 in Tarsos Selbstmord[22]. Erst damit endete die schwere Zeit der Bedrängnis und Verfolgung für die Christen des Ostens.

Es ist keineswegs erwiesen, dass Trdat ein „begeisterter" Christenverfolger war, möglicherweise suchte er um 312 auch um ein besseres Verhältnis zu den Sāsāniden nach – die angebliche Verwandlung in einen Eber könnte so gedeutet werden[23]. Auch der Kampf des Maximinus Daia gegen nicht näher bestimmte „Armenier", den Eusebios für diese Zeit

[18] Am 23. 2. 303 erließ Diokletian im Namen der Tetrarchen ein erstes Edikt, dem bald weitere folgten; vgl. J. Vogt, Christenverfolgung I (historisch, Bewertung durch Heiden und Christen), in: *RAC* II. Stuttgart 1954, 1195–1198.

[19] Griechisch Γρηγόριος (byzantinisch Grigorios ausgesprochen), armenisch Grigor Lusaworič', „der das Licht (der Offenbarung) brachte", lateinisch Gregorius Illuminator, der „Erleuchter".

[20] Vgl. dazu den Beitrag von M. van Esbrœck in diesem Band, u. S. 171–179.

[21] Vgl. Vogt, a.O. 1198–1201; H. Lietzmann, Geschichte der Alten Kirche. Bd. III. Berlin 1938 (Ndr. Berlin – New York 1999) 55–59; 63–65.

[22] Vgl. A. H. M. Jones – J. R. Martindale – J. Morris, The Prosopography of the Later Roman Empire I. Cambridge 1971, 579, Nr. 12 (Galerius Valerius Maximinus Daia).

[23] Auf den Eber als Emblem des sāsānidischen Königssiegels verweist M. van Esbrœck, Agathangelos, in: *RAC*, Suppl.-Lieferung 1/2. Stuttgart 1985, 247. Dass bei der Ausgestaltung dieser „Story" die dem Lukianos zugeschriebene Geschichte Λούκιος ἢ ὄνος über die Verwandlung eines Lucius in einen Esel und die schlussendliche Entzauberung (die ihrerseits auf die Metamorphosen des Lukios von Patrai zurückgeht und auch in einer Bearbeitung des Apuleius vorliegt) Pate gestanden ist, betont mit Recht Mahé, a.O. 108.

erwähnt[24], mag in obigen Zusammenhang gehören. Als sich die Toleranz im römischen Reich, besonders auch in dessen Osthälfte, durchsetzte (also 313), endeten auch die Verfolgungen in Armenien, und Gregor wurde frei.

Die Vita lässt ihn alsbald in missionarischen Eifer verfallen, es fällt aber auf, dass die Ortsnamen, die in diesem Zusammenhang genannt werden, im wesentlichen ein eher kleines Gebiet im Westen Armeniens, an der römischen Grenze betreffen, Δαραναλί[25]/ Δαρανάλεως χώρα[26] /Δαραναλιτῶν πατρίς[27] (Daranałik‘[28]), Ἐρήζ[29]/μεγάλη κώμη Ἐρίζων[30]/ Ἔρηζ[31] in Ἐκελισηνή[32] (Ekełeac‘[33]) und Δερζανή[34]/Δερζῶν χώρα[35]/Δερζανιτῶν πατρίς[36] (Derǰan, in der Gegend des heutigen Erzincan, westlich von Erzurum). Hatte dort ein besonders toleranter oder sogar christenfreundlicher Nacharar das Heft in der Hand? Gab es dort schon stärkere Christengemeinden? Dass auch König Trdat irgendwie in die Erzählung hereingenommen wird, wirkt dagegen fast gekünstelt, wie eine Vorwegnahme späterer Entwicklungen.

Dann ist von der Reise Gregors nach Kaisareia die Rede[37], wo er durch Erzbischof Leontios – inmitten einer großen Zahl von Bischöfen[38] – im Jahre 314 die Bischofsweihe erhält[39]. Dass das im Zusammenhang einer „Synode von Kaisareia" geschah, ist zwar fast *communis opinio*, aber doch nicht sicher[40]. Ich möchte unterstreichen, dass Gregor zum Bischof geweiht wurde, was nicht unbedingt von Anfang an „Bischof von Großarmenien"

---

[24] Hist. Eccl. IX 8, 2; 8, 4; vgl. KETTENHOFEN, a.O. 81–84.

[25] Vo 117 (S. 282 GARITTE).

[26] Vg 108 (S. 77, 15 GARITTE, Documents).

[27] Ag 131 (S. 300, 11 LAFONTAINE).

[28] Hier wurde Gregor später auch begraben, vgl. Buzandaran patmut‘iwnk‘ III 2 (S. 67 trad. GARSOÏAN).

[29] Vo 118 (S. 283 GARITTE).

[30] Vg 111 (78, 15 GARITTE, Documents).

[31] Ag 132 (S. 301, 8 LAFONTAINE).

[32] Ag 132 (S. 301, 6 LAFONTAINE).

[33] Hier wurde später Aristakēs, der jüngere Sohn Gregors, begraben, s. Buzandaran patm. a.O.

[34] Vo 119 (S. 284 GARITTE).

[35] Vg 115 (80, 7 GARITTE, Documents).

[36] Ag 133 (S. 302, 14 LAFONTAINE).

[37] Während Vo 121 (286 GARITTE) nur allgemein von den höchsten Würdenträgern des Reiches als Begleitern spricht, ohne konkrete Angaben zu liefern, wird Vg 124 (83, 12f. GARITTE, Documents) schon deutlicher, indem Artavasd Mamikonean als Anführer namhaft gemacht wird: Ἀρτάβα<σ>δος, ὁ τῶν Μαμακουνιανῶν γενεάρχης καὶ ἀσπαραπέτης ὁ πάσης Ἀρμενίας; Ag 135 (304f. LAFONTAINE) dagegen nennt 16 Würdenträger, teilweise mit der von ihnen verwalteten Provinz, wobei offenbar die Satrapien einen wichtigen Anteil ausmachen, obiger Mamikonean dagegen nicht erscheint – als erster wird vielmehr der ἄρχων τῶν Ἀγγελιτῶν οἴκου aufgeführt. Die Zahl 16 ist allerdings auch Vg bekannt, wie etwas später erhellt (131 [86, 1 GARITTE, Documents]). Vielleicht ist es aber gar nicht so sicher, dass Gregor wirklich mit großem Gefolge nach Kaisareia zog – möglicherweise hat der Hagiograph nur seinem Wunschdenken Ausdruck verliehen.

[38] Vo 122: Καὶ κατὰ κέλευσιν τοῦ ἁγιωτάτου ἐπισκόπου Λεοντίου συνήχθη ἐπισκόπων πλῆθος. Ag 139 wird deutlicher: γίνεται σύνοδος ἐπισκόπων ἐν τῇ Καισαρείων πόλει. Vg 133 (86, 10–12 GARITTE, Documents) gibt die Zahl der anwesenden Metropoliten und Bischöfe mit 20 an und hebt explizit den Metropoliten von Chalkedon hervor. Dass alle diese Hierarchen allerdings ὑπ' αὐτὸν (sc. Λεόντιον) gestanden wären, kann wohl als Übertreibung gewertet werden, ebenso wie die überhöhte Bezeichnung πατριάρχης, die gelegentlich erscheint (z. B. Vg 145 [91, 2 GARITTE, Documents]).

[39] Vo 120–123 (S. 285–287 GARITTE). Mit Recht wies R. THOMSON in der Einleitung zur englischen Übersetzung (LXVI) darauf hin, dass so manche Einzelheit der Erzählung bei Agathangelos Koriwns Bericht über die Reise von Maštoc‘ nach Konstantinopel entlehnt ist.

[40] Vgl. dazu auch KETTENHOFEN 87–89. M. van Esbrœck wies kürzlich in einem Vortrag in Halle darauf hin, dass viele Einzelheiten, die dieser Synode zugeschrieben werden, eher auf die etwas später abgehaltene Synode von Neokaisareia zu beziehen sind.

bedeuten musste! Dennoch wurde Kaisareia durch diesen Akt in gewissem Sinne „Mutterkirche“ Armeniens, jedenfalls für eine gewisse Zeitspanne, bis eben Armenien nach Autokephalie verlangte. Gregor selbst als Katholikos oder als Patriarchen zu bezeichnen, wäre anachronistisch, aber Agathangelos entwirft sein Bild von Gregor als Modell für alle späteren Patriarchen, zugleich auch als Integrationsfigur für ein einheitliches, großes, christliches Armenien[41].

Nach dieser Synode kehrte Gregor in den Osten zurück, aber nicht zum armenischen König, wie man nach so manchen Andeutungen der Vita postulieren würde, sondern in eine andere Grenzprovinz, nach Tarōn (Ταραυνή[42]/Ταραυνῶν χώρα[43]), westlich des Van-Sees, um dort kraftvoll zu missionieren bzw. gegen heidnische Kulte anzukämpfen, nun auch eifrig die Taufe zu spenden, Priester zu weihen und Kirchen sowie Baptisterien zu errichten, mit Astišat/Aštišat/Yaštišat[44] (᾿Αστισάτ[45]/᾿Αστισατῶν κώμη[46]/τόπος ᾿Αστισάττου[47]) als erstem Stützpunkt. Astišat blieb auch später ein sehr wichtiges kirchliches Zentrum, bei Ps.-Faustus (Buzandaran patmutʿiwnkʿ) ist von der „großen und ersten Kirche, der Mutter der Kirchen ganz Armeniens“ die Rede[48]. Möglicherweise gab es hier in Tarōn schon früher Christen, eher aus dem syrischen Raum bzw. über die Satrapien her missioniert, vielleicht sogar bereits mit einer gewissen kirchlichen Hierarchie[49]. Sollten etwa mit der Betonung der missionarischen Aktivität Gregors auch in dieser Region zwei konkurrierende Traditionen über die Christianisierung armenischer Territorien „auf einen gemeinsamen Nenner“ gebracht werden? Auf Tarōn, wo die mächtige Familie Mamikonean den Ton angab und auch die Nachkommen Gregors über umfangreiche Besitzungen gebieten sollten, hatte der König von Großarmenien, dessen Herrschaftszentrum eher im Norden Armeniens lag, wohl nur eingeschränkten Einfluss.

Erst jetzt wird der König Großarmeniens persönlich aktiv, er begibt sich mit großem Gefolge[50] in Richtung Tarōn, und trifft am Murat, bei Bagavan[51] (im Kanton Bagrevand),

---

[41] In einer Zeit, als Armenien zwischen Byzanz und dem Iran geteilt war, als das Königtum der Arsakiden/Aršakuni in beiden Teilen des Landes bereits Geschichte war, als die Kirche – unter der Führung mächtiger Patriarchen – zum wichtigen, integrierenden Bindeglied der Nation geworden war. Vgl. dazu auch Thomson, Introduction XCIIf.

[42] Vo 124 (S. 287 Garitte): ἐν τῇ πατρίδι Ταραυνῆς. Von einem längeren Aufenthalt Grigors und allfälliger Begleiter in Sebasteia, den Ag 139 erwähnt, findet sich in Vo nichts.

[43] Vg 154 (95, 9 Garitte, Documents); vgl. Ag 140 (S. 310 Lafontaine).

[44] Letztere Form findet sich bei Aa 809 (346 Thomson); vgl. dazu S. 490, Anm. 6.

[45] Vo 124 (287 Garitte).

[46] Vg 155 (95, 10 Garitte, Documents).

[47] Ag 140 (311, 9 Lafontaine).

[48] Buzandaran patm. III 14 (S. 47), (S. 86 trad. Garsoïan). Vgl. Garsoïan, Schisme 26f. Zur wichtigen Rolle von Astišat als religiöses Zentrum der Armenier vgl. auch Thomson, Introduction LXXVI; dens., Mission, Conversion, and Christianization: The Armenian Example. *Harvard Ukrainian Studies* 12/13 (1988/89) 35 = Studies in Armenian Literature and Christianity. Aldershot 1994, III 35: Astišat war der Sitz des Oberhauptes der armenischen Kirche bis zur Teilung Armeniens zwischen Byzanz und Iran, erst dann zogen die Patriarchen nach Vałaršapat.

[49] Zur Bedeutung der „syrischen Komponente“ für die Christianisierung insbesondere Südarmeniens, nicht zuletzt von Edessa aus, vgl. R. W. Thomson, Syrian Christianity and the Conversion of Armenia, u. S. 159–169.

[50] Während bei Vo 126 und Ag 143 nur vom militärischen Gefolge des Königs sowie von dessen Gattin und Schwester die Rede ist, bindet die jüngere griechische Version Vg ebenso wie Va, die arabische Version (Garitte, Documents 97), – sicher unhistorisch – auch die Könige der Iberer, der Lazen und der Albaner ein: ἅμα … καὶ ᾿Ιβέροις, Λαζοῖς καὶ ᾿Αλβανοῖς βασιλεῦσιν καὶ φυλάρχαις τε καὶ γενεάρχαις. Dementsprechend werden nach der Taufe des Königs und seines Gefolges auch gleich Priester zu den Iberern, Lazen (in der arabischen Version finden sich anstelle der Lazen die Abchazen!) und Albanern geschickt (l.c. 98f.)!

[51] Vo 126 (S. 288f.): εἰς πόλιν καλουμένην Βαγαβάν, ἔνθα τὴν ἀρχὴν τῆς πορείας ὁ Εὐφράτης ποταμὸς ἔχει. Vgl. Ag 143 (S. 314, 11): ἐν κωμοπόλει Βαγαυάν.

mit Gregor zusammen. In einem großen Staats- und Festakt lässt er sich, seine Familie und die anwesenden Würdenträger des Reiches taufen. Damit kommen wir in ein Datum frühestens 314, eher bereits 315.

Natürlich ist es denkbar, dass Trdat schon deutlich früher Sympathien für die Christen empfand und so in seinem Herzen bereits vor 314 zumindest ein „halber Christ" war, aber getauft wurde er erst damals, und erst mit dem danach herausgegebenen Edikt[52] wurde das Christentum zur verbindlichen Staatsreligion in Großarmenien[53].

Wenn man die Zahlen 15 und 17, die in der Überlieferung eine wichtige Rolle spielen, als Regierungsjahre Trdats interpretiert, wurde Gregor im 15. Jahr[54], also ca. 313 aus dem Kerker befreit, und Trdat im 17. Jahr, ca. 315 getauft[55]. Das alles fügt sich m.E. sehr schön zu einem Mosaik zusammen.

Damals hatte sich im Römischen Reich der Toleranzgedanke, wie oben dargelegt, voll durchgesetzt, es bedeutete keineswegs einen Affront gegen die Römer, wenn sich ein Vasallenkönig zum Christentum bekannte – hätte er es um 303 oder um 310 gewagt, Trdat wäre innerhalb kürzester Zeit gestürzt gewesen.

Der gläubige Christ sieht in der Bekehrung eines Volkes primär das Walten des Heiligen Geistes, das Wirken göttlicher Gnade. Es ist ferner durchaus denkbar, dass sich Trdat nicht zuletzt aufgrund der Erkenntnis der moralischen Überlegenheit der neuen Religion gegenüber dem traditionellen Heidentum bekehrte, der Historiker möchte jedoch auch fragen, was die Entscheidung Trdats als Realpolitiker zusätzlich beeinflusst haben könnte. Da waren zunächst die iranischen Priester und Kultstätten mit enormem Reichtum, zu denen Trdat, der römische Vasall, kaum ein positives Verhältnis aufgebaut hatte; auch die altarmenischen Priesterschaften und Tempel hatten sehr reiche Besitzungen, deren sie aufgrund des neuen Rechtsstatus verlustig gingen. Die Vita betont zwar in ähnlichem Zusammenhang gelegentlich, dass Gregor solche Reichtümer an die Armen verteilte, aber bei einer Neuverteilung, die ja auch die neue Kirche ökonomisch absichern sollte, kamen die königlichen Interessen wohl nicht zu kurz. Und dann gab das Mäntelchen des religiösen Eifers und der missionarischen Begeisterung einen idealen Vorwand, mit der iranfreundlichen Opposition im Lande abzurechnen – dass sich diese allerdings nicht kampflos geschlagen gab, kommt in der Geschichte der folgenden Jahrzehnte immer wieder zum Vorschein.

Es fällt auf, dass Gregor in der Folge zwar Bischöfe für Armenien weihte[56] und durch sein mönchisches Vorbild in Askese und Enthaltsamkeit junge Männer für diese Lebens-

---

52 Ein solches Edikt nennt auch Sozomenos II 8, 1 ausdrücklich: Λέγεται γὰρ Τηριδάτην … Χριστιανὸν γενέσθαι καὶ πάντας τοὺς ἀρχομένους ὑφ' ἑνὶ κηρύγματι προστάξαι ὁμοίως θρησκεύειν.

53 Es soll jedoch nicht verschwiegen werden, dass Trdat wohl nicht der erste Herrscher war, der sich taufen ließ. Wahrscheinlich war das Abgar VIII. von Edessa (177–212), auch wenn die entsprechende Überlieferung legendenhaft ist. Vgl. dazu Mahé a.O. 111; Lietzmann (s. A. 21) II. Berlin 1936, 266f.

54 Z. B. Vo 90 (S. 267 Garitte): ὅτι σήμερον δεκαπέντε ἔτη ἔχει ἐν λάκκῳ βαθυτάτῳ.

55 Vgl. Movsēs Xorenacʿi II 91: Im 17. Jahr der Regierung Trdats nahm Grigor den Thron des Apostels Thaddaeus ein.

56 Während es Vo 129 (290 Garitte) bei einer ganz allgemein gehaltenen Notiz bewenden lässt, werden spätere Fassungen schon deutlicher. Ag 153, 15 u. 154, 1–2 (324f. Lafontaine) nennt an erster Stelle Ἀλβῖνος, der zum Bischof τοῖς μέρεσιν Εὐφράτου τοῦ ποταμοῦ eingesetzt wurde, dann aber auch zum „Hofbischof" wurde (ἐν τῷ παλατίῳ τοῦ βασιλέως ἐπιστάτην ἔταξεν). Er sollte später – der Legende nach – auch Trdat, Gregor und Aristakēs zu Konstantin d. Großen begleiten: Ag 164, 8 (335 Lafontaine). Das entspricht der Darstellung in Aa, nur dass der Mann dort Ałbianos heißt (§ 845f. u. 873, S. 378, 380 u. 406 Thomson). Schwieriger werden die Verhältnisse bei Vg 172 (102f. Garitte, Documents), da hier sowohl an erster Stelle ein Ἀλβιανός als Bischof τῇ χώρᾳ Βαγραυανδῶν als auch – erheblich später – ein Ἄλβιος als Bischof des Hauses Mamikonean (τοῦ γένους τῶν Μα<μα>κονιανῶν) erscheint, die ihre Besitzungen in

art begeisterte[57], die später zum „missionarischen Sauerteig" werden konnten – denn mit der Taufe allein war es ja noch längst nicht getan –, dass Gregor aber nicht in die armenische Hauptstadt zog oder sonst als Erzbischof von Armenien nachdrücklich in Erscheinung trat[58]. Die Vita betont klar, dass er in Zurückgezogenheit lebte, in der Einsamkeit der Berge, vorwiegend wieder im westlichen Grenzgebiet des Reiches, in den Quellgebieten des Euphrat[59].

Vielleicht klingt für manchen die Frage provokant, welcher Herkunft denn Gregor überhaupt war. Die Legende von der Abstammung aus dem parthischen Königsgeschlecht der Arsakiden, dem ja auch die meisten Könige Großarmeniens angehörten, ist wohl eine späte Erfindung[60], um einerseits für seine Nachkommen den Anspruch auf den Patriarchenthron Armeniens abzusichern[61], und andererseits die sāsānidischen Oberherren späterer Zeit zu beruhigen, denen allzu starke Verbindungen der armenischen Kirche mit der byzantinischen politisch höchst bedenklich erscheinen mussten. Man machte sich dabei nicht einmal die Mühe, einen schönen iranischen Namen für den Vater Gregors zu erfinden, sondern nannte ihn einfach Anak, den Übeltäter, ja selbst die Identifikation mit einem Königsmörder wog leichter als der Verdacht zu großer Nähe zu Rom bzw. Byzanz.

Wir wissen, dass Gregor aus Kappadokien kam, verheiratet war[62] und Kinder hatte[63]. War er Armenier, war er „Grieche", stammte er aus dem kappadokisch-armenisch-pontischen Grenzgebiet[64]? Sicher war er griechisch gebildet, wahrscheinlich konnte er

---

Tarōn und Taik' hatten; da dieses Haus den Generalissimus Großarmeniens stellte (τοῦ μεγάλου στρατηγοῦ καὶ ἀσπαραπέτου), der sich zumeist in der Nähe des Königs aufhielt, sollte auch dieser Albios stets in der Nähe des Königs sein.

Zu späteren Verdiensten dieses Hofbischofs bzw. zu Nachkommen, die auch zu patriarchalen Ehren gelangten, vgl. z. B. GARSOÏAN, Schisme 38–41.

57 Insbesondere bemühte man sich offenbar um die Söhne der heidnischen Priesterschaft.

58 Ein kurzer, doch recht allgemeiner Absatz (Vo 128) berichtet, dass das Evangelium durch Gregor ἐν πάσῃ τῇ τῶν Ἀρμενίων χώρᾳ ἄχρι Κλιμηδῶν καὶ Ἀλβανῶν verkündet wurde, und dass er Bischöfe und Kleriker weihte, ja sogar Klöster gründete. Das erstaunliche Κλιμηδῶν wurde von Garitte ansprechend zu καὶ Μήδων korrigiert. Ag 152 (S. 323, 5 – 324, 12) gefällt sich in einer deutlichen Steigerung: Καὶ ἐν πάσῃ τῇ χώρᾳ τῆς Ἀρμενίας … ἀπὸ Σαταλῶν τῆς πόλεως μέχρι τῆς χώρας Χάλτων καὶ Καλαρσῶν, ἕως ὁρίων Μασαχουτῶν Οὔννων καὶ πυλῶν Ἀλανῶν καὶ μερῶν Κασπίων καὶ Φατακαρανῆς πόλεως Ἀρμενίων βασιλείας. Καὶ ἀπὸ τῆς τῶν Ἀμιδηνῶν πόλεως μέχρι Νισίβεως παρὰ τὰ ὅρια Ἀσσυρίων ἕως Νορσιράκων γῆς καὶ Κορδουΐτων καὶ τῆς ὀχυρωτάτης χώρας τῶν Μήδων καὶ τοῦ οἴκου Μαχούρτων τοῦ ἄρχοντος καὶ μέχρι Ἀτραπατακάν. Dieses geographische Konzept geht schon deutlich über die Grenzen Großarmeniens hinaus – allerdings ist tatsächlich anzunehmen, dass das Christentum allmählich von Armenien aus auch in den Nachbarländern an Bedeutung gewann. Damit soll aber nicht vorschnell postuliert werden, dass auch schon die allerersten Kontakte – etwa nach Albanien – über Armenien gelaufen sein müssen.

59 Vo 129 (S. 290). Vgl. dazu auch Ag 154 (S. 325f.).

60 Ebenso ist die Legende, die selbst Movsēs Xorenac'i (II 74) nur mit Vorbehalt bietet, dass Anak den Gregor im Gau Artaz (in der Provinz Vaspurakan, westlich des Araxes, gegenüber von Naχičevan, demgemäß südlich bzw. südöstlich des Ararat; vgl. R.H. HEWSEN, The Geography of Ananias of Širak. Wiesbaden 1992, 63, 63 A u. 66), in der Nähe des Grabmals für Thaddaeus, gezeugt habe, ein spätes Konstrukt, um die beiden Hauptmissionare der armenischen Tradition in einen gewissen Zusammenhang zu bringen.

61 In diesem Sinne wäre ein zölibatäres Leben – zumindest vor der Erhebung zum Patriarchen – sogar „kontraproduktiv" gewesen.

62 Seine Gattin hieß Iulitta: GARITTE, Documents 72, § 97, 10.

63 Seine beiden Söhne Aristakēs und Vrt'anēs wurden Oberhirten Armeniens.

64 In dem angeblichen Antwort-Brief des Königs Trdat an Kaiser Diokletian, der um Nachforschungen bezüglich Rhipsimes ersucht hatte, erwähnt der Armenier den eingekerkerten Gregor einfach als Γρηγόριόν τινα καππαδόκην: GARITTE, Documents 37, 9 (Vg § 40); vgl. S. 218 u. 287. Der entsprechende Passus in der Ohrider Handschrift ist nicht ediert. Die arabische Version der Vita erwähnt diesen Brief nicht. Sollte andererseits die enge Verbindung zu den Gauen am Ursprung des Euphrat (Fırat N.) ein Indiz auf seine Heimat bedeuten? Vgl. auch M.-L. CHAUMONT, Sur l'origine de Saint Grégoire d'Arménie. *Muséon* 102 (1989) 115–130.

oder lernte zumindest später Armenisch – armenisch schreiben konnte er natürlich nicht, denn die armenische Schrift wurde bekanntlich ja erst fast ein Jahrhundert später erfunden. Viele Völker wurden durch Missionare, die von außen kamen, bekehrt ...

Ein letzter Hinweis sei noch gestattet. Während Konstantin d. Gr. im Westen des Imperium Romanum nach seinem großen Sieg das Christentum und die Kirche nachhaltig förderte, ja zu einer der Säulen seiner Herrschaft erkor[65] (was natürlich auch Gefahren für die weitere Entwicklung der Kirche in sich barg), rückte Licinius, der Herrscher des Ostens, von seiner anfänglich ebenfalls toleranten Politik allmählich wieder ab und gerierte sich etwa ab 321 eher als Gegner der Christen[66]. Möglicherweise hatte das auch gewisse Auswirkungen auf die Position der neu gegründeten Kirche in Armenien und das Verhalten Gregors. Aber mit dem Endsieg Konstantins (324) war auch dieser Stein des Anstoßes beseitigt, obgleich sich Konstantin wohl erst auf dem Totenbett taufen ließ. Staatsreligion wurde das Christentum im Imperium Romanum (bzw. bereits im frühbyzantinischen Staat) erst im späten 4. Jh., also viel später als in Armenien.

[65] Vgl. dazu auch A. Kee, Constantine versus Christ. The Triumph of Ideology. London 1982; T. D. Barnes, Constantine and Eusebius. Cambridge, Mass. 1981.

[66] Vgl. Vogt, *RAC* II 1201f.; Lietzmann (s. A. 21) III 65f.

MICHEL THIERRY / ÉTAMPES

L'HISTOIRE DE SAINT GRÉGOIRE PEINTE DANS L'ÉGLISE SAINT-GRÉGOIRE DE TIGRAN HONENCʿ À ANI (1215)

L'église Saint-Grégoire de Tigran Honencʿ que ce riche propriétaire, proche de l'amir spasalar Zakare, a fondée à Ani en 1215 est de plan typiquement arménien en croix inscrite ouverte, variante réduite des salles à coupole. Elle a été ornée d'un important décor sculpté (peut-être œuvre d'artistes musulmans) et peint (exécuté par des artistes géorgiens). Elle est encore en assez bon état pour que son analyse contribue a enrichir de façon substantielle notre connaissance de l'art arménien au début du XIIIe siècle.

Le bras ouest de l'église est consacré à un cycle de la conversion de l'Arménie par saint Grégoire, l'Illuminateur. Les épisodes occupent les parois des niches nord et sud, ainsi que les parties du mur ouest, qui encadrent la porte d'entrée.

Le récit hagiographique, développé ici en 17 scènes, est à notre connaissance, le premier exemple connu[1]; il est donc impossible pour l'instant d'en discerner les sources iconographiques; en revanche, les sources littéraires sont plus claires car les images traduisent assez fidèlement les événements contenus dans l'Histoire du règne de Tiridate et de la prédication de saint Grégoire l'Illuminateur écrite par Agathange. On ne sait que peu de chose de ce dernier qui fut, au dire de Moïse de Khorène, secrétaire de Tiridate et dont le nom suggère une origine grecque[2]. En fait le récit ne semble pas antérieur au Ve siècle. Il associe trois histoires, assez logiquement articulées entre elles, à savoir la biographie de Tiridate III, roi d'Arménie[3], le martyre de saint Grégoire, le martyre des Vierges hripsimiennes.

Toutefois les textes d'Agathange qui nous sont parvenus présentent des variantes assez notables entre elles pour que G. Garitte ait pu les répartir en deux groupes relevant de deux traditions différentes:

---

1 Il existait certes, à titre de figures isolées, des images de saint Grégoire dès le haut moyen âge et peut-être de Tiridate (transformé en sanglier), bien que les figures de saint affublé d'une tête animale soient, selon certains auteurs celles de saint Christophe cynocéphale. Des cycles décrivant «ses tourments, ses vertus» et les saintes hripsimiennes sont cités dans les églises arméniennes par une Apologie des Images du VIIe siècle, mais ils ont disparu (DER NERSESSIAN 1973, 384). Deux scènes figurent exceptionnellement dans le Psautier de Londres, daté de 1066 et dû à un miniaturiste de Césarée de Cappadoce; elles illustrent le verset 3 du Ps. 39 (40): «Il m'a tiré de la fosse de misère et du bourbier fangeux. Puis sur le roc, il a placé mes pieds et affermi mes pas»; on voit Grégoire retiré du Puits Profond et une scène symbolique de la conversion de Tiridate que Grégoire mène à l'église (DER NERSESSIAN 1973, 59–60; EADEM, L'Illustration des Psautiers grecs du Moyen Âge, II. Londres add. 19.352, Paris, 1970, 12, 29, 96, fig. 82). Les cycles développés sont beaucoup plus tardifs, des XVIIe et XVIIIe siècles, notamment en Italie (à San Grigorio de Naples par le peintre Francesco Francazano en 1635 et à l'église des Arméniens de Livourne par le peintre François Rivière en 1718) ainsi qu'à la Nouvelle-Djoulfa en Iran dans les églises de Bethléem (1627), du Saint-Sauveur (1660) (où le peintre Yovhannēs Merkʿuz est nommé) et de Saint-Grégoire (1728). J. CARSWELL, New Julfa. The Armenian Churches and Other Buildings, Oxford 1968, 21–6, 33, 50, 62.

2 Cf. H. AČAŘYAN, Hayocʿ anjnanunneri bařaran, s.v., nr. 1.

3 Sur ce roi, cf. ibid., nr. 4.

1. D'une part l'«Agathange» arménien (Aa) et l'«Agathange» grec (Ag) avec les recensions dérivées, en particulier une arabe (Ar) et plusieurs géorgiennes.

2. D'autre part des versions indépendantes de Aa qu'on réunit sous le sigle V: recensions arabes (Va et Var) et recensions grecques (Vg et Vo) auxquelles il faut ajouter une version *karšuni* (Vk)[4]. Le cycle de Saint-Grégoire de Tigran Honencʿ ne se rattache expressément à aucune de ces versions.

Nous donnons ci-dessous un tableau de concordance entre le cycle de notre église et les principaux épisodes du Livre d'Agathange[5]:

1	2	G	E	Aa	Ag	Vg	Va	Vk	Vo
Prologue. Introduction. Enface	–	1/2	I–III						
Vie de Tiridate	–	3	IV–V						
Martyre de Grégoire	**1–6**	4	VI–VII	48–122	22–55	1–28	1–8	50–71	
Histoire des Hripsimiennes	**7–8**	5	VIII–X	137–210	57–89	30–50	10–37	74–135	91
Prédication. Vision	**9–11**	6/7	XI–XIV	211–777	90–127	51–82	38–52	136–206	91
Epuration de l'Arménie	–	8	XV						
Sacre de Grégoire à Césarée	**12**	9	XVI	791–808	134–9	116–53	104–41	219–41	120–129
Christianisation de l'Armenie	**13–14**	10	XVII–XVIII	806–66	140–61	154–73	142–56	243–63	124–129
Retraite et Succession	**15–16**	11	XIX	858–62	157–9	192–8	112–6	264–74	129
Visite à Constantin. Concile	–	12/3	XX						
Fin de la vie de Grégoire	**17**	14	XXI	888	169		187	287–92	129

On notera d'abord qu'à Saint-Grégoire de Tigran Honencʿ l'ordre du récit n'est pas respecté. On remarquera ensuite que le cycle de l'église concorde avec les textes mais qu'il comporte des lacunes plus ou moins explicables. C'est ainsi qu'il manque l'enfance de Grégoire qui aurait pu être utile pour l'intelligence des événements suivants.

En revanche, que fasse défaut la vie de Tiridate jusqu'à son accession au trône se justifie dans un récit axé sur la vie de Grégoire. Dans le développement du martyre du saint, le peintre s'est arrêté au quatrième supplice, les huit autres sont supprimés, soit par manque de place, soit peut-être par crainte d'une certaine monotonie.

Dans l'épisode du martyre des Vierges hripsimiennes, le châtiment de Tiridate est omis et c'est d'autant plus surprenant que la figure du roi transformé en sanglier est justement un thème fréquent dans l'art arménien dès le VIe siècle[6]. Il semble qu'ici la

[4] Les recensions, éditions et études de cet ouvrage sont nombreuses et nous nous contenterons de citer les principales et les plus récentes. Pour la recension arménienne d'Agathange (Aa), cf. l'édition et traduction anglaise Thomson 1976; pour la grecque (Ag): Lafontaine 1973 et Garitte 1946 et aussi (Vo): Garitte 1965; pour les arabes (Va, Ar, Aar) ibidem et Ter-Levondyan 1973, pour les géorgiennes Muradyan 1982. Cf. aussi *BHO* s.v. Gregorius et Tiridatus. Pour les études cf. Peeters 1942; Garitte 1946 avec la nouvelle version grecque (Vg) et van Esbroeck 1971 avec la version karšuni (Vk). Pour les origines et les filiations voir aussi Muradyan 1982, 10 et Garsoïan 1985, XII.

[5] Colonne 1: Les épisodes du récit; colonne 2: Numération des scènes figurées dans l'église Saint-Grégoire de Tigran Honencʿ; colonne G: classement des épisodes par G. Garitte; colonne E: classement des épisodes par M. van Esbroeck; colonne Aa: Paragraphes de Aa; colonne Ag: Paragraphes de Ag; colonne Va: Paragraphes de Va; colonne Vg: Paragraphes de Vg; colonne Vk: Paragraphes de Vk; colonne Vo: Paragraphes de Vo.

[6] Encore que ce point soit contesté et que, pour certains, le saint à tête animale figuré sur les stèles paléo-arméniennes ne soit point celle (à tête de sanglier) de Tiridate, mais celle (à tête de chien) de saint Christophe.

punition soit seulement suggérée par le départ à la chasse de la cour royale. Un autre omission insolite est celle de l'éradication du paganisme en Arménie, pourtant facile à figurer par une destruction d'idoles comme c'est fréquent dans l'iconographie chrétienne. Enfin la suppression de la visite de Tiridate et de Grégoire à l'empereur Constantin et au pape Sylvestre[7], comme le silence sur le concile de Nicée, peuvent-ils avoir une signification religieuse ou politique? Ce serait là une contradiction avec le chalcédonisme ambiant de l'époque géorgienne et, du reste, les Arméniens se sont toujours et sans restriction déclarés fidèles aux canons du concile de Nicée. D'autre part on a remarqué que Sylvestre est présent dans l'abside à côté d'Aristakés, tous deux réunis par les circonstances du concile de Nicée. Nous pensons donc que les omissions sont sans caractère dogmatique et qu'elles tiennent peut-être à l'ignorance que l'on avait des événements lointains.

Depuis les affirmations de N. Marr qui rattachait les peintures de cette église à une version arabe de l'Agathange, traduite d'un texte grec, et celui-ci d'un original arménien «chalcédonien», la connaissance des textes a bénéficié de découvertes et recherches qui ont largement battu en brèche les conclusions de cet auteur, lequel avait pour but avoué de prouver l'existence «d'affinités religieuses entre l'Arménie et la Géorgie». Le qualificatif «chalcédonien» attribué par N. Marr à l'original du Vᵉ siècle n'a guère de sens parce qu'il est antérieur au schisme. Le texte est, en fait, anti-nestorien, anti-perse[8].

Comme nous le verrons le cycle peint s'écarte du Livre d'Agathange, moins par des éléments descriptifs que par les lacunes qu'il comporte et l'addition d'une image-clé de la Conversion de la Géorgie, la légende de la Colonne vivante de Nino. Ainsi, on peut se demander si le peintre n'a pas suivi librement, plutôt que telle version connue du texte, un récit hagiographique tardif[9], voire des traditions orales, résumés plus ou moins fidèles du texte ancien.

Nous allons maintenant décrire et analyser l'iconographie du cycle.

1. Comparution de saint Grégoire devant le roi Tiridate[10]

ႼႤ ႧႰႣႠႲႨႱ:ႼჂ:ႢႢႪ:ႼႠႰႨႣႢႨႬႠ:ႢႬႩႨႧႾ
ႥႠႣ
წ<ინაშ>ე თრდატის წ<მიდა>ჲ გ<რი-
>გ<ო>ლ წარიდგინა გ<ა>ნკითხვად

«Devant Tiridate (Trdat'i), st. Grégoire (Grigol) est présenté pour être jugé»

Le roi Tiridate est revêtu d'une longue robe à empiècements et porte la couronne royale[11]. Son visage à courte barbe et cheveux massés derrière les oreilles est semblable à celui de Constantin représenté dans le bras sud, ce qui n'est pas fortuit, le peintre ayant ainsi assimilé les deux souverains, tous deux convertis au christianisme, tous deux propa-

---

[7] On sait que les deux traditions littéraires (cf. n. 4) présentent des différences, la série Va et Vg dit que c'est Constantin qui invita Tiridate, alors que la série Aa-Ag présente le voyage à Rome comme une initiative de Tiridate.

[8] Marr 1905, 64; Garitte 1946, 347–50; N. Adontz, Armenija v epochu Iustiniana, St. Pétersbourg 1908, 351–3, et trad. anglaise dans: Garsoïan 1970, 231–2, 266–7.

[9] Comme le *Synaxaire de Tēr Israyēl*, compilé au XIIIᵉ siècle, publié dans *PO*, en particulier 6/2, 309–16 (saint Grégoire) et 16/1, 131–4 (saint Tiridate).

[10] Aa 48–68; Ag 21–8; Vg 1–11; Vk 50–2. Cf. pl. 5.

[11] Il s'agit de la couronne (Tʻag) géorgienne dérivée du *stemma* byzantin. C'est celle de la reine Tamar dans les peintures de Vardzia (1184–6). On en trouve des exemples arméniens, comme celles des rois dans un manuscrit de 1269 (Jérusalem nr. 1925, f. 241. Cf. Armenian Art Treasures of Jerusalem, New Rochelle

gateurs de la foi et finalement sanctifiés[12]. Tiridate est assis sur son trône et derrière lui se trouve la foule des courtisans dont se détache un homme âgé debout (même robe, mais de couleur plus foncée, haut bonnet à bouton)[13]. Il pourrait s'agir d'Agathange, secrétaire du roi (Moïse de Khorène, 2, 67). Deux gardes (longs cheveux blonds, tuniques courtes, bas-de-chausses richement brodés et bottines) entraînent Grégoire à comparaître. Le saint est nimbé[14] et vêtu d'une longue robe.

L'image traduit fidèlement le texte du Livre d'Agathange. La scène se passe au camp de Tiridate, près du fleuve Gayl (= Λύκος), non loin d'Erez-Eriza[15], l'été 298[16]. Le roi venait d'accomplir son pélerinage annuel au temple d'Anahit et d'y faire ses dévotions. Il demanda à Grégoire de faire l'offrande de guirlandes à la statue. Celui-ci refusa arguant de sa foi chrétienne. Tiridate tenta encore de le persuader de rendre hommage à la «noble dame Anahit, gloire et vie de notre nation, sous peine de se voir retirer dignités, charges et honneurs», sans compter de multiples tourments à subir. Grégoire s'obstina et la discussion s'envenima. Il refusa d'apostasier, dans les termes habituels à la tradition hagiographique, niant tout pouvoir aux fausses divinités Aramazd et Anahit, comparant à des ânes ceux qui les adorent.

2. Premier supplice (du sel et pendaison)[17]

ႠႵႠ ႼჂ ႢႢႪ ႨႼႠႫႤႡႨႱ ႫႠႰႨႪႨႧႥႰႧ
ႧႠႥႱ ႣႠႵႺႤ
ႥႨႧ
აქა წ<მიდა>ჲ გ<რი>გ<ო>ლ იწამების
მარილითჳრთ თავს დავსდაქცევით

«Ici st. Grégoire est martyrisé avec le sel, la tête en bas»

Le saint (non nimbé semble-t-il) est ligoté et porte une lourde charge de sel fixée dans son dos[18]. Il est hissé la tête en bas par un système de poulies. Les bourreaux (robes courtes, bas et bottes) exécutent la manœuvre.

1979, 72, fig.86), celle du prince Ēač'i Prošean sur un reliquaire de 1300 (Ibidem, fig.158) ou encore celle du même Tiridate sur une bannière de 1441 (Der Nersessian 1977, fig.173). Cette coiffure a été adoptée au XVe siècle par certains patriarches arméniens, cf. J. Muyldermans, Le costume liturgique arménien. Étude historique, *Le Muséon* 39 (1926) 296–7.

[12] Au Moyen Age, qualifier le souverain de «nouveau Constantin» était un cliché cf. C. Jovilet-Levy, L'image du pouvoir dans l'art byzantin à l'époque de la dynastie macédonienne, *Byz* 57 (1987) 457–59.

[13] Coiffure de l'aristocratie géorgienne dont on connaît des équivalents au XIe siècle à Zemo-K'rixi, où il est réhaussé de fourrure, et au XIIe à Pavnisi (Alibegašvili 1979, fig. 25; Eka Privalova, Pavnisi, Tbilisi, 1977, fig. 15, 16). Nous en reverrons des exemples sur des cavaliers accompagnant Tiridate dans une scène suivante (n° 8).

[14] On verra par la suite que le peintre tantôt le dote d'un nimbe tantôt non, sans aucune raison apparente.

[15] Il faut l'identifier au Çardaklı suyu (G. Siwrmenean, Erznka, Le Caire 1947, 429) cours d'eau dont le nom n'est pas porté sur les cartes. Il passe par T'il et se jette dans l'Euphrate à une dizaine de km à l'ouest d'Erzincan. D'après S. Eremyan (S. Eremyan, Hayastanë ëst «Ašxarhac'oyc'»-i (L'Arménie d'après la «Géographie»), Erivan 1963, 155), il naît de la montagne Yediderelar (sic). Gelzer l'identifie au Kuru çay, affluent de l'Euphrate à 75 km en aval d'Erzincan (H. Gelzer, Ungedruckte und ungenügend veröffentlichte Texte der Notitiae Episcopatuum. *Abh. München* 21/3, 1901, 582) et Markwart au Munzur çay (J. Markwart, Südarmenien und die Tigrisquellen nach griechischen und arabischen Geographen. Wien 1930, 429, n. 1).

[16] Marie-Louise Chaumont, Recherches sur l'Histoire d'Arménie, Paris 1969, 135. Mais cf. W. Seibt, au dessus, p. 128.

[17] Aa 69–73; Ag 29–30; Vg 12; Vk 53.

[18] Cette charge de sel fixée à son dos comme on fait pour les ânes, est un raffinement de vengeance infligé par Tiridate, furieux d'avoir été comparé à un âne par Grégoire.

L'image s'inspire des deux recensions du Livre d'Agathange. Il est hissé par poulies comme dans Aa et Ag, la tête en bas comme dans Vk. Il ne semble pas porter de mors, comme dans Ag; il n'est pas enfumé comme dans Vk et sa peau n'est pas raclée comme dans Vg.

Le site des tourments infligés à Grégoire n'est pas précisé dans les textes. Selon la tradition locale, il aurait eu lieu près du temple d'Anahit, sur la rive gauche de l'Euphrate, là où s'élèvent maintenant les ruines du couvent des Supplices[19].

3. Deuxième supplice (pendaison sur immondices et coups)[20]

Ⴀ႕Ⴀ ႼႫ ႢႢႪ ႫႲႤႰႧႠ
ႫႰ ႠႰႱ ႼႠႫႤႡႠႣ
აქა წ<მიდა>ჲ გ<რი>გ<ო>ლ მტერთა
მ<იე>რ არს წამებად

«Ici st. Grégoire va être martyrisé par les ennemis»

Le saint non nimbé est suspendu par un pied à l'aide d'une corde passant sur une poulie que tire l'un des bourreaux. Au-dessous de sa tête des fumées s'échappent d'un tas d'immondices en flammes. De part et d'autre, deux groupes de cinq tortionnaires le flagellent à l'aide de badines mouillées.

Le texte des recensions Aa et Ag est fidèlement respecté, même dans le nombre des bourreaux. Les recensions Vg et Vk sont seulement moins riches en détails.

4. Troisième supplice (des brodequins)[21]

... ႼႫ ႢႢႪႨ ႣႠႢႰႠႢႧႠ ႫႰ ႨႼႠႫႤႡႨႱ
[აქა] წ<მიდა>ჲ გ<რი>გ<ო>ლი დაგრაგ-
თა მ<იე>რ იწამების

«[Ici] st. Grégoire est martyrisé au moyen d'étaux»

La scène est incomplète. Grégoire, cette fois nimbé, est assis, sans qu'on distingue son siège. Il paraît bénir de la main droite ses éxecuteurs. Un bourreau s'incline pour enserrer ses chevilles dans des étaux de bois, trois autres assistent en spectateurs. L'image est conforme à l'ensemble des versions: «Tiridate commanda qu'on apportât des entraves de bois pour lui appliquer sur les os de ses jambes et qu'on les serrât à l'aide de fortes cordes qui faisaient sourdre le sang des extrémités des orteils».

5.Quatrième supplice (des clous)[22]

... ႢႢႪႨ ....ႴႤႰႩႧႠ ႧႠ
ႠႨႻႳႪႡႣႨႱ
[აქა წმიდაჲ] გ<რი>გ<ო>ლი.......ფერკთა
თ<ან>ა აიძულბდის

«[Ici st.] Grégoire .... avec les pieds est obligé de ...»

---

[19] Sur ce couvent, cf. M. Thierry, Voyage archéologique en Turquie orientale. II, *HA* 103 (1989), 31–3.

[20] Aa 74–99; Ag 31–46; Vg 14; Vk 56.

[21] Aa 100–2; Ag 47; Vg 19; Vk 59.

[22] Aa 103; Ag 47; Vg 21; manque à Vk.

Le saint, dont la souffrance est bien rendue, est tiré par un des bourreaux (cheveux blonds, bottines rouges) qui l'invite du geste à se hâter, tandis qu'un autre (petite barbe blonde, tunique noire) le pousse aux épaules. A gauche, un groupe compact d'assistants; à droite un personnage en longue robe et chaussons rouges est assis et désigne Grégoire. Il est entouré de deux serviteurs en robe courte.

La scène est conforme aux textes: «On lui enfonça des coins de fer dans la plante des pieds. Puis on le prit par la main et on le faisait courir çà et là d'un côté à l'autre. Le sang coulait de ses pieds arrosant la terre en abondance». Le personnage assis est certainement Tiridate dirigeant les tortures.

Avec cette image s'interrompt la série des supplices[23].

6. Saint Grégoire dans le puits profond (Xor Virap)[24]

Pas d'inscription visible.

Cette image réunit deux scènes en un même lieu[25]:

a) En haut, le trou quadrilobé du puits[26] sur la margelle duquel Grégoire, non nimbé, cou et chevilles liées par une même corde, est basculé, poussé par deux bourreaux (courtes tuniques foncées, bas brodés) et par un personnage plus âgé, portant barbe blonde et turban dont le pan retombe du côté droit de la tête. Ce dernier, à l'aspect bien typé, qu'on retrouvera dans les scènes 8 et 10, pourrait être identifié au satrape Ōta Amatuni, premier ministre de Tiridate[27]. Plus loin à gauche le roi assis commande l'exécution tandis qu'en face de lui un personnage lui adresse la parole: il s'agit probablement du satrape Tačat lui apprenant que Grégoire est le fils d'Anak, meurtrier de son père. A droite, devant des architectures (la ville d'Artašat), une femme en longue robe et voile retombant sur l'épaule tend un pain.

b) En bas l'image est très déteriorée mais on reconnaît le saint tombé au fond du puits figuré comme une voûte claire. Ici, il est nimbé. Il est assis, à demi-vêtu de guenilles. Il élève ses deux mains en signe de prière cependant que de chaque côté des serpents lovés ou déjà tendus dardent leurs têtes fines vers lui.

Dans l'ensemble la peinture traduit le texte du Livre d'Agathange dans les versions Aa, Ag et Vk. Après avoir été informé par Tačat de l'identité de Grégoire, Tiridate fit jeter le saint, pieds et mains liés, carcan au cou, dans le Puits Profond, véritables oubliettes du château d'Artašat d'où nul n'est jamais sorti vivant et qui était réservé à «ceux qui s'étaient rendus coupables d'homicide». Ils mouraient en effet de faim, à moins qu'ils ne soient mordus par les serpents qui grouillaient au fond. Mais le saint sera respecté par les reptiles comme Daniel par les lions et une veuve viendra chaque nuit lui apporter du pain. L'illustration s'écarte de Va et Vg qui ne mentionnent pas le dénonciateur Tačat et décrivent dans la fosse, Grégoire recevant aussi à boire, et les serpents qui s'éloignent de lui.

---

[23] Pour la suite des supplices cf. VAN ESBROECK 1971, 123.

[24] Aa 121–4; Ag 54 (AG 1867, 132–3); Vg 28; Vk 69–73; Va 8.

[25] On désigne ainsi une des oubliettes du château royal d'Artašat situé sur la rive gauche de l'Araxe, au sud-est d'Erivan. Par la suite, il fut arasé et sur ses fondations fut élevé le couvent de Xor Virap reconstruit presque entièrement au XVIIe siècle, mais qui a conservé du haut moyen âge la chapelle bâtie sur le puits. C'est, de nos jours l'un des buts de pélerinage les plus appréciés des Arméniens (Cf. ĒPʿRIKEAN 1903/ 1, 331–7; 1905/2, 205–9; voir aussi P. CUNEO et collab., Architettura Armena, Roma 1988, nr. 20).

[26] L'orifice est semblable à celui d'un baptistère et ne ressemble en aucune façon à celui du puits qu'on peut encore voir aujourd'hui au monastère de Xor Virap.

[27] Ou Awta (Vg Αὐταῖας). Connu par Moïse de Khorène (2, 77, 82, 84) (Moïse de Khorène 1993, 228, 233, 235). Cf. AČAṘYAN, Hayocʿ anjnanunneri baṙaran, s.v. Ōta.

7. Supplice des saintes Hṙipʿsimē et Gayanē[28]

ႠႵႠ ႨႼႠႫႬႤႱ ႰႨႴႱႨႫႤ ႣႠ ႢႠႢႠႬႤ
აქა იწამნეს რიფსიმე და გაჲანე

«Ici furent martyrisées Ripsime et Gajane»

La composition rectangulaire se divise en trois scènes[29]:

a) En haut et à gauche, un bourreau, tenant par les cheveux une des moniales, s'apprête à lui porter un coup d'épée tandis qu'une autre gît à terre le col tranché et qu'un petit groupe attend le supplice. Derrière un personnage âgé, barbu, portant un turban dont un pan descend sur son épaule droite semble diriger l'exécution. Il s'agit probablement du satrape Óta Amatuni que nous avons vu dans la scène précédente.

b) A droite, on voit un bourreau (cheveux blonds, courte tunique noire, bas de chausse rouges ornés de broderies blanches) tranchant la gorge de Hṙipʿsimē vêtue de noir. Elle est accompagnée d'une douzaine de nonnes aux visages à peine esquissés, comme elle debout et penchées en avant.

c) En bas, sur un fond jaune qui figure peut-être une grotte, un dernier bourreau (cheveux blonds, courte tunique bleue, bas de chausses rouge foncé à losanges blancs) décapite Gayanē qui est à genoux, les mains liées. Devant elle une moniale est étendue, cou tranché et une autre à genoux attend la mort.

Cette composition s'écarte quelques peu des recensions connues du Livre d'Agathange où l'exécution s'est accomplie en deux ou trois temps: d'abord Hṙipʿsimē avec la plupart de ses compagnes, puis la nonne malade qui était restée dans la réserve aux tonneaux, enfin Gayanē avec deux autres religieuses. Ici l'exécution est simultanée, mais le peintre a suggéré la chronologie par la séparation en trois tableautins. On remarquera d'autre part qu'il a répugné à représenter certains détails cruels, comme l'écartèlement, l'arrachage de la langue.

8. Chevauchée du roi Tiridate[30]

Pas d'inscription visible.

Le roi Tiridate, portant le même costume que dans la scène 1, monte un cheval gris verdâtre. De la main gauche il tient les rênes et de la droite il fait un geste d'allocution. Il est accompagné de trois hauts personnages portant des coiffures à bouton, couvre-chef bien connu en Géorgie d'après divers portraits de donateurs[31]. En arrière, deux cavaliers portent l'un une lance, l'autre un bouclier; en avant deux autres portent à la fois lances et boucliers. Que représente cette scène dont l'intérêt narratif ou symbolique n'est pas évident?

---

[28] Aa 197–201; Ag 83–4; Vk 117–23; Va 32–7; Vo 83–8.

[29] Il n'y a aucun rapport iconographique avec les ménologes byzantins, où la scène est plus sobrement figurée, par exemple le Ménologe de Basile II (fin Xe siècle). Il menologio di Basilio II, Torino, 1907, pl. 75. Cf. aussi ALIŠAN, Ayrarat, Venise 1890, 237.

[30] Aa 211; Ag 86–90; Vg 51; Vk 124–5; Va 34; Vo 86. Sur la signification de la chasse occupation du prince dans le monde iranien et arménien, GARSOÏAN 1985, XI, 50–54.

[31] On la rencontre chez les aznavours au XIe siècle à Zemo K'rixi (Rača) et au XIIe–XIIIe à Adiši (Svanetie). Cf. The Treasure of Georgia, London 1984, pl. 72; Nicole THIERRY, Notes d'un voyage archéologique en Haute-Svanétie, *BK* 37 (1979) 172–73, fig. 23. Notre exemple s'ajoute à ceux rassemblés dans E. PRIVALOVA, Pavnisi, Tbilisi 1977, fig. 15 et 16. Voir n. 12 à propos de la coiffure d'un dignitaire proche de Tiridate.

a) Selon N. Marr, il s'agirait du départ de Tiridate pour une de ces campagnes militaires signalées au cours du Livre d'Agathange[32]. Cet auteur pensait que c'étaient les rois des Ibères, des Lazes et des Albaniens qui étaient représentés. Il en déduisait que l'iconographie de cette vie de Grégoire en image avait pour origine Va ou son archétype[33].

b) Une autre hypothèse est d'y voir les princes allant préparer le voyage de Grégoire à Césarée ou encore le cortège royal partant pour accueillir le saint à son retour[34].

c) A notre avis, il s'agirait plutôt du départ de Tiridate et de sa cour pour une chasse qu'il avait organisée afin de se consoler de la mort de Hṙipʿsimē. Pour ce faire, «il avait ordonné à la garde royale de s'y préparer», ce qui explique la présence de «soldats»[35]. On sait que c'est au cours de cette randonnée que le roi fut transformé en sanglier furieux. Le peintre qui n'a pas représenté cette célèbre métamorphose s'est peut-être contenté de la suggérer de cette façon. Le choix de cet épisode pourrait avoir été influancé par une scène analoque de l'Histoire de sainte Nino: la chasse du roi de Géorgie Mirian[36].

9. Libération de saint Grégoire[37]

....ႣႠ ႨႼႷႠ ႧႰႣႠႲႨ ႣႠ ႠႶႫႭႨ..
.... და იწყა თრდატი და აღმოი[ყვანა]..

«... Tiridate commença et fit re[monter Grégoire de la fosse] ...»

De l'orifice tétralobé du puits émerge Grégoire nimbé et vêtu d'une tunique claire. Il s'accroche à deux cordes tirées par des jeunes gens blonds à tuniques courtes de couleur verdâtre et bas rouges brodés de losanges. A droite, un vieillard debout et le bras droit tendu dirige la manœuvre. En bas, à gauche, dans un puits latéral se dressent encore des reptiles. Dans l'ensemble la scène est assez fidèle au texte d'Agathange: Dieu ayant, par un songe, averti la sœur du roi que seule la délivrance de Grégoire lui permettrait de reprendre figure humaine, ce dernier chargea le satrape Ōta Amatuni de cette mission. Celui-ci se rendit à Artašat et fit extraire le saint qui apparut nu et noir «comme du charbon». Ici la durée de l'incarcération est rendue par le vieillissement du visage: cheveux blancs et barbe. En revanche ses téguments sont restés clairs contrairement à toutes les versions du Livre d'Agathange. Enfin il est habillé ce qui suppose qu'Ōta lui a fait jeter des vêtements comme il est dit seulement dans Vk. Ōta (cheveux et barbe foncés) est vêtu d'une longue robe verte et porte un turban dont un pan retombe sur l'épaule gauche. Nous avons rencontré ce personnage dans deux scènes antérieures, alors que dans le Livre d'Agathange, son rôle est plus limité.

---

32 Ag 55, 57.

33 Marr 1905, 180–1, n. 2. Kakovkin adopte l'hypothèse de Marr car l'image lui paraît le symbole de l'évangélisation de toute la Transcaucasie par Grégoire (Kakovkin 1989, 81–2). Mais la coiffure des compagnons de Tiridate n'a rien de spécifiquement royal.

34 Va 147; Vg 159.

35 Peeters 1942, 112. Dans les textes du groupe V, l'initiative de la chasse revient aux nobles, dont le rôle est ainsi mis en évidence et Vk (125) précise qu'ils accompagnent le roi. Ce sont peut-être les mêmes qui sont énumérés à propos du départ pour Césarée, Aa 795, Ag 135, Vg 98 et Va 86 .

36 M. Tamarati, L'Église géorgienne des origines jusqu'à nos jours, Rome 1910, 171.

37 Aa 214–9; Ag 91–2; Vg 58; Vk 130–40; Vo 91. Cf. n. 1, à propos de la miniature du Psautier de Londres, qui montre le saint extrait par deux hommes, mais déjà revêtu du costume d'évêque.

10. Acclamation de saint Grégoire à la sortie du puits[38]
Inscription illisible.

Le saint auréolé et désormais barbu, cheveux blancs et visage foncé, légèrement tourné vers sa gauche tend les mains en signe d'allocution vers un groupe de trois femmes, portant un voile blanc autour de la tête et du cou[39], qui l'acclament devant des architectures figurant la ville d'Artašat. Symétriquement à sa droite une foule d'hommes, la plupart blonds et jeunes tendent les mains vers lui. Au premier plan, on retrouve Ōta Amatuni. L'image est conforme au Livre d'Agathange qui décrit Grégoire, habillé par Ōta mais le visage encore noir, acclamé par les habitants d'Artašat puis de Vałaršapat. Peut-être l'image se rapproche-t-elle de Vk plus que des autres.

11. Vision de saint Grégoire[40]
Pas d'inscription visible.

La scène s'inscrit dans un champ en L renversé. Grégoire, nimbé et barbu, a été figuré deux fois: dans la partie inférieure gauche, il apparaît de face, les bras levés; il est en prière et un peu plus loin, à droite, le même personnage, tourné légèrement sur sa gauche, tend les bras vers le ciel. Il est entouré d'une foule, hommes et femmes mélés devant un décor d'architecture, un portique surmonté de deux édifices à coupole, l'une sommée d'une croix sous les écritures(?). Tout à fait en haut de la composition, dans une sorte de croissant rose se trouve un buste. En partie effacé, mais semblant nimbé et barbu, il tend vers la terre deux doigts de la dextre. De la convexité du croissant partent deux bandes: une rouge légèrement courbe s'effile au-dessus de Grégoire en prière et une autre plus étroite et rigide juste à côté et à droite tombe en direction de la seconde représentation du saint. Deux anges vêtus de vert volent sous le croissant. Celui de droite tend en avant ses mains couvertes d'un linge, celui de gauche tient une longue tige oblique, munie d'une petite traverse supérieure.

Il était difficile pour le peintre de rendre exactement la vision du Livre d'Agathange. Fidèle à son procédé de représentation simultanée d'événements séquentiels, il montre dans la même scène Grégoire lors de sa vision (à gauche), puis le même l'exposant au peuple (à droite). Il a peint sous forme de croissant «la voûte du ciel ouverte comme une tente d'où apparaît un homme éclatant de lumière[41]» qui lui enjoint de contempler les phénomènes célestes: la lumière et les eaux inondant la terre et «l'homme frappant le sol». Ici on ne peut pas savoir si le peintre a voulu se conformer à la version V où l'ange porte un bâton ou à la version A où il tient un marteau d'or. Quant à la «cohorte des hommes étincelants et ailés[42]», elle est représentée par l'ange qui tend ses mains voilées, en signe de dévotion.

Les architectures représentent le «palais du roi» avec son portique et sa porte monumentale, les «piédestaux rouges surmontés des mausolées des saintes hripsimiennes sommés de croix[43]». Le ciel bleu du fond est hachuré de traits rouges qui, peut-être, figurent

[38] Aa 219; Ag 92; Va 40; Vg 61; Vk 141; Vo 91.

[39] Cette coiffure qui était d'usage en Arménie au moyen âge (V. Hacʻuni, Patmutʻiwn hin hay tarazin, patkerazard [Histoire illustrée du costume arménien],Venise 1923) est encore porté de nos jours en Turquie où il est nommé *başlık*.

[40] Aa 731–56; Ag 112–21; Va 53–62; Vg 76–82.

[41] V. Langlois, Collection des historiens anciens et modernes de l'Arménie, I, Paris 1867, 156.

[42] L. c., 1867, 157.

[43] Sur ce type de mausolée et son iconographie cf. A. Khatchatrian, Données historiques sur la fondation d'Edjmiatsin à la lumière des fouilles récents, *HA* 76, 1962, 158–70; idem, L'Architecture arménienne du IVe au VIe siècle, Paris 1971, 104–5.

«la colonne de feu» de la vision, mais qui correspondent probablement au fond rouge de l'apprêt.

La construction des églises et l'ensevelissement des saintes martyres auraient dû suivre; or l'on a placé là le miracle de la Colonne vivante, tirée de l'histoire de la Conversion de la Géorgie par sainte Nino. Après cette interruption, le récit de la christianisation de l'Arménie reprend.

12. Sacre de saint Grégoire à Césarée[44]

Pas d'inscription visible.

Le «catholicos» Léonce est debout tête nue et cheveux noirs, revêtu d'une chasuble blanche[45]. Grégoire, non nimbé, est déjà vêtu en évêque. Il serre dans sa main un objet indistinct (vraisemblablement un rouleau) et s'incline devant Léonce. Celui-ci tient de la main gauche l'évangile ouvert et de l'autre pose sur la tête du saint le pan de son omophorion[46]. Derrière Grégoire apparaît une foule d'assistants dont un évêque qui tient un rouleau, et un diacre identifiable à l'orarion qui pend sur l'épaule droite[47] et les objets qu'il porte: l'encensoir et la boite[48].

Derrière Léonce se trouve un groupe de prêtres et en tête un évêque qui tient une châsse ou plutôt l'étui de l'évangile. Le fond d'architecture figure sans doute la grande basilique de Césarée de Cappadoce.

L'image est conforme aux textes: l'évangélisation de l'Arménie, en dépit du zèle de Grégoire et de Tiridate, se heurtait à un obstacle liturgique, à savoir l'impossibilité de dresser des autels et de conférer le baptême sans être prêtre. Il était donc indispensable que Grégoire se rendit à Césarée pour s'y faire ordonner. Le voyage, organisé par Tiridate, fut triomphal. Grégoire, accompagné de dignitaires, était acclamé par la population massée sur son passage. Un synode fut spécialement convoqué à Césarée et l'exarque Léonce procéda à l'intronisation. La composition de la scène est conforme à l'iconographie géorgienne et assez proche de la byzantine[49].

---

[44] Aa 791–808; Ag 134–8; Vg 117–41; Va 105–28; Vk 219–40; Vo 120–3. L'épisode se place lors du Concile de Césarée, en 314 (VAN ESBROECK 1971, 17, 142). Cf. pl. 5.

[45] En arménien moderne Շուրջառ (Šurjar).

[46] Sur cette étole, attribut principal des évêques, WALTER 1982, 9–13. Il est semblable chez les Byzantins, Géorgiens et Arméniens, décrit pour ces derniers sous le nom d'*emip'oron*, avec les autres éléments du costume épiscopale du XIIIe siècle. S. ORBÉLIAN, Histoire de la Siounie, trad. M. BROSSET, I, Saint-Pétersbourg 1864, 69–70 et n. 4.

[47] G. DE JERPHANION, L'attribut des diacres dans l'art du moyen âge en Orient. *La Voix des Monuments*, Nouvelle série, Paris 1938, 283–296.

[48] Dans cette scène, on peut penser aussi que la pyxide était destinée au myron, huile d'onction consacrée par le patriarche qui le distribue aux évêques (ibidem), mais il n'est pas impossible qu'il ne s'agisse des reliques de saint Jean cédées par Léonce à Grégoire (Vg 147).

[49] Sur une miniature du manuscrit géorgien A-109 de Tiflis, le rituel est plus compréhensible car l'omophorion est plus long et bien objectivé par l'ornement de grandes croix noires; l'Evangile est sous forme de rouleau déployé (S. AMIRANAŠVILI, Gruzinskaja miniatjura, Moskva, 1966, pl. 54; ALIBEGAŠVILI 1979, pl. 75). Chez les Grecs, si l'imposition de l'Evangile est bien attestée, il n'en est pas de même pour celle du pan de l'omophorion, cf. la miniature du Paris. gr. 510 (ca 883) où seul l'Evangile ouvert est posé sur la tête de l'évêque à consacrer, WALTER 1982, 130–36, fig. 34.

13. Rencontre de Tiridate et de saint Grégoire à Bagawan[50]

Pas d'inscription.

Suivi d'écclésiastiques, Grégoire, debout et nimbé, bénit par imposition de la main Tiridate incliné devant lui. Ce dernier, revêtu d'une riche robe rouge brodée, est accompagné d'une foule parmi laquelle on identifie la reine Askēn, portant une robe à col rond brodé, une couronne[51] et le *thorakion*[52]. Derrière elle, la sœur du roi, Xosroviduxt, la tête ceinte d'un voile formant turban.

Ce tableau représente l'entrevue de Grégoire revenu de Césarée avec Tiridate et sa famille venus à sa rencontre. Cette entrevue eut lieu à Bagawan, sur les bords de l'Euphrate[53]. Il n'est pas exclu que le peintre ait, dans son esprit, plus ou moins confondu cette scène avec celle du baptême.

14. Le Baptême dans l'Euphrate[54]

Pas d'inscription visible.

Sur le fond sombre de la nuit, le saint revêtu du *šurjar*, baptise la foule. Les catéchumènes du premier rang ont le torse nu, le bassin caché par un linge. D'un demi-anneau blanc peint en haut de la composition descend vers Grégoire un rayon clair. L'image traduit le texte d'Agathange: après un délai de jeûne et de dévotions, la foule des Arméniens, estimée à plusieurs centaines de milliers, fut baptisée. Il semble que le peintre soit plus proche des recensions V à cause de l'image du ciel d'où descend la lumière[55].

15–16. Grégoire dans le désert et sacre d'Aṙistakēs[56]

ႠႵႠ ႢႢႪ ႠႩႳႰႧႾႠ
ႫႶႣႤႪႧ ႫႭႻႶႰႠႣ
ႠႰႭႱႲႠႩႤႱ ႫႱႨ ႸႥႨႪႨ
აქა გ<რი>გ<ო>ლ აკურთხა მღდელთ
მოძღ<უ>რად აროსტაკეს მ<ი>სი შვილი

«Ici Grégoire bénit comme patriarche son fils Arost'ak'es»

Le panneau est divisé en deux parties cernées par un épais trait rouge.

a) A droite (scène 16), le buste du saint nimbé, en habit d'ascète, apparaît dans une grotte creusée dans une montagne de couleur ocre; une échelle en permet l'accès. En bas

---

[50] Aa 817–31; Ag 143–4; Vg 159; Va 147; Vk 252–3; Vo 126. Cf. n. 1, à propos de l'image symbolique du Psautier de Londres: Grégoire a saisi la main du roi que suit la reine, le menant à l'église et lui montrant l'image du Christ.

[51] A peu près semblable à celle que nous avons décrite plus haut (cf. n. 11).

[52] Pièce du vêtement royal.

[53] D'après Vk, la rencontre aurait eu lieu à Arzn. Pour toutes les autres recensions à Bagawan (= le village des idoles) sur le rive gauche de l'Euphrate près de sa source. Grégoire y fonda une église nommée Šołat'ak (Ag 149), refaite au VIIe siècle et détruite en 1916.

[54] Aa 832–6; Ag 148–57; Vg 164–73; Va 132–61; Vk 254–63; Vo 127.

[55] Vg 167; Va 155; surtout Vk 255. L'image rappelle le nom de l'église; Šołat'ak en effet signifie «où est descendu la lumière de vie» (VAN ESBROECK 1971, 85, 150–2).

[56] Aa 858–62; Ag 158–60; Vg 192; Va 161; Vk 264; Vo 129. Cf. M. THIERRY 1988, 393. La localisation de cette première retraite n'est pas précisée par Agathange qui dit seulement qu'il se trouve dans le désert, sur la montagne de Maneay ayrk', c'est-à-dire de «la grotte de Manē». Vk 262 parle de retraite «dans les montagnes», entre des périodes de précidation (VAN ESBROECK 1971, 86).

et à gauche, sortant des limites de la scène voisine, un personnage tête nue, richement vêtu, tend vers lui ses mains en signe d'imploration. Grégoire esquisse un geste de refus.

Cette image illustre un événement important du premier séjour de Grégoire dans le désert de Daranałik sur le mont Sepuh[57]. Sa retraite posait en effet le problème urgent de sa succession. Le choix de Tiridate s'étant porté sur Aristakes, fils de Grégoire, c'est le roi en personne qui «ayant rejeté la couronne de sa tête (Vk 272)», vint implorer Grégoire d'introniser son fils.

b) A gauche (scène 15) est figurée le sacre d'Aristakes, proche de celui de Grégoire à Césarée (cf. supra scène 12[58]). Le décor change: la cérémonie ayant eu lieu à Vałaršapat, le peintre, en effet, a figuré la cathédrale à coupole et le palais royal.

Les deux scènes, quoiqu'audacieusement confondues dans le temps selon un procédé goûté par le peintre, suit le Livre d'Agathange, au demeurant assez bref sauf dans la version Vk.

17. La fin de la vie de saint Grégoire[59]

Pas d'inscription visible.

Grégoire représenté en ascète amaigri à barbe allongé prie dans une cavité ménagée dans les racines d'un arbre maladroitement figuré qui tend vers le haut son extrémité feuillue. De part et d'autre de l'arbre se trouvent deux anges, l'un debout à gauche désigne le saint, l'autre plane à droite, les mains couvertes d'un linge[60]. La scène illustre les derniers moments du saint qui, après l'intronisation d'Aristakes, est retourné au mont Sepuh où, à sa mort, «son âme fut emportée par les anges»[61].

Ainsi se termine le cycle de la vie de Grégoire, dont la mort elle-même n'est pas représentée conformément aux recensions A.

Bibliographie

Sources

Aa	=	Texte arménien du Livre d'Agathange. Cf. THOMSON 1976.
Ag	=	Version grecque de Aa. Cf. LAFONTAINE 1973.
Moïse de Khorène 1993	=	Moïse de Khorène, Histoire de l'Arménie, trad. Annie et J. P. MAHÉ, Paris.
Va	=	Version arabe du Livre d'Agathange. Cf. GARITTE 1966, 27–116.
Vg	=	Version grecque du Livre d'Agathange. Cf. GARITTE 1966, 23–116.
Vk	=	Version karšuni du Livre d'Agathange. Cf. VAN ESBROECK 1971.
Vo	=	Version d'Okhrid du Livre d'Agathange. Cf. GARITTE 1965.
YE	=	Yovhannēs Erznkacʻi, Nerboli surbn Grigor Lusaworičʻ (Panégyrique de saint Grégoire l'Illuminateur), *Sopʻerkʻ Haykakankʻ*, nr. 5, Venise 1853, 85–164.

[57] Cette scène donnerait à penser que le peintre s'est inspiré de traditions tardives, comme le *Synaxaire de Tēr Israyēl*, où Grégoire vit dans une grotte ou dans un genévrier creux du vivant de Manē et n'occupe la grotte de cette dernière qu'après sa mort (*PO* 16/1, 66–7; Cf. M. THIERRY 1988, 393–4; M. THIERRY et B. OUTTIER, Histoire des saintes Hripsimiennes, *Syria* 77, nr. 3.4, 1990, 710–11.

[58] On remarquera qu'Aristakes est agenouillé, contrairement à Grégoire.

[59] Dans le groupe A, la mort est citée sans aucun détail (Ag 169–71; cf. aussi Vo 129), alors que dans les recensions V, le sujet est développé (Vg 173; Va 61, Vk 292), ainsi que chez Moïse de Khorène (2, 91 [Moïse de Khorène 1993, 245–6]) et dans les synaxaires tardifs. Cf. pl. 6.

[60] L'attitude est celle des anges psychopompes dans les Dormitions.

[61] Cf. n. 57 et 58. Il semble que le peintre ait fait une confusion puisqu'en dernier lieu il se trouvait dans la grotte.

Études

ALIBEGAŠVILI 1979 = Gayanē ALIBEGAŠVILI, Svetskii portret v gruzinskoi srednevekovoi monumental'noi živopisi (Le portrait laïque dans la peinture monumentale géorgienne du Moyen Age), Tbilisi.

DER NERSESSIAN 1937 = Sirarpie DER NERSESSIAN, Manuscrits arméniens illustrés des XIIe, XIIIe et XIVe siècles de la bibliothèque des Pères Mekhitharistes de Venise, Paris.

DER NERSESSIAN 1965 = Sirarpie DER NERSESSIAN, Aght'amar. Church of the Holy Cross, Cambridge (Mass.).

DER NERSESSIAN 1977 = Sirarpie DER NERSESSIAN, L'Art arménien, Paris.

DRAMPIAN – KOTANJIAN 1990 = Irina DRAMPIAN et N. KOTANJIAN, The Frescoes in the Church of St. Gregory the Illuminator Founded by Tigran Honents in Ani, *Armenian Review* 43/4 (172) 41–65.

ĒP'RIKEAN 1903–1905 = S. ĒP'RIKEAN, Patkerazard Bnašxarhik Bararan (Dictionnaire illustré de la patrie), Venezia, 1903–1905, 2 vol.

GARITTE 1946 = G. GARITTE, Documents pour l'étude du livre d'Agathange,Vatican.

GARITTE 1965 = G. GARITTE, La Vie grecque inédite de saint Grégoire d'Arménie, *AnBoll* 83, 233–90.

GARSOÏAN 1970 = N. ADONTZ, Armenia in the Period of Justinian: The Political Conditions Based on the Naxarar System, éd. et trad. Nina G. GARSOÏAN, Louvain.

GARSOÏAN 1985 = Nina GARSOÏAN, The Iranian Substratum of the «Agat'angelos» Cycle, dans: Armenia between Byzantium and the Sasanians, London.

HADERMAN-MISGUICH 1979 = Lydie HADERMAN-MISGUICH, La peinture monumentale tardo-comnène et ses prolongements au XIII siècle, Actes du XVe Congrès International d'Études byzantines, Athènes, 255–84.

KAKOVKIN 1985 = A. KAKOVKINE, De la datation des fresques de la chapelle, du parvis et de l'église Saint-Grégoire (1215) d'Ani, Quatrième Symposium International sur l'Art Arménien 174–7.

KAKOVKIN 1987 = A. KAKOVKIN, O datirovke rospisej chrama sv. Grigorija (1215 g.) v Ani, ego časovni i pritvora (De la datation des fresques de l'église, de la chapelle et du parvis Saint-Grégoire (1215) d'Ani), *VV* 48, 108–14.

KAKOVKIN 1989 = A. KAKOVKIN, Scena «Čudesnoe javlenie životvorjaščego stolpa» v rospisi chrama Grigorija (1215 g.) v Ani (La scène du «Miracle de la colonne vivante» peinte à l'église de Grégoire à Ani, en 1215), *Zograph* 20, 30–2.

KAKOVKIN 1990 = A. KAKOVKIN, Zametki ob osobennostjach žitijnogo cikla Grigorija prosvetitelja v cerkvi Tigrana Onenca (Notes sur les particularités du cycle de Grégoire l'Illuminateur dans l'église de Tigran Honenc', *PBH* 1990/2 (129) 227–36.

LAFONTAINE 1973 = G. LAFONTAINE, La version grecque ancienne du livre arménien d'Agathange, Louvain.

LYNCH 1901 = H. F. LYNCH, Armenia. Travels and Studies, London, 2 vol.

MARR 1905 = N. MARR, Kreščenie Armjan, Gruzin, Abxazov i Alanov svjatym Grigoriem (Baptême des Arméniens, Géorgiens, Abkhazes et Alains par saint Grégoire), *Zapiski Vostočnogo otdelenija Russkogo archeologičeskogo obščestva* 16, 63–211 (Saint-Pétersbourg).

MORA – PHILIPPOT 1977 = P. et Laura MORA –P. PHILIPPOT, La conservation des peintures murales, Bologne.

MURADYAN 1982 = P. MURADYAN, Agat'angełosi hin vrac'eren xmbagrut'yunnerë (Anciennes recensions géorgiennes d'Agathange), ed. et trad. (en arménien oriental), Erivan.

MURAVJEV 1848 = A. MURAVJEV, Gruzija i Armenija, Saint-Pétersbourg, 3 vol.

NAGATSUKA 1979 = Y. NAGATSUKA, Descente de Croix. Son développement iconographique des origines jusqu'à la fin du XIVe siècle, Tokyo.

PEETERS 1932 = P. PEETERS, Les débuts du christianisme en Géorgie d'après les sources hagiographiques, *AnBoll* 50, 5–58.

PEETERS 1942 = P. PEETERS, S. Grégoire l'Illuminateur dans le calendrier lapidaire de Naples, *AnBoll* 60, 91–130.

PEETERS 1951 = P. PEETERS, A propos de la version arménienne de l'historien Socrate, *Subsidia hagiographica* 27, 310–36.

PELEKANIDIS – CHATZIDAKIS 1985 = S. PELEKANIDIS – M. CHATZIDAKIS, Kastoria, Athens.

SYČEV 1912 = N. SYČEV, Anijskaja čerkov' raskopannaja v 1892 g. (Église d'Ani fouillée en 1892), *Christianskij Vostok* 1, 212–9.

TER-ŁEVONDYAN 1973 = A. TER-ŁEVONDYAN, Agat'angełosi arabakan xmbagrut'yan norahayt bnagirë (Nouvelle recension arabe d'Agathange), *PBH* 1973, 209–28, ed. et trad. (en arménien oriental), Erivan.

M. THIERRY 1988 = M. THIERRY, Le mont Sepuh, *REArm* NS 21 (1988–1989) 385–453.

Nicole et M. THIERRY 1993 = Nicole et M. THIERRY, L'église Saint-Grégoire de Tigran Honenc' à Ani (1215), Louvain–Paris.

THOMSON 1976 = R. W. THOMSON, Agathangelos: History of the Armenians, trad. et comm., Albany.

VAN ESBROECK 1971 = M. VAN ESBROECK, Un nouveau témoin du Livre d'Agathange, *REArm* NS 8, 13–167.

WALTER 1982 = Ch. WALTER, Art and Ritual of the Byzantine Church, London.

WEITZMANN 1980 = K. WEITZMANN, The Origin of the Threnos, dans: Byzantine Book Illumination and Ivories, Variorum Reprints, London.

Distribution des peintures dans le bras ouest. Côté S. Cycle de st Grégoire. Scènes 1-2-4/12-13-14

Distribution des peintures dans le bras ouest. Côté N. Cycle de st Grégoire. Scènes 8/10-11 et Miracle de Nino

Scènes 6-7/9

Distribution des peintures dans le bras ouest. Côté O. Cycle de st Grégoire

Scènes 3-5/15-16-17

NICOLE THIERRY / ÉTAMPES

SUR LE CULTE DE SAINTE NINO

I. Le miracle de la Colonne vivante dans le programme des peintures de Saint-Grégoire de Tigran Honenc‘ à Ani (c. 1220)[1]

Les peintures de l'église de Saint-Grégoire de Tigran Honenc‘ sont postérieures de peu à la fondation attestée en 1215. Sur le tympan de la porte d'entrée on voit encore des traces de peintures: à gauche Grégoire l'Illuminateur, les mains levées vers le ciel, et à droite le haut d'un visage masculin nimbé: le donateur, peut-être Tigran. On imagine mal, en effet, qu'il ait négligé de faire peindre ce monument de prestige, lui qui se disait «serviteur de l'amir spasalar Zakaré» alors gouverneur d'Ani.

Ce dernier était resté grégorien alors que son frère Ivané s'était converti au chalcédonisme, tous deux s'étant également illustrés au service de la reine Tamar. On sait qu'Ivané était le commanditaire de l'église d'Axtala et de ses peintures.

L'église d'Ani était entièrement peinte, le programme général étant celui de tradition au début du XIIIe siècle dans les églises géorgiennes. Cependant, l'histoire de la conversion de l'Arménie illustrée dans le bras ouest en fait un monument unique et témoigne de la foi grégorienne du commanditaire.

Les 17 illustrations de cette conversion par Grégoire l'Illuminateur est le premier exemple de cycle développé. Il ne se rattache expressément à aucune des versions du texte original, s'écartant du Livre d'Agathange moins par des éléments descriptifs que par les lacunes qu'il comporte et par l'addition de l'image-clé de la conversion de la Géorgie, la légende de la Colonne vivante de Nino[2].

La présence du sujet géorgien dans le récit hagiographique arménien peut surprendre. En fait, il témoigne de la culture régnant à Ani sous domination géorgienne au début du XIIIe siècle. On sait d'ailleurs que Zakaré voulut alors rapprocher l'Arménie du chalcédonisme sans cependant se couper de son Église grégorienne et que les autorités arméniennes, comme la plupart des évêques, se plièrent sans protester à quelques entorses aux règles, par exemple sur les dates des fêtes et l'introduction des images dans les églises.

Le miracle de sainte Nino s'inscrit entre les scènes 11 et 12, en parallèle à la vision de saint Grégoire.

Les deux compositions sont juxtaposées à l'entrée de l'église, dans l'angle nord-est, manifestement pour exalter les théophanies dont furent favorisés les deux évangélisateurs respectifs de l'Arménie et de la Géorgie (schéma). Grégoire voit «un homme éclatant de lumière» qui lui enjoint de contempler les phénomènes célestes, la lumière et les eaux «les piédestaux rouges surmontés des mausolées des saints martyres hripsimiennes», et

---

[1] Cet article reprend en partie le texte de notre monographie, N. et M. THIERRY, L'Église Saint-Grégoire de Tigran Honenc‘ à Ani (1215), École Pratique des Hautes Études, Ve Section, Archéologies I, Louvain-Paris 1993, 53–56, 60–6.2 (cité N. et M. THIERRY 1993).

[2] Les recensions, éditions et études de cet ouvrage sont nombreuses et nous nous sommes contentés de citer les principales et les plus récentes; bibliographie dans N. et M. THIERRY, op. cit., 42, n. 4.

Nino voit un homme semblable au Christ qui semble s'adresser aux deux anges qui descendent la colonne sur les fondations de l'église.

Cependant, on a privilégié le miracle de Nino représenté face au visiteur qui pénètre dans l'église, alors que la vision de Grégoire est de côté, sur la paroi gauche.

Le miracle de la «Colonne vivante»

La scène, étrangère au Livre d'Agathange, est empruntée au cycle de la *Vie de sainte Nino*, évangélisatrice de la Géorgie[3].

Sur le fond bleu-nuit, on voit en bas et à gauche, sainte Nino enveloppée du maphorion (*fig. 1 et 2*). Elle est debout, tournée de trois-quarts, les mains levées, priant devant une colonne suspendue au-dessus de deux lits de pierres préparées comme base (schéma). La colonne est rouge-feu, haute et massive, tenue par deux anges volant en haut et à droite de l'image. En face d'eux, dans l'angle supérieur gauche apparaît dans un arc de cercle le buste nimbé d'un homme jeune à barbe fine, semblable à un Christ juvénile; son geste est celui de l'allocution et de la bénédiction. En bas et à droite se trouve un groupe de sept femmes vêtues comme Nino; accroupies au pied de la colonne, elles paraissent endormies, sauf deux d'entre elles. La signification de la scène était précisée par une légende en géorgien, fragmentaire aujourd'hui.

On sait que le miracle de la Colonne vivante est une des plus remarquables preuves du pouvoir thaumaturge de l'évangélisatrice de la Géorgie, bien qu'elle ait été peu représentée. Une relation assez sobre avait été ajoutée par Rufin à sa traduction latine de l'*Histoire ecclésiastique* d'Eusèbe[4] et le texte fut repris par Socrate et Sozomène mais non par Théodoret[5].

Dans la *Vie de sainte Nino*[6] et dans les deux recueils parallèles, l'*Histoire de la Géorgie* et *Kartlis Cxovreba* (*La vie de la Géorgie*), le récit est très enrichi et jumelé à d'autres, comme ceux de la tunique du Christ conservé à Mcxeta et de la croix lumineuse dressée sur la montagne voisine, dérivés de la légende de Longin[7].

De plus, Nino a été introduite dans l'histoire de Hripsimé et Gayané: après avoir vécu dans leur couvent, elle s'enfuit avec les saintes femmes et, échappant au massacre, arrive alors en Géorgie[8]. À côté de la traduction enrichie de l'*Histoire ecclésiastique* de Socrate par Philon de Tirak (696), des recensions arméniennes ont lié l'évangélisatrice de la Géorgie à la conversion de l'Arménie[9]. Des additions arméniennes ont été plus ou moins précoces et adoptées par les Géorgiens, ce qui explique la couleur arménienne du *Livre des*

---

[3] L'événement, conté pour la première fois par Rufin dans les toutes premières années du Ve s. (Thélamon 1981, 13, 87–90; Tamarati 1910, 160–63), se retrouve enrichi dans la *Vie de sainte Nino* (Pätsch 1985, 322–24) et dans la *Vie des Rois*, de Leonti Mroveli, première partie de la chronique géorgienne (Brosset 1849, 116–18; Pätsch 1985, 166–70; encore Takaišvili 1891). Cf. aussi J.-P. Mahé, au dessus p. 113–16.

[4] Son récit provenait du témoignage d'un prince géorgien, Bak'ur, historiquement attesté, qu'il rencontra à Jérusalem, 50 ans après les faits racontés (Thélamon 1981, 93–96).

[5] Tarchnišvili 1947, 31; Thélamon 1981, 91 et n. 10; Mahé, au dessus, 114.

[6] Pätsch 1975, 304–37.

[7] Brosset 1849, 89–136 (116–8); Pätsch 1985, 131–89 (166–70). La partie qui comprend le miracle, nommée *Le Livre des Rois*, du moine Mroveli, est attribuée au VIIIe s., cf. Tarchnišvili 1947, 37–41; Pätsch 1985, 12–13; Thélamon, 91; Mahé, 115–16.

[8] Pätsch 1975, 308–09; Brosset, 97–99.

[9] Tarchnišvili 1947, 30, 33, 41–50; Thélamon, 91 et n. 11; Mahé, 114. Dans Moïse de Khorène, ch. 86, c'est à saint Grégoire que Nino demande des instructions une fois en Géorgie, alors que dans Rufin, c'est à l'empereur Constantin qu'elle fit demander des prêtres.

Rois et du texte assez proche constitué par la *Vie de sainte Nino*; les échanges eurent sans doute lieu là où les deux communautés se côtoyaient, ce qui a suscité diverses hypothèses[10]. Dernièrement M. van Esbroeck plaçait le «jumelage de Nino avec les Hripsimiennes, voire avec Grégoire l'Illuminateur, à Jérusalem et à une époque où il ne faisait pas de difficulté (à propos du chalcédonisme), c'est-à-dire dans le contexte hénotique du premier Concile de Dwin de 506. Un des effets de la politique de Zénon, ayant été de ne supprimer aucune légende appartenant à quelque parti que ce soit»[11].

Une fois en Géorgie, Nino, grâce à quelques miracles, gagna la confiance du roi Mirian qui finit par se convertir et se proposa de construire une église[12]. Les textes composites racontent comment, l'endroit ayant été choisi et les six premières colonnes mises en place, il fut impossible de dresser la plus grande «réservée pour le centre de l'édifice»[13].

Après maints efforts, tout le monde se retira découragé sauf Nino qui resta à prier avec ses compagnes. Celles-ci s'endormirent, à l'exception de Sidonie, la narratrice du récit de l'événement. À la fin d'une nuit pleine de visions terribles, un jeune homme apparut à Nino, vêtu de «lumière et de feu», il éleva la colonne «resplendissante de lumière» qui vint se poser doucement sur son socle[14]. L'édifice put alors se construire et de nombreux miracles eurent lieu.

La peinture représente assez librement cette aurore où Nino voit sa prière exaucée. En haut, le jeune homme semble donner aux anges l'ordre de descendre la colonne sur les fondations: plusieurs lits de moellons bien individualisés et non pas sur la racine d'un arbre (comme sur les images du XIXe siècle).

La scène se passe devant Sidonie et ses compagnes. Contrairement aux textes qui s'accordent pour en dénombrer douze[15], les femmes ne sont que sept. Il faut donc y reconnaître les premières disciples de Nino: Sidonie, la fille du prêtre juif Abiathar et les six autres juives converties en secret. Les originalités de la composition sont peut-être dues à une contraction de la légende ou à un texte de base qui ne nous est pas connu[16].

Il est tout à fait remarquable de trouver ce sujet introduit dans le cycle consacré à Grégoire l'Illuminateur. Certes, Nino, sous le nom de Nuné, n'est pas inconnue des sources arméniennes et Moïse de Khorène lui consacre une courte biographie, mais il ne fait pas allusion au miracle de la Colonne (2, 86)[17].

---

[10] Bibliographie dans N. et M. Thierry 1993, p. 61, n. 71.

[11] M. van Esbroeck, La place de Jérusalem dans la Conversion de la Géorgie, texte aimablement communiqué en 1992.

[12] C'était une église de bois dont on retrouva quelques traces sous le pavement de la cathédrale de Mcxeta, V. Cincadze, Sveti-cxoveli à Mcxeta, *Ars Georgica* 9A (1987) 15–21. Le miracle est omis par Moïse de Khorène qui lui préfère celui de la croix lumineuse élevée sur le lieu de l'idole détruite d'Aramazd, le dieu du tonnerre: Annie et J.-P. Mahé, Histoire de l'Arménie par Moïse de Khorène, Paris 1993, 239.

[13] Brosset 1849, 116; Pätsch 1985, 166–67; eadem, 1975, 322.

[14] Brosset 1849, 117; Pätsch 1985, 169–70; eadem, 1975, 324. Les modalités varient: dans Rufin, c'est la troisième colonne qui reste oblique, Nino est seule en prière toute la nuit, au matin, le roi trouva la colonne suspendue en l'air (Thélamon, 89–90). Dans la *Vie des Rois de Géorgie*, comme dans la *Vie de sainte Nino*, la colonne se fixe sur le tronc du cèdre dont elle est faite (Brosset 1849, 117; Pätsch 1985, 167; eadem 1975, 324). Dans le Synaxaire arabe, c'est une série de colonnes de réemploi qui sont transportées (Tamarati 1910, 169).

[15] Brosset 1849, 116; Pätsch 1985, 167; eadem, 1975, 322. Dans la *Chronique arménienne* de Juanšer qui traduit à peu près la *Vie de sainte Nino*, les femmes sont douze également.

[16] Le dépouillement des textes n'est pas de notre ressort et nous nous sommes contentés des travaux publiés. Dans une lettre du 4-4-1981, M. van Esbroeck nous disait avoir déjà rassemblé plus de 250 titres sur Nino, considérant le dossier comme un des plus complexes de toute l'hagiographie.

[17] Annie et J.-P. Mahé, op.cit., Paris 1993, 238–39.

On a noté que le peintre, indiscutablement géorgien, a mis le sujet en bonne place, frappant le regard pour qui entre dans l'église. D'autre part, il en a fait le pendant de la vision de Grégoire, plaçant les deux théophanies côte à côte, bien que ce soit en contradiction avec la chronologie des événements.

Iconographie du sujet

Enfin, cette composition est un sujet rarement représenté et la plus ancienne qu'on connaisse aujourd'hui. Cependant la popularité de l'histoire de Nino a commencé à se développer à partir de la fin du XIe siècle, aux XIIe et XIIIe. Les références au miracle de la Colonne vivante faisaient alors partie des formules imprécatoires, et le catholicos Arsène écrivit des hymnes à sainte Nino qui passèrent dans un canon de l'office[18].

Il faut donc citer la thèse annoncée de Ketevan Abramichvili-Tcholokachvili, relative à la décoration du mur de l'apside centrale de la cathédrale Sveti Tsxoveli de Mcxeta (1010–1029), de l'église-reliquaire du premier sanctuaire de bois. L'auteur pense que primitivement, on avait représenté la Colonne vivante portée par les anges, au chevet de l'église, là où souvent figure une grande croix. Il est de fait que sur cette façade, aujourd'hui très remaniée et ornée de divers réemplois, on voit sur les côtés deux anges volant symétriquement l'un vers l'autre, les mains tendues et serrées sur un fragment de pierre mal définissable (*fig. 1*). Il se pourrait donc qu'ils soient les reliquats d'une composition frontale, vision triomphale d'un type comparable à celle qu'on a peinte plus tard à Saint-David d'Udabno.

Quelques scènes d'un cycle de Nino ont été illustrées sur le mur ouest de cette église à la fin du XIIIe siècle. Aujourd'hui presque effacées, elles représentaient la Vierge et la sainte, le miracle de la Colonne vivante et la guérison du fils de Riev, petit-fils du roi Mirian; la colonne était portée dans une mandorle par quatre anges, comme une image théophanique de la croix (*fig. 2*)[19]. C'est dire que l'illustration de l'église de Tigran Honencʿ était bien caractéristique de son temps.

Rappelons comme particularité de la composition, le groupe des sept femmes qui assistent Nino. On a mis en valeur les liens de la sainte avec l'antique communauté juive de Mcxeta, jadis détentrice de la tunique du Christ. Les premières conversions de Nino furent celle du grand-prêtre, de sa fille et de ses compagnes, et la légende de Nino précise qu'elle parlait l'hébreu[20]. On peut y voir le rappel des relations privilégiées entre la chrétienté de Géorgie et la Terre Sainte, marquée dès l'origine par l'histoire du Juif de Mcxeta qui rapporta la tunique du Christ de Jérusalem[21]. Sans compter que c'est dans la Ville sainte, c. 390 que le prince Bakur fit connaître à l'auteur latin l'évangélisation de l'Ibérie par une captive.

L'étude de l'architecture et des décors sculptés de l'Église Saint-Grégoire de Tigran Honencʿ met en évidence la valeur de ce monument comme témoin de la civilisation cosmopolite qui régnait à Ani. Les maîtres d'œvre étaient venus d'horizons divers, et les peintres notamment, de terres géorgiennes. Dans la ville, importante place d'échanges, centre artisanal et commercial très prospère, Arméniens, Géorgiens, Kurdes et Iraniens se

---

[18] D'après Jordania, Chroniques, II, Tiflis 1893, 97, cité par Tamarati 1910, 360–61. Arsène correspond au règne de Roussoudane (1223–1245). Infra B. Martin Hisard, n. 23.

[19] S. Amiranašvili, Histoire de la peinture monumentale géorgienne (en russe), Tbilisi 1957, 53, pl. 27, 28. Les scènes sont en seconde couche et datées entre 1272 et 1289. L'érection de la colonne par quatre anges, composition symétrique du type triomphal, est très différente de la scène peinte à Ani.

[20] Brosset 1849, 104–09; Pätsch 1985, 150–57.

[21] Brosset 1849, 106–07.

côtoyaient sans trop de mésentente. Cependant, les rapports entre grégoriens et chalcédoniens restaient délicats. L'archevêque d'Ani était sous la dépendance du catholicos géorgien; le petit clergé et les moines arméniens étaient plus ou moins hostiles à cet état de chose, alors que les élites religieuses et laïques s'en accommodaient.

C'est pourquoi le programme des peintures de l'église de Tigran est si intéressant, chalcédonien pour l'ensemble, mais grégorien si l'on en juge d'après le cycle développé de la conversion de l'Arménie par Grégoire. D'autant plus que les deux fils du saint, patriarches à sa suite (Aristakès et Vertanès), figurent dans le sanctuaire, encadrant la file des saints évêques. Quant à la juxtaposition des visions de Grégoire et de Nino, on peut la considérer comme un trait d'union entre les deux confessions. Rappelons d'autre part, qu'à l'époque, le culte de Nino avait pris un caractère officiel sous le règne de la reine Tamar (1184–1213), les portraits de la sainte se multipliant[22]. Aussi peut-on voir également dans cette représentation du miracle de la Colonne vivante, une prise en considération de la pensée monarchique géorgienne par le commanditaire arménien du décor.

II. Rapport du culte de Nino et des régions du Tao-Clardjeti et d'Ani

Un article récent de Bernadette Martin-Hisard sur «Les jalons pour une histoire de culte de sainte Nino (fin du IVe–XIIe s.)» reprend certaines données relatives aux lieux saints: Sveti Tsxoveli de Mcxeta édifiée sur le site de l'église du roi Mirian, Samtavro, église épiscopale, Djvari abritant la croix de bois de la sainte[23].

Si l'historicité de la sainte est attestée depuis le IVe siècle et son rôle d'évangélisatrice reconnu au cours du haut Moyen Âge (VIe–VIIIe s.), l'auteur a noté qu'en revanche, son culte n'apparaît qu'au Xe siècle, le jour de sa commémoration n'étant pas encore fixé. Des sermons lui sont attribués et elle apparaît dans le manuscrit de Šatberd, *La conversion du Kartli* (973), qui reste sans écho. L'œvre est ignorée à l'Athos.

À cette étude qui insiste sur l'intérêt du manuscrit de Šatberd[24], nous rattachons une représentation contemporaine de sainte Nino orante (*fig. 3*). Elle est sculptée en buste sur le pilier de la galerie sud de la cathédrale d'Öşk (Tao), datée de 963–973. C'est un pilier à programme sur lequel divers saints sont associés aux anges, séraphins et tétramorphes qui accompagnent la *Déisis*[25].

Enfin, une légende arménienne de la croix de Nuné nous ramène à Ani par le Tao. Elle est relatée dans l'*Histoire Universelle* de Vardan: lors de l'apostasie du roi de Géorgie Vazgen (l'époux de sainte Susan[26]), la croix de bois de Nino fut emportée de Mcxeta et cachée dans la montagne de Parhal, gardée durant sept ans par un ermite Andréas.

Informé de cela, Grigor Mamikonean la transporta dans son château de Kapoytberd (fin de VIIe siècle) d'où elle fut transférée dans le canton de Vanand où un couvent fut fondé à son intention. Elle prit alors le nom de Croix de Vanand (voir la carte). Quand la

---

22 Sur le sujet, A. Eastmond, Royal Imagery in Medieval Georgia, Pennsylvania St. Univ. Press 1998, 119–21.

23 Dans: From Byzantium to Iran. In Honour of Nina G. Garsoïan, Columbia University, Program in Armenian Studies 5, (Atlanta 1997), 53–76.

24 La localisation du couvent reste incertaine, une dernière hypothèse propose avec vraisemblance le site de Yeni Rabat (communication de Kétino Abachidzé); de toute façon, dans le district d'Ardanuç (carte).

25 E. Takaišvili, Expedition archéologique de 1917 dans les provinces méridionales de Géorgie (en russe), Tbilisi 1952, 52, pl. 78; D. Winfield, Some Early Medieval Figure Sculpture from North-East Turkey, *J. of the Warburg and Courtauld Institutes* 31 (1968), 33–72 (48, fig. 19a). En 1991, nous lisions encore le nom de Nino. L'an 2000, on a détruit ou emporté le buste de Nino et la *Déisis*.

26 Sur le martyre de la sainte reine, aperçu dans J. Karst, Littérature géorgienne chrétienne, Paris 1934, 74–76.

maison des Mamikonean fut anéantie par Sukʿman, la croix fut portée à Ani, à l'époque du catholicos Barseł (1080–1113). Sa fête fut fixée le dimanche suivant l'octave de l'Exaltation de la Croix[27]. Malgré l'incohérence chronologique du récit à propos de l'apostasie du roi d'Ibérie (milieu du Ve siècle) et du transport de la croix près de Parhal (VIIe), certaines données sont très évocatrices, comme la notion du Tao-Clardjeti en tant que montagne-refuge, les transferts successifs de la relique en raison des hasards de la guerre, et l'arrivée à Ani, capitale régionale et place forte importante.

Ces trois données disparates constituent des indices en faveur d'un foyer de culte de sainte Nino dans la zone géographique du Tao-Clardjeti et de la région voisine de Kars et Ani (carte). Elles témoignent, une fois de plus, de l'importance de la province ibère comme source historique du haut Moyen Âge arméno-géorgien. La représentation du miracle de la Colonne vivante dans l'église de Tigran Honencʿ s'inscrit peut-être également dans une tradition locale.

Illustrations

Schéma (N. Thierry): Les deux visions théophaniques, celle de Grégoire l'Illuminateur de l'Arménie et celle de la Colonne vivante de Nino
Carte (M. Thierry):. Régions arméno-géorgiennes

Fig. 1 (Pl. 7): La Colonne vivante entre Nino et ses compagnes (N. Thierry)
Fig. 2 (Pl. 8): Détail: Nino en prière (N. Thierry)
Fig. 3 (Pl. 8): Öşk: Nino en orante (P. Couprie) – Sujet disparu en l'an 2000.
Fig. 4 (Pl. 9): Un des anges porteur du mur oriental de Mcxeta (N. Thierry)
Fig. 5 (Pl. 9): La Colonne, portée par quatre anges à Udabno (d'opus Amiranašvili, pl. 27)

Abréviations bibliographiques

Brosset 1849: M. Brosset, Histoire de la Géorgie depuis l'Antiquité jusqu'au XIX siècle, Saint-Pétersbourg.

Pätsch 1975: Gertrud Pätsch, Die Bekehrung Georgiens, Mokcevay kartlisay (Verfasser unbekannt), *Bedi Kartlisa* 33, 288–337.

Pätsch 1985: Gertrud Pätsch, Kartlis cxovreba. Das Leben Kartlis. Eine Chronik aus Georgien 300–1200 , Leipzig.

Peeters 1932: P. Peeters, Les débuts du christianisme en Géorgie d'après les sources hagiographiques, *AnBoll* 50, 5–58.

Peeters 1951: P. Peeters, A propos de la version arménienne de l'historien Socrate, *Subsidia hagiographica* 27, 310–36.

Tamarati 1910: M. Tamarati, L'Église géorgienne des origines jusqu'à nos jours, Rome.

Takaišvili 1891: E. Takaišvili, La conversion du Kartli. Une nouvelle recension de sainte Nino, Tiflis.

Tarchnišvili 1947: M. Tarchnišvili, Sources arméno-géorgiennes de l'histoire ancienne de l'Église de Géorgie. *Museon* 60, 29–50.

Thélamon 1981: Françoise Thélamon, Païens et chrétiens au IV siècle. L'apport de l'Histoire ecclésiastique de Rufin d'Aquilée, Paris.

[27] Eprikian, Dictionnaire illustré de la patrie (en arménien) 1905, 2, 141–42; R. W. Thomson, The Historical Compilation of Vardan Arewelcʿi, *DOP* 43 (1989) 199.

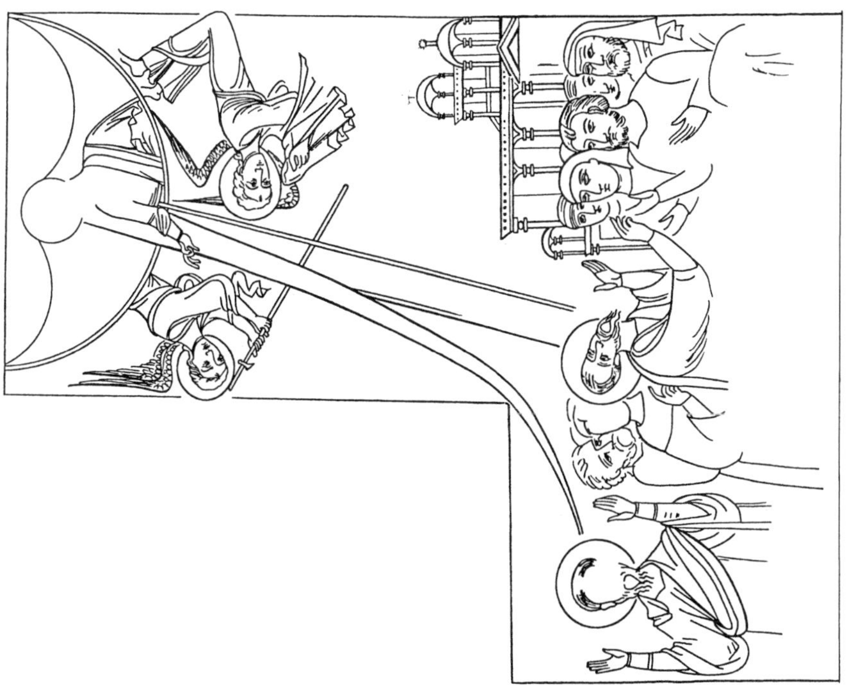

Vision de Grégoire (N.T.)

Vision de sainte Nino. (N.T.)

Les deux visions théophaniques

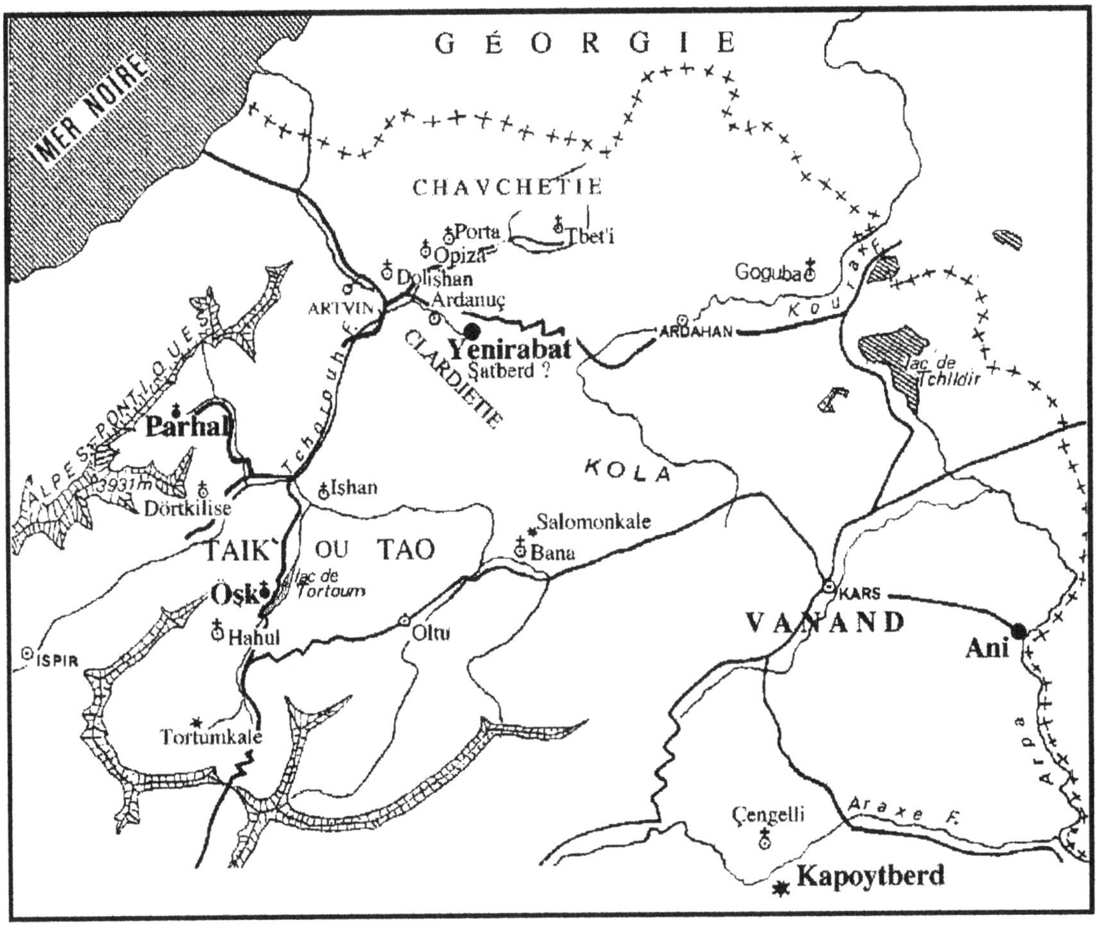

Carte (M. Thierry): Régions arméno-géorgiennes

ROBERT W. THOMSON / OXFORD

SYRIAN CHRISTIANITY AND THE CONVERSION OF ARMENIA

The Armenian historian Agatʿangełos describes the conversion of king Trdat early in the fourth century in terms of his turning away from ancient Armenian roots, which were closely related to Iranian religious traditions, towards the west, to the Christian church of the Roman empire and to an alliance with the emperor Constantine[1]. He stresses the role of Saint Gregory the Illuminator, his consecration as bishop for Armenia at Caesarea, the establishment of a regular hierarchy, and the presence of Gregory's son, Aristakēs, at the council of Nicaea. But whatever the motivation or the precise date for this dramatic shift in Armenian policy and the events surrounding it, and however accurate or fanciful the account in Agatʿangełos, the king's acceptance of Christianity and the establishment of a regular ecclesiastical hierarchy in Armenia are but two steps in the conversion of Armenia – or, to be more precise, the conversion of the Armenians.

This is not the place to analyse or date the various recensions of the *History* attributed to Agatʿangełos[2]. We may regard with scepticism the claim in the Armenian version that in seven days after Gregory's return as bishop more than four million Armenians were baptized, and that during his lifetime Gregory actually established a church "in every place," and consecrated more than four hundred bishops[3]. It is quite clear from the *Epic Histories* of the *Buzandaran* that Christianity met with much opposition in Armenia. In his first book that author laments of his fellow-countrymen: "When they had taken on the name of Christian ... they did not receive it with ardent faith, but as some human folly [and] under duress ... Those who were acquainted with Greek or Syriac learning [were able] to achieve some partial inkling of it. As for those who were without skill in learning and who were the great mass of the people ... not one of them could keep in mind a single thing of what he had heard." He continues with a description of their traditional, pagan practices[4]. Referring to the situation at the end of the same century, Koriwn points to the need for missionary activity in the countryside[5]. General acceptance of a Christian outlook would take some time to achieve.

---

[1] For the Iranian background see Garsoïan, Prolegomena, Iranian Substratum, The Two Voices. The alliance with Constantine plays a major role in later Armenian tradition and was influential in the development of apocalyptic themes; for a general view of the literary evidence see Thomson, Constantine and Trdat.

[2] The standard version is the surviving Armenian text. An earlier recension lies behind some of the Greek and Arabic renderings. For an overview of the complicated textual transmission of the story of Trdat and Gregory see van Esbrœck, Agathangelos, and Winkler, Our Present Knowledge. Details of the editions of Armenian texts cited are given in the Bibliography at the end of this article; more information on modern translations and secondary sources may be found in Thomson, A Bibliography of Classical Armenian Literature.

[3] See Agatʿangełos, § 835, 856. Cf. also Harutyunyan, Die Diözesan-Gliederung, above, p. 81–98.

[4] *Buzandaran*, III, 13; I quote from the recent translation by Garsoïan, Epic Histories. The author of the *Buzandaran* was familiar with the History of Agatʿangelos (or at least a version of it), and regarded his own work as a continuation, "as a brick set in the wall (III, 1)."

[5] His biography of Maštocʿ is as much concerned with the master's missionary travels as with his invention of the script and the beginnings of Armenian literature. Later Armenian historians also emphasize the importance of the script in the conversion of the populace at large.

Here I shall concentrate on two related points: the role of Syrian Christians in the process of Armenia's conversion (as opposed to the activity of Gregory and his Greek-oriented policies), and the continuing influence of Syrian traditions in the development of the early Armenian church. Agatʿangełos ignores the former, though ironically the impact of the latter may be seen in the Armenian version of his *History*[6]. The theological questions involved in the relationship of the Armenian and Syrian churches in the fifth and sixth centuries are not my present concern. These were first discussed as a whole in the famous work by Ervant Tēr-Minaseancʿ, "Die armenische Kirche in ihren Beziehungen zu den syrischen Kirchen", which deals with the question from the beginnings to the thirteenth century. This study was epoch-making, since he was able to use the extensive correspondence between Armenians and Greeks, Syrians and Georgians, the famous "Book of Letters," that was not published until 1901[7]. We now have an even more detailed study of the early Armenian-Syrian relationship based on all the original documents in Nina Garsoïan's, "L'église arménienne et le grand schisme d'Orient", published in 1999. This is the most comprehensive investigation of the question to date, and her conclusions will take a while to be assimilated[8].

That many Armenians were familiar with Syriac is indicated by the fact that when Maštocʿ sent pupils to Edessa to make translations after the successful invention of the script, they did not need to learn Syriac first; whereas they had to learn Greek before embarking on translations from that language[9]. Syriac was widely used in areas of Armenia subject to the Iranian shahs, especially in the provinces along the frontier in northern Mesopotamia[10], while in northern and western Armenia that language was less well known, Greek being the dominant tongue for reading and writing. However, it is hardly the case that linguistic ability in Greek or Syriac was strictly divided in accordance with the frontiers established in 387.

Although Agatʿangełos claims that schools were established by king Trdat where children were to be instructed in the art of writing, some being set to Syriac and others to Greek, it is noticeable that the text in this section shows the strong influence of Koriwn's biography of Maštocʿ. The same actions are attributed to the Catholicos Nerses I in the *Buzandaran*[11]. However, in the time of Maštocʿ Koriwn merely says that some of his disciples were sent to Syria in order to make translations from that language into Greek, not that schools for Syriac existed in Armenia. At the turn of the fifth and sixth century Łazar Pʿarpecʿi, describing the concern of Maštocʿ that Armenian could not be written down, emphasizes that the youth of Armenia had to go on long journeys to learn Syriac[12]. He explains: "For the worship of the church and the readings of scripture were conducted in Syriac in the hermitages and churches of the Armenian people. But the congregations of such a large country were quite unable to comprehend or profit from it." This too implies a lack of facilities for instruction in the language.

---

[6] For the influence of motifs from Syriac texts available in Armenian translation by the end of the fifth century see the Introduction to the English translation of Agatʿangełos by THOMSON.

[7] The original German edition of Tēr-Minaseancʿ' work appeared in 1904; the Armenian version was published in 1908 (and reprinted in 1998). The second edition of the *Book of Letters* by N. POŁAREAN, based on a broader range of textual evidence, provides better readings in many places; but the order of the items has been changed from that of the original in accordance with Połarean's own views concerning their dating.

[8] The very detailed Bibliography is also valuable.

[9] See Koriwn, ch. 19.

[10] This is discussed in GARSOÏAN, Schisme, ch. 1.

[11] *Buzandaran*, IV, 4.

[12] Łazar, History, p. 13.

Nonetheless, Armenian writers did think that Syriac would have been well known. Movsēs Xorenacʻi claims that king Vałaršak's envoy, the enigmatic Mar Abas Catina, brought back from the archives in Nineveh extracts in both Greek and Syriac. And he implies that Syriac was not used only at court but also by Maštocʻ in his preaching activity. Referring to the establishment of schools by Maštocʻ and Sahak, he declares: "Maštocʻ instructed the entire area of the Persian sector, but not the Greek part where they used the Greek script and not Syriac"[13].

Armenians of the fourth century were not only familiar to some degree with Syriac as a language, but also with the more tangible presence of Syrian Christians. The claim in the so-called *History of Taron* attributed to Zenob of Glak that Saint Gregory summoned many helpers from among the Syrians, and that he even asked Zenob to reduce his emphasis on Syrians, may be discounted in view of the late tenth century date and the tendentious character of this curious text[14]. Stepʻannos Orbelean claims that Gregory sent one of the Syrians in his entourage to Siwnikʻ; while Movsēs Dasxurancʻi refers to Syrian priests burying the relics of an unnamed disciple of Grigoris in Ałuank[15]. We are on surer ground with Koriwn and the early historians. Koriwn paints a clear picture of the work of Maštocʻ as preacher and missionary. He first devoted himself to spiritual discipline as an ascetic hermit. As he gained renown, pupils began to attach themselves to him in order to learn from the master the path of spiritual progress. They moved around as a group, and by their preaching endeavoured to turn the local inhabitants from their pagan traditions. Koriwn describes how Maštocʻ went first to Gołtʻn. The prince of that region, Šabitʻ, was already a Christian and gave these visiting holy men his support[16]. Koriwn does not suggest that Šabitʻ himself had previously put any pressure on his people to convert; at the end of the fourth century the Christians among the nobility needed outside help in imposing their ideals on the general populace.

Now the role of the itinerant holy man, working miracles that authenticated his mission, did not begin with Maštocʻ. Disregarding apocryphal traditions in Syriac, such as the supposed missionary activity of Mari, disciple of Addai, in Arzanene and along the Tigris[17], I shall mention only fourth century examples in the *Buzandaran*. The majority of such persons there described were Syrian, or were associated with Syria. The visit to Armenia by Jacob of Nisibis to reform prince Manačihr Ṙštuni, whatever its historicity, did not result in any conversions[18]. More important was the later work of Daniel, the bishop of Taron, a Syrian by origin. He was famous for preaching not only in his own diocese, but also in foreign parts under Persian control. His ability in both Syriac and Armenian must therefore be assumed[19]. The author of the *Buzandaran* describes his amazing ascetic prodigies, and refers elsewhere to several of his pupils. They operated principally in southern Armenia, in the regions bordering on Syriac-speaking Christian-

---

[13] Movsēs Xorenacʻi, History, I, 9; III, 54.

[14] See p. 18 and 25 of the Armenian text; for the date see the Introduction to AVDOYAN's translation.

[15] Stepʻannos, ch. 5; Movsēs Dasxurancʻi, I, 14. Both of these historians of border provinces give traditions about the early evangelisation of their areas which diverge greatly from the accounts in mainstream Armenian historians. For missionary activity in norther regions and the death of Grigoris, grandson of Gregory the Illuminator, see the *Buzandaran*, III, 5–7; and for traditions about Maštocʻ and his journeys, TER-PETROSYAN, Maštocʻyan Avandnerë.

[16] Koriwn, ch. 5.

[17] See CHAUMONT, Christianisation de l'empire iranien, Appendix 5.

[18] *Buzandaran*, III, 10. On this passage see PEETERS, La légende de saint Jacques, and the comments in GARSOÏAN, Epic Histories, p. 252, 431. Jacob's renown in Armenia is reflected in the attribution of Afrahat's *Homilies* to him.

[19] *Buzandaran*, III, 14.

ity, but also in the north and west, in the region of Erzinjan, in Basean and in Ayrarat. The work of Daniel's disciples Šaɫita in Korduk', Epip'an in Cop'k', and the general oversight of the eremitic communities in Armenia by Gind are particularly emphasized. The *Buzandaran* notes that they lived in hermitages and that Epip'an had a very large following devoted to an ascetic life[20]. Syrian missionaries were still active much later, as emerges from the Life of Aḥo, who died circa 560. His biographer notes that he attempted to convert a pagan Armenian village[21].

In other words, the author of the *Buzandaran* does not imply that the spread of a Christian ethos in Armenia was primarily brought about by the bishops of the different dioceses founding local churches. There was no diocesan network along the lines of the organised system in the Roman empire. Such an urban configuration was foreign to Armenia[22]. The leading noble families provided the bishops, though their number was quite modest to judge from those named in the *Buzandaran*, other early texts, and the signatories to Armenian church councils. In contrast to the claim in Agat'angeɫos, we may note that at the gathering at Artašat in 450 in time of crisis, only seventeen bishops are named by Eɫišē[23]. No list of signatories is attached to the canons of the council of Šahapivan held in 444; the large number of forty unidentified bishops appears only in the much later Introduction[24]. At the first council of Dvin in 506 twenty-one bishops are named[25]; and in the letter of Nersēs before the second council in 555, eighteen – though it is implied that this was not a complete listing[26].

Of parish organization, as opposed to the episcopal hierarchy or ascetic groupings, we have little evidence from this early period. Canons and the much later lawcode of Mxit'ar Goš imply that the local priests were drawn from their communities and not imposed from outside. The number of 390 priests appears in the canons associated with the council of Dvin held in 607[27], but it is not indicated what proportion of the total number in Armenia this represents. In any event, during the fourth century the task of bringing the populace at large into the Christian fold was carried out primarily by itinerant preachers. And their leaders were quite likely to be of Syrian origin. The seriousness of their activity in Armenia is further indicated by the effort of the bishop Daniel to adapt an older, presumably semitic, script for the Armenian language before Maštoc' had successfully created his own. Daniel's sphere of activity is not mentioned by Koriwn, but it is tempting to place him in Arzn on the Tigris and to identify him with the Daniel mentioned as attending the Syrian councils of 410 and 424[28].

It is in this context that Maštoc's' own work must be viewed. He did not hold episcopal rank with attendant obligations, but was the independent holy man *par excel-*

---

[20] See the Prosopographical Index of GARSOÏAN's translation for full references. Organised coenobitic monasticism had not yet developed in fourth century Armenia. The terminology of Armenian texts (of the fifth century or later) is confusing and anachronistic. See THOMSON, Łazar P'arpec'i, p. 269–271, Monks and Monasteries, and GARSOÏAN, Schisme, p. 439–440, n. 11, on *vanakan*, "solitaire".

[21] PALMER, Monk and Mason, p. 127.

[22] See GARSOÏAN, The City.

[23] Eɫišē, History, p. 27–28. Łazar, History, p. 44–45, gives the same number, though in a different order, with only one variation in name. Cf. HARUTYUNYAN, l.c., above, p. 83–94 and M. K. KRIKORIAN, Addendum, above p. 95–98.

[24] *Kanonagirk' Hayoc'*, I, p. 424–449.

[25] Girk' T'ɫt'oc', p. 41–47; translation in GARSOÏAN, Schisme, p. 438–446.

[26] Girk' T'ɫt'oc', p. 70–71; translation in GARSOÏAN, Schisme, p. 474–476.

[27] Girk' T'ɫt'oc', p. 146–148.

[28] See WINKLER's commentary to Koriwn, p. 235–252, for all Armenian references to Daniel. Daniel of Arzon appears in the *Synodicon Orientale*, p. 272 (synod of 410, where he signs as no. 16, his see being the ninth in canon 21), and p. 285 (synod of 424, where he is the ninth in the list).

lence. The importance of his invention of the script was not to bring literacy to the nobility, who already possessed it in Greek or Syriac, and still less to teach the peasants to read. It was to provide texts which could be read publicly in Armenian, so that the peripatetic missionary preachers no longer had to rely on extemporary translation. Furthermore, by creating the proper medium, he enabled the previously variant traditions of Greek and Syriac origin to be welded into an original and specifically Armenian amalgam. What were the main Syrian strands in this new entity?

Several points come immediately to mind. The first is linguistic, namely, the continuing use of Syriac words and expressions taken over into Armenian. More general vocabulary from Aramaic had entered Armenian prior to the advent of Christianity[29]. But many specifically Christian terms were adopted by the fledgling Armenian church, some of which remain in use to the present day. For example, *kʿahanay* for "priest," *com* for "fast," *abełay* for "monk," as opposed to borrowings from Greek such as *katʿołikos*, originally used for a "metropolitan bishop," *episkopos*, and many others. Sometimes a Syriac expression has been literally translated, bringing a new sense into Armenian. Thus the verb *pahel*, "to hold, keep," takes on the sense of "fasting," from the use of the equivalent in Syriac *nʿtar*.

Another interesting Syriacism is the use in early canons of the expression *uxti mankunkʿ*, "children of the covenant," for the lesser clergy[30]. In Syriac this expression, *bnai qyama*, originally referred to a category of laity rather than clergy; they were people who had devoted their lives to ascetic practices and chastity, but lived in the world rather than in seclusion[31]. In the Armenian translation of the *Homilies* of the Syrian Afrahat, *bnai qyama* is rendered by *uxtaworkʿ*, "those who had made a vow," which is a fairly exact translation. But after the fourth century the Syriac expression *bnai qyama* lost its narrow meaning, and the Armenian calque *uxti mankunkʿ* could reasonably be used for clergy.

In addition to the influence of Syriac terminology, the impact of Syrian Christian writings in Armenia is obvious in several areas. Koriwn emphasizes that the pupils of Maštocʿ were active in translating, though he does not name the individual Syrian authors translated. Their first concern was with the bible. We cannot go into this complicated question, to which attention has been given by many scholars; nor do I have any new conclusions to present on that subject[32]. We may merely note that the first rendering of the gospels and of many other books of the bible was from Syriac – though precisely which Syriac version is disputed in certain cases – and that this first translation was later revised on the Greek text. It would have taken many years to render into Armenian not only the biblical texts mentioned by Koriwn, but also the works of noted Syrian authors such as Ephrem and Afrahat, in addition to the large number of Lives of saints and martyrs that found their way into Armenian.

Not surprisingly, then, Armenians continued to study in Edessa after the visits by Maštocʿ and his pupils in the early fifth century. This is clear from a non-Armenian source. One of the documents submitted to the second coucil of Ephesus in 449 was signed by local Edessan authorities, including representatives of the "schools" of the Syrians, Persians (i.e. Christian Syrians from Persian territory) and "Armenians"[33]. Although there is little other evidence for a permanent Armenian presence in Edessa until very

---

29 The list in Hübschmann's Grammatik, p. 281–321, does not distinguish the varying dates of adoption into Armenian of the foreign vocabulary. See also Greppin, Syriac Loanwords.

30 *Kanonagirkʿ*, I, p. 129: Nicaea, 18; p. 370, 393, 398: Canons of Sahak.

31 See Griffith, Asceticism in the Church of Syria.

32 See in general Metzger, The Early Versions, and Renoux, Langue et littérature.

33 See the Akten der Ephesinischen Synode, ed. Flemming, p. 25.

much later, that city does figure as a stage on the route from Armenia to Jerusalem. The importance of Jerusalem for Armenians as a centre of pilgrimage is well known[34]. According to the Itinerary (*Młonačapkʿ*) associated with the Armenian Geography known as the *Ašxarhacʿoycʿ*[35] if a traveller started from Dvin, he passed through the Kleisourai (i.e. the Bitlis Pass), then Urha (i.e. Edessa), before reaching the Euphrates; the route then led via Damascus and Mount Tabor to Jerusalem. From Jerusalem the traveller could proceed to Alexandria. It may be no coincidence that the route described by Movsēs Xorenacʿi in the account of his own travels runs from southern Armenia to Edessa, then on to Palestine and Egypt[36].

Before turning to the impact of Syriac writings on Armenian authors, we might just note that some works originally composed in Greek, but already available in Syriac, were translated from that rendering and not directly from the original. The most influential of these secondary translations was probably the *Ecclesiastical History* by Eusebius of Caesarea, who was regarded by later Armenian writers as the Greek historian *par excellence*, with whom Movsēs Xorenacʿi could be compared among the Armenians[37]. And one might mention, *inter alia*, that the popular *Hexaemeron* by Basil of Caesarea came into Armenian via its somewhat expanded Syriac version[38].

As for the impact in Armenia of texts by Syrian authors, unfortunately we still lack studies similar to those of Kim Muradyan on Basil and Gregory of Nazianzus[39]. Nonetheless, a few comments can be hazarded. The impact of Syrian hagiography, notably the Acts of the Persian Martyrs (*Vkaykʿ Arewelicʿ*), on Ełišē has been noted by Levon Ter-Petrosyan[40]. In Agatʿangełos imagery from the Lives of the Edessene martyrs is discernible[41]. The influence of Afrahat's *Homilies* in their Armenian version has not yet been investigated, though there are several legendary Armenian Lives of their supposed author, Jacob of Nisibis[42]. Ephrem's renown was even greater. Of particular significance was the *Commentary on the Diatessaron* – that it may not be by the hand of Ephrem himself, but the work of a close disciple, is not directly relevant here[43]. Ter-Petrosyan has noted several close parallels with the Armenian version of this Commentary in the long *Teaching of Saint Gregory*, which appears in the Armenian version of Agatʿangełos; but they are not verbatim quotations[44]. There are parallels also in the *Homily on the Passion* attributed to Ełišē, where the narrative often follows the order of events in the Diatessaron and details in Ephrem's commentary rather than one of the gospels[45]. In addition to the early close renderings of Ephrem's compositions, there are later reworkings, such as

---

34 See the works of Hunt, Maraval and Stone in the Bibliography below.

35 The Armenian text is included in the works of Anania of Širak; translation in Hewsen, The Geography of Ananias of Širak, p. 320–321.

36 Movsēs Xorenacʿi, III, 61. The date of this History and the authenticity of the author's claim to have made this journey, remain hotly disputed. See the Introductions to the translations by Mahé and Thomson for a review of opinions.

37 See the introductory chapters to the Histories by Stephen of Taron (Asołik) and Samuēl of Ani. Eusebius's even more influential Chronicle was translated into Armenian directly from the Greek.

38 See Thomson, The Syriac and Armenian Versions.

39 See Muradyan, Barseł and Grigor.

40 Ter-Petrosyan, Abrahamu Xostovanołi.

41 See the translation by Thomson, notes to § 99, 102, 111, 119.

42 See Peeters, *BHO*, p. 93–94, for the texts; and in general Krüger, Jakob von Nisibis.

43 See Petersen, Some Remarks. For the Armenian version see Leloir, Commentaire, and his edition of the text.

44 Ter-Petrosyan, Grigor Lusavorčʿi.

45 See the Introduction to the translation by Thomson.

the *Commentary on Genesis*, which passed under his name[46]. And the false *Canons of Ephrem* appear in the later collection of canons printed as the second volume of the *Kanonagirkʿ*[47].

It is noteworthy that Ephrem is not often mentioned by name in early Armenian texts, and that the *Lives* of Ephrem were not translated until much later[48]. He is not cited in the Armenian-Syrian correspondence found in the *Book of Letters*, although later texts in that collection do mention him as an authority. The earliest of these is the *Treatise against the Dyophysites* attributed to Sahak III, which does not predate the late seventh century[49]. In the catena known as *Knikʿ Hawatoy*, "Seal of Faith", which was compiled in the time of the Catholicos Komitas of the seventh century, there are three quotations from Ephrem[50]; though in the later *Armat Hawatoy*, "Root of Faith"[51], quotations ascribed to him are more prominent. But this apparent neglect is not surprising, because the dogmatic works of Ephrem were not translated into Armenian; his popularity there was reflected more in the hymns and commentaries[52].

Another sphere of Syrian influence is that of liturgical usage. In this regard the Armenians developed a unique tradition, drawing from both Greek and Syrian practices and influenced by the ritual of Jerusalem. Gabriele Winkler has shown how early Armenian rites, especially those of initiation, reflect Syrian models[53]. Even the description of Trdat's baptism in the Greek-oriented Agatʿangełos reflects aspects of Syrian practice. Some of the earliest formulations of Armenian credal statements also follow Syriac wording[54]. Liturgical usage, of course, cannot be disconnected from liturgical space. Here one cannot neglect the impact of Syrian church architecture in Armenia, notably the early basilica types before the domed cross became more or less the standard Armenian style. Of these Ereruk is the most significant example[55]. But ecclesiastical architecture and liturgical practice go beyond my present concerns.

Perhaps the most striking aspect of Syrian influence on the early Armenian church is the adaptation of the tradition concerning the origin of the Edessan church to Armenia. Even by the year 200 only one small church building is recorded at Edessa, despite the later importance of that city which gave its local dialect to the burgeoning Syrian church as Syriac[56]. But here, as elswhere, the desire for a foundation associated with the apostles prompted pious imagination to fill a void. By the beginning of the fourth century the historian Eusebius, the importance of whose *Ecclesiastical History* for Armenia we have already noted, records the story of correspondence between king Abgar of Edessa and Jesus, and the subsequent visit of Thaddaeus to convert Abgar. As time passed the tale became ever more elaborate, involving a portrait of Jesus which was kept at Edessa, and numerous other expansions. Although attempts have been made to associate this story

---

[46] See the edition by MATHEWS, and his Introduction to the volume of translation for the date and origin of this text.

[47] *Kanonagirkʿ Hayocʿ*, II, p. 55–58.

[48] See OUTTIER and TER-PETROSYAN, Textes arméniens.

[49] For the date and circumstances of this treatise see most recently VAN ESBRŒCK, Le discours.

[50] *Knikʿ Hawatoy*, p. 4, 257, 299; the analysis in LEBON, Les citations, deals only with quotations from Greek authors.

[51] See THOMSON, The Shorter Recension.

[52] Further details of published texts in THOMSON, Bibliography, p. 46–48.

[53] See WINKLER, Das armenische Initiationsrituale, especially p. 106–129 for the ritual at Trdat's baptism.

[54] WINKLER, Armenian Anaphoras and Creeds.

[55] KHATCHATRIAN, L'Architecture arménienne, p. 45–48.

[56] See the brief *Chronicle of Edessa*.

with a later king Abgar, not the one living in the time of Jesus, this foundation myth has no basis in fact[57].

Armenians no doubt became familiar with this tradition even before Maštocʿ went to Edessa in his quest for a script. In the fifth century they certainly could read about it in the Armenian translation of Eusebius; and the more elaborate Syriac version of the tale, known as the *Teaching of Addai*, where Addai is the Syriac for Eusebius's Thaddaeus, was also translated into Armenian. In the process, however, a very significant addition was made. According to the Syriac tradition Addai died in Edessa after ordaining his successor; the Armenian version has him go to the north and found the first church in Armenia. There he was martyred by king Sanatruk. Thus in the *Buzandaran* the patriarchal throne is called the "throne of Tʿadēos," even though there was a hiatus of more than two centuries between this legendary visit and the activity of Saint Gregory the Illuminator[58]. The two were later linked by the tradition of Gregory's conception at the grave of Thaddaeus[59].

As is well known, Movsēs Xorenacʿi actually makes Abgar an Armenian king, which was generally accepted by later Armenian writers. But his identification of figures in the story of Edessa's conversion with Bagratuni nobles did not enter the mainstream of Armenian tradition. Nor did the later Tʿovma Arcruni's counter-claim gain general acceptance, that it was an Arcruni who was baptised by Thaddaeus to become the first Armenian Christian.

The adaptation of the foundation myth of Edessa, which was the centre of Syriac-speaking Christianity, illustrates well the deep and persistent influence in Armenia of Syrian Christian traditions and the close interaction between Armenians and Syrians in the early centuries of the Armenian church. Once the legends of the other apostles' extensive travels had gained credence, then Bartholomew was also appropriated as an apostolic founder of the church in Armenia – though again there was a long hiatus between his time and the work of Saint Gregory, who by universal agreement was considered the real father of Armenian Christianity[60]. By contrast, the Ałuankʿ traced their church back to a disciple of Thaddaeus named Elisaeus, who became for them "the Illuminator of the lands of the East." This tradition is aggressively pushed by Movsēs Dasxurancʿi in the tenth century[61]. But to pursue these developments would take us beyond the scope of the present theme.

---

[57] See Brock, Eusebius and Syriac Christianity.

[58] *Buzandaran*, III, 12; IV, 3, 4. The author begins his *History*, III, 1, by stating that the period from the martyrdom of Thaddaeus by Sanatruk to the deaths of Gregory and king Trdat had been written down "by others". For a review of opinions regarding these unnamed authors see Garsoïan, Epic Histories, p. 1–22. Since the *Buzandaran* begins with Book III, likely preceding texts are the Acts of Thaddaeus and a recension of Agatʿangelos.

[59] This tradition first appears in the Syriac version of Agatʿangelos, § 8 in van Esbrœck, Le résumé syriaque. In Armenian Movsēs Xorenacʿi, II, 74, attributes his knowledge of the tradition to "a wonderful old man".

[60] Movsēs Xorenacʿi, II, 34. See further van Esbrœck, La naissance du culte de saint Barthélemy.

[61] Movsēs Dasxurancʿi, I, 6, 28; III, 8.

Bibliography

Texts

Agatʿangełos: *Patmutiwn Hayocʿ*, ed. G. TĒR-MKRTČʿEAN and S. KANAYEANCʿ, Tiflis 1909; reprinted Delmar, NY, 1980, Erevan 1983. English translation: R. W. THOMSON, Agathangełos: History of the Armenians, Albany, NY, 1976. This omits the Teaching of Saint Gregory, for which see R. W. THOMSON, The Teaching of Saint Gregory (*Harvard Armenian Texts and Studies* 3), Cambridge, MA, 1970.

Anania Širakacʿi: *Anania Širakacʿu Matenagrutʿyunē*, ed. A. ABRAHAMYAN, Erevan 1944. English translation of the Geography: R.H. HEWSEN, The Geography of Ananias of Širak (Ašxarhacʿoycʿ) (*Beihefte zum Tübinger Atlas des Vorderen Orients*, Reihe B, Nr. 77), Wiesbaden 1992.

Asołik: See *Stepʿannos Taronecʿi*.

Book of Letters: See *Girkʿ Tʿłtʿocʿ*.

Buzandaran: *Pawstosi Buzandacʿwoy Patmutʿiwn Hayocʿ*, ed. Kʿ. PATKANEAN, St. Petersburg 1883; reprinted Delmar, NY, 1984. English translation: N. G. GARSOÏAN, The Epic Histories attributed to Pʿawstos Buzand (*Buzandaran Patmutʿiwnkʿ*) (*Harvard Armenian Texts and Studies* 8), Cambridge, MA, 1989.

Chronicle of Edessa: in I. GUIDI, Chronica Minora (*CSCO*, III, 4), Louvain 1903, p. 1–13.

Ełišē: History. Armenian text: *Vasn Vardanay ew Hayocʿ Paterazmin*, ed. E. TER- MINASYAN, Erevan 1957. English translation: R. W. THOMSON, Elishe. History of Vardan and the Armenian War (*Harvard Armenian Texts and Studies* 5), Cambridge, MA, 1982.

Ełišē: Homily on the Passion. Armenian text in Ełišēi *Matenagrutʿiwnkʿ*; Venice 1859, p. 240–354. English translation: R. W. THOMSON, A Homily on the Passion of Christ attributed to Elishe (*Eastern Christian Texts in Translation* 5), Leuven 2000.

Ephesus: Akten der Ephesinischen Synode vom Jahre 449, ed. J. FLEMMING (Abh. Göttingen, Phil.-Hist. Kl. N.F. 15/1), 1917.

Ephrem: Commentaire de l'Evangile concordant, version arménienne, ed. L. LELOIR (*CSCO*, 137, 145), Louvain 1953.

Ephrem: The Armenian Commentary on Genesis attributed to Ephrem the Syrian, ed. E. G. MATHEWS, JR., (*CSCO*, 572, 573), Leuven 1998.

Girkʿ Tʿłtʿocʿ, ed. Y. IZMIREANCʿ, Tiflis 1901; second edition, ed. N. POŁAREAN, Jerusalem 1994.

Kanonagirkʿ Hayocʿ, ed. V. HAKOBYAN, 2 vols., Erevan 1964, 1971.

Knikʿ Hawatoy, ed. K. TĒR-MKRTČʿEAN, Ējmiacin 1914; reprinted as "Sceau de la Foi", Louvain 1974.

Koriwn: Varkʿ Maštocʿi, ed. M. ABELEAN, Erevan 1941; reprinted Cairo 1954, Erevan 1981, Delmar, NY, 1984. German translation: G. WINKLER, Koriwns Biographie des Mesrop Maštocʿ (*Orientalia Christiana Analecta* 245), Rome 1994.

Łazar Pʿarpecʿi: History and Letter: *Patmutʿiwn Hayocʿ ew Tʿułtʿ aṙ Vahan Mamikonean*, ed. G. TĒR-MKRTČʿEAN, Tiflis 1904; reprinted Delmar, NY, 1985. English translation: R. W. THOMSON, The History of Lazar Pʿarpecʿi (*Columbia University Program in Armenian Studies. Suren D. Fesjian Academic Publications* 4), Atlanta, GA, 1991.

Movsēs Dasxurancʿi (or Kałankatuacʿi): Patmutʿiwn Ałuanicʿ Asxarhi, ed. V. AṘAKʿELYAN, Erevan 1983. English translation: C. J. F. DOWSETT, The History of the Caucasian Albanians (*London Oriental Series* 8), London 1961.

Movsēs Xorenacʿi: *Patmutʿiwn Hayocʿ*, ed. M. ABELEAN and S. YARUTʿIWNEAN, Tiflis 1913; reprinted Delmar, NY, 1981; facsimile edition with additional collations by A. B. SARGSEAN, Erevan 1991. English translation: R. W. THOMSON, Moses Khorenatsʿi. History of the Armenians *(Harvard Armenian Texts and Studies* 4), Cambridge, MA, 1978; French translation: A. and J.-P. MAHÉ, Histoire de l'Arménie par Moïse de Khorène, Paris 1993.

Samuēl Anecʿi: *Hawakʿmunkʿ i grocʿ Patmagracʿ*, ed. A. TER-MIKAĒLEAN, Ējmiacin 1893. Translation: A. MAI, Samuelis presbyteri Aniensis Temporum usque ad suam aetatem Ratio, in *PG*, 19.

Stepʿannos Orbelean: *Patmutʿiwn nahangin Sisakan*, ed. N. EMIN, Moscow 1861. French translation: M. BROSSET, Histoire de la Siounie par Stépannos Orbélian, St. Petersburg 1864 [Introduction, 1866].

Stepʿannos Taronecʿi (Asołik): *Patmutʿiwn tiezerakan*, ed. S. MALXASEAN, St. Petersburg 1885. Translation of parts I and II: E. DULAURIER, Etienne Açoghig de Daron. Histoire Universelle, Paris 1883; of part III: F. MACLER, Etienne Asolik de Taron. Histoire Universelle, Paris 1917, 1920.

Synodicon Orientale, ed. J. B. CHABOT, Paris 1902.

Zenob Glak: *Patmutʿiwn Taronoy*, ed. A. ABRAHAMYAN, Erevan 1941. English translation: L. AVDOYAN, Pseudo-Yovhannes Mamikonean. The History of Taron (*Columbia University Program in Armenian Studies. Suren D. Fesjian Academic Publications* 6), Atlanta, GA, 1993.

Secondary Literature

S. P. Brock, Eusebius and Syriac Christianity, in: Eusebius, Christianity and Judaism, ed. H. W. Attridge, Detroit 1992, p. 212–234; reprinted in Doctrinal Diversity (*Recent Studies in Early Christianity* 4), ed. E. Ferguson, New York 1995.

M.-L. Chaumont, La christianisation de l'empire iranien des origines aux grandes persécutions du IVe siècle (*CSCO*, 499, Subsidia 80), Louvain 1988.

N. G. Garsoïan, Armenia between Byzantium and the Sasanians (Variorum, CS 218), London 1985.

eadem, Church and Culture in Early Medieval Armenia (Variorum, CS 648), Aldershot 1999.

eadem, The Early-Mediaeval Armenian City: an Alien Element? *Journal of the Near Eastern Society* 16–17 (1984–85) = Ancient Studies in Memory of Elias Bickerman, p. 67–83; reprinted in her: Church and Culture in Early Medieval Armenia.

eadem, Epic Histories. See *Buzandaran*, (s.v. Texts).

eadem, L'Eglise arménienne et le grand schisme d'Orient (*CSCO*, 574, Subsidia 100), Leuven 1999.

eadem, The Iranian Substratum of the Agatʿangelos Cycle, in: East of Byzantium: Syria and Armenia in the Formative Period, eds. N. G. Garsoïan, Th. F. Mathews and R. W. Thomson, Dumbarton Oaks, Washington, D.C., 1982, p. 151–189; reprinted in her: Armenia between Byzantium and the Sasanians.

eadem, Prolegomena to a Study of the Iranian Elements in Arsacid Armenia, *HA* 90 (1976), p. 1–46; reprinted in her: Armenia between Byzantium and the Sasanians.

eadem, The Two Voices of Armenian Mediaeval Historiography: The Iranian Index, *Studia Iranica* 25 (1996), p. 7–43; reprinted in her Church and Culture in Early Medieval Armenia.

J. A. C. Greppin, Syriac Loanwords in Classical Armenian, in: Humanism, Culture and Language in the Middle East. Studies in Honor of G. Krotkoff, eds. A. Afsaruddin and A. H. Mathias Zahniser, Winona Lake, 1997, p.247–251.

S. Griffith, Asceticism in the Church of Syria, in: Asceticism, eds. V. L. Wimbush and R. Valantasis, New York 1995, p. 220–248.

H. Hübschmann, Armenische Grammatik. Erster Teil: Armenische Etymologie, Leipzig 1897; reprinted Hildesheim 1962.

E. D. Hunt, Holy Land Pilgrimage in the later Roman Empire AD 312–460, Oxford 1982.

A. Khatchatrian, L'Architecture arménienne du IVe au VIe siècle (*Bibliothèque des Cahiers Archéologiques* 7), Paris 1971.

P. Krüger, Jakob von Nisibis in syrischer und armenischer Überlieferung, *Le Muséon* 81 (1968), p. 161–179.

J. Lebon, Les citations patristiques grecques du 'Sceau de la foi', *Revue d'histoire ecclésiastique* 25 (1929), p. 5–32.

L. Leloir, Commentaire de l'Evangile concordant ou Diatessaron, traduit du syriaque et de l'arménien (*Sources chrétiennes* 121), Paris 1966.

P. Maraval, Lieux saints et pélerinages d'Orient, Paris 1985.

B. M. Metzger, The Early Versions of the New Testament, Oxford 1977.

K. Muradyan, Barseł Kesaracʿin ev nra "Vecʿoryan" hay matenagrutʿyan meǰ, Erevan 1976.

idem, Grigor Nazianzacʿin hay matenagrutʿyan meǰ, Erevan 1983.

B. Outtier, Textes arméniens relatifs à saint Ephrem, traduits par B. Outtier (*CSCO* 474), Louvain 1985 (cf. Ter-Petrosyan).

A. N. Palmer, Monk and Mason on the Tigris Frontier. The Early History of the Tur ʿAbdin, Cambridge 1990.

P. Peeters, Bibliotheca Hagiographica Orientalis (*Subsidia Hagiographica* 10), Bruxelles 1910; reprinted 1954.

idem, La légende de saint Jacques de Nisibe, *AnBoll* 28 (1920), p. 285–373.

W. L. Petersen, Some Remarks on the Integrity of Ephrem's Commentary on the Diatessaron, *Studia Patristica* 20 (1989), p. 197–202.

Ch. Renoux, Langue et littérature arméniennes, in: Christianismes orientaux, ed. M. Albert et al., Paris 1993, p. 109–166.

M. E. Stone, Holy Land Pilgrimage of Armenians before the Arab Conquest, *Revue Biblique* 93 (1986), p. 93–110.

idem, Three Observations on Early Armenian Inscriptions from the Holy Land, in: From Byzantium to Iran: Armenian Studies in Honour of Nina Garsoïan, eds. J.-P. Mahé and R. W. Thomson, Atlanta, GA, 1996, p. 417–424.

E. Ter-Minassiantz, Die armenische Kirche in ihren Beziehungen zu den syrischen Kirchen (*Texte und Untersuchungen*, N.F. XI, 4), Leipzig 1904. Armenian version: E. Tēr-Minaseancʿ, Hayocʿ Ekełecʿu Yaraberutʿiwnnerë Asorwocʿ Ekełecʿineri het, Eǰmiacin 1908; reprinted Erevan 1998.

L. Ter-Petrosyan, Abrahamu Xostovanoł Vkaykʿ Arewelicʿë, Erevan 1976.

idem, Grigor Lusavorčʿi Vardapetutʿyan asorakan ałbyurnerë, *Banber Matenadarani* 15 (1986), p. 95–109.

IDEM, Maštoc'yan Avandnerë ev Hayoc' Arak'elut'yunë Honac' Ašxarhum, *Patmabanasirakan Handes* 92 (1981, pt.1), p. 107–119.
IDEM, Textes arméniens relatifs à saint Ephrem, édités par L. TER PETROSSIAN (*CSCO* 473), Louvain 1985 (cf. OUTTIER).
R. W. THOMSON, A Bibliography of Classical Armenian Literature to 1500 AD (*Corpus Christianorum*), Turnhout 1995.
IDEM, Constantine and Trdat in Armenian Tradition, *Acta Orientalia* 50 (1997), p. 201–213.
IDEM, The Shorter Recension of the *Root of Faith*, *REArm* 5 (1968), p. 249–260.
IDEM, The Syriac and Armenian Versions of the *Hexaemeron* by Basil of Caesarea, *Studia Patristica* 17 (1993), p. 113–117.
M. VAN ESBROECK, Agathangelos, *Reallexikon für Antike und Christentum*, Supplement Band 1 (1985), 241ff.
IDEM, Le discours du Catholicos Sahak III, in: The Council in Trullo Revisited, eds. G. NEDUNGATT and M. FEATHERSTONE (*Kanonika* 6), Rome 1995, p. 323–454.
IDEM, La naissance du culte de saint Barthélemy en Arménie, *REArm* 17 (1983), p. 171–205.
IDEM, Un nouveau témoin du livre d'Agathange, *REArm* 8 (1971), p. 13–167.
IDEM, Le résumé syriaque de l'Agathange, *AnBoll* 95 (1977), p. 291–358.
G. WINKLER, Armenian Anaphoras and Creeds: A Brief Overview of Work in Progress, in: The Armenian Christian Tradition, ed. R. F. TAFT, S. J. (*Orientalia Christiana Analecta* 254), Rome 1997, p. 41–55.
EADEM, Das armenische Initiationsrituale (*Orientalia Christiana Analecta* 217), Rome 1982.
EADEM, Der armenische Ritus, in: The Christian East (*Orientalia Christiana Analecta* 251), Rome 1996, p. 265–298.
EADEM, Our Present Knowledge of the History of Agat'angelos and its Oriental Versions, *REArm* 14 (1980), p. 125–141.

MICHEL VAN ESBRŒCK / MÜNCHEN

DIE STELLUNG DER MÄRTYRERIN RHIPSIME IN DER GESCHICHTE DER BEKEHRUNG DES KAUKASUS

Wer sich mit der Bekehrung des Kaukasus beschäftigt, wird bald feststellen, dass in beiden Ländern, in Armenien und Georgien, keine Persönlichkeit tiefer in den legendären Quellen verwurzelt ist als die heilige Rhipsime. Im Norden ist in den georgischen Quellen die Anwesenheit von Nino in Georgien nur durch die Vermittlung der Sara Miaphor aus Dwin möglich, welche dann der Nino Rhipsime als Begleiterin zuweist. Im Süden hätte man Gregor den Erleuchter nie aus dem Brunnen herausgeholt, wenn nicht König Tiridates und seine Adeligen zu wilden Schweinen verwandelt worden wären, nachdem der König Rhipsime nicht für sich hatte gewinnen können. Diese Feststellung ist ein ausreichender Grund, um uns mit diesem Thema im Rahmen der Bekehrung des Kaukasus so weit wie möglich zu beschäftigen.

(1) Als Ausgangspunkt freue ich mich zunächst die Methode anzuwenden, die der Bollandist Paul Peeters entwickelt hat, als er dieses Thema im J. 1942 behandelte[1]. Es geht dort um die literarische Gattung der Hagiographie. Alfred von Gutschmid[2], der das Buch Agathangelos nur durch die kleinformatige Ausgabe der Mechitharisten und seine griechische Übersetzung durch die Edition von Paul de Lagarde kannte[3], bemerkte bereits im J. 1871, dass das Datum des Martyriums, 26. und 27. Hoṙi, wirklich plausibel ist. Er schrieb: „Etwas Derartiges pflegt in Legenden nicht zu fehlen, die zum Vorlesen an Festtagen der Heiligen bestimmt sind“[4]. Paul Peeters erweiterte diese Feststellung, indem er bemerkte, dass es bei dem Sterben Gregors selbst nicht möglich ist, ein solches Datum zu finden. Die inzwischen erschienenen Versionen bekräftigen diese Ansicht: in der griechischen Fassung findet man das Datum 26. September[5], und in den arabischen Viten 26. und 28. Oktober[6]. Hier sieht man, wie der zweite Monat Hoṙi pauschal einmal als September und einmal als Oktober übersetzt wurde. Wegen des beweglichen Kalenders der Armenier, der keine Schaltjahre kannte, wäre dabei die griechische Vorlage der arabischen Version potentiell ungefähr 120 Jahre älter als die griechische Version. Es geht jedoch hier, wie Peeters bereits bemerkt hat, um eine spätere Korrektur, die versucht, das Datum mit den Gegebenheiten des 4. Jahrhunderts zu harmonisieren[7]. Die griechische Übersetzung des offiziellen armenischen Agathangelos liefert auch als Datum den 26. September[8].

---

[1] P. PEETERS, Saint Grégoire l'Illuminateur dans le calendrier lapidaire de Naples. *AnBoll* 60 (1942) 91–130 [im folgenden PEETERS, Grégoire].

[2] A. von GUTSCHMID, Agathangelos. *ZDMG* 31 (1871) 1–60.

[3] Über diese Ausgabe s. G. GARITTE, Documents pour l'étude du livre d'Agathange, Città del Vaticano, 1956, 1–4 [im folgenden GARITTE, Documents].

[4] A. VON GUTSCHMID, Kleine Schriften, ed. F. RÜHL, Bd. III, Leipzig 1892, 404.

[5] GARITTE, Documents, S. 47, § 50 im griechischen Text von Vg [*Vita graeca*].

[6] Ibid., S. 47, § 37 der lateinischen Übersetzung von Va [*Vita arabica*], und S. 123.

[7] PEETERS, Grégoire 11.

[8] Heute bei G. LAFONTAINE, La version grecque ancienne du livre arménien d'Agathange, Louvain 1978, 254 [Ag].

Paul Peeters stützt sich auf die Geschichte des Eusebius, um die Verfolgungen zu datieren. Weil Eusebius im 8. Buch seiner Geschichte Februar 303 für den Anfang der Folterungen ausweist, gibt es keinen Anlass, ein Märtyrertum davor in Armenien als geschichtlich anzusehen. Vielmehr wird man dieses höchstwahrscheinlich unter Maximinus Daia ansetzen, der sich im J. 311–312 tatsächlich nach Armenien begab[9], wo er eine noch härtere Verfolgung gegen die Christen durchführte als jene, die durch Galerius und Diokletian begonnen worden war. Es gibt also gute Gründe, sich vorzustellen, dass in den Jahren nach 303 eine Gruppe junger Nonnen vor der Unterdrückung des Diokletian nach Armenien geflohen ist, und dann am 26. September 312 dort das Martyrium erlitt. Im J. 312 wäre der 26. Hoṙi der 4. November gewesen. Dass dieser Gedächtnistag im westlichen Byzanz nie vorkommt, zeigt, dass der Kult der Rhipsime ursprünglich lokal war. Weiters wird in Agathangelos die Weihe der Kirche Johannes des Täufers am 7. Sahmi gefeiert, was auf Griechisch als 7. Oktober wiedergegeben wird. Die zwei Daten, 26. Hoṙi als 26. September und 7. Sahmi als 7. Oktober, passen genau in die Jahre 464–468[10]. Natürlich ist die Periode, in der der Monat Hoṙi pauschal als September übersetzt werden kann, ausgedehnter als nur diese vier Jahre. Eine zweite chronologische Festlegung gewinnt Paul Peeters mit dem Fest des heiligen Gregor am 11. Kʿałocʿ, dem 5. Monat des beweglichen armenischen Jahres. Dieses Fest ist im armenischen Synaxar in Bezug auf die Rhipsime-Feier verständlich, während gemäß Agathangelos zwischen beiden Ereignissen 75 Tage verflossen waren. Hier verfügt man über eine unerwartete Quelle im Marmorkalender von Neapel. Den gemischten griechisch-lateinischen Heiligenkalender, der dort verwendet wird, darf man auf das Ende des 8. Jahrhunderts datieren[11]. Dort findet sich eine sehr rätselhafte Memoria am 2. und 3. Dezember, nämlich zuerst die *passio Gregorii episcopi*, und dann die *passio Gregorii Armeniae*. Wenn diese Feier mit der von Gregor am 11. Kʿałocʿ zusammengebracht wird, ergeben sich als Synchronismen die Jahre 496–504. Gemäß der Grundhypothese von Gutschmid, dass dem ursprünglich isolierten Martyrium Rhipsimes und ihrer Gefährtinnen eine Geschichte Gregors hinzugefügt wurde, bekommt man hier zwei Hinweise auf die Datierung der Zusammenführung. Auf die Verdoppelung des Namens Gregor kommen wir am Ende dieses Beitrags zurück.

Nun gibt es für Rhipsime und ihre Gefährtinnen drei Erwähnungen in der armenischen Literatur. Die *Historischen Kommentare*, die einem gewissen Faustus zugeschrieben wurden, sagen im Buch III, 14 ausdrücklich, dass die ersten Märtyrer Gayane und Rhipsime waren und ihre erste Kirche im Distrikt Ayrarat errichtet wurde, auch wenn in diesem Passus der südliche und nördliche Ursprung des Christentums am deutlichsten wird[12]. Sebeos und Johannes Draschanakertetsi (Drasxanakertcʿi) berichten, dass Komitas im J. 618 die Kirche in Vałaršapat vergrößert hat, und dass der heilige Sahak († 437) als erster diese Martyriumskapelle gebaut hatte, wo tatsächlich ihr ausgemergelter Leib durch Komitas gefunden wurde[13]. Die Geschichtlichkeit dieses Martyriums könnte kaum besser belegt sein. Konsequenterweise sind die Daten des Festes wirklich als geschichtlich zu bewerten.

---

[9] Dieser Punkt wurde durch R. Laqueur, Eusebius als Historiker seiner Zeit, Giessen 1929, 123 angezweifelt. Doch stimmt ihm Ernest Stein, Histoire du Bas-Empire, t. I. De l'état romain à l'état byzantin (284–476), Amsterdam 1968, 88–90 und Anm. S. 456 u. 125* nicht zu.

[10] Peeters, Grégoire107–108.

[11] Ibid. 113–114 u. 125–128.

[12] N. Garsoïan, The Epic Histories Attributed to Pʿawstos Buzand, Cambridge-Massachusets 1989, 86–87 und 257–258.

[13] G. V. Abgaryan, Patmutʿiwn Sebēosi, Erevan 1979, 121, Kap. 37, und Yovhannu Katʿolikosi Drasxanakertcʿoy Patmutʿiwn Hayocʿ , ed. M. Emin, Moskau 1853, 46.

(2) Wenn man sich die Folterungen des heiligen Gregor vorstellt, ist es schwierig zu denken, dass diese Grausamkeit in den sehr friedlichen Jahren zwischen 284 und 303 stattgefunden habe. Diese Zeit war für die Kirche ziemlich günstig. Andererseits wäre sie nach dem J. 303 durchaus möglich. Die heilige Rhipsime und ihre Gefährtinnen wären dann tatsächlich ungefähr 10 Jahre später in Armenien gefoltert worden. Diese Darstellung ist wahrscheinlich der erste Versuch gewesen, Gregor mit den jungen Nonnen in Verbindung zu bringen. Aber sobald es notwendig wurde, den Sasaniden gegenüber einen parthischen Ursprung für Gregor zu schaffen, musste das Ganze anders modelliert werden. So hat man für beide Fälle persönliche Gründe gefunden, die es ermöglichen, alles zu erklären. In der ersten Fiktion wurde für Diokletian eine hübsche Frau gesucht. Da Diokletian gemäß den *Consularia Constantinopolitana ad annum 405* im Jahr 316 gestorben ist[14], gab es einen beachtlichen Zeitraum, um diese Episode zwischen 285 und 316 als etwas Akzeptables erscheinen zu lassen, besonders deswegen, weil die Ereignisse tatsächlich im J. 311/312 stattgefunden haben. Garitte hat bereits bemerkt, dass gegenüber Agathangelos die griechische Vita nichts von einem kaiserlichen Schönheitswettbewerb weiß[15]. Ein Porträt der Jungfrau ist hier nicht notwendig. In der syrischen Fassung wird zuerst das Porträt gemalt, und erst anschließend werden die Boten in das ganze Imperium ausgesandt, um diese Schönheit für den Kaiser zu gewinnen[16]. Dieses Bündel aus Varianten zeigt einsichtig, dass hier eine Fiktion vorliegt. Übrigens hätten die Hagiographen, die die Geschichte von Rhipsime und ihren Gefährtinnen und die von Gregorios zusammengefügt haben, das Märtyrertum erst im J. 303, während der großen Verfolgung, situiert und dann sicher nicht den Umweg über einen persönlichen Heiratsversuch des Diokletian wählen müssen. Hingegen ist Gregorios selbst für den Hagiographen um 303 während der großen Verfolgung gefoltert worden, weil er zuerst nur für sein Christentum leidet. Davon ist die Bemerkung übriggeblieben, dass die Rhipsimianerinnen ihre Abenteuer zuerst anlässlich der Verfolgung Diokletians erleben[17]. Diese chronologische Angabe kommt natürlich erst von der selbständigen *Passio Gregorii*, die verschollen ist. Erst nach den Folterungen wird seine Verwandtschaft mit Anak und Tiridates selbst enthüllt, und deswegen wird er für 13/15 Jahre in den Brunnen geworfen. Damit sind zwei Stufen zu unterscheiden. Zuerst wird die Verbindung Rhipsimes mit Diokletian in einen friedlichen Kontext gebracht – sie wird vom Jahre 312 weg zwischen 285 und 303 angesetzt –, und zum zweiten scheint die Folterung Gregors um 303 begonnen zu haben. Aber um Tiridates sein Königtum wiederzugeben, vermittelt der Hagiograph eine Geschichte, die von Johannes Malalas für die Zeit von Vahram V. und Theodosios Junior erwähnt wird[18]. Dort geht es um die Gründe für einen 50-jährigen Frieden, der von den Persern den Römern zugestanden wurde. Damals wurde der Patrikios Prokopios zum Schah geschickt. Sie handelten aus, dass jedes Heer einen einzelnen Kämpfer entsenden sollte, um die Schlacht zu entscheiden. Die Römer wählten den Goten Areobindos aus und die Perser den Ardazanes aus dem Bataillon der Unsterblichen. Areobindos gewann, und die Perser schlossen einen Friedensvertrag. Es ist kaum zu glauben, dass diese Geschichte dem Verfasser des Agathangelos nicht bekannt gewesen sein sollte. Zwar wird

[14] Th. Mommsen, Monumenta Germaniae Historica. Auctores antiquissimi, t. IX, Berlin 1892, 231.

[15] Garitte, Documents 292–293.

[16] M. van Esbrœck, Un nouveau Témoin de l'Agathange. *REArm* 8 (1971) 127 [im folgenden *Nouveau Témoin*]. Vk = Vita karšuni und ist identisch mit Vs (Vita Syriaca) in M. van Esbrœck, Le résumé syriaque de l'Agathange. *AnBoll* 95 (1977) 291–358.

[17] So in Aa 61, Ag 142 und Vk / Vs 74, aber nicht in den übrigen Vitae.

[18] Ioannis Malalae Chronographia 285, 65–286, 81 [+23–+39] (Thurn); 364, 3–21 (Dindorf).

von Malalas der ursprüngliche Name Ardabur durch den in der Zeit Justinians bekannteren Areobindos ersetzt. Doch dieser Friede ist wohl der von 422 gewesen, als Ardabur bei Nisibis den Persern gegenüberstand[19]. Diese kleine Heldengeschichte wurde vom Hagiographen geschickt benutzt – also nach 422 –, um die Rechte des Tiridates in Armenien zu begründen und das Märtyrertum der Rhipsime in Armenien um 490 glaubwürdig darzustellen.

(3) Andere Indizien plädieren für eine jüngere Datierung der Hauptereignisse des Agathangelos: die Taufe der Armenier im Euphrat. Diese beeindruckende Szene findet direkt im Fluss statt. Die griechische Fassung hat noch Angaben erhalten, die im offiziellen Agathangelos verschwunden sind. Zum Beispiel erwähnt sie den Namen der Gattin des Gregorios und Mutter von Vrthanes und Aristakes, Julitta, die eine Griechin war[20]. Die syrische Zusammenfassung weiß, dass Gregor von seiner Amme nicht nach Kaisareia, sondern nach Neokaisareia gerettet wurde, und dort scheint auch die Ehe stattgefunden zu haben, da die beiden Söhne aus Neokaisareia abgeholt wurden, nachdem Gregor sich zurückgezogen hatte[21]. J. Markwart bemerkte einmal auch, dass die Reliquien von Athenogenes, die von Gregor nach Aštišat gebracht wurden, eher über eine Verwandschaft Gregors mit Neokaisareia verstanden werden können, als durch seine Beziehungen mit Kaisareia[22]. Immerhin erscheinen hier Elemente, die sich nicht so leicht mit der These des „parthischen" Gregor in Verbindung bringen lassen. Aber selbst in dieser ursprünglichen Fassung lautet die große Taufszene auf griechisch: Καὶ λαβὼν μύρον καὶ ἔλαιον ἐπὶ τὸ ποταμὸν κατέχεεν, σταυροῦ τύπον ἐκτελέσας[23]. „Er nahm das Myrrhon und das Öl und goss sie auf das Wasser, indem er ein Kreuzeszeichen machte".

Für diese Liturgie gibt es zwei unabhängige Zeugnisse; Theodoros Anagnostes weiß, dass Petrus der Walker den Gebrauch des Myrrhon in die Liturgie eingeführt hat: Πέτρον φησὶ τὸν Κναφέα ἐπινοῆσαι τὸ μύρον ἐν τῇ ἐκκλησίᾳ ἐπὶ παντὸς τοῦ λαοῦ ἁγιάζεσθαι, καὶ τὴν ἐπὶ τῶν ὑδάτων ἐν τοῖς θεοφανίοις ἐπίκλησιν ἐν τῇ ἑσπέρᾳ γίνεσθαι[24], und dasselbe wurde von Cyrus von Edessa in der Chronik von Zuqnīn geschrieben:

ܘܗܘ ܥܝܕܐ ܕܢܬܩܕܫܘܢ ܡܝܐ ܒܠܠܝܐ ܡܩܕܡܗ̈، ܒܥܐܕܐ ܕܒܝܬ ܕܢܚܐ . ܘܟܠ ܡܫܚܐ ܕܡܫܝܚܘܬܐ
ܒܚܡܫܐ ܒܫܒܐ (ܢܝܣܠܐ) ܠܥܝܢ ܟܠܗ ܥܡܐ

„Er begründete den Brauch, das Wasser am frühen Morgen vor der Epiphanie zu weihen und das Öl zur Weihe am Gründonnerstag in Anwesenheit des ganzen Volkes zu weihen".[25]

Es ist kaum zu bezweifeln, dass sich beide Zeremonien im ursprünglichen Agathangelos widerspiegeln. Cyrus von Edessa und Petrus der Walker wurden erstmals im Jahre 471 Bischöfe, aber ihre liturgische Nachwirkung kann sich kaum schon seit dieser Zeit entwickelt haben, da Kaiser Leo Petrus sofort absetzte. Um 475, als Petrus zwei Jahre Bischof war, und vor allem im J. 485, als Petrus der Walker endgültig von seinem Exil (bis zum Tod im J. 488) zurückkam, müssen diese neuen Bräuche aufgekommen sein. Dabei gewinnt man einen guten *terminus post quem* für die Entstehung des Agathangelos. Dies ist besonders günstig, um die Anzahl der Rhipsimianerinnen zu betrachten.

---

19 A. Demandt, Die Spätantike, München 1989, 168 und 205.

20 Garitte, Documents 216 und 308, Vg 97.

21 van Esbrœck, Nouveau Témoin 26, Vk 17 und 152, Vk 265 und 268.

22 J. Markwart, Die Entstehung der armenischen Bistümer. *OCP* 17 (1932) 187.

23 Garitte, Documents 100, Vg 167.

24 Theodoros Anagnostes, *Kirchengeschichte*, ed. G. C. Hansen, Berlin 1971, 155, n° 547.

25 *Incerti Auctoris chronicon pseudo-dionysianum vulgo dictum*, ed. J. B. Chabot, Louvain 1927, 258.

(4) Da wir nun in der Zeit des Henotikons angekommen sind, in der sich ein aktiver Antichalkedonismus verbreitet hat, ohne dass das Konzil je erwähnt wurde, möchten wir den Forscher zuerst auf die zahlreichen Gruppen von vierzig Märtyrern, die in diesen Zeiten auftauchen, aufmerksam machen. Am wichtigsten scheint uns das Panegyricum der XL Märtyrer von Sebasteia durch Sisinnios von Sebasteia zu sein[26]. Dieses Panegyricum hängt von einer griechischen Vorlage ab und wurde wahrscheinlich um das 10. Jahrhundert ins Armenische übersetzt. Eine kritische Ausgabe aufgrund der elf vorliegenden Handschriften steht heute zur Verfügung[27]. Neben der normalen Überlieferung des Martyriums findet sich in diesem Text ein starker theologischer Einschlag. Die geistlichen Vorstellungen von Evagrius Ponticus werden besonders geschickt benutzt, um die Bedeutung der Zahl *Vierzig* zu eruieren. Diese Zahl ist nicht nur zehn mal vier, wodurch die Ausdehnung des Kultus angezeigt wird, sondern auch acht mal fünf, um die Laster zu Tugenden zu transformieren, und zwar von den fünf leiblichen zu den fünf geistlichen Sinnen. Die Buchstaben der vierzig Eigennamen der Märtyrer sind gerade 318, d.h. die Anzahl der heiligen orthodoxen Väter von Nizäa, was von großer Bedeutung für die Henotiker ist, die sich ausdrücklich auf Nizäa stützten, um die Erwähnung Chalkedons zu vermeiden. Weiters enthält 318 die drei Buchstaben T, I, H: die Anzahl 18 wird durch 6 mal 3 interpretiert. Dort bekennen die Seraphim mit ihren sechs Flügeln den dreifachen Heiligen Gott und das T des Kreuzes steht in der Anzahl 318, um die himmlische Zustimmung zu dem Zusatz „der Du für uns gekreuzigt worden bist“ im Trishagion zu bestätigen. Eine solche Spekulation verrät ein Datum um 475. Die sinaitische Inschrift über die Vierzig Märtyrer vom Sinai erwähnt ausdrücklich die Vorgänger von Sebasteia[28], und man darf nicht vergessen, dass der Gegenbischof von Jerusalem, Theodosios, zuerst im Sinai-Kloster eine Zuflucht gefunden hat. Offensichtlich sind die Märtyrer von Sinai und Raithu eine bloße orthodoxe Widerspiegelung der Vierzig von Sebasteia.

Lassen Sie uns jetzt die Gruppe der Rhipsimianerinnen analysieren. Im offiziellen Agathangelos zählt man zuerst Rhipsime mit 32 Gefährtinnen (Ag 83, 9–10 und Aa 199); dann Gaiane und zwei Gefährtinnen (Ag 86, 52 und Aa 204); schließlich 37 insgesamt (Ag 88, 8 und Aa 209). Die *Vita Syriaca* zählt Gaiane mit drei Gefährtinnen, und Rhipsime erscheint mit einer Gruppe von 33 Gefährtinnen, was zusammen 38 ergibt[29]. So findet man es auch in den anderen Viten. Aber die vollständige Überlieferung weiß, dass eine Gefährtin, Mani, geflohen ist, und dass sie später durch Gregor begraben werden sollte, wie einst Maria die Ägypterin durch den Mönch Paramon[30]. Die vierzigste ist Nino, die ja erst dann die Gruppe verlässt, um nach Georgien zu reisen. Tatsächlich gibt es auch vierzig Rhipsimianerinnen, und in der Zeit des Henotikons hat diese Anzahl sicher eine Bedeutung. Die syrische Vita zählt 77 junge Nonnen, die Rom verlassen, um der Eifersucht Diokletians zu entfliehen, und der offizielle Agathangelos sagt, dass es über siebzig waren[31]. Der Grund dafür ist einfach zu verstehen: Vierzig gehen nach Dwin, und 37 nach Awan, dem Ort des Katholikos Yovhannes Bagaranetsi nach der Teilung Armeniens

---

[26] Über diesen wichtigen Text hielten wir einen leider noch nicht gedruckten Vortrag, „The Forty Martyrs of Sebasteia in the Armenian Tradition“ im Rahmen einer Konferenz, die in Queen's University, Belfast, vom 11. bis 16. April 1986 stattgefunden hat. Cf. *AnBoll* 109 (1991) 253, Anm. 13.

[27] Sisianosi Hayocʻ Vardapeti nerbołean i surb kʻarasuns, ed. Th. Dasnabedean, Antelias 1995.

[28] I. Ševčenko, The Early Period of the Sinai Monastery in the Light of Its Inscriptions. *DOP* 20 (1966) 258 u. 263.

[29] van Esbrœck, Nouveau Témoin 132.

[30] Ibid. 157.

[31] Ibid. 127–128: Aa 199, 10 u. 209, 11 sowie Vk 77.

unter Kaiser Maurikios im J. 591. Da diese Verteilung noch immer vierzig Rhipsimianerinnen für Dwin angibt, zeigt sie, dass die ursprüngliche Zahl vierzig grundsätzlich von Bedeutung bleibt.

(5) Man kann ältere Züge der Agathangelos-Legende durch andere Varianten weiter analysieren. Gemäß der Hauptfassung haben sich die Rhipsimianerinnen sofort in Vałaršapat niedergelassen (Aa 150), sobald sie nach Armenien gekommen waren. Eine genauere Untersuchung des Textes zeigt, dass vielleicht auch hier diese Auffassung eigentlich die letzte Vorstellung gewesen ist. Bereits G. Garitte hatte in der griechischen Vita und ihren arabischen Verwandten notiert (Vg 92 und Va 65), dass, nachdem Gregor in Vałaršapat gepredigt und die Kirche der Märtyrerinnen erbaut hatte, der Text dann hinzufügt: „Und er fuhr dann nach Vałaršapat". In einer Fußnote erkennt jedoch Garitte an, dass die Vision Gregors in Artašat stattgefunden hat (Vg 77 und Va 54)[32]. Die beiden Viten sagen nicht ausdrücklich, wohin die Rhipsimianerinnen zuerst gekommen sind, aber die syrische Fassung schickt die vierzig sofort nach Dwin und die 37 anderen nach Awan. Hätte Yovhannes von Bagaran die letzte Auffassung gekannt, dann hätte er sicher im J. 591 seine Kathedrale direkt in Vałaršapat errichtet. Tatsächlich dient diese letzte Vorstellung den Zielen des Komitas, der die drei Kirchen dort ansiedeln wird. Die Vision Gregors fand in Artašat statt, mit drei Fundamenten und der Lichtsäule. Diese drei Kirchen sind die von Rhipsime, die von Gaiane und die der Gefährtinnen, inklusive der kranken Nonne, die im Kelter geblieben war, also in Dwin (Vg 76–82, Va 53–62 und Aa 737)[33]. Da Dwin viel näher bei Artašat liegt, ist es auch leichter zu verstehen, warum der geheilte König zwölf Steine für drei Pforten aus dem Berg Masis holt (Vg 87, Va 80). Der Berg Ararat, früher Masis genannt, befindet sich genau gegenüber von Artašat. Doch die letzte Fassung spricht von acht Steinen (Ag 124, Aa 765 und Vo 113 [34]), also für zwei Kirchen. Man darf zuerst von drei Kirchen reden, und danach nur von zwei für die Märtyrerinnen. Die Hauptkirche für Gregor selbst ist die dritte Kirche geworden, und sie wurde durch Komitas auch dem herabgestiegenen Eingeborenen gewidmet und deswegen Ējmiacin genannt. Es besteht kein Zweifel, dass die völlig verlorengegangene Hauptkirche zuerst in Dwin erbaut wurde. So wird klar, dass die Bedeutung der Märtyrerinnen unter Maximinus Daia sich mit der Zeit etwas verändert hat, bis zu der Zeit, als Komitas in der von Sahak gebauten Martyriumskapelle die neun Handlängen und vier Finger ihrer Reliquien messen konnte.

(6) Im letzten Teil unserer Analyse wollen wir uns mit der Rolle Rhipsimes bei den Georgiern beschäftigen. Wie ist man dazu gekommen, Rhipsime als Vermittlerin zu benutzen, um die Reliquie Christi in Mzchetha (Mcxeta) durch Nino auffinden zu lassen? Zur Klärung dieser Frage sind wir gezwungen, eine Reihe von fünf Legenden zu erwähnen[35], da sie zusammen eine Datierung ermöglichen, und zwar noch vor oder während des Konzils von Dwin im J. 506.

Die erste Legende ist nur lateinisch, armenisch und georgisch erhalten[36]. Sie betrifft Longinus, den Soldaten, der mit seiner „Λογχής" oder Lanze den Tod Christi am Kreuz festgestellt hat. Man erzählt, wie Longinus in seine Heimat Kappadokien zurückgekehrt

---

[32] Garitte, Documents 306 u. Anm. 1.

[33] Ibid. 58–61.

[34] Vo ist die griechische Vita von Ochrid: G. Garitte, La vie grecque inédite de saint Grégoire d'Arménie. *AnBoll* 85 (1965) 233–290.

[35] Eine grundsätzliche Analyse dieser Legenden findet man in M. van Esbroeck, Invention des reliques comme attribut impérial: La tunique du Christ à Moscou et son symbolisme, in: Roma fuori di Roma. Istituzioni e immagini, ed. P. Catalano, 5 (21 aprile 1985) [1974], S. 225–243.

[36] Georgische Version: K. Kekelidze, Monumenta hagiographica georgica, Tiflis 1918, 188–192. Armenische Version: Vark' ew Vkayabanut'iunk' Srboc', [ed. L. Ališan], I, Venedig 1874, 715–721. Lateinische Version in: Acta Sanctorum mensis Martii, Bd. II, Antwerpen 1668, 384–386.

ist, wahrscheinlich mit dem Mantel Christi (aber hier wird darüber noch nichts gesagt). Nach einigen Jahren wird er wegen seines Glaubens vor Gericht geführt und in Kappadokien hingerichtet, wo man für ihn ein kleines Martyrion errichtet. Diese sehr klassische hagiographische Legende liefert nichts, das nicht in den meisten ähnlichen Texten zu finden ist, ein Verhör, ein Glaubensbekenntnis und eine Hinrichtung. Diese sehr einfache Erzählung ist jedoch notwendig, um die Ausweitung des Themas zu verstehen.

Die zweite Legende ist nur auf griechisch erhalten und wird dem großen Redner Hesychius von Jerusalem zugeschrieben[37]. Doch dieser Name gilt eher als Deckmantel. Sehr wahrscheinlich hat Hesychius das Konzil von Chalkedon selbst nicht mehr erlebt. Die Legende entwickelt sich in folgender Weise: Zuerst findet man in Jerusalem den Schädel des Longinus. Der Heilige erschien einer blinden Witwe, die mit ihrem Sohn die heilige Stätte besuchte. Der Schädel befand sich deswegen in Jerusalem, weil die Gesandten von Herodes und Pilatus den Longinus in Kappadokien wiedergefunden hatten. Der Heilige empfing sie sehr freundlich, da er die Gelegenheit, Märtyrer zu werden, nicht verpassen wollte. Er wurde enthauptet, und sein Haupt wurde in Jerusalem auf eine Lanze gebunden, um alle Gläubigen abzuschrecken.

Die dritte Legende ist auch nur griechisch auffindbar und wird ebenfalls Hesychius zugeschrieben[38]. Longinus erhält hier eine erweiterte Bedeutung: Noch vor dem heiligen Stephanus wird er zum Protomartys erhoben. Tatsächlich wurde ihm in der Zeit Herodes' des Großen die Gelegenheit gegeben, sich als Märtyrer zu bekennen, als Herodes die kleinen Kinder von Bethlehem ermordete. Denn schon als die Magier durch Jerusalem zogen, hatte Longinus geglaubt. Als ihn aber die Schergen des Herodes verfolgen wollten, wurde er durch den Mantel, den er trug, so abgeschirmt, dass ihn niemand mit einer Waffe erreichen konnte. So wurde er durch diesen Mantel vor dem Tod errettet. Später war er als „Primanius" beim Kreuz Christi anwesend.

Die vierte Legende ist nur ein kurzer Brief des Dorotheus, Comes von Palästina, an Mari, den Oberen des Akoimetenklosters am Bosporus[39]. Es geht um die Sendung des Mantels Christi, den Dorotheus mit seinem Brief zu den Mönchen weiterschickt. Der Brief erzählt, wie dieser Mantel ihm von einem konvertierten Rabbiner von Jerusalem anvertraut wurde. Dies geschah kurz nach dem Konzil von Chalkedon.

Die fünfte Legende ist nur armenisch erhalten. Der Titel lautet: „Rede des Johannes Chrysostomus über die nahtlose Tunika und die Geschichte Abgars, des Königs der Armenier"[40]. Dort geschieht alles vor der Kreuzigung. Die Zahl der unmündigen Opfer von Bethlehem beträgt 1462. Abgar schickt Jesus durch Addaeus den Mantel. Doch Addaeus wirft ihm vor: „Wie kann man ein Kleid für Gott schaffen?" Plötzlich kommen Kaufleute mit einer nahtlosen Tunika. Abgar kauft sie und fragt, wo sie dieses Kleid gefunden haben. Sie antworten, sie hätten es von Hirten aus Bethlehem gekauft. Abgar läßt die Hirten zu sich kommen, und diese erzählen, dass sie in einer Nacht drei leuchtende Personen gesehen haben, die über die nahtlose Tunika wachten. Hierzu darf man noch anmerken, dass die armenische Übersetzung Michaels des Syrers von Ephrem wissen sollte, dass die nahtlose Tunika am Fuß des Kreuzes von einem Soldaten namens Longinus durch Los erworben wurde. Er nahm sie und brachte sie in seine Heimat Makson in

[37] M. Aubineau, Les homélies festales d'Hésychius de Jérusalem, Bd. II, Bruxelles 1980, 778–844.

[38] Ibid. 845–901.

[39] M. van Esbroeck, Une lettre de Dorothée comte de Palestine à Marcel et Mari en 452. *AnBoll* 91 (1983) 35–75.

[40] N. Marr, Chiton Gospoden v knižnych legendach Armjan, Gruzin i Siricev, in al-Mużaffariyyat. Sbornik statej učennikov professora barona Viktora Romanoviča Rozena, Sankt-Petersburg 1897, 67–96.

Galatien. Einen anderen Teil davon nahm ein Laze und brachte ihn in seine Stadt Pud in Mingrelien[41]. Das findet man auch unter der Regierung von Aderki in „Kartlis Cxovreba", wonach Longinus die Reliquie nach Mingrelien trug, und dann Elioz, sein Gefährte, nach Armazi, was später in Mzchetha umgewandelt wurde[42]. Man braucht kaum daran zu erinnern, dass Elioz die zentrale Persönlichkeit ist, dank deren Nino die Reliquie in Mzchetha finden wird.

Mehrere Passagen dieser vielseitigen Legende können datiert werden. Am Anfang der zweiten Hesychius-Legende wird ausdrücklich gesagt, dass Longinus größer als Stephanus und Johannes der Täufer gewesen ist. Er hat sich tatsächlich eine Reliquienauffindung geschaffen, die weit über die auf 415 datierte Auffindung des Stephanus hinausgeht[43], und zwar dadurch, dass sein Haupt auf eine Lanze gebunden wurde, genau wie für Johannes den Täufer, dessen Reliquien Kaiser Markian um 455 gefunden hat[44]. Der einfache Mantel, der ursprünglich ihm anheimgegeben wurde, ist ebenfalls höher geschätzt worden, da auch der Chalkedoniker Dorotheus den Mantel gefunden haben soll. Jetzt ist ihm der Mantel jedoch ausschließlich vom Himmel gegeben worden, und es ist kein Wunder, dass der, der diesen Mantel nach Armazi bringt, sich selbst Elioz nennt, während der himmlische Mantel eigentlich derjenige ist, der auch in Zusammenhang mit dem Propheten Elias gekommen ist. Tatsächlich stammen Abiathar und Sidonie aus der Familie des Propheten Elias, und sie haben Nino zur Reliquie von Mzchetha geführt.

Nach diesem langen Exkurs kommen wir jetzt zu Rhipsime zurück. Sie führt Nino zuerst nach Armenien, wo Nino zwei Jahre mit ihren Gefährtinnen verbringt, bis sie umgebracht wurden. Sehr bedeutsam scheint uns die Anzahl der Rhipsimianerinnen bei den Georgiern: sie sind gewöhnlich 52, aber eine Variante sagt ausdrücklich, dass sie mit der Prinzessin Rhipsime in Rom vierzig Adelige waren[45]. Diese Art, die Legende umzudeuten, scheint uns ein Zeichen für eine ziemlich frühe Komposition, als das Bewusstsein der mystischen antichalkedonischen Bedeutung dieser Anzahl noch nicht vergessen war. Dazu darf man auch bemerken, dass Rhipsime zuerst aus Ephesus kommt, der Stadt der „guten" Konzilien von 431 und 449.

Es ist gewiss nicht leicht gewesen, diese so deutlich festgelegte antichalkedonische Legende wieder in den Chalkedonismus hineinzuziehen. Dies gelang durch eine unwahrscheinliche Umdeutung: Juvenal, der chalkedonische Bischof von Jerusalem, wird zum Onkel der Nino gemacht[46]. In diesem Kontext findet man auch die wunderbare Vorstellung, dass Mirian der Enkel des Tiridates und Großvater des Vachtang gewesen sei[47], was die Berichte von Rufinus über Nino ziemlich richtig auf die Jahre um 380 verschiebt. Rhipsime hat mit Nino zuerst eine zufällige Verwandtschaft, indem Nino sie ausschließlich durch Sara Miaphor von Dwin gekannt hat. Noch besser erfunden ist, dass Sara Miaphor dem Bischof Juvenal die Vermählung seiner Schwester Suzanna mit Zabilon empfohlen hat. Durch ihre Eltern ist Nino dabei erst durch die fromme Armenierin aus Dwin im Schatten von Chalkedon vollständig erzogen worden. Eine klarere Abweichung

---

[41] Ibid. 79–80 und 82.

[42] Kartlis Cxovreba, ed. S. Qauchtschischvili, Bd. I, Tbilisi 1955, 99–100.

[43] M. van Esbrœck, Jean II de Jérusalem et les cultes de S. Étienne, de la Sainte-Sion et de la Croix. *AnBoll* 102 (1984) 99–134.

[44] M. van Esbrœck, Les plus anciens homéliaires géorgiens, Louvain-la-Neuve 1975, 93.

[45] Kartlis Mokcevay, ed. I. Abuladze, Dzveli kartuli agiograpiuli lit'erat'uris dzeglebi, Bd. I, Tbilisi 1964, 84, B-Version und 114, Zeile 24, A-Version.

[46] Durch seine Schwester Suzanna, Mutter der Nino.

[47] Kartlis Cxovreba (zit. Anm. 42), S. 160 und 132.

von der früheren antichalkedonischen Tendenz konnte man kaum erfinden.

Zum Schluss erwähne ich noch Movses Chorenatsi (Xorenacʿi), der weiß, dass Nino mit den Rhipsimianerinnen zuerst nach Valaršapat gekommen ist. Er zitiert dafür das Buch Agathangelos. Doch findet man diese Auslegung nur in dem syrischen Résumé, dessen ausgedehnte Redaktion Movses offensichtlich benutzt hat[48]. Diese Version stammt aus der Zeit des Yovhannes Bagaranetsi, ist also nach 591 zu datieren. Hier findet man nur ein zusätzliches Buch auf Movses' Regalen, die bereits sorgfältig von Robert Thomson beschrieben worden sind[49]. Diese Bibliothek war wirklich eine Reise wert.

Lassen Sie mich noch einen einzigen Punkt erwähnen, der für die Bekehrung des Kaukasus von Bedeutung ist. Der Kalender aus Neapel erwähnt am 2. und 3. Dezember zwei Gregorii, einen Bischof Gregor und Gregor von Armenien. Beiden wird eine Passio zugeschrieben. Das scheint wirklich gut belegt zu sein, durch die georgische Passio Gregors des Wundertäters[50], und durch Agathangelos; und dies geschah, wie oben gesehen, in den Jahren 495–504. Meines Erachtens sind die beiden großen Martyrien nie unabhängig voneinander zu betrachten. Aber darüber zu sprechen würde den vorgegebenen Rahmen sprengen.

---

[48] van Esbrœck, Nouveau Témoin 132.

[49] R. Thomson, Moses Khorenatsi. History of the Armenians, Cambridge Massachusetts, 1978, 10–61.

[50] van Esbrœck, Le martyre géorgien de Grégoire le Thaumaturge et sa date. *Le Muséon* 112 (1999) 129–185.

KAREN N. YUZBACHIAN / ST. PETERSBURG

EINIGE BEMERKUNGEN ÜBER DIE ENTWICKLUNG DER NATIONALEN BEWUSSTSEINSBILDUNG IM KAUKASISCHEN ALBANIEN

Das Studium des kaukasischen Albanien, das auf dem politischen Hintergrund Transkaukasiens zusammen mit Armenien und Georgien eine stabile Trias ausmachte, begann erst im 19. Jh.[1] Bis in die letzten Dezennien war dieses Studium rein akademischen Charakters und kam nicht auf die globalen Probleme zu sprechen. Die armenische Philologie hat sich nicht näher mit literarischen Texten auseinandergesetzt, die albanische Herkunft hatten oder mit albanischen Realien verbunden waren. Auch die Geschichte der albanischen Kirche wurde nicht systematisch untersucht.

Die Erforschung Albaniens als spezifisches Phänomen beginnt erst nach dem 2. Weltkrieg, in einer Atmosphäre, als die Völker der noch real existierenden UdSSR einige Freiheiten erlangten, ihre nationalen – und nicht selten nationalistischen – Ideologien zum Ausdruck zu bringen. In dieser Zeit haben die Azerbaidshaner der Republik Azerbaidshan (oder vielmehr ihre wissenschaftliche Elite) begonnen, sich als Abkömmlinge der Albanier aufzufassen und ihre Geschichte entsprechend zu interpretieren[2]. Um den Standard einiger Arbeiten zu charakterisieren, möge ein Beispiel genügen. Man behauptete ernstlich, dass die „Geschichte der Albanier" von Movsēs Kałankatuacʻi (Dasxurancʻi, 10. Jh.), die nur armenisch bekannt ist, eine Übersetzung aus dem Albanischen wäre. Es handelt sich um ein Schriftdenkmal in armenischer Sprache, wo die Bibelzitate wörtlich mit der armenischen Version der Hl. Schrift übereinstimmen, die Textstellen aus den armenischen Autoren getreu wiedergegeben sind und die Strophen eines Lobliedes der Ordnung des armenischen Alphabets folgen! Eine kritische Besprechung der modernen Arbeiten enthält die Monographie von A. Akopjan[3], die derzeit überhaupt als bester Ausgangspunkt für albanische Forschungen dient.

Einen Begriff über die Mentalität der Albanier kann man sich heute nur in Bezug auf die christliche Epoche machen, wobei man sich praktisch immer auf armenische Quellen stützen muss. Die Dechiffrierung der albanischen Inschriften und besonders der neulich entdeckten Texte in dieser Sprache[4] können vielleicht wesentliche Korrekturen unserer Vorstellungen bringen, aber derzeit sind wir gezwungen, uns auf die traditionellen Nachrichten zu beschränken. Möglicherweise sind unsere Vorstellungen über die albanische Mentalität etwas einseitig, wahrscheinlich entsprechen sie aber doch im allgemeinen der Wirklichkeit.

---

[1] ANASSIAN 1969, 299f. mit Anm.; TREVER 1959, 24–40 (s. die Bibliographie am Ende des Beitrages).

[2] Z. B. MAMEDOVA 1986 und die Bibliographie S. 263–281. Vgl. die wertvolle, korrekte Kritik, die die Monographie von A. A. Akopjan (AKOPJAN 1987) enthält. – Ich gebrauche die Form „Albanier" (in Analogie zu „Armeniern" neben „Armenien" usw.), um einer Verwirrung bezüglich der Albaner des Balkans zu entrinnen.

[3] AKOPJAN 1987.

[4] S. ALEKSIDZE 1999.

Nachrichten über Albanien und seine Bevölkerung finden sich schon in den ältesten Denkmälern der armenischen Literatur, aber nichts reicht an die „Geschichte der Albanier" von Movsēs Kałankatuacʿi oder Dasxurancʿi (?) heran[5]. Viele Forscher datierten und datieren diesen Text noch immer in das 7. Jh.[6], aber die Argumente für das 10. Jh. sind doch überzeugender. Die dreiteilige „Geschichte der Albanier" (im folgenden GA) ist in mehreren Schichten komponiert, viele Quellen sind wörtlich zitiert. A. Akopjan zufolge hat dieses Werk folgende Blöcke:

a. Erzählung über den König Vačʿagan (I 14 und 16–23);
b. Geschichte des Katholikos Viroy (II 9–16);
c. Geschichte des Jahres 684 (I 27–30 und II 18–45);
d. Abschnitte, die aus der Feder von Movsēs Dasxurancʿi selbst stammen (I 1–9, 12–13, 15; II 3, 5, 8, 17, 47; III 3, 7, 12–13, 15–16, 19–23).

Die anderen Abschnitte kann man nicht zuverlässig identifizieren[7].

Das kaukasische Albanien erscheint in griechisch-lateinischen wie auch in frühharmenischen Quellen als Territorium nördlich von Armenien, östlich von Iberien (Georgien), südlich des Kaukasusgebirges, mit Zugang zum Kaspisee. Die klassischen Autoren nennen es Ἀλβανία, *Albania*, die armenischen *Ałuankʿ*, für die Georgier ist es *Hereti* (von den *Herni* bevölkert), für die Perser *Ran* (hieraus arabisch *Arran*). Nach Strabo besteht die Bevölkerung aus 26 Stämmen (jeder mit seiner eigenen Sprache), wovon man etwa 20 identifizieren kann. Arrian berichtet über die Teilnahme von Albaniern an der Schlacht von Gaugamela (331 v. Chr.), natürlich auf Seiten der Perser. 283–282 besuchte Patrokles die westliche Küste des Kaspisees und verfasste einen ausführlichen Bericht, dessen Angaben von Eratosthenes und Strabo benützt wurden. Als Königreich ist Albanien ab dem 1. Jh. v. Chr. bezeugt. An der Seite des armenischen Königs Tigranes II. leisteten die Albanier 69 v. Chr. der römischen Expansion Widerstand, ihr Land wurde aber 66–65 von Pompeius okkupiert. Plutarch, Plinius Junior, Cassius Dio und Ammianus Marcellinus überliefern viele historische Episoden, die Albanien betreffen, Ptolemaios nennt 28 albanische Städte bzw. Dörfer, aber nur Strabo gibt ein allgemeineres Bild des Landes[8].

Das Zivilisationsniveau der Albanier war niedriger als das der Armenier und Georgier, aber auch sie folgten denselben Entwicklungssträngen. Ähnlich wie ihre Nachbarn bekannten sich die Albanier zum Zoroastrismus, wahrscheinlich in einer lokalen Form. Die quasi-feudale Gesellschaft der Albanier hat sich – ebenso wie die der Armenier und Georgier – im kulturellen Umkreis des Iran formiert, die politische Abhängigkeit dauerte – bei wechselnden Grenzen – bis zum Sturz des Sasaniden-Reiches (651).

Ende des 4. oder Anfang des 5. Jh. (genauer wissen wir es nicht) trat ein Ereignis ein, das prinzipielle Folgen für die politische und kulturelle Entwicklung hatte und die ethnische Struktur des Staates veränderte: zwei armenische Provinzen, Utikʿ und Arcʿax, kamen zum albanischen Königreich. Kurz danach wurde Utikʿ zu einem administrativen und religiösen Zentrum. Die „neuen Albanier" beginnen, eine spezifische Rolle in der Entwicklung des nationalen Selbstbewusstseins, des albanischen Patriotismus, zu spielen. Ein Parallelismus zu den Vorstellungen der Nachbarn ist ganz offensichtlich, manchmal auch eine verdeckte Rivalität. Diese Erscheinungen finden sich immer – oder fast

[5] GA 1983. Bedauerlicherweise gibt es in dieser neuesten Ausgabe nicht wenige Druckfehler.

[6] So z. B. Aleksidze 1999, 5: „albanischer Historiker des 7. Jh., dessen Werk in einer Version des 10. Jh. in Armenisch erhalten ist". Aber diese Geschichte ist nicht nur in Armenisch erhalten, sondern wurde auch in dieser Sprache geschrieben!

[7] Akopjan 1987, 177–211; vgl. auch J.-P. Mahé, Die Bekehrung Transkaukasiens, o. S. 118–120.

[8] Trever 1959, 7–11, 41ff. – Die oben gebotene Einschätzung der Spezialliteratur über Albanien trifft auf das Werk von K. V. Trever nicht zu.

immer – auch im religiösen Bereich. Das Hauptthema ist die Geschichte der Predigt, der Verbreitung des Christentums und besonders der albanischen Kirche überhaupt. Schon von allem Anfang an konstruiert der Autor der GA den Stammbaum von Japhet und seinen Nachkommen her und bestimmt sein Volk in einem quasi-biblischen Kontext. Die ersten drei Kapitel des I. Buches der GA folgen fast wörtlich einer armenischen Chronik des 7. Jh., die ihrerseits in diesem Abschnitt eine Übersetzung der Chronik von Hippolytos dem Römer (ca. 170–235) ist[9]. Der Urquelle folgend zitiert auch die GA das Ethnonym Chittier (Κίτιοι Gen 10, 4) und fügt hinzu, dass nördlich von ihnen ihre Stammesgenossen sind, von denen die Albanier (Ałuankʿ) abstammen. Und weiter unten nennt der Autor unter den Nachkommen Japhets nochmals die Albanier[10]. Aber das Thema der Christianisierung seiner Heimat interessiert ihn unvergleichlich mehr.

Bekanntlich identifiziert sich die armenische Kirche als apostolisch. Die Grundlage dieser Idee ist die Legende über die Taufe des syrischen Königs Abgar, die „Lehre Addaïs“. Der kranke König hatte Erkundigungen über die Wunder Christi eingezogen und lud daraufhin den Retter in seine Hauptstadt Edessa ein, damit Er ihn heile und in seinem Land Zuflucht fände. Jesus antwortete, dass Er alle seine Taten vollendet habe und nun die Himmelfahrt erwarte. Er werde aber einen seiner Schüler zum König schikken, damit dieser den Kranken heile. Und wirklich schickte der Apostel Thomas den Apostel Addaï, einen der LXX (Lc 10, 1) zum König. Addaï vollbringt Wunder, stellt die Gesundheit des Königs wieder her und beginnt zu predigen. Die königliche Familie und viele Einwohner der Stadt werden getauft. Umringt von Schülern stirbt der Apostel dann in Edessa.

Die syrische Abgar-Sage bildet die Grundlage der Erzählung des Eusebius von Cäsarea über dieselben Ereignisse; hier figuriert ein Sendbote nach Jerusalem, auch hier ist ein Apostel aus der Schar der LXX anwesend, der aber bereits Thaddäus genannt wird.

Der König, der in dieser Legende auftrifft, ist Abgar V. Oukkâmâ (4 v. Chr. – 7 und 13–50 n. Chr.), aber den historischen Hintergrund der Erzählung gibt die (historisch glaubwürdige) Bekehrung eines anderen Königs, Abgars VIII. (177–212) und seiner Familie ab.

Bei der Verpflanzung dieser Legende auf armenischen Boden hat sie einen grundsätzlichen Wandel erfahren. Während Addaï/Thaddäus in der syrischen Urschrift und der griechischen Darlegung in der Stadt Edessa verschieden ist, weiht er dort einen anderen Addaï (in den syrischen und griechischen Texten wird er Aggaï genannt) zum Bischof und begibt sich selbst in den Orient (d. h. nach Armenien), „um das Evangelium Christi zu predigen“.

In Armenien ist Thaddäus als einer der XII bekannt (Mt 10, 3; Mc 3,18; Lc 6, 16). Er kommt in den Kanton Artaz (im Süden des Landes) und bekehrt viele Menschen zum christlichen Glauben, darunter Sanduxt, die Tochter des armenischen Königs Sanatruk. In der armenischen Sage ist Sanatruk ein Neffe Abgars, der als armenischer König figuriert. Sanatruk verfolgt die Proselyten grausam, Sanduxt – und nach ihr auch Thaddäus – beenden ihr Leben als Märtyrer. Einer anderen Sage folgend habe Thaddäus in Armenien den Apostel Bartholomäus getroffen, der mit ebensolchem Ziel gekommen war. Auch Bartholomäus fand das gleiche Ende. In der armenischen Version ist Thaddäus also vom armenischen, nicht vom syrischen König Abgar eingeladen worden.

Die heutige Wissenschaft zweifelt nicht am legendären Charakter beider Sagen. Die Erzählungen über die Apostel – in ihren verschiedenen literarischen Varianten – haben

[9] Bartikian 1967.
[10] GA 1983, S. 5. 2, 9.

aber einen wichtigen Platz im religiösen Bewusstsein der Armenier eingenommen. Hier spiegelt sich die große Rolle wider, die das syrische Element bei der Gestaltung des armenischen Christentums gespielt hat[11].

Die Thaddäus-Sage hat auch auf albanischem Boden eine weitere Entwicklung erfahren. Die lokale Legende erzählt vom Apostel Thaddäus, der nach Armenien, in den Kanton Artaz gekommen und als Märtyrer gestorben ist. Sein Schüler, der hl. Ełišay, geht nach Jerusalem und teilt den anderen Aposteln den Tod des Thaddäus mit. Daraufhin wird er vom hl. Jakob, dem Bruder Jesu und ersten Bischof in Jerusalem, geweiht und kommt nochmals nach Albanien. Seine Predigt beginnt er in Čʻołay, nördlich der Kura, unter den Mazkutʻ (Massageten), und beendigt sein Leben ebenfalls als Märtyrer. Seine Reliquien werden später entdeckt[12].

Ełišay ist das wichtigste Symbol des Christentums in Albanien. Die armenische Kirche verehrte ihn auch, aber die literarischen Quellen vor dem 10.-11. Jh. erwähnen ihn noch nicht. Eine kurze Vita Ełišays findet sich in einem armenischen Synaxar des 13. Jh.[13]

Die albanischen Hierarchen bekamen ihre Weihe von den armenischen Katholikoi, so dass die albanische Kirche zumindest formell von der armenischen abhing. Zugleich akzentuierte die albanische Kirche jene Umstände, die ihr Anspruch auf eine gewisse Gleichheit, ja sogar Priorität verleihen könnten. Der neue Glaube sei durch Vermittlung Ełišays direkt aus Jerusalem gekommen[14], in dieser Stadt sei er zum Bischof geweiht worden, und zwar durch den hl. Jakob, Jesu Bruder[15]. Das Jerusalem-Thema kommt in der „Geschichte der Albanier" mehrfach vor. Der Schöpfer der Alphabete, Mesrop (Maštocʻ), sei wie ein Pilger nach Jerusalem gegangen[16], nach dessen Tod haben seine albanischen Schüler diesen Weg wiederholt: „Die Anfangserleuchtung Albaniens ist doch durch den hl. Ełišay aus Jerusalem gekommen!"[17] Ein Kapitel enthält eine Beschreibung der berühmtesten Kirchen der Heiligen Stadt[18] und ein anderes die der Klöster, die die Albanier erbaut haben[19].

Unsere Kenntnisse über die ersten reellen Schritte auf dem Wege der Verbreitung des neuen Glaubens sind sehr knapp. Agathangelos, der so ausführlich über die Christianisierung Armeniens unter Gregor dem Erleuchter erzählt, nennt die Albanier nur einmal, in Zusammenhang mit dem Krieg des armenischen Königs „Chosrow" gegen den Usurpator Ardaschir Papakan[20]. Aber das *Leben Gregors*, das in seiner griechischen Variante erhalten ist, teilt uns mit, dass während der allgemeinen Taufe der Armenier auch die Könige der Lazen, der Iberer und der Albanier getauft wurden[21]. Weiters hätte Gregor Priester und Bischöfe in die benachbarten Gebiete delegiert, und es war Thomas, ein frommer Bischof aus Satala (Kleinarmenien), der nach Albanien ging. Pʻawstos Buzand erzählt über

---

[11] Zur Position der armenischen Kirche s. z.B. Ormanian 1912, §§ 5–16; Angaben zu den armenischen Quellen, die das Thema betreffen: Adjarian, Personennamen II 6–8, Nr. 1 (Abgar); IV 185, Nr. 1 (Oguhi); 392f., Nr. 1 (Sanatruk); 393f., Nr. 4 (Sanduxt). Über die syrischen und armenischen Legenden: Carrière 1895; Segal 1970, 62–84; Meščerskaja 1984; Van Esbrœck 1972, 241–283; ders. 1983, 171–175; Epic Histories 406 (Sanatruk), 411f. (Tʻadēos); Doctrine d'Addaï 1997, 1473–1525. Vgl. auch Mahé, o. S. 111–112.

[12] GA I 6f.

[13] Synaxaire 1911.

[14] GA 1983, S. 97, 20–98, 1–2.

[15] GA 1983, S. 342, 8–9.

[16] A.O., S. 95, 9–10.

[17] A.O., S. 97, 18–98, 2.

[18] A.O. II 51.

[19] A.O. II 52.

[20] Agathangelos 1976, § 19.

[21] Über die Details Akopjan 1987, 125–127.

Grigoris, den Engel Gregors d. Erleuchters, der die Kirchen in Albanien restauriert und dort sein Leben als Märtyrer beendigt hat[22]. Diesem Autor gemäß gab es also schon vor der Ankunft des Grigoris einige Kirchen in Albanien.

Die albanische Version über die Predigt in dieser Periode ist davon wesentlich verschieden. In der Zeit des Kaisers Konstantinos, erzählt der Autor der „Geschichte der Albanier", sind die Bewohner des Orients, d.h. die Albanier, zum zweiten Mal erleuchtet worden. Diese „zweite Einsicht" hat durch den albanischen König Uṙnayr, den Schwiegersohn oder Schwager des iranischen Königs Schapuhr, stattgefunden. Uṙnayr bekommt die „zweite Geburt" durch Gregor den Erleuchter, kehrt nach Albanien zurück und klärt die Bevölkerung auf. Ein Römer, der mit ihm gekommen ist, wird Bischof. Nach dessen Tod erbittet man den jungen Grigoris für Albanien[23].

Die Figur des ersten albanischen Königs Uṙnayr ist auf albanischem Boden entstanden, nicht früher als im 7.–8. Jh.[24] Die armenischen Quellen kennen einen albanischen König Uṙnayr, einen Verbündeten des persischen Königs, einen Feueranbeter, der ein Zeitgenosse des armenischen Königs Pap (368–374) war und bei einer Schlacht verwundet wurde[25]. Diese Angaben sprechen gegen eine Identifikation der beiden Personen. Jedenfalls wurde das Bild Uṙnayrs in den albanischen Quellen wie ein Analogon zum ersten christlichen armenischen König Trdat (298–330) und mit derselben transparenten Tendenz geschaffen – um eine Gleichstellung zwischen beiden christlichen Gemeinschaften zu sichern.

Die Bedeutung ihres Alphabets haben die Armenier nach Gebühr gewürdigt, der Schöpfer des armenischen Schrifttums, Maštocʿ, wurde hoch geehrt und sofort nach seinem Tod kanonisiert. Bei all seiner wissenschaftlichen Bedeutung war Maštocʿ in den Augen seiner Landsleute vor allem ein Prediger des christlichen Glaubens, und die Bezeichnung „Zweiter Erleuchter" (nach Gregor) wurde später üblich. Sein Schüler Koriwn hat eine *Vita* geschrieben (443–449), wo er die Tätigkeit seines Lehrers sehr pragmatisch darstellte.

Die Schöpfung der georgischen und albanischen Alphabete ist mit dem Namen des großen Philologen verbunden, auch für die Albanier ist er ein Held gewesen. Nach Koriwns lakonischer Nachricht[26] hat der Autor der GA viele Details in sein Werk aufgenommen, die die Biographie des Maštocʿ noch hervorragender machen. Die Leistung von Maštocʿ wird nachdrücklich als Heldentat im christlichen Sinne hoch geschätzt, das Alphabet vor allem als Instrument der Predigt gesehen. Auch die albanischen Schüler des Maštocʿ sind in demselben Sinne ruhmgekrönt[27], ja die Erzählung über Maštocʿ und seine albanischen Schüler dient ihrerseits zu deren Glorifizierung.

Gleich am Beginn der GA gibt es ein Kapitel „Über die Völker, die das Schrifttum haben". Unter diesen Völkern sind auch die Albanier genannt[28]. Dieses Kapitel ist eine Übersetzung aus der Chronik des Hippolytos[29]. Im 7. Jh. wurde dieses Werk ins Armenische übersetzt, und der Übersetzer hat in die Liste der Völker, die das Schrifttum kennen,

---

[22] Buzand 1933, III 6–7; Epic Histories 72–75.

[23] GA 1983, I 9.

[24] Ein Brief unter dem Namen des Katholikos Giwt (461–478; s. GA I 11) erzählt auch über Uṙnayr, aber viele Forscher lehnen seine Authentizität ab und datieren diese Schrift in 7.–8. Jh. Die GA kennt diesen Uṙnayr nicht.

[25] Epic Histories, S. 417, s.v. Uṙnayr. – Vgl. auch Mahé, o. S. 121.

[26] Koriwn 1981, cap. 16–17. S. auch Koriwn 1994.

[27] GA 1983, I 17. 18. 19; II 3 u. a.

[28] GA 1983, S. 6, 8.

[29] Vgl. o. S. 183.

auch die Armenier eingeschlossen. Diese Übersetzung wird auch vom Autor der GA benützt, unter Hinzufügung der „Albanier".

So war es auch mit den Grundlagen der konfessionellen Selbstbestimmung der Albanier. Die Vorstellungen über die Herkunft der albanischen Kirche waren stabil und unabhängig vom allfälligen Schwanken zwischen „monophysitischen" und „dyophysitischen" Lehren der offiziellen Kirche.

Die ethnische Struktur des kaukasischen Albanien war immer kompliziert. Der Anschluss der armenischen Provinzen hat diese Lage noch erschwert. Die Einwohner von Utikʿ und Arcʿax verstanden den Wandel ihres Status klar, aber sie kamen mit ihrer eigenen Sprache und ihren eigenen Traditionen und wollten sich nicht mit den anderen vermischen. Im ethnischen Sinne sind sie Armenier geblieben. Bezeichnend ist, dass der Autor der GA selten über die nordischen Völker spricht, die Stämme am linken Ufer der Kura. Gleichzeitig nahmen sie aber schon den Unterschied zu den Armeniern Armeniens wahr, die für sie nicht mehr „wir" sondern „sie" waren[30]. Ihre „Nationalität" (im modernen Sinn) wurde verändert, sie wurden zu „Albaniern". Die GA bringt vor allem die Geistesverfassung dieser Teile der Bevölkerung zum Ausdruck.

Die GA berichtet hauptsächlich von den Albaniern der christlichen Epoche. Die Zugehörigkeit zur Kirche der Albanier wird auch als Staatsangehörigkeit interpretiert. Eine solche Begriffsverwirrung ist durchaus eine gewöhnliche Erscheinung, man vergleiche nur das Schrifttum, wo die Termini „Jude" und „Hellene" in derselben Zeit sowohl im ethnischen als auch im religiösen Sinn verwendet werden. Auch die Ethnika „Armenier" und „Georgier" konnten im Sinne der Zugehörigkeit zur armenischen bzw. georgischen Kirche verwendet werden. Die Ῥωμαῖοι waren sowohl die Byzantiner als auch die Söhne der orthodoxen Ostkirche. Auch in unserem Fall bedeutet der Terminus „Albanier" nicht nur die Bewohner des Landes Albanien, sondern auch die Gläubigen der albanischen Kirche, die in den Augen ihrer Gegner „monophysitisch" war. Auch in diesem Sinne konnten Armenier, die „Albanier" geworden waren, diesen Namen tragen, ohne in Widerspruch mit der Wirklichkeit zu geraten.

Bibliographie

Adjarian, Personennamen

Hr. Adjarian, Wörterbuch der armenischen Personennamen. Bd. I–V. Erevan 1942–1962 [arm.].

Agathangelos 1976

Agathangelos. History of the Armenians. Translation and Commentary by R. W. Thomson. Albany 1976.

Akopjan 1987

A. A. Akopjan, Albanien-Aluank in den griechisch-lateinischen und armenischen Quellen. Erevan 1987 [russ.].

Aleksidze 1999

Z. Aleksidze, Some newly discovered texts of Caucasian Albania. *Christianskij Vostok* 1 (7) (1999) 3–13 [russ.]

Anassian 1969

H. S. Anassian, Une mise au point relative à l'Albanie Caucasienne (Ałuankʿ). *REArm* 6 (1969) 299–330.

Bartikian 1967

H. M. Bartikian, A propos de la Chronographie attribuée à Anania Chirakatsi et de son véritable compilateur. *Banber Matenadarani* 8 (1967) 57–77 [arm. mit russ. u. franz. Resümees].

[30] Im Altarmenischen bezeichnet Haykʿ „Armenien" und „Armenier" (Plural), daneben gibt es ein Fachwort Hayastaneaykʿ für „Bewohner Armeniens". Letzterer Terminus wird in der GA oft benützt und bezeichnet jeweils nur Bewohner Armeniens: S. 10, 12; 14, 16; 120, 1–2; 122, 17–18 (in einem Brief des armenischen Katholikos); 274, 11; 314, 2; 318, 13; 325, 7; 335, 13–14.

Buzand 1933
Geschichte der Armenier von Pʻawstos Buzand. Venedig 1933.
Carrière 1895
A. Carrière, La légende d'Abgar dans l'Histoire de Moïse de Khoren. Paris 1895.
Doctrine d'Addaï 1997
Doctrine de l'apôtre Addaï. Texte traduit, présenté et annoté par A. Desreumaux, in: Ecrits apocryphes chrétiens, ed. F. Bovon u. a. Paris 1997, 1473–1525.
Epic Histories
The Epic Histories Attributed to Pʻawstos Buzand (*Buzandaran Patmowtʻiwnkʻ*). Translation and Commentary by N. G. Garsoïan. Cambridge, Mass. 1989, S. 406 (Sanatruk); 411–412 (Tʻadēos).
GA 1961
The History of the Caucasian Albanians by Movsēs Dasxurancʻi. Translated by C. J. F. Dowsett. London 1961.
GA 1983
Movsēs Kałankatuacʻi. Geschichte des Landes Albanien. Kritischer Text und Einführung von V. Arakeljan. Erevan 1983.
GA 1984
Movses Kalankatuaci, Geschichte des Landes Albanien. Übersetzung aus dem Altarmenischen, Vorwort und Kommentar von Š. V. Smbatjan. Erevan 1984 [russ.].
Koriwn 1981
Koriwn, Das Leben von Maštocʻ. Erevan 1981 [Text mit neuarmen., russ. u. engl. Übersetzungen].
Koriwn 1994
G. Winkler, Koriwns Biographie des Mesrop Maštocʻ. Überlieferung und Kommentar (*OCP* 245). Rom 1994.
Mamedova 1986
F. Mamedova, Politische Geschichte und historische Geographie des Kaukasischen Albanien (III. Jh. v. – VII. Jh. n. Chr.). Baku 1986 [russ.].
Meščerskaja 1984
E. N. Meščerskaja, Die Legende über Abgar – ein altsyrisches Literaturdenkmal. Moskau 1984 [russ.].
Ormanian 1912
M. Ormanian, Nationale Geschichte. Konstantinopel 1912 [arm.].
Segal 1970
J. B. Segal, Edessa, „The blessed City". Oxford 1970.
Synaxaire 1911
Le synaxaire arménien de Ter Israel, publié et traduit par G. Bayan. *PO* VI, 1911, S. 302–304.
Trever 1959
K. V. Trever, Studies on the History and Culture of Caucasian Ałbania. Moskau-Leningrad 1959 [russ.].
Van Esbrœck 1972
M. van Esbrœck, Le roi Sanatrouk et l'apôtre Thaddée. *REArm* 9 (1972) 241–283.
Van Esbrœck 1983
M. van Esbrœck, La naissance du culte de saint Barthélémy en Arménie. *REArm* 17 (1983) 171–175.

BOGHOS LEVON ZEKIYAN / VENEDIG

DIE CHRISTIANISIERUNG UND DIE ALPHABETISIERUNG ARMENIENS ALS VORBILDER KULTURELLER INKARNATION, BESONDERS IM SUBKAUKASISCHEN GEBIET

Der Prozess der Christianisierung und der Alphabetisierung Armeniens hat als Ergebnis die Formation einer lokalen Kirche, welche eine ausgeprägte ethnische Charakterisierung aufweist. Es wäre nicht irreführend, glaube ich, die armenische Erfahrung in der Kirchengeschichte als die Erscheinung eines neuen, sich wohl unterscheidenden kirchlichen Vorbildes zu betrachten, welches man als „ethnische Kirche" definieren kann. Ein Vorbild, das zwischen dem V. und VIII. Jahrhundert in einem bestimmten Sinne auf das ganze subkaukasische Gebiet ausstrahlte.

Geschichtliche Vorbilder der Kirche und der kulturelle Begriff von „Nation/Ethnos"

Dieses Vorbild stellt sich neben die großen geschichtlichen Vorbilder, welche das Sein und das Leben der Kirche, im Laufe der Jahrtausende, in ihren vielfältigen Aufgliederungen moduliert haben. Ich hatte in einer früheren Arbeit[1] die wichtigsten dieser Vorbilder als „imperiale Kirche" und „rituell-konfessionelle Kirche" gekennzeichnet. Man sollte darüber nicht erstaunen, wenn hier von einer „ethnischen Kirche" die Rede ist. Die ethnische Realität ist ein wesentlicher Teil der evangelischen Botschaft. Die letzten Worte Christi vor seiner Himmelfahrt, die letzte Anweisung des auferstandenen Herrn, betreffen unmittelbar und ausdrücklich *„panta ta ethne*[2]*"*. Die Heilsbotschaft wendet sich zum Menschen nicht bloß als zu einem einzelnen und isolierten Individuum, vielmehr als zu einer Person, die in einen lebendigen Zusammenhang von vielseitigen gemeinschaftlichen und sozialen Wechselbeziehungen eingefügt ist. Die Realität des *Ethnos* bildet den geschichtlichen Höhepunkt dieses Zusammenhanges[2].

Die armenische Erfahrung bietet eine gültige Hilfe, um das Phänomen der Verkörperung des Wortes Christi in den ethnischen und kulturellen Eigentümlichkeiten der Völker, seine Notwendigkeit und Vorgänge, seine Bedingungen, seine Risken und Vorteile, besser begreifen und verstehen zu können. Ein Prozess, den die heutige Theologie auch „christliche Inkulturation" nennt oder mit äquivalenten Ausdrücken beschreibt[3]. Zudem

---

[1] Das Verhältnis zwischen Sprache und Identität in der Entwicklung des armenischen Nationalbewusstseins. Versuch einer begrifflichen Formulierung aus geschichtlicher Erfahrung, in: Gerd Hentschel (Hrsg.), Über Muttersprachen und Vaterländer. Zur Entwicklung von Standardsprachen und Nationen in Europa, Frankfurt am Main 1997, 277–297.

[2] Für eine weitere Verarbeitung des Begriffes siehe Boghos L. Zekiyan, Vangelo, Chiese e culture, *Presenza pastorale* 65 (1995) 15 [1047] – 23 [1055].

[3] Vgl. unter anderen: Karl H. Neufeld (Hrsg.), Problemi e prospettive di teologia dogmatica, Queriniana, Brescia, 1983, bes. Parte terza: Il compito della teologia dogmatica nelle diverse regioni del mondo, S. 373–493; Heinrich Fries, Kirche und Kirchen, in: René Latourelle – Gerald O'Collins (Hrsgg.), Probleme und Aspekte der Fundamentaltheologie, Hrsg. der deutschen Ausgabe … Johannes Bernard, Leipzig, 1985, 366–383, übersetzt aus dem Italienischen: Problemi e prospettive di teologia fondamentale, Queriniana, 1980; François Kabasélé – Joseph Doré – René Luneau (Hrsgg.), Chemins de la

wäre es möglich, weiter zu behaupten, dass uns das armenische Vorbild eine anregende Gelegenheit bietet, eine Theologie vom Ethnos zu entwickeln, gerade am Beispiel des modernen theologischen Nachdenkens, das fast von allen irdischen Tatsachen eine organische theologische Auffassung formuliert hat. Die armenische Erfahrung bietet uns im besonderen ein Vorbild, in dem die Idee von „Nation" keineswegs diejenige ist, die das westliche Denken, vor allem das französische, auf den Spuren der Aufklärungsphilosophie im Sinne der „Staatsnation" gebildet hat. Es ist eher die Realität des Ethnos, die, im Rahmen dieser kirchlichen und sozial-kulturellen Erfahrung, einfach als „Nation" gilt: eine Gesprächspartnerin der Heilsbotschaft Jesu, in deren Zusammenhang der Mensch das Heil erreicht[4].

christologie africaine, Paris 1986; Germano PATTARO, La svolta antropologica. Un momento forte della teologia contemporanea, opera postuma, a cura di M. Cristina BARTOLOMEI e Alberto GALLAS, Bologna, 1990.

[4] Ich habe diese Ideen in den folgenden früheren Arbeiten weiterentwickelt: Prémisses pour une méthodologie critique dans les études arméno-géorgiennes, *Bazmavep* 139 (1981) 460–469; P'akman xōsk' Yovsēp' Ašrafeani ogekoč'man handēsin aṙt'iw [Schlusswort anlässlich der Gedenkfeier an Yovsēp' Ašrafean], *Bazmavep* 140 (1982) 206–210; Italahay mec k'nnadat Yovsēp' Ašrafean (Glauco Viazzi), 1920–1980 [Der große armenisch-italienische Kritiker Yovsēp' Ašrafean (Glauco Viazzi), 1920–1980], *Haratch. Mitk yev Arvest*, N° 62, 6. Juni 1982, nachgedruckt *Haratch* [Yaraǰ] 60, (Matenašar Haratch, 17), Paris, 1985, 298–316; Le croisement des cultures dans les régions limitrophes de Géorgie, d'Arménie et de Byzance, *Annali di Ca' Foscari*, (Serie Orientale 17), 25/3, 1986, S. 81–96; Da Konstantiniye a Venezia", *Studi Eurasiatici in onore di Mario Grignaschi*, a cura di Giampiero BELLINGERI e Giorgio VERCELLIN, (Eurasiatica 5, Quaderni del Dipartimento di Studi Eurasiatici, Università degli Studi di Venezia), Libreria Universitaria Editrice, Venezia, 1988, 17–35; L'«idéologie» nationale de Movsēs Xorenac'i et sa conception de l'histoire, *Handes Amsorya* 101 (1987), Sp. 471–485; Ellenismo, ebraismo e cristianesimo in Mosè di Corene (Movsēs Xorenac'i). Elementi per una teologia dell'etnia, *Augustinianum* 28 (1988): *XVI. Incontro di Studiosi dell'Antichità Cristiana. Cristianesimo e giudaismo: eredità e confronti, 7–9 maggio 1987*, Roma, 1988, 381–390; Hrand Nazariantz, gli Armeni e l'Italia. Da una vicenda interculturale verso una nuova tipologia di confronto etnoculturale, *Annali di Ca' Foscari* 29/3 (Serie Orientale 21), 1990, 135–150; Les identités polyvalentes et Sergueï Paradžanov. La situation emblématique de l'artiste et le problème de la polyvalence ethnique et culturelle, *Filosofia Oggi* 16 (1993) 217–231; Lo studio delle interazioni politiche e culturali tra le popolazioni della Subcaucasia: alcuni problemi di metodologia e di fondo in prospettiva sincronica e diacronica, in: Il Caucaso: cerniera fra culture dal Mediterraneo alla Persia (secoli IV–XI). *Atti della Quarantatreesima Settimana di studio del Centro Italiano di Studi sull'Alto Medioevo (aprile 1995)*, Bd. I, Spoleto, 1996, 427–482; In margine alla storia. Dal fenomeno dell'emigrazione verso un nuovo concetto dell'identità e dell'integrazione etnoculturale, in: Ad limina Italiae, Aṙ druns Italioy. In viaggio per l'Italia con mercanti e monaci armeni, a cura di B. L. ZEKIYAN, Padova, 1996, 267–286; The Armenian Way to Modernity. Armenian Identity between Tradition and Innovation, Specificity and Universality, *Eurasiatica* 49, Quaderni del Dipartimento di Studi Eurasiatici, Università degli Studi Ca' Foscari di Venezia, Venezia, 1997, bes. 15–26, 83–96.

Die wissenschaftliche Diskussion über den Begriff von Ethnizität und die vielseitigen diesbezüglichen Fragen ist heute hochaktuell und lebhaft. Von einer umfangreichen Literatur möchte ich auf die folgenden Titel aufmerksam machen: Über die allgemeine Problematik: Richard MARIENSTRAS, Être un peuple en diaspora, *Mosaïques* 1, Paris, 1975; Theodor VEITER, Nationalitätenkonflikt und Volksgruppenrecht im 20. Jahrhundert, München, 1977; Ronald A. REMINICK, Theory of Ethnicity. An Anthropologist's Perspective, Lanham, MD – London, 1983; A. MELUCCI, Nazioni senza Stato: i movimenti etnico-nazionali in Occidente, Torino, 1983; B. GILSON, The Conceptual System of Sovereign Equality, (Philosophie du Droit International), Leuven, 1984; Pier Giovanni DONINI, Le minoranze nel Vicino Oriente e nel Maghreb. Problemi metodologici e questioni generali, Salerno, 1985; William H. MCNEILL, Polyethnicity and National Unity in World History, *The Donald G. Creighton Lectures* 1985, University of Toronto Press, 1986; Hannah ARENDT, Ebraismo e modernità (raccolta di saggi sparsi tradotti in italiano), Milano, 1986, Milano, 1993^2; DIES., La lingua materna. La condizione umana e il pensiero plurale, a cura di Alessandro DAL LAGO, Milano, 1993; Alain FINKELKRAUT, La défaite de la pensée, Paris, 1987; Etienne BALIBAR – Immanuel WALLERSTEIN, Race, Nation, Classe. Les identités ambiguës, Paris, 1988; AA. VV., Ebrei moderni. Identità stereotipi culturali, a cura di D. BIDUSSA, Torino, 1989; Tzvetan

Armenien, das erste christliche Königtum, und der epistemologische Begriff von historischem „Vorbild"

Wenn wir die chronologische Abfolge der offiziellen Verbreitung des Christentums, nämlich die Bekehrung der einzelnen Königreiche im subkaukasischen Gebiet, betrachten, dann erscheint das armenische Königtum als das erste, das die neue Religion offiziell annahm. Das geschah spätestens im Jahre 314/315[5]. Obwohl es unter den Gelehrten bezüglich des genauen Datums der Bekehrung des armenischen Königtums große Unterschiede gibt, ist von niemandem dafür ein späteres Jahr vorgeschlagen worden. Hinzu kommt, dass eine solche Hypothese aufgrund der vorhandenen geschichtlichen Daten unvorstellbar wäre. Natürlich ist die Frage nicht: *post hoc, ergo propter hoc*. Methodologisch wäre eine solche Argumentation ein grober Fehler. Die Frage ist anders zu stellen, ob nämlich eine Reihe von aufeinanderfolgenden Ereignissen als geschichtlicher Kontext erklärt werden darf, ob es möglich ist, die Dynamik Ihrer Entwicklung aufgrund geschichtlicher kontextueller Faktoren besser zu verstehen.

Ich glaube, dass uns der moderne Begriff von „Vorbild" (*pattern, modèle*), der in der zeitgenössischen Wissenschaft sehr weit und vielschichtig gebraucht wird, in der Suche

---

Todorov, Nous et les autres. La réflexion française sur la diversité humaine, Paris, 1989; James G. Kellas, The Politics of Nationalism and Ethnicity, London, 1991; Alain Minc, La vengeance des nations, Paris, 1991; M. Wieviorka, La démocratie à l'épreuve. Nationalisme, populisme, ethnicité, Paris, 1993; Zwischen Nationalstaat und multikultureller Gesellschaft: Einwanderung und Fremdenfeindlichkeit in der Bundesrepublik Deutschland, hgg. v. M. Hessler, Berlin, 1993; Questioni di etnicità, a cura di Vanessa Maher, Torino, 1994; Ugo Fabietti, L'identità etnica. Storia e critica di un concetto equivoco, Roma, 1995; Ph. Poutignat – J. Streiff-Fenart, Théorie de l'ethnicité, Paris, 1995; Carlo Tullio-Altan, Ethnos e civiltà. Identità etniche e valori democratici, Milano, 1995; Charles Taylor, The Politics of Recognition, Princeton University Press, 1992, Jürgen Habermas, Kampf um Anerkennung im demokratischen Rechtsstaat, Frankfurt am M., 1996; beide Schriften zusammen in italienischer Übersetzung: Multiculturalismo. Lotte per il riconoscimento, Milano, 1998.

Über die religiös-kirchlich-theologischen Dimensionen der betreffenden Begriffe und Fragen: Nations et peuples: *Concilium. Revue Internationale de Théologie* 121; Dietrich Mendt, Christsein – Bereitschaft zur Diaspora. Zur Problematik Volkskirche, Minoritätskirche, Bekenntniskirche, in: Als Boten des gekreuzigten Herrn. Festgabe für Bischof Dr. Dr. Werner Krusche ..., hgg. v. Heino Falcke ..., Berlin, 1982, 179–184; Luigi Sartori, Teologia dei popoli, Trento, 1984; die monographischen Faszikel der Zeitschrift *Parola, spirito e vita*: N° 26, 1992/2, *Le genti nel piano di salvezza*; N° 27, 1993/1, *L'altro, il diverso, lo straniero*; N° 28, 1993/2, *Chiesa straniera e pellegrina*; Maria Campatelli, I cristiani tra nazioni e nazionalismi, in: Novità della soglia. Aperture della nuova evangelizzazione, Roma, 1995.

Mit besonderem Bezug auf die Armenier: La struttura negata: Cultura armena nella diaspora, Convegno-Seminario Internazionale: I, Milano, 1978, Atti / The Proceedings, redazione: Marc Nichanian – Remo Pomponio, Venezia, 1979; II, Milano, 1979, Atti / The Proceedings, Infrastructure de la Culture Arménienne Diasporique. La Culture: Mouvement socio-culturel ou structure figée?, red.: M. Nichanian, Venezia, 1981; A. Der-Karabetian, Multiple Social Identity as a Reflection of Modernity, *Armenian Review* 36 (1983), N° 1–141, S. 100–105, in deutscher Fassung: Vielfältige soziale Identität als Reflektion der Moderne, *Identität in der Fremde*, zitiert *infra*, S. 25–32; What is to be asked, Proceedings / Colloquium I, 2nd ed, Cambridge, MA, 1986; Viada A. Arutjunova-Fidanjan, The Ethno-confessional Self-Awareness of Armenian Chalcedonians", *REArm* 21 (1988–89) 345–363; Aleksej Lidov, L'art des Arméniens chalcédoniens, in: Atti del V Simposio Internazionale di Arte Armena (Venezia 1988*)*, B.L. Zekiyan (Hrsg.), Venezia, 1992, pp. 479–495; Giusto Traina, Il complesso di Trimalcione. Movsēs Xorenacʿi e le origini del pensiero storico armeno (*Eurasiatica* 27), Venezia, 1991, bes. 69–109; Identität in der Fremde, hgg. v. Mihran Dabag – Kristin Platt, Bochum, 1993.

5 Vgl. Paolo Ananian, La data e le circostanze della consecrazione di S. Gregorio Illuminatore, *Le Muséon* 74 (1961) 43–73, 317–360 (mit umfassender Besprechung der verschiedenen älteren Stellungnahmen); für die nachfolgende Diskussion siehe Marie-Louise Chaumont, Recherches sur l'histoire de l'Arménie de l'avènemenet des Sassanides à la conversion du Royaume, Paris 1969 (die Verfasserin stellt die Bekehrung zwischen 305–311); B. MacDermot, The Conversion of Armenia in 294 A.D., *REArm* 7 (1970), S. 281–359. Siehe nun auch W. Seibt, Der historische Hintergrund ..., o. S. 130f.

nach einem solchen Verständnis zu Hilfe sein kann. Zwar ist der Begriff von „Vorbild" in den Natur- und Sozialwissenschaften eng mit dem von „Struktur" und „System" verbunden. Das impliziert aber nicht einen schicksalhaften Determinismus. Übrigens hat der Begriff in den verschiedenen Zweigen der Wissenschaft keinen eindeutigen Gebrauch und funktioniert von Fall zu Fall nach geeigneten semantischen Besonderheiten und eigenen methodologischen Prinzipien und Prozeduren[6]. Die Geschichte selber ist die Bewegung der menschlichen Gemeinschaft durch die Zeit, mit ihren verschiedenen Strukturen, Modellen, Kräften, Funktionen usw., die das besondere Objekt der anthropologischen und soziologischen Untersuchung darstellen. Dieselben sind also auch unter die bestimmenden Faktoren der geschichtlichen Entwicklung zu zählen.

Aufgrund dieser Voraussetzungen können wir mit folgenden Worten definieren, was wir mit „Vorbild" im Prozess der geschichtlichen Entwicklung, mit besonderer Berücksichtigung des Prozesses der christlichen Inkulturation der Völker des subkaukasischen Gebietes, meinen. Der Begriff schließt grundsätzlich diese zwei Funktionen ein: *a)* das Vorbild wirkt als eine Inspirationsquelle, das heißt als ein Modell, an das man sich, auch wenn nur implizit, anlehnt; *b)* es wirkt als ein Faktor, der imstande ist, das Erscheinen einiger nachfolgender Entwicklungen zumindest teilweise zu erklären. Es ist aus dieser Formulierung selbst klar, dass sich erstens die beiden Funktionen in einem bestimmten Sinne gegenseitig einschließen, und dass sie zweitens keineswegs in einer exklusiven, das heißt monopolisierenden und totalisierenden Bedeutung verstanden werden dürfen, sondern nur in einer inklusiv-konnotativen Bedeutung. Wenn wir uns auf die Terminologie der klassischen Logik beziehen, sollten wir sagen, dass die beschriebenen Funktionen des „Vorbildes" mit Bezug auf die Wirkung eventueller anderer Faktoren in einem gegebenen geschichtlichen Kontext nicht *in signo diviso*, sondern *in signo composito* zu betrachten sind.

Über die Bekehrung Georgiens: Kornel Kekelidze, Die Bekehrung Georgiens, Leipzig 1928; Joseph Markwart, Die Bekehrung Iberiens, *Caucasica* 7 (1931) 111–167; Paul Peeters, Les débuts du christianisme en Géorgie, *AnBoll* 50 (1932) 5–58; Michel Tamarati, Die heilige Nino, *Analecta Ordinis Sancti Basilii Magni*, Romae 1953, 572–581; Tamila Mgaloblishvili (Ed.), Ancient Christianity in Caucasus (*Iberica Caucasica* 1), Curzon, Surrey, 1998.

Über den Kaukasus im allgemeinen mit besonderem Bezug auf kaukasisches Albanien: Bernard Outtier, La christianisation du Caucase, in: Il Caucaso: cerniera fra culture dal Mediterraneo alla Persia (secoli IV–XI), Bd. I, S. 553–570.

[6] Im folgenden einige Titel für eine allgemeine Einführung in den Begriff; aus anthropologisch-ethnologischer, kultureller Sicht: Claude Levi-Strauss, Anthropologie structurale, Paris, 1958 et 1974; Jurij M. Lotman – Boris A. Uspenskij, Tipologia della cultura, a cura di Remo Faccani e Marzio Marzaduri, Bompiani, Sonzogno, 1975, Milano 1995; Giuseppe Padovani (Hrsg.), Antropologia socio-culturale. Una introduzione ai concetti di sistema e di struttura sociale, Roma, 1979; Elémire Zolla, Archetypes, London–New York, 1981, italienische Version mit „alcuni tagli e numerose aggiunte" vom Verfasser: Archetipi, Venezia, 1988.

Aus soziologischer Sicht: Michel Crozier – Erhard Friedberg, L'acteur et le système. Les contraintes de l'action collective, Paris, 1977.

Aus epistemologischer Sicht: Giuseppe Barbieri – Paolo Vidali (Hrsg.), La ragione possibile. Per una geografia della cultura, Milano, 1988, bes. Parte quinta: I linguaggi della teoria, mit Beiträgen von Aldo G. Gargani, Ignacio Matte Blanco, Giulio Giorello, Edgar Morin, Mauro Ceruti, Renato Nobili und René Thom.

Aus philosophisch-ontologischer Sicht: Marcel François, Processions, dialectiques, structures, Paris, 1977, Livre IV: Structures et structuralisme, S. 329–423.

Die Bedeutung des Alphabetisierungsprozesses in Armenien und das Neue daran

Jedenfalls ist die Erfindung des armenischen Alphabets das entscheidende Ereignis, das der armenischen Christenheit ihren eigenen Charakter einer „ethnischen Kirche" gab. Diese Erfindung steht ohne Zweifel in enger Verbindung mit dem Prozess der Vertiefung der Wurzeln der neuen Religion im armenischen Boden. Es ist ganz deutlich, dass die missionarische Sorge mit ihren kerygmatischen und katechetischen Anliegen als eine grundsätzliche Begründung von Mesrops Tätigkeit fungierte. Aber es ist schwer sie zu erklären, ohne sie in ihrem konkreten geschichtlichen Umfeld und ohne die ihr zugrundeliegende Auffassung der Beziehung zwischen Religiosität und profanem Kontext, zwischen Religiosität und den nationalen und kulturellen Dimensionen des Individuums und der Gesellschaft in Betracht zu ziehen.

Was ich meine, möchte ich mit einem Beispiel „vom Gegenteil her" klarer zu machen versuchen. Wenn sich die Lokalsprachen und -liturgien im westlichen Christentum bis zur Reformation nur sehr wenig entwickelten und noch weniger von ihnen übriggeblieben ist, beruhte dies sicher auf der dort herrschenden Grundauffassung von der Beziehung zwischen Religion, Identität und Sprache. In einer imperialen Staats- und Religionsideologie[7] wie es sie im Römischen Reich gab, hatte eine lokalsprachliche religiös-nationale Identität natürlich wenig oder gar keinen Platz. Dies war aber nicht der Fall bei den kleineren christlichen Gemeinden, die außerhalb des byzantinischen Reiches blühten, auch wenn sie vom religiös-kulturellen Einfluss dieses Reiches stark gezeichnet waren, wie vor allem bei den nicht-griechischen orthodoxen Kirchen – z.B. der georgischen –, aber in bestimmtem Maße auch bei nicht-orthodoxen, wie der armenischen.

Es wäre gut hier anzumerken, dass die geschichtlichen Ereignisse im allgemeinen, und erst recht diejenigen, die am meisten originär und schöpferisch erscheinen, keine Geschöpfe des Augenblicks sind, ohne Schritte, die sie vorbereiteten. In ähnlicher Weise sind auch die Ursprünge einer ethnisch gefärbten Entwicklung des Frühchristentums im syrischen Gebiet zu identifizieren[8]. Eine solche Vorgeschichte bietet auch einen Schlüssel zur Lösung der Legitimitätsfrage, die weder Mesrop noch dem Katholikos Sahak entgehen konnte. Im geistlichen Kontext der Zeit konnte die Legitimitätsfrage eine Lösung nur im Rahmen einer solchen Auffassung der Sprache und ihrer ethnischen Träger finden, die sie nicht als etwas dem Bereich des Heiligen oder Sakralen Entferntes bzw. ihm Fremdes begriffen[9]. Dass die Sprache für die Syrer des 4. und für die Armenier des 5. Jahrhunderts, wie später für die Slavenapostel Kyrill und Method, wirklich etwas Sakrales war, ist keine Frage. Der Mensch der Spätantike und des Mittelalters bewahrte noch vieles vom Erbe der alten Menschheit, für die alles, was die Natur und den Menschen betrifft, heilig war.

Doch nur in der schöpferischen Erfindung von Mesrop Maštocʿ ist, so glaube ich, ein voll entwickeltes Bewusstsein von der dreifachen Wechselbeziehung zwischen Religion, Sprache und nationaler Identität zu finden. Was dem Werk Mesrops zugrundeliegt, ist

---

[7] Das Wort „Ideologie" gebrauche ich in dem Sinne, in welchem es François Châtelet und seine Mitarbeiter verwenden, nähmlich als ungefähre Entsprechung des deutschen Begriffs „Weltanschauung": François CHÂTELET (Hrsg.), Histoire des Idéologies, Bd. I, Introduction, Paris, 1978, bes. S. 10–11.

[8] Vgl. Winfried BOEDER, Identität und Universalität: Volkssprache und Schriftsprache in den Ländern des alten christlichen Orients, *Georgica* 17 (1994) 66–84.

[9] Gustave BARDY, La question des langues dans l'Église ancienne (*Études de Théologie Historique* 1), Paris, 1948, für Syrien und Armenien siehe insbes. S. 18–38; Claudio GUGEROTTI, Un testo kerigmatico-mistagogico di tradizione bizantina, *Oriente Cristiano* 32 (1992) 59–61; DERS., L'invenzione dell'alfabeto in Armenia: teologia della storia nella *Vita di Maštocʿ* di Koriwn, in: Claudio MORESCHINI – Giovanni MENESTRINA (Hrsgg.), La traduzione dei testi religiosi, Brescia, 1994, 101–126.

eine neue Auffassung dieser Wechselbeziehung und im besonderen eine neue Vorstellung von der kulturellen und nationalen Identität. Die neue Auffassung stellte gegenüber der der Syrer nicht nur eine reifere Entwicklungsstufe dar, sondern führte auch etwas qualitativ Neues ein. Es gibt etwas in Mesrops Werk, das neu, fast revolutionär ist. Dieses Neue besteht darin, dass Mesrops Werk zugleich *einen allgemeinen Plan für die ethnokulturelle Rettung und das Überleben des Volkes und der Nation enthielt.* Mesrop und seine engsten Mitarbeiter bemühten sich nach diesem Plan, das Problem der Bewahrung der armenischen Identität durch die Einführung einer nationalen Schriftsprache, einer nationalen Literatur zu lösen. Der Plan bewirkte eine grundsätzliche Verlagerung der Überlebensbestrebungen des armenischen Volkes von der politischen auf eine echt kulturelle Ebene. Die Identitätsfrage wird für die Armenier von da an tatsächlich eher eine kulturelle als eine politische Frage darstellen.

Wir würden nicht übertreiben, wenn wir sagen, dass Mesrop, mindestens in unserer mittelmeerischen *Oikumene*, einer der ersten großen Geister ist, der die Einheit und das Überleben des Volkes von dem sozial-politischen Grund der Einheit des Clans, des Stammes, des Königtums, mit einem Wort von einem primitiven oder entwickelten staatlichen oder städtischen administrativen Kern von Gewalt, auf den Grund der Kultur, ihrer Organisierung und demnach ihrer einheitlichen Wirkungen verlagert hat. Vorher war eine analoge Verlagerung der Einheit des Volkes vom Grunde der politischen Gewalt auf einen geistlichen Grund, nämlich den Grund des religiösen Glaubens in der nationalen Erfahrung der Juden nach der Verlust der politischen Macht geschehen: Von den Exilpropheten zuerst behauptet, wurde diese Verlagerung von den großen jüdisch-alexandrinischen Denkern als das Prinzip der Einheit des Volkes in einer grundsätzlich diasporischen, das heißt Zerstreuungssituation, theoretisch ausgearbeitet.

Die tiefste Charakterisierung der Idee Mesrops: ein allgemeiner Plan für das ethno-kulturelle Überleben des Volkes

Diese Betrachtungen und deren eingehende Analyse helfen uns, den großen Unterschied zwischen dem Werk des syrischen Bischofs Daniel einerseits, mit seinem für die armenische Sprache geschaffenen "danielischen" Alphabet[10] – wie auch immer man sich dieses vorstellen mag –, sowie auch allen ähnlichen Bemühungen, z.B. des gotischen Bischofs Wulfila, die im spätantiken und mittelalterlichem *orbe christiano* blühten, und dem Werk Mesrops andererseits besser zu verstehen. Daniel und Wulfila kümmerten sich um ein schlicht kerygmatisch-katechetisches Ergebnis, ohne eine allgemeine Auffassung bezüglich des Schicksals des Volkes, der Probleme seiner Identität und seines Überlebens, der Wechselbeziehungen zwischen den Komponenten dieser Identität vor Augen zu haben.

Das syrische Christentum hatte im Laufe des 4. und 5. Jahrhunderts allmählich einen Modus friedlicher Koexistenz mit dem sasanidischen Reich gefunden. Diese Koexistenz stützte sich darauf, dass die Syrer das Reich als ihren eigenen Staat akzeptierten. Dies war, wenn man so sagen darf, eine Art politischer Symbiose. Aber das Ergebnis einer solchen dauernden Symbiose war, dass sich das Nationalbewusstsein der Syrer entspre-

---

[10] Über das Danielische Alphabet vgl. Nerses Akinean (Akinian), S. Maštocʿ Vardapeti keankʿn ew gorcunēutʿiwnë handerj kensagrutʿeamb S. Sahakay (Der hl. Maschtots Wardapet. Sein Leben und sein Wirken nebst einer Biographie des hl. Sahak), (*Nationalbibliothek* 158), Wien, 1949, 232–241, deutsches Resümee S. 431–473; Pełos Ananean (Ananian), Varkʿ Maštocʿi (Biographie von Maštocʿ),Venedig, 1962, 61–95; Serge N. Mouraviev, Les caractères daniéliens (Identification et reconstruction), *REArm* 14 (1980), 55–85.

chend den wechselnden Umständen nicht entwickeln konnte, und sich mit der arabischen Eroberung des Landes fast gänzlich verdünnte. Tatsächlich haben sich die echte syrische Kultur und die syrische Sprache seit jener Zeit hauptsächlich als Sprache und Kultur der Kirche, des religiösen Lebens und Tuns erhalten, während zugleich im Profanen und im Alltag eine sehr starke Arabisierung der Kultur stattfand. Nur in einigen kleinen Enklaven hat die syrische bzw. aramäische Sprache im Alltag überlebt, ohne jedoch die Bildung einer allgemein wirkenden und sich weiter entwickelnden Volkskultur bestimmen zu können[11]. Die Armenier dagegen wollten sich mit keiner fremden politischen Einheit identifizieren. Das heißt jedoch nicht, dass sie zum Schutz ihrer nationalen Identität absolut und in jedem Fall die politische Unabhängigkeit als Grundprinzip gehabt hätten. Wenn es so gewesen wäre, so wären sie schon seit langem verschwunden. Es bedeutet nur, dass das Grundprinzip, das für die Armenier ihr Verhältnis zur herrschenden Macht regeln sollte, lediglich in der Loyalität gegenüber einem gegenseitigen, ausdrücklich formulierten oder selbstverständlichen Vertrag zwischen Souveränen und Untertanen, nach Maßgabe einiger lebenswichtiger und absolut unverzichtbarer Bedingungen, bestand. Bedingungen, die während der schweren politischen Auseinandersetzung mit den Sasaniden, die im Jahre 451 zur Schlacht der *Vardanankʿ* führte, mit größter Klarheit formuliert wurden. Ein so deutliches, starkes und tiefes Identitätsbewusstsein wäre ohne das Werk von Mesrop Maštocʿ und seinen Mitarbeitern unvorstellbar[12].

Dieselben oben entwickelten Betrachtungen helfen uns auch besser zu verstehen, warum auf die Schaffung des georgischen und des kaukasisch-albanischen Alphabets nicht unmittelbar eine gleiche oder ähnliche literarische Blüte in den betreffenden Ländern folgte wie in Armenien. Der Hauptgrund liegt, so meine ich, darin, dass sich der Alphabetisierungsprozess in Georgien und im kaukasischen Albanien in der ersten Hälfte des 5. Jahrhunderts eher auf Grund eines äußeren Vorbildes, als eine von außen inspirierte Bewegung entwickelte, mit praktischen, pastoralen Sorgen missionarischer Art, wie es der Fall bei Daniel dem Syrer oder bei dem Goten Wulfila war, ohne jene starke nationalideologische Begründung, die im Geist seines armenischen Bahnbrechers, Mesrop Maštocʿ, wirksam war. Etwas Ähnliches wird sich in Georgien erst am Anfang des 7. Jahrhunderts ereignen, natürlich mit dem Ziel einer graduellen Entwicklung: mit der Trennung der georgischen Kirche von der armenischen unter der Führung der entschlossenen und weitblickenden Persönlichkeit des Katholikos Kyrion, des Quirinus der Lateiner. Diese Trennung, die das iberische Christentum dem Einflussbereich einer stärkeren Kirche, wie es damals die armenische war, endgültig entzog, bedeutete den entscheidenden Schritt auf dem Weg zur völligen Ausbildung eines religiös-nationalen Selbstbewusstseins georgischer Identität[13]. Dieser Prozess wird sich gegen das 10. Jahrhundert mit einer

---

[11] Vgl. Antoine Meillet et Marcel Cohen (Hrsg.), Les langues du monde, nouvelle édition, Paris, 1952, 128–129.

[12] Zu einer detaillierten Behandlung der Schlacht der *Vardanankʿ* (oder im armenischen Genitiv *Vardanancʿ*), den grundsätzlichen Bedingungen, die die Armenier zur Bewahrung ihrer Identität als unverzichtbar betrachteten, und zu dem sich darauf beziehenden Begriff des „Ahnengesetzes“, vgl. B.L. Zekiyan, Riflessioni preliminari sulla spiritualità armena. Una cristianità di ‘frontiera’: martyria ed apertura all'oikumene, *OCP* 61 (1995) 337–341, 346–355; ders., Das Verhältnis zwischen Sprache und Identität, l.c. (Anm. 1), S. 285.

[13] Zwar „war der dogmatische Waffengang zwischen dem Katholikos Kyrion und den Würdenträgern der armenischen Kirche zu Beginn des 7. Jahrhunderts nichts anderes als der sichtbare letzte Akt einer innerlich schon längst vollzogenen Handlung“ (Geschichte der kirchlichen georgischen Literatur auf Grund des ersten Bandes der georgischen Literaturgeschichte von K. Kekelidze, bearbeitet von P. Michael Tarchnišvili mit Dr. Julius Assfalg (*Studi e Testi*, 185), Città del Vaticano, 1955, 186), trotzdem scheint mir die Rolle, die in diesem Prozess dem Katholikos Kyrion zukommt, von großem Gewicht zu sein, von größerem jedenfalls, so glaube ich, als ihm von einigen georgischen Historikern

klaren und endgültigen Formulierung vollziehen. Eines der Hauptergebnisse dieser Vollendung war gerade die bemerkenswerte literarische Blüte, die Georgien von jener Epoche an im späten Mittelalter erfahren hat.

Was Albanien betrifft, weiß man nicht einmal, ob es in der Sprache dieses Landes je eine Literatur im engeren Sinne gegeben hat. Selbstverständlich genügen einige Inschriften, einzelne seltsame literarische Werke nicht, um von einer organischen und entwickelten Literatur sprechen zu können. Aber selbst wenn es irgendeine „Literatur" auf Albanisch gab, spielte sie keine Rolle, die mit jener vergleichbar wäre, die das Schrifttum in Armenien und Georgien hatte[14]. So sollte ein ausgeprägtes Nationalbewusstsein in dieser Christenheit aus besonderen Gründen, die wir hier nicht weiter diskutieren können, nie zur Reife kommen – vielleicht mit Ausnahme einiger einzelner Persönlichkeiten oder kleinerer Gruppen –, um die notwendigen Bedingungen zur Bildung einer eigenen nationalen literarischen Kultur und einer nationalen Ideologie zu schaffen.

Ein positiv-konstruktiver Versuch der Identität, die nicht bloß aus Entgegenstellungen besteht

Ein wichtiger Aspekt, auf den ich an dieser Stelle hinweisen möchte, der des Prozesses der Formulierung und Behauptung der christlich-armenischen Identität durch das Werk von Mesrop, Sahak und ihren Mitarbeitern im Laufe des 5. Jahrhunderts besteht darin, dass sowohl der Ausgangspunkt als auch der Zielpunkt dieses Vorganges von keinem Willen inspiriert waren, sich jemandem zu widersetzen, um die eigene Identität behaupten zu können. Die armenische christliche Ideologie bildete sich im 5. Jahrhundert keineswegs in einer Perspektive von Entgegenstellungen, weder gegenüber den Griechen, noch den Syrern, nicht einmal gegenüber den Persern. Mesrop und Sahak sowie ihre Helfer waren nicht nur in der griechischen und syrischen Kultur erzogen worden, sondern sie hatten auch gute, sogar ausgezeichnete Beziehungen zu den Griechen und den Syrern. Es genügt hier zu erwähnen, wie Mesrop in Syrien vom Klerus und den Laien, und wie er in Konstantinopel vom Kaiser selbst mit hohen Ehren aufgenommen wurde, wie er sich für die Verwirklichung seines Planes mit der Bitte um Mitarbeit an Syrer und Griechen wandte, wie sehr er sich darum kümmerte – in absoluter Übereinstimmung mit dem Katholikos Sahak –, den Schülern und Jüngern eine hervorragende Erziehung in den besagten Kulturen zu sichern. Das alles erhellt eindeutig nicht nur von Koriwns Zeugnis, sondern auch von fast allen darauf folgenden Dokumenten, die von Mesrop und seinem

---

zugeschrieben worden ist (z. B. Michel TAMARATI, L'Église géorgienne des origines jusqu'à nos jours, Rome, 1910; Kalistrat SALIA, Histoire de la nation géorgienne, 1980, 1983², engl. Übersetzung nach der 2. franz. Aufl. v. K. VIVIAN: History of the Georgian Nation).

[14] Vahan INGLISIAN, Die armenische Literatur, in: Handbuch der Orientalistik, 1963, 167, 171–172, 183–184; Serge MOURAVIEV, La forme interne de l'alphabet albanais caucasien et la phonologie de l'oudien, *Le Muséon* 93 (1980) 345–374; DERS., Tri etjudy o kavkazko-albanskoj pis'mennostij, *Ežegodnik iberijsko-kavkazkogo jazikoznanija* 8 (1981) 222–320; Robert HEWSEN, Ethno-History and the Influence of the Armenians upon the Caucasian Albanians, in: Classical Armenian Culture, Influences and Creativity. Proceedings of the First Dr. H. Markarian Conference on Armenian Culture, ed. by Thomas J. SAMUELIAN (*University of Pennsylvania Armenian Texts and Studies* 4), Delmar, 1982, 27–40; Aleksan A. AKOPJAN (HAKOBYAN), Albanija-Aluank v greko-latinskich i drevnearmjanskich istočnikach, Erevan 1987; Patrick DONABÉDIAN, Une nouvelle mise au point sur l'Albanie du Caucase, *REArm* 21 (1988–1989) 485–495 (eine ausführliche Besprechung von Akopjans Buch mit weiterer Bibliographie von Armeniern und Azeris); B. L. ZEKIYAN, Lo studio delle interazioni politiche e culturali tra le popolazioni della Subcaucasia, l.c. (Anm. 4). Jedoch ist es nicht ausgeschlossen, dass in Hinkunft – nach den neu entdeckten sinaitischen Palimpsesten – noch Weiteres auf Albanisch entdeckt wird, wie es von P. Ananian schon vor Jahren ausdrücklich behauptet wurde (op. cit., S. 208).

Werke reden. Was die Perser betrifft, war die schwere Krise um die Mitte des 5. Jahrhunderts in den persisch-armenischen Beziehungen klar durch das Bestreben des sasanidischen Reiches verursacht, den Armeniern den Mazdeismus aufzuzwingen.

Sogar nach dem verräterischen Gesinnungswechsel des byzantinischen Reiches zur Zeit der Krise der *Vardanankʿ*, und noch am Anfang des 6. Jahrhunderts, am ersten Konzil von Duin, in den Jahren 506–508, unter dem Katholikos Babgēn von Othmus, war es ein grundsätzliches Prinzip für die Armenier, selbst in den Fragen des Glaubens, „mit dem gelobten Könige der Römer einig“ zu sein[15]. Die Lage änderte sich wesentlich erst um die Mitte des 6. Jahrhunderts, aller Wahrscheinlichkeit nach unter dem entscheidenden Einfluss der justinianischen Politik in Armenien, wie ich früher, an anderer Stelle, zu beweisen versucht habe[16]. Von jener Periode an wirkt der Gegensatz zu den Byzantinern jahrhundertelang fast wie ein charakteristisches Merkmal des Armeniertums. In diesem historischen Kontext erreichte auch – durch einen ähnlichen, gleichsam umgekehrten parallelen Prozess – die Behauptung der georgischen Identität gegenüber den Armeniern ihren endgültigen Ausdruck.

Der Begriff von „Vorbild“ und die Philologie

Der Begriff von Vorbild, wie wir ihn bestimmt und erklärt haben, hilft uns m. E., auch neues Licht in verschiedene philologische Debatten zu bringen, und zwar in jene über die Ursprungsbeziehung zwischen den drei subkaukasischen Alphabeten, insbesondere dem armenischen und dem georgischen. Bekanntlich hat Koriwns viel diskutierte, aber nicht ganz klare Aussage über Mesrops Rolle beim Entstehen der georgischen und albanischen Alphabete zu verschiedenen Auslegungen Anlaß gegeben[17]. Was im besonderen die georgische Schrift betrifft, reichen die Interpretationen von ziemlich radikalen Haltungen, die für eine fast globale Rolle Mesrops Stellung nehmen oder andererseits jede Beziehung zwischen den beiden Schriften absolut ablehnen, bis zu mehr nuancierten oder unbestimmten Auslegungen, die eventuelle gegenseitige Einflüsse vermuten[18]. Hier ist nicht der richtige Ort, um die verschiedenen Hypothesen einer gründlichen Untersuchung bzw. Kritik zu unterziehen. Ich möchte nur darauf hinweisen, dass zwar einige davon keine seriösen Grundlagen besitzen, andere dagegen Argumentationen anführen können, die nicht jeder Wahrscheinlichkeit entbehren. Als Beispiele wollen wir zwei Ansätze betrachten. Koriwns Zeugnis aus irgendwelchen Gründen radikal abzulehnen, ist zwar ein leichterer Weg, aber gerade deswegen schwerlich überzeugend. Andererseits sollten die Unterschiede in der Auffassung der beiden Alphabete nicht unbeachtet bleiben[19]. Die rein philologischen Beweise sind wohl beim jetzigen Stand der Daten nicht in der Lage, den Engpass mit vernünftiger Sicherheit zu überwinden. Ich meine aber, dass der oben eingeführte Begriff von „Vorbild“ eine neue Chance bietet.

Um diese Vermutung besser illustrieren zu können, ziehen wir den Prozess der Entstehung des armenischen Alphabets in Erwägung, wie er von Koriwn und diesem nachfol-

---

[15] *Girkʿ Tʿłtʿocʿ*, Tiflis, 1901, S. 49: „*Zenoni, barebaneloy tʿagaworin Hoṙomocʿ*“, 2. Ausg. Jerusalem, 1994, S. 159.

[16] B. L. ZEKIYAN, La rupture entre les Églises géorgienne et arménienne au début du VIIe siècle. Essai d'une vue d'ensemble de l'arrière-plan historique“, *REArm* 16 (1982) 155–174.

[17] Für einen ganz allgemeinen Hinweis auf die verschiedenen Meinungen siehe: Gabriele WINKLER, Koriwns Biographie des Mesrop Maštocʿ. Übersetzung und Kommentar (*OCA*, 245), Roma, 1994, 288–292.

[18] Z.B. Thomas GAMKRELIDZE in: Thomas Gamkrelidze's Reply to John Greppin, *Bazmavep* 139 (1981) 458: “It goes without saying that the Old Georgian and the Mesropian scripts, being Christian scripts of roughly the same epoch, may have influenced each other“.

[19] Dazu vgl. z.B. Thomas GAMKRELIDZE, l.c., S. 457–459.

gend von den wichtigsten armenischen Geschichtsschreibern erzählt wird[20]. Alle sind sich darüber einig – wenngleich mit Nuancen, die jedem eigen sind -, dass die Schrift Gottes Geschenk ist und es in ihrer Schaffung etwas Wunderbares, Übernatürliches, ja fast Göttliches gab. Die Schaffung des Alphabets scheint in diesem panegyrisch-theologischen Kontext das Resultat eines Augenblicks, eines Wunder-Augenblicks, gewesen zu sein. Das ist aber nur ein Aspekt des Phänomens und der diesbezüglichen Erzählung. Es wird sogar eine oberflächliche Lektüre der übrigen Teile derselben Texte genügen, um der Tatsache bewusst zu werden, dass die Schaffung des Alphabets nicht nur jahrelange Bemühungen und methodische, genaue Untersuchungen verlangte, sondern auch in hohem Maße ein kollektives Werk, eine Teamarbeit gewesen ist. Sogar das tatsächliche Erscheinungsbild der Buchstaben verdanken wir nicht so sehr Mesrop selber, sondern dem berühmten Kalligraphen Rufinos aus Samosata. Doch verkleinert all dies keineswegs das einzigartige Verdienst, die außerordentliche Größe, in einem Wort das Genie Mesrops. Ihm gehört die Idee, die grundsätzliche und revolutionär schöpferische Auffassung dieser Idee, die wunderbar funktionierende Methode zur Vollziehung derselben Idee.

Wenn wir jetzt dieses Paradigma, *mutatis mutandis*, zu Koriwns Bericht anwenden, dass nämlich Mesrop eine bestimmte Rolle bei der Schaffung der georgischen und albanischen Alphabete spielte, sehe ich keine zwingende Notwendigkeit, diese Rolle in einem eindeutigen und engen Sinne so zu verstehen, dass man alles Mesrop selbst verdanken müsse. Andererseits würde es nicht zu einer größeren und tieferen historischen Verständlichkeit führen, sondern in eine diametral entgegengesetzte Richtung, wollte man die Entstehung der beiden in Frage kommenden kaukasischen Alphabete so auslegen, dass sie von dem historisch-literarischen Kontext des Christianisierungs- und Alphabetisierungs-, sowie dem nachfolgenden Inkulturationsprozess Subkaukasiens, der sich vor allem in der Übersetzung der Bibel ausdrückte, herausgerissen würden. Ein Prozess, in dem Armenien und seine christlichen Heroen, von Gregor dem Erleuchter bis zu Mesrop Maštocʿ, die Rolle eines wirksamen und bedeutenden „Vorbildes" übernahmen.

Abschluss

Wir können die wesentlichen Elemente, die, nach diesem Überblick, an der Bestimmung der armenischen christlichen Identität und Weltanschauung teilhaben, in folgenden Punkten zusammenfassen:

a) dem christlichen Glauben kommt eine grundsätzliche Rolle in der geschichtlichen Bildung der armenischen Identität zu;
b) eine deutliche Wahrnehmung der nationalen Identität, auf Grund derer die Armenier sich nicht nur von ihren nichtchristlichen Nachbarn, sondern auch von den christlichen Völkern unterschieden;
c) eine bestimmte Vorstellung, welche Elemente eigentlich bei der Bildung der wesentlichen Struktur dieser Identität zusammenfließen: der Sprache und ihrem schriftlichen Ausdruck kommt unter diesen Elementen eine hervorragende Stellung zu;
d) der sakrale Charakter der Sprache, der Kultur und all dessen, was zum Bereich des Lebens und Überlebens eines Volkes gehört;
e) die Bestimmung der Identität aufgrund von zunächst eher kultureller Eigenart als politischer Zugehörigkeit.

[20] Für einen detaillierten Überblick vgl. G. Winkler, l.c., insbes. S. 226–228.

SIGLENVERZEICHNIS

A.	Anmerkung
AASS	*Acta Sanctorum*
Abb.	Abbildung
AnBoll	*Analecta Bollandiana*
Anm.	Anmerkung
A.O.	Angegebenen Orts
ArmRev	*Armenian Review*
BK	*Bedi Kartlisa. Revue de Kartvélologie*
Byz	*Byzantion*
BZ	*Byzantinische Zeitschrift*
bzw.	beziehungsweise
ChristVost	*Christianskij Vostok*
CSCO	*Corpus Scriptorum Christianorum Orientalium*
e.g.	exempli gratia
HA	*Handes Amsorya*
ibid.	ibidem
JbAC	*Jahrbuch für Antike und Christentum*
Jh.	Jahrhundert(s)
JÖB	*Jahrbuch der Österreichischen Byzantinistik*
l.c.	loco citato
m.	metre(s)
OCA	*Orientalia Christiana Analecta*
OCP	*Orientalia Christiana Periodica*
ÖAW	Österreichische Akademie der Wissenschaften
op. cit.	opere citato
p.	page
PBH	*Patma-banasirakan Handes/Istoriko-filologičeskij žurnal*
PG	*Patrologia Graeca*
PL	*Patrologia Latina*
PLRE	*Prosopography of the Later Roman Empire*
PO	*Patrologia Orientalis*
RAC	*Reallexikon für Antike und Christentum*
REArm	*Revue des Études Arméniennes*
ROC	*Revue de l'Orient Chrétien*
S.	Seite
s.o.	siehe oben
StT	*Studi e Testi*
s.u.	siehe unten
T.	Tafel
TAPA	*Transactions of the American Philological Association*
TIB	*Tabula Imperii Byzantini*
u.z.	und zwar
VKByz	*Veröffentlichungen der Kommission für Byzantinistik* (ÖAW)
VV	*Vizantijskij vremennik*
z.B.	zum Beispiel

INDIZES

1. PROSOPOGRAPHISCHER INDEX (incl. Autoren)

2. GEOGRAPHISCHER INDEX

3. RES ET VERBA MEMORABILIA (incl. anonyme Werke)

4. MODERNE AUTOREN

TAFELN

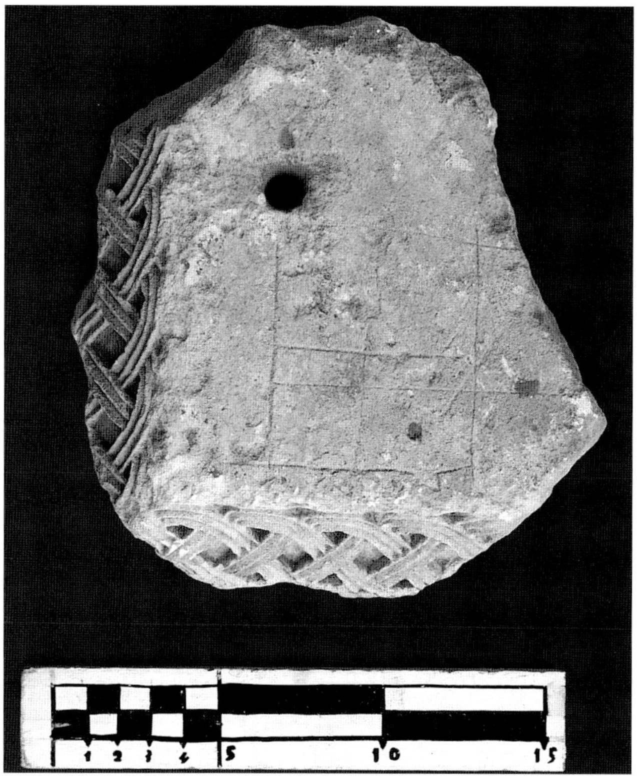

Fig. 1: St. Barlaam's Monastery, Small Impost or Base

Fig. 2: St. Barlaam's Monastery, Fragment of a Colonette

Fig. 3: St. Barlaam's Monastery, Fragment of a Colonette

Fig. 4: Wood of Life, Bundle Column of Porch

Fig. 5: Wood of Life, Bundle Column of Porch

Fig. 17: St. Barlaam's Monastery, Pantile Fragment Bearing Inscription "Barlaam"

Fig. 18: St. Barlaam's Monastery, Inscribed Stele with Inscription

Fig. 19: St. Barlaam's Monastery, *Eucharistic* Bread Mold

Fig. 20: St. Barlaam's Monastery, *Eulogia* Bread Mold

Église Saint-Grégoire de Tigran Honenc' à Ani
Scène 1: Comparution de saint Grégoire devant le roi Tiridate (détail)

Scène 12: Sacre de saint Grégoire à Césarée

Scène 17: La fin de la vie de saint Grégoire

Fig. 1: La Colonne vivante entre Nino et ses compagnes (N. Thierry)

Fig. 2: Détail: Nino en prière (N. Thierry)

Fig. 3: Öşk: Nino en orante (P. Couprie)

Fig. 4: Un des anges porteur du mur oriental de Mcxeta (N. Thierry)

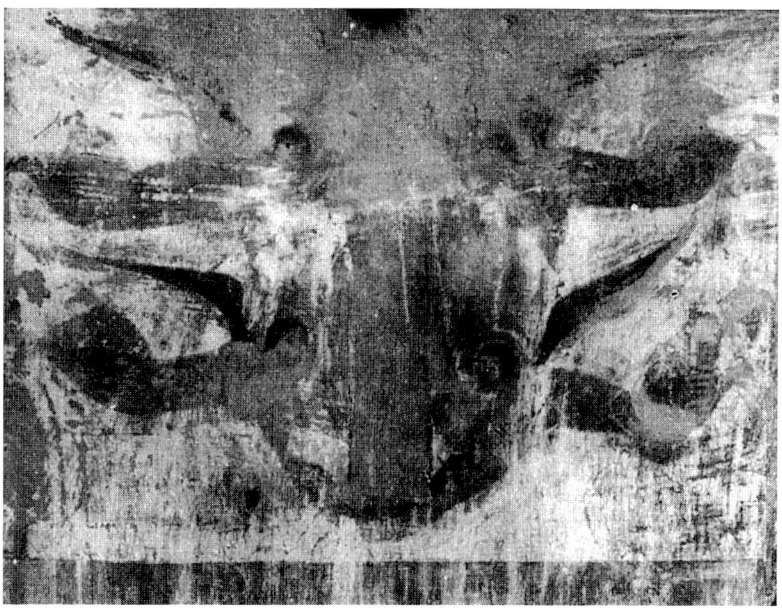

Fig. 5: La Colonne, portée par quatre anges à Udabno (d'opùs Amiranašvili, pl. 27)